Praise for

FOR GOD AND COUNTRY

"In *For God and Country*, Ralph Reed dismantles liberal media false-hoods and provides a compelling analysis of why Evangelical Christians back Donald Trump—because his policies reflect their values and he is a champion for their beliefs."
  —**Mark Levin,** host of *The Mark Levin Show*, host of *Life, Liberty & Levin* on Fox News, and bestselling author

"For decades, Evangelicals have wanted to defend their rights and answer their critics. In this terrific book, Ralph Reed shows them how. And he correctly argues they are right to support Donald Trump and his policies."
  —**Mark Meadows,** congressman from North Carolina and former chairman of the House Freedom Caucus

"As Ralph Reed makes clear in his brilliant new book, Christians stand with Trump because he stands for important biblical principles including the right to life and religious liberty."
  —**Dr. Robert Jeffress,** pastor at First Baptist Church in Dallas, Texas, and author of *Courageous: 10 Strategies for Thriving in a Hostile World*

"Donald Trump may not have been my first choice for president (I was!), but I joined tens of millions of Evangelicals in supporting him. In this rollicking account, Ralph Reed shows how these God-fearing, patriotic voters made the difference for Trump in 2016—and will likely do so again . . ."
  —**Mike Huckabee,** former governor of Arkansas, host of *Huckabee* on the Trinity Broadcasting Network (TBN), and bestselling author

"Many wonder why and how Evangelical Christians can support Donald Trump. Patriot and Christian leader Ralph Reed answers that question in *For God and Country*. Life, liberty, and faith hang in the balance, and this terrific book gives me hope for America."

—**Dr. Jack Graham,** pastor at Prestonwood Baptist Church in Plano, Texas

For GOD AND

THE CHRISTIAN CASE FOR TRUMP

COUNTRY

FOR GOD AND
THE CHRISTIAN CASE FOR TRUMP
COUNTRY

RALPH REED

Since 1947
REGNERY
An Imprint of Skyhorse Publishing, Inc.

Visit our website at www.regnery.com.
Please follow our publisher Tony Lyons on Instagram @tonylyonsisuncertain.

10 9 8 7 6 5 4 3 2 1

Hardcover ISBN: 978-1-68451-057-3
Paperback ISBN: 978-1-5107-8268-6
eISBN: 978-1-68451-064-1
Library of Congress Control Number: 2020931953

Cover photograph by Kevin Lamarque/Reuters

Printed in the United States of America

To Jo Anne

CONTENTS

INTRODUCTION TO
THE 2024 EDITION

Nothing has made liberals—and even some of their coreligionists—lose their sanity quite like evangelicals supporting Donald Trump. Beginning in June 2015, when Trump rode down an escalator in New York city to announce his candidacy, many have wondered: How could born-again, Bible-believing Christians support a thrice-married, playboy billionaire from Manhattan who owned casinos and was pro-choice for most of his life? Today, following a liberal lawfare campaign that has resulted in Trump's conviction in a kangaroo court in New York City in a trial that featured testimony about payments to a porn star prior to the 2016 election, the critics add that he is a convicted felon.

I sought to answer this question and refute what I saw as unfair criticism of evangelicals for their support of Trump in *God and Country* when it was first published in 2020. As someone who has known Donald Trump for years and worked closely with his administration, I believe evangelicals were vindicated in their decision to support Trump because of his policies and remarkable record as president. Nevertheless, the critics of evangelicals continue to hurl abuse at them, claiming they are hypocrites who have compromised their spiritual witness and their moral authority by backing Trump.

It is important to remember that these attacks are nothing new. In the four decades since evangelical Christians broke upon the beaches of the American political scene after a half-century of self-imposed exile, few constituencies have been subjected to greater vitriol and abuse. The *Washington Post* once called politically active evangelicals "poor, uneducated, and easy to command." One liberal columnist once labeled them "Shiite Baptists." A *Wall Street Journal* columnist claimed that "demagogic intolerance is central to the religious right's political agenda," citing a liberal cleric who denounced religious conservatives for the "manipulation of people of faith for the purposes of building support for a partisan political agenda."[1]

Recently, the media and the far Left has engaged in an updated smear campaign against what they term "Christian nationalists," alleging that conservative people of faith are predisposed to authoritarianism and even political violence. James Carville, who once hung a sign in the Clinton campaign headquarters saying, "It's the economy, stupid," now claims it's about religion. He says Christian "nationalists" pose "a bigger threat than al-Qaeda to this country."[2] Senator Raphael Warnock of Georgia recently compared them to Christians who supported slavery and segregation, asking, "Who really is their God?"

The answer is Jesus Christ. Unlike some of their opponents, they are not seeking a political messiah because they already have a Savior. They do not seek political power in the narrowly partisan sense, but rather a voice in the conversation of democracy that reflects their numbers in the electorate and society at large. Their voices and votes express the values that beat in the hearts and give meaning to the souls of tens of millions of Americans: faith in God, hard work, individual self-initiative, the centrality of family, the freedom to express their religious beliefs, and caring for the poor, the orphan, the prisoner, and the immigrant.

As for Trump, evangelicals were clearly more comfortable with presidential candidates who came from their community like Ted Cruz,

Mike Huckabee, and Marco Rubio. Then Trump surprised almost everyone by winning the nomination by the sheer force of his personality and the power of celebrity. As I document in great detail in *God and Country*, he did so while aggressively seeking the backing of evangelicals. He swore fealty to their pro-life and pro-family agenda, courted evangelical leaders, and released a list of conservative jurists from whom he pledged that he would fill the seat on the U.S. Supreme Court left vacant by the death of Anontin Scalia. Faced with Hillary Clinton's radical pro-abortion agenda and the danger of her filling the vacant seat with a younger version of Ruth Bader Ginsberg, evangelical Christians warmed to Trump and gave him 81 percent of their votes in 2016.

Their decision was not without risk—or criticism. But it has been completely vindicated by Trump's policies and record as president. Trump was the most pro-life president in American history, keeping his promise to appoint pro-life judges to the federal judiciary, including the U.S. Supreme Court, leading to the achievement of the pro-life movement's penultimate goal after a half-century of struggle with the 2022 *Dobbs* decision overturning *Roe v. Wade*. Trump also reinstituted and strengthened the Mexico City policy prohibiting the use of U.S. taxpayer funds to promote and perform abortions overseas, defunded abortion giant Planned Parenthood through executive action, became the first president to address the March for Life in person, and protected the conscience rights of pro-life physicians and health-care providers.

Second, Trump was strongly supportive of the First Amendment right to religious freedom, suspending enforcement of the Johnson Amendment, which threatened churches and Christian ministries with harassment by the Internal Revenue Service and the revocation of their tax-exempt status if they spent any amount on electioneering activity. (Interestingly, this may be the only Trump policy that Biden has not sought to reverse. One presumes because many black churches and pastors have long been politically engaged and also don't want to be harassed by federal tax bureaucrats for exercising their freedom of speech.) His Justice Department provided guidance to school administrators making it clear that students could voluntarily pray and organize Bible clubs and other religious activity in public schools. The Trump administration made religious freedom one of its top priorities in foreign policy as well, based on a simple understanding that countries that violate religious freedom will also violate the right to political freedom.

Trump was the most pro-Israel president in history, moving the U.S. Embassy from Tel Aviv to Jerusalem and recognizing the eternal city as the indivisible capital of Israel. Trump recognized Israeli sovereignty over the Golan Heights on the border with Syria that provides a strategic defense against future invasions and made it official U.S. policy that Israelis living in Judea and Samaria (or the West Bank) does not violate international law. There is no doubt in my mind that had Donald Trump been reelected Hamas and Hezbollah would have never invaded Israel on October 7 or fired numerous missiles at civilians in northern Israel. Trump also imposed harsh sanctions on Iran, crippling its oil revenues and therefore its ability to fund and foment terrorism through its various proxies in the Middle East and elsewhere. Joe Biden weakened those sanctions and provided $10 billion in relief for Iran, with disastrous consequences for the entire civilized world.

My point was and remains that public policy has a moral dimension, either allowing evil things to proliferate or promoting what is good and praiseworthy. So whatever one thinks of the personal character of Donald Trump—and my experience with him is that he is a good man, a devoted husband and father, and a straight shooter—his policies advanced not only our cherished values, but what was best for the people of the United States and their allies.

Second, politics in a free society offers citizens flawed and imperfect choices that are often binary. Whatever one's views of Trump, Joe Biden's policies have resulted in an open border that at this writing has led to the entry of an estimated 10 million illegal aliens, including some on the terrorist watch list. It is a national security and humanitarian crisis that has no precedent in the history of our nation. Fueled by runaway stimulus spending and liberal monetary policies, inflation has spiked under Biden, with consumer prices increasing by roughly 20 percent during this presidency and the cost of owning a home roughly doubling. For example, the median price of a home in the U.S. was roughly $355,000 when Joe Biden assumed the presidency; today it is $439,716. In the same period, mortgage rates have more than doubled, putting the American dream of home ownership out of the reach of many young couples and middle-class families. As Governor Joe Lombardo of Nevada recently pointed out in an op ed in the *New York Times*, the median home listing price in Las Vegas, one of the fastest growing cities in one of the most rapidly growing states in the nation, was $342,995 in January 2021, and skyrocketed to $460,000 in 2024. In this critical battleground state, assuming a home mortgage financed at the average rate of 6.9 percent, the cost of owning a home has roughly doubled under Joe Biden from $1,500 to $2900 a month.[3]

This matters because while man does not live on bread alone, man cannot live without bread. If families can't afford to put a roof over their heads or buy a new home, that is damaging to the institution of the family. If millions of workers are surviving paycheck to paycheck, unable to adequately provide for their families or save for their children's education, this is not just an economic problem, it is a moral concern. This is the reality in the U.S. today. An estimated one out of every eight U.S. households, or over 44 million people, cannot afford an adequate, nutritious diet for their families. Biden inflation adds to this food insecurity because it makes it harder to buy more expensive groceries like fresh produce and quality protein that is essential to good health.

When Jesus entered a village, before he preached the good news, he always met people at the point of their need. If they were hungry, he fed them. If they were thirsty, he gave them water to drink. If they were lame, they walked. Wherever Jesus went, the blind saw, the deaf heard, the mute had their tongues loosened and spoke. The health and welfare of the people mattered to Jesus. When his critics questioned his ministry or claimed he was a servant of the Devil, he told them that even if they didn't believe his words, they should believe his works (John 10:38). This should be our concern as Christians as well, doing works that feed the hungry, heal the sick, strengthen families, and provide for the common good. The economic and financial catastrophe for working-class families wrought by Biden's policies stands in dramatic contrast with the stronger economy under Donald Trump, when inflation was 2 percent, gas prices were $2.50, and unemployment for Hispanics, Blacks, and women were at historic lows.

Biden, a professing Roman Catholic who once claimed to be pro-life, is the most pro-abortion president in history. He advocates a national law that repeals almost all common-sense restrictions on abortion at the state level and mandates a national standard of abortion on demand at any stage of pregnancy, even after the unborn child can feel pain and survive outside the womb. He also favors repealing the Hyde Amendment, which has forbidden the use of taxpayer funds to pay for abortion for forty-six years, and allowing Medicaid to pay for elective abortions, which would lead to hundreds of thousands of additional abortions of unborn children.

If the taking of innocent human life is a moral issue, not just a political issue, then concerned Christians are required as both moral actors and citizens to assess the impact of these policies on the innocent, the working poor, and the vulnerable. To fail to oppose them is to acquiesce to evil; to decline to support a candidate who would end and reverse them is to accept evil by one's inaction. Voting or speaking out in the public square are not just political acts; they hold moral content for which we are answerable and accountable.

What about character? While voters evaluate the personal character of candidates and render a judgment as individuals all the time, the choice is often not usually between the perfect and the good. Jimmy Carter was a born-again Baptist and a Sunday school teacher who could also be petty and vindictive, often micromanaging his administration while losing sight of the big picture. His failure to act decisively after the Soviets invaded Afghanistan and Iranian radicals took fifty-two American hostages made the U.S. look weak and impotent. Ronald Reagan was the first divorced man to ever be elected president and had once signed the most liberal abortion law in the country as governor of California. But evangelical Christians backed him strongly against their fellow evangelical Carter because he had become profoundly pro-life and pledged to roll back Soviet advances and pursue a strategy that would lead to victory in the Cold War. The loss of his movie career and first marriage also imbued Reagan with a profound belief that God had a plan for his life, one far greater than movie stardom or merely seeing his name in lights. It transformed him as a man and a leader.

I do not judge either Trump or Biden spiritually. But Biden seems to have outsourced the policies of his administration to the most radical and progressive wing of his party, including in his weak and vacillating support for Israel as it faces an existential war with Hamas and other Iranian military proxies. In terms of public character, he promised in his Inaugural address to unify the American people and bring us together as a nation. "My whole soul is in this—bringing America together," he pledged. Biden vowed that it was time to end "our uncivil war." Instead, he exacerbated our divisions, using the Justice Department to indict, bankrupt, and jail his leading political opponent, Donald Trump, in ways that are among the most deeply divisive in our history. He has denounced his political opponents as fascists and racists, turning perfectly honest policy differences into a polarizing conflict in which he routinely questions the motives of his opposition. This is destructive of national unity and purpose.

It has also been proven that his family received an estimated $19 million from Ukrainian, Russian, and Chinese corporations, including an infrastructure company controlled by the Chinese military. These countries had business before Joe Biden as vice president, knew he planned to run for president, and have business before him today as president. No president or vice president in the history of our country has ever had family members who were the recipients of millions of foreign funds, including from hostile foreign powers. Whether or not it is a crime, it was certainly corrupt. It has also come to light that contrary to his claims during the 2020 campaign, Biden was involved in his son Hunter's business dealings, including attending private dinners and participating in numerous phone calls with clients who paid millions for access to the future president. Biden also mishandled classified documents as a U.S. Senator and Vice President, even purloining a top-secret memorandum he penned as vice president on the war in Afghanistan, in clear violation of the law. Some of the classified documents Biden removed from the White House were found in boxes in his garage near his vintage Corvette. Even the special counsel who investigated Biden's mishandling of classified documents acknowledged in his report to Attorney General Merrick Garland that he could have indicted Biden but feared that a jury would see him as a sympathetic old man with a faulty memory. The double standard is obvious. Given all these facts, Joe Biden and his Justice Department have no credibility in leveling charges at Donald Trump.

Most troubling of all the policies of Joe Biden is the weaponization of the judiciary and the criminalization of political differences. The deliberate targeting of Donald Trump by Biden's Department of Justice, by liberal Democratic prosecutors in Georgia and New York city, and by the state attorney general of New York constitute an abuse of power without precedent in our history and have undermined respect for the rule of law in a way that may be beyond repair. It is commonplace for the leaders of Third World countries to indict their political opponents and put them in jail after show trials. It has never happened in the United States until now. One prosecutor once told me he could indict Santa Claus on Christmas eve. And especially in the deep-blue precincts of New York city and Washington, DC, where Trump received only five to fifteen percent of the vote, it is almost impossible to select a jury from a pool of registered voters that will allow for a fair trial. For many Christians but also millions of independent or swing voters of good will, the loss of the rule of law is so dangerous that it will lead them to support Trump in 2024 because the abuse of power by the Biden administration poses such a grave threat to the country they love.

In 2020, self-identified evangelical Christians voted for Donald Trump by a margin of 84 percent, the largest ever received by a presidential candidate in the modern era. I believe there is a real possibility Trump will receive an even greater share of the votes of conservative Christians in 2024. The reason is laid out in this book. While some of the politics have changed since originally published—the millions of illegal aliens pouring across an open border, two wars raging in Europe and the Middle East—the basic arguments remain the same. Christians, like all citizens, are moral actors who support candidates who share their values, are qualified for office, and are uniquely able to advance a policy agenda they support. Donald Trump is that candidate, and the Christian case for supporting him on the issues and his policies is stronger than ever.

May God richly bless our nation and find us faithful as both Christians and citizens.

Ralph Reed
Atlanta, Georgia
June 18, 2024

CHAPTER 1

DONALD TRUMP CALLING

"Mr. Reed? Please hold. I have Donald Trump on the line."

I had never met or spoken with Donald Trump. Why was he calling me? How did he get my cell phone number? It was March 31, 2011, and I was sitting by a pool at a Miami Beach resort making phone calls and firing off emails. My family was flying down the next day for spring break. As it turned out, there was an explanation for Trump's call.

That morning, I had been on a treadmill at a hotel in Washington, D.C., watching the rerun of Fox News' *The O'Reilly Factor* at five o'clock in the morning. The guest was Donald Trump. I wasn't necessarily a huge Donald Trump fan. I had caught snippets of *The Celebrity Apprentice*, his hit television show, and viewed him more as a political gadfly than as a serious candidate. Trump had toyed with running for president as far back as 1988, and he did so again in 2000, when I worked on George W. Bush's presidential campaign. But he never took the plunge. Like most political observers, I was skeptical. Still, I was keenly interested in the 2012 presidential election, so I watched the interview and was pleasantly surprised with Trump's skill and aplomb as he parried back and forth with the famously aggressive Bill O'Reilly.

"Mr. Trump has made millions building and selling real estate," O'Reilly said. "But he has not been closely questioned about policy until tonight."

O'Reilly began with Obamacare: If it were repealed, would Trump provide health care to those who needed it?

"I have a great, big, fat, beautiful heart. And when people are in trouble, I like to help them out," Trump replied. "We have a moral obligation to help people. I really believe that. I believe that strongly, and not everybody does."

So would it be replaced with Trumpcare? "Well, it would be a form of much better."

How did Trump intend to deal with illegal immigration? "Well, you either have a country or you don't," Trump vowed. "You either have a line and a boundary or you don't." He called for deploying U.S. military forces on the border and deporting illegal aliens on a case-by-case basis, allowing those who obeyed the law and contributed to society to remain—a law-and-order stance that would shortly rock the political establishment.

"What about abortion?" O'Reilly asked.

"As you know, I'm pro-life," Trump replied matter-of-factly.

"OK, so you're pro-life on abortion. Would you outlaw abortion?"

"Well, I'd go a pretty strong step. I used to not be pro-life. I have become pro-life." Then Trump got personal. "I have seen friends that had children that they didn't want. And now they have children, and they are the apple of the eye. So I really have changed in my views over the years, and I am pro-life."

Donald Trump was...pro-life? I was floored; I had assumed that Trump's tabloid past and gilded Manhattan social status had shaped him into a social liberal. Trump sidestepped the question of whether he would outlaw abortion while promising to take "a pretty strong step" to protect life. He shifted the discussion to the personal, revealing that he had friends who had had unwanted pregnancies but did not have abortions. The children later born were "the apple of the eye." This was similar to the advice I had given candidates for decades: Explain your pro-life views in personal terms, such as an adopted child in one's family. When it comes to the highly polarizing and emotional issue of abortion, people can argue all day about politics or the law, but they cannot argue about your own story. Many of those candidates didn't follow my advice. But Trump's was one of the better pro-life answers I had heard in my career.

O'Reilly then asked about gay marriage. "I'm against it," Trump shot back without hesitation.

"Why?"

"I just don't feel good about it," Trump replied. "I don't feel right about it. I'm against it and I take a lot of heat because I come from New York. You know, for New York it's like, how can you be against gay marriage? But I'm opposed to gay marriage."

So Donald Trump was a social conservative! This was news to me. Yet there he was in the flesh on the highest-rated program on cable television unapologetically expressing his pro-life, pro-family views. And it meant two things were clear: First, Trump was serious about running for president. Second, there was no downside to having a candidate of Trump's high-watt celebrity advocating the pro-life cause. Whatever the outcome of the presidential contest, he could theoretically bring the pro-life message to millions of Americans who might not otherwise have received or embraced it.

Two hours later, I caught a flight to Miami. When I landed, I received a call from David Brody of the Christian Broadcasting Network. Brody had been poking around and had heard Trump was interviewing people to staff a possible presidential campaign. Had I heard anything?

"No, but it makes what I saw this morning add up," I told him.

"How's that?" Brody asked.

I told him about Trump's appearance on Fox News and what he had said about abortion and marriage. If he did throw his hat in the ring, I suggested, he might make an aggressive play for Evangelical votes. With his money and celebrity, combined with a socially conservative message aimed at Evangelicals, he could make a serious run at the Republican presidential nomination. Brody agreed that this was newsworthy, and he asked me if I'd give him a quote.

I was neutral in the GOP presidential race and knew that saying nice things about Trump might be misinterpreted as an endorsement. But Brody was a fair and honest reporter who wouldn't burn me. So I decided to give Trump a big bear hug.

"There is a nascent and growing curiosity in the faith community about Trump," I told Brody. "Evangelicals will like his pro-life and pro-marriage stances, which combined with his business record and high-wattage celebrity all but guarantee he will get a close look from social conservatives as well as other Republican primary voters."

Soon after that, my cell phone rang again. Strangely, it was a 212 area code with the rest of the numbers blocked. I didn't usually answer blocked numbers, but for some reason I did in this case.

Donald Trump came on the line, announcing himself with an easy familiarity that revealed a preternatural confidence, as if we'd known each other for years. He said he was calling to thank me for the nice things I had said about him.

Trump had already seen Brody's blog post! I hadn't even seen it yet and didn't know Brody had posted it. My mind raced. *That didn't take long!*

"Well, thank you for what you said," I fired back. "I saw your interview on Fox News. I must tell you I was pleasantly surprised and impressed by what you said about life and other social issues. I didn't know that's where you were on those issues."

Trump said he meant every word of it. A lot of people might think I'm socially liberal, but I'm not, he said. If I run for president, I'll be a pro-life candidate.

Contrary to my expectations, I liked Trump instantly. He was confident, relatable, personable, and a natural at connecting one-on-one; he definitely had charisma. I had sized up a lot of political horseflesh in my career, and Trump was a thoroughbred. He could flatter with the best and was an engaging and entertaining conversationalist, easily toggling between substantive issues and breezy gossip. Based on this first impression, I felt it would be a mistake to underestimate him and thought he should be welcomed into the conservative and pro-family movement. After all, I was in the business of making converts—and Trump joining the cause of protecting life and the traditional family would be a game changer.

"Donald, I don't know you, and you don't really know me," I said, "and I have to be honest with you, I've not always had a high opinion of you." Trump greeted my confession with silence. "But last year I was at a conference in Park City, Utah, and my wife and I spent a lovely evening over dinner with your daughter Ivanka. And I must tell you, she is one of the most beautiful, gracious, intelligent, and charming young women I have just about ever met. I know something about women of that quality and caliber because I have two daughters myself, and I know the apple doesn't fall too far from the tree. So I have to tell you, it forced me to revise my opinion of you."

I had attended a conference with my wife, Jo Anne, called "Dialogue" during the previous winter in Park City, Utah, and we were coincidentally seated next to Ivanka and her husband, Jared Kushner. They were then newlyweds. Given their pedigree as children of privilege, I suppose I had expected them to put on airs. The exact opposite was true. I was impressed by how engaging and solicitous Ivanka was, asking about how we met, our children, and other aspects of our lives. Jared was mostly quiet and said little. (I would later learn that his low-key demeanor belied a big heart and a quick mind.) When we walked back to our room that night, I told my wife that I might have to change my opinion of Donald Trump. As the parents of two daughters who were charming, gracious, and intelligent, we knew young people like that didn't happen by accident. Her father had to have had something to do with it. Jo Anne agreed, and we filed it away for future reference. I never thought I would be speaking to him on the phone and sharing this story.

Trump waxed enthusiastic at the mention of Ivanka. Everyone tells me that, he said. He told me that people he didn't know stopped him to tell him they had met Ivanka and found her to be a remarkably gifted woman. He asked me if I could guess who had told him something similar just the other day.

"Who?" I asked. Of course, I had no idea.

Oprah Winfrey, Trump replied. Ivanka had gone on Oprah's television show to promote her fashion line, and Oprah had called Trump after the taping. He revealed that Oprah, who he said was a friend, had told him she had been doing her show for decades and had interviewed literally thousands of guests and had never met a more confident and poised woman than Ivanka. He said he considered it a remarkable statement from one of the most respected women in the world. (I would learn later that the deep love and emotional bond between Trump and his children was an amazing thing to witness.)

How do you not like this guy? I thought to myself. He was really a stitch. In political parlance, he was the kind of guy you'd want to have a beer with, though he did not drink alcohol. I figured I'd made enough of a personal connection to risk offering some unsolicited political advice. "Far be it from me to tell you how to run your campaign, but if you're really serious about running for president—"

Trump interrupted me. He told me he was dead serious about running for president. He repeated it slowly for emphasis.

"Well, if that's the case, then you need to get to know the Evangelicals," I replied. "They're half of all Republican primary voters, and there's no path to the Republican nomination without them."

Trump said he wanted Evangelicals to know him better.

"Then you should come to the Faith & Freedom Coalition policy conference in June in Washington," I suggested. Trump had spoken at the Conservative Political Action Conference (CPAC), the annual conservative confab in D.C., but not yet to a major Evangelical gathering.

"There will be thousands of grassroots activists and pastors there," I told Trump. "My organization is neutral in the primary. There are a lot of candidates coming. I'll give you a prominent platform and a chance to make your case. I promise you'll be treated with fairness and respect."

Trump asked for the dates; I gave them to him. He asked what day I wanted him to speak, and I suggested Friday—a good time for media coverage and maximum attendance. He asked what time, and I suggested an evening time slot. He said he had just put it on his calendar, and he would see me there.

I told Trump I'd have my staff reach out to his office to coordinate. After an exchange of farewells, Trump asked me stop by and see him the next time I was in New York City. I told him I would take him up on the offer.

I hung up in disbelief. Trump had confirmed his appearance at a major political event without consulting a single staffer, scheduler, political strategist, or straphanger. Apparently, he was his own strategist! I had met a lot of instinctive politicians in my life, but Trump was in a category all his own. I pictured him sitting behind a gold-leafed desk in a midtown Manhattan tower that bore his name, working the phones like a stock trader, booking his own speaking gigs, and hopscotching around the country on his jumbo jet. I shook my head. *You can't make this up!* The last time a take-charge candidate of wealth and fame had grabbed the wheel of his own campaign was Ross Perot in 1992. That had not ended well. Would the Trump candidacy flame out like Perot's, or would it be historic and transformational, changing our politics and the course of American political history? I didn't know. One thing was certain: it wasn't going to be boring.

I speed-dialed my team at Faith & Freedom Coalition and told them to get ready for a bigger crowd at the policy conference. One of the world's most famous businessmen and highest-rated television stars, whose personal and professional exploits had provided fodder for the New York tabloids for decades, was going to appear before an Evangelical Christian audience and pledge his fealty to biblical values and the pro-family issues agenda. I didn't know it at the time, but American politics would never be the same.

Thus began my journey as one of tens of millions of Evangelical Christians who would come to support the presidential candidacy and pro-life, pro-family policies of Donald Trump. How it unfolded is one of the most unlikely stories of our time—a tale stranger than fiction, and one that has never been fully told until now. As we know, Trump chose not to run for president in 2012, something to which we will turn later. But his escalator ride to the lobby of Trump Tower three years later would lead to his victory over sixteen Republican primary opponents and culminate in his shocking upset of Hillary Clinton. Trump's election as president was made possible in no small measure by his winning an astonishing 81 percent of the Evangelical vote—the highest total won by a presidential candidate in the history of modern American politics. It has been a roller-coaster ride without precedent in American history, with no president so upending the furniture of our political system and rewriting the rules of politics since the election of Andrew Jackson in 1828.

The only thing that has driven the liberal media more nuts than Trump's presidency (for which they were totally unprepared, confident that Hillary Clinton's coronation was guaranteed) is the fact that it was achieved with the full backing of Evangelical Christians. Liberal opinion elites claim that Evangelicals are hypocrites who sold their souls to Trump for thirty pieces of silver, trading their spiritual integrity for access to power and a few items on their policy agenda. These self-appointed cultural elites point the finger at Christians who support Trump, accusing them of bastardizing their faith and cheapening the Gospel by backing the Manhattan billionaire. They assert that Christians have surrendered their moral authority as a result and are disqualified from ever speaking out on matters of public morality again. In the simplest of terms, the media and the Left twist the Trump-Evangelical alliance into a weapon with which they hope to bludgeon people of faith into shame and silence.

MSNBC host Joe Scarborough has accused Evangelicals of being "rank hypocrites" plagued by a "robotic mindset" who acted as if "everything that they grew up reading in the Gospels now does not apply to their life since a guy named Donald Trump got into politics."[1] *New York Times* columnist Frank Bruni faulted Evangelicals for supporting a man who "personifies greed" and "radiates lust," proving yet again "how selective and incoherent the religiosity of many in the [Republican] party's God squad is."[2] A *Washington Post* columnist accused them of climbing "the heights of hypocrisy" by backing Trump, "blessing the destruction of public norms on civility, decency and the importance of public character."³ A former religion columnist for the *New York Times* charged that by backing a "casino mogul and all-purpose bigot," the social conservative movement "has laid bare its hypocrisy, and indeed its heresy."⁴ Never to be outdone, HBO host Bill Maher skewered Evangelicals as "the shameful hypocrites they've always been." Maher declared that "Trump has nothing in common with Jesus." Evangelicals, he charged, "went for the foul-mouthed, p***y-grabber."⁵

These attacks on Christians reveal a troubling ignorance about the civic aspirations of people of faith and a profound misunderstanding about the proper role of faith in God in a pluralistic society. Taken to their logical extremes, these attacks suggest that Christians should support only candidates without past sins who subscribe to (and live up to) our religious or moral precepts, but we are precluded from voting for a candidate who has made mistakes and has come up short in his life but now advances policies that protect life, defend the First Amendment right to freedom of religion, strengthen the family, and support Israel. This argument removes the heart of the Gospel message from our civic discourse—the grace and forgiveness available to us all through faith in Christ. These critics wish to turn us into Pharisees who harshly judge and condemn those who have sinned. But we are all sinners saved by grace. In their formulation, therefore, the citizenship of Christians is reduced to a function of their piety—not love for America, advancing sound public policy, or a desire for the common good. Their argument *reductio ad absurdum* is that voters of faith should have stayed home in 2016 or cast a protest vote for a write-in or third-party candidate who had no chance of winning. And now they aim to shame conservative Christians into staying home or throwing their votes away in 2020.

If I believed their intention was to restore the moral greatness of America and elevate leaders of character, I might take their critique a little more seriously. But many of these media elites were cheerleaders and defenders of Bill Clinton, which makes their attacks on Trump (and the Christians who support him) ring hollow. Make no mistake—their true goal is to defeat Trump in 2020 by demoralizing Christian voters, and the reason is because they oppose the pro-life, pro-family, pro-Israel policies of his administration, not to mention the hundreds of conservative judges he has appointed.

If fifty million Evangelical and pro-life Catholic voters had followed their advice in 2016, Hillary Clinton would be in the White House. Had that occurred, people of faith would have been culpable by their moral and civic negligence in electing as president a woman who had corrupted every position of public trust she previously held, including as secretary of state (third in line to the presidency under the Constitution), conducting sensitive government business on a home-brewed email server, exposing our nation's secrets to surveillance by hostile foreign powers, destroying evidence, and hindering a criminal investigation by the FBI. Even worse, they would have borne responsibility for Hillary Clinton's appointing two liberal Supreme Court justices (or more), appointing hundreds of other pro-abortion and radical federal judges, restricting religious freedom, promulgating pro-abortion policies, increasing taxpayer funding for Planned Parenthood, and undermining Israel while allowing Iran—the leading state sponsor of terrorism in the world—to obtain the most destructive weapons on earth.

Had Evangelical Christians followed the deceptive advice of the media elites (and sadly, some Christian and conservative Never Trumpers), they would have helped put a woman in the presidency who, when asked in a televised presidential debate whether she opposed late-term abortion when the unborn child could survive outside the womb, blithely dismissed any objection to what can only be described as infanticide. "I strongly support *Roe v. Wade*, which guarantees a constitutional right to women to make the most intimate, most difficult in many cases, decisions about her healthcare that one can imagine," she said. Clinton defended her vote as a U.S. senator against a ban on late-term abortion. *Vogue* magazine, edited by Hillary fundraiser Anna Wintour, celebrated her for "awesomely" defending abortion, which is perhaps the first time the taking of the life of a child just hours before birth has been described as "awesome." Had those of faith failed to vote for Donald Trump in 2016, this is who would have become president. And someone with even more extreme views will occupy the White House if conservative Christians do not turn out in record numbers to the polls to support Trump in 2020.[6]

If Evangelical voters had sat on their hands and allowed Hillary Clinton to prevail in 2016, it would have been open season on Christian ministries, leaders, colleges, and churches—and even Christian-owned businesses. Hillary attacked the Supreme Court's decision in *Burwell v. Hobby Lobby*, which upheld the right of closely held businesses owned by Christians from being forced to provide medical services that violated their faith. That decision was decided by a vote of five to four. With Antonin Scalia gone and his seat vacant, Clinton would have appointed his successor, and the high court would have shifted to a liberal majority opposed to religious freedom—probably for a generation.

What about President Trump? By executive order, he suspended enforcement of the Johnson Amendment, an obscure provision of the Internal Revenue Code that prohibits churches and pastors from speaking out on political matters and public policy. If Evangelical Christians and pro-life Catholics stay at home in 2020 or throw their vote away on a protest candidate, a future Democratic president will reinstate the Johnson Amendment, and the IRS will swiftly revert to its previous posture of harassment, persecution, invasive audits, and litigation against faith-based ministries. The BOLO ("Be On the Look Out") list created by Lois Lerner and others at the IRS under Barack Obama will look tame by comparison. Under Elizabeth Warren or anyone else in the Democratic presidential field, one can also expect reinstatement of the conscience regulations under Obamacare (which were repealed by the Trump administration) that required faith-based charities to provide medical services they objected to because of their faith—including abortion. The Little Sisters of the Poor, dragged into federal court by the Obama Justice Department for not wanting to pay for contraception and abortion (ironically for Roman Catholic nuns who had taken a vow of celibacy), would likely be sued again. Christian colleges like Liberty University and the University of Notre Dame could see their tax-exempt status endangered if they sought to remain true to their statements of faith and religious doctrine.

This is not an empty threat. During an LGBTQ community forum broadcast on CNN during the 2020 Democratic presidential primary campaign, Beto O'Rourke vowed to revoke the tax-exempt status of any house of worship or religious institution that did not repudiate traditional Christian teaching on marriage and family and adopt positions favoring same-sex marriage and special rights for gay and transgender individuals.

"There can be no reward, no benefit, no tax break for anyone or any institution or organization that denies the full human rights, and full civil rights, of everyone in America," O'Rourke promised.

The anti-Christian bigotry inherent in such a policy is clear. When criticized, O'Rourke tried to backpedal, claiming only that no Christian church or other religious institution would be able to "discriminate" in delivering social services to the poor, needy, and others. But it is clear that the secularist agenda of the modern Democratic Party is a dagger aimed at the heart of our freedom to express our faith in America. In the dogma of modern liberalism, the First Amendment protects the right of believers to speak and share their faith only if that faith is politically correct. But if their Christian faith violates the speech codes and secularist agenda of the Far Left, expect the machinery and enforcement power of the federal government to be used to harass and persecute Christians, including denying them nonprofit tax status, suing them, and fining them into bankruptcy and financial ruin.

Most critics of Evangelicals do not dispute these facts. Their response is essentially: So what? They see it as no big deal if Christian Americans have their First Amendment rights trampled upon by their own government. After all, they claim, wasn't the early Church similarly persecuted, and did it not thrive in the midst of that persecution? They also contend that it is not a senseless tragedy for hundreds of thousands of additional unborn children to lose their lives to abortion because of taxpayer funding, including to Planned Parenthood. They argue by implication that American Christians should not do all they can to elect a president who will defend Israel against its mortal enemies, including Iran, whose ruling mullahs have killed Americans and vowed to wipe the Jewish state off the face of the earth. They assert that Christians should reject Donald Trump as a political ally, despite his stalwart defense of unborn life and religious liberty, primarily because of his allegedly suspect character, sordid personal past, and Darwinian ethics. Instead, they should by their inaction allow the radical Left to take power and deny them their God-given constitutional rights.

The fallacy in this argument is obvious. Although it is true that the early Church thrived in the midst of persecution and that Christians around the world are persecuted for their faith every day, the Bible does not teach that we should actively seek our mistreatment when we can avoid it. There is a difference between accepting persecution and allowing it. The former is pious; the latter is spiritual masochism. The Apostle Paul was beaten, imprisoned, shipwrecked, and ultimately died for the Gospel, but he asked others to pray for his deliverance. "And pray that we may be delivered from wicked and evil people," Paul urged his fellow Christians, "for not everyone has faith. But the Lord is faithful, and he will strengthen and protect you from the evil one" (2 Thessalonians 3:2–3). Why would the early apostles ask God to deliver them from evil people if they were supposed to welcome persecution? Nor does the Bible teach that believers should reject deliverance by a governor, president, or judge, however flawed. After all, Paul argued his case before corrupt and venal Roman officials, and even appealed his case to Caesar, who happened to be a sexual deviant and a bloodthirsty tyrant. Critics of Evangelicals today argue that we should spurn assistance from political leaders who are not perfect or have committed sins. But as a citizen of Rome, Paul pleaded for the help of the most disreputable political leaders the world has ever known. Did this signal he was a hypocrite or compromise his witness for Christ? Of course not. In fact, it did the opposite, and the

Bible records that members of Herod's and Caesar's households became Christians as a result.

A mother trapped with her innocent children in a burning building does not refuse assistance from a firefighter because he may have short-comings. She is trying to escape the fire. Oskar Schindler, who saved 1,200 Jews from the ovens of Nazi concentration camps, was a notorious philanderer and Nazi spy. But because he spared so many Jewish lives, Schindler's name is enshrined in the Avenue of the Righteous at the Yad Vashem memorial in Jerusalem, and he is buried on Mount Zion, the only member of the Nazi Party to be so honored. His many flaws and shortcomings did not rob his righteous acts of their rich moral content.

In a legal and political culture that is often hostile to their faith and First Amendment rights to express it, Christians should welcome defend-ers and allies wherever they can be found. That is wisdom. But a handful of Christian Never Trumpers implore their fellow believers to reject the assistance of Donald Trump. "The American church isn't so weak that it needs Trump's version of secular salvation," insisted former *National Review* staff writer David French. "Yet the church is acting as if it needs Trump to protect it. That's not courageous. It's repulsive."[7]

This is a straw man. The issue isn't whether we should seek a secular savior like Donald Trump or Ronald Reagan in his time; it is whether we should defend our rights under the Constitution as Americans. If we take seriously our rights as citizens of the United States and if we believe those rights come from God (as they surely do), then we are obligated to defend them with all our might and to support candidates who will also defend them. This is also why calling on Christians to avoid mud-dying their boots with the compromises that accompany civic engage-ment and withdraw from politics is so misguided. Rod Dreher, author of *The Benedict Option*, urged Christians to "quit looking for a political white knight to save us and open our eyes to the stark reality of Chris-tianity's exile status in our American Babylon in our own modern Dark Age."[8] But advocating the surrender of our God-given rights as Ameri-cans is correcting the evil of political idolatry with a blinkered, monkish self-righteousness. Healthy and spiritually mature political engagement recognizes the limits of politics while celebrating its possibilities. It embraces the responsibility of earthly citizenship with all its attendant rights while looking and yearning for true salvation in a heavenly kingdom that is not of this world.

The argument for civic withdrawal or refusing to vote for like-minded candidates is really a cop-out to keep from making difficult and imperfect decisions in a free society and fallen world. It seeks heavenly perfection and is of little earthly good, leading to the advance of evil by abandoning the field of battle. Perhaps most perplexing, it ignores the enormous human progress of two thousand years of recorded history. Do we really want the model for American society to be ancient Rome, with its unrivaled venality, corruption, and brutal denial of human rights? Or the Middle Ages, with its caste society, bloody sectarian conflict, and civil disorder? I pray not. Medieval Christians retreated to cloisters and monasteries to shelter themselves from barbarism. Fortunately, that is not our lot. Our inheritance as Americans is freedom (which ultimately belongs to all humanity). We possess hard-won rights sanctified by the blood of patriots and enshrined in the Magna Carta, the Constitution, and the Bill of Rights. We do not need to return to the cultural strategies of the Dark Ages. We are free men and women, and we should act accordingly.

Our forebears paid a great price—many of them with their lives—so we can live and thrive in a nation that respects our God-given rights to freedom of speech, association, and religion. Christians escaped persecution in Europe by crossing an ocean to worship God as they pleased, rebelled against Great Britain to lay claim to their God-given rights as free men and women, and ultimately enshrined those rights in the U.S. Constitution. We do not rely on political saviors to deliver us. But throughout history, God has used political leaders to accomplish His purposes and deliver His people. In His wisdom, He has placed us in our nation at this moment in history, and I believe God expects us to defend and assert the rights that He (not the government) has granted us—with our lives, if necessary. Christians should do so not because we are afraid of being persecuted (for the Bible teaches us that persecution is our lot here on earth) or because we require a human savior (for the yearning for a political messiah is a form of idolatry), but because we honor God and bear witness to His sovereignty and goodness when we defend the human rights that He has ordained.

No one is arguing that Donald Trump is a perfect man, because we are all imperfect, or that he is without sin, because we are all sinners and all fall short of God's glory. But as president, Trump has led with great moral clarity as he has protected the right of Christians to express their faith, defended religious liberty at home and around the world, successfully fought for the release of Pastor Andrew Brunson in Turkey and other Christians held in the prisons and gulags of authoritarian regimes, used the bully pulpit and the power of his office to protect the unborn, and appointed hundreds of federal judges who respect the Constitution and the Bill of Rights. In so doing, he has kept his campaign promises, revealing much about his heart and character not only to Christians, but to the American people. If keeping one's word is central to one's character—and it clearly is—then Donald Trump has shown he has far more character than his critics.

Christians are not seeking a political savior in Donald Trump. But they are acting in their capacity as citizens in supporting a leader who defends their First Amendment rights to freedom of speech and religion, which, after all, are their rights as Americans. They did not surrender those rights on the day they came to Christ. They are not lesser Americans by virtue of their religious faith. As John F. Kennedy said in his famous speech to the Houston Ministerial Association in 1960, if "40 million Americans lost their chance of being president on the day they were baptized, then it is the whole nation that will be the loser…in the eyes of history, and in the eyes of our own people." Kennedy spoke of Roman Catholics in an election in which bigotry was directed at Catholics. Today, a similar bigotry is directed at Evangelical Christians, and they are well within their rights to oppose it and seek protection wherever it can be found. This is not a form of political idol worship; it is the defense of their God-given rights that are inherent to their very humanity. Christians who support Trump are not pining for a political savior; they are defending Thomas Jefferson's idea as articulated in the Declaration of Independence that we are endowed by our Creator with inalienable rights (that is, rights inherent to their humanity), including the right to life, liberty, and the pursuit of happiness. The sole purpose of government is to safeguard those rights. Christians who back Trump because he shares these beliefs and supports public policies that advance them are acting as American citizens, not only as Christians. They were not drawn to Trump because they need a messiah; they already have one, and His name is Jesus.

Followers of Jesus are taught by Scripture to fear God alone and look only to Him for their salvation and deliverance—not to any politician, king, or parliament. "You are not to fear what they fear or be in dread of it," God told His people. "It is the Lord of hosts who you should regard as holy. He shall be your fear, and He shall be your dread" (Isaiah 8:12–13). Elsewhere, God warned Israel not to rely on the armies or kings of other nations to defend it, for "the Lord of hosts will protect Jerusalem. He will protect and deliver it, He will rescue it" (Isaiah 31:5). But it is also true that God has ordained that we live in a nation that recognizes certain inalienable rights, including the right to petition our government. We would be poor stewards of our civic responsibilities if we failed to exercise that right.

The African-American Christians who flocked to the March on Washington in August 1963 were not merely appealing to the Kennedy administration and Congress to deliver them from the oppression of segregation and racial injustice; they were also issuing a call to the conscience of the nation. They lobbied for their constitutional right to equal protection under the law. They were appealing to elected officials to do the right thing. And why not? The Bible teaches that a ruler who leads righteously is "like a refuge from the wind and a shelter from the storm, like streams of water in a dry country, like the shade of a huge rock in a parched land" (Isaiah 32:2). The New Testament urges that "prayers, petitions and thanksgivings be made on behalf of all men, for kings and all who are in authority, so we may lead a tranquil and quiet life in all godliness and dignity" (1 Timothy 2:1–2). Praying for leaders who will govern righteously is not the defensive crouch of a timid and frightened Church; it is the faithful supplication of a confident Church that is fired up with enthusiasm and hope, relying entirely on God's promises as found in the Bible.

The Civil Rights Movement was steeped in the Christian faith, with leaders like Martin Luther King Jr. and Ralph David Abernathy, who were Baptist preachers, and citizen action organizations whose names bore witness to their faith, such as the Southern Christian Leadership Conference. They put their ultimate trust in God, but they pricked the conscience of the nation, as well, calling the American people to act in a way that was consistent with the better angels of their nature and live up to the promises of the Declaration of Independence and the U.S. Constitution. Theirs was not merely a prophetic movement; it was a political endeavor. Civil rights leaders lobbied Congress and the White House, sued in the courts, and appealed to the executive and legislative branches to pass legislation and take action to defend their right to equal protection under the Fourteenth Amendment. The March on Washington, it should be remembered, was part of a lobbying campaign to break a filibuster of the Civil Rights Act that was led by segregationist Democratic senators.

African-American Christians also sought the assistance of flawed and imperfect allies, including President Lyndon Johnson. Johnson was a corrupt man who profited from his public service; a known philanderer who was unfaithful to his wife; a crude man who used racial epithets and profanity, sometimes forcing aides to meet with him in the bathroom while he relieved himself; a former segregationist; and a protégé of Georgia senator Richard Russell Jr., the leader behind the Southern Manifesto, which sought to deny equality to black Americans. But for all his flaws and past racist views, Johnson became a champion for civil rights as president. African-American Christians joined with him as U.S. citizens, seeking *civil* rights, which required civic action as political actors. Johnson was not a perfect man, but he occupied the most powerful office in the land and was willing to defend their rights. So they worked with him to advance what was right and just. Making an alliance with Johnson on civil rights did not compromise their moral beliefs or their Christian faith. Indeed, King would later differ with Johnson on Vietnam while continuing to make common cause with him on fighting poverty, pushing for civil rights, and other pressing moral concerns.

I am not comparing Trump to Johnson, or our movement to the cause of civil rights. They are each quite different. Every epoch is unique, with its own distinct challenges, circumstances, and personalities. But as Christians, effective citizenship requires that we work with individuals with whom we sometimes disagree and with whom we have theological and moral differences—some of them deep and abiding. That is not compromising spiritual integrity; it is democracy. As our African-American brothers and sisters in Christ did the right thing by engaging in the rough-and-tumble of politics, lobbying, litigation, and the necessary and normal compromises that accompany political involvement, so do today's Evangelicals. None of us can know the future. But if progress continues to be made on protecting innocent human lives, preserving religious freedom, and shifting the federal courts to a position of respect for the First Amendment's right to religious liberty, then I believe history will vindicate Evangelicals for working with and supporting the policies of Donald Trump. They are called by their faith and compelled by their moral beliefs to resist evil and advance good. Given that the agenda offered by the Democratic nominees in 2016 (and again in 2020) is openly hostile to and completely antithetical to the principles of their biblical Christian faith, and most certainly to the right to life, Evangelicals and pro-life Roman Catholics are fully justified in supporting Trump for president. Now let's dive into the full ramifications of the stark choice now facing Christians—and all Americans—to see why this is the case.

CHAPTER 2

DEEDS VERSUS WORDS

"Please hold for the president."

Donald Trump had been president for ten days, and I was sitting in my home study at around nine o'clock on a January evening.

President Trump came on the line, and we talked briefly about the executive order he had recently issued that prohibited travel to the U.S. from seven countries that could not verify the background of visa applicants, including state sponsors of terrorism like Iran and failed states like Yemen and Syria. The elite media pummeled Trump over the order and falsely labeled it a "Muslim ban"—even though non-Muslim countries like North Korea and Venezuela were on the list, no one was excluded based on their religion, and Muslims from India, Malaysia, and other countries with large Muslim populations were free to enter. Far-left groups erupted in angry opposition, staging sit-ins and protests that wreaked havoc at airports and government buildings. Trump asked me if I supported his action.

"As long as it's not based on religious beliefs, yes," I replied. "I don't support a ban on religion. But your policy is based on protecting the homeland from the dangerous terrorist networks in those countries. So I support it, and have publicly said so."

Trump said the American people overwhelmingly supported his efforts to defend the country and protect the homeland. (Trump was vindicated when the Supreme Court upheld the travel ban in 2018 as fully within the president's authority to control U.S. borders and regulate immigration, despite the dishonest distortions of the media and the opposition of the Left.)

News accounts indicated that Trump would announce his Supreme Court nominee the following evening at the White House. I gingerly raised the topic.

"Mr. President, let me ask you a question," I began. "Am I going to be happy tomorrow night?"

Trump replied that I wouldn't be happy. He paused. You're going to be thrilled, he said. The president said he could not tell me who it was, but he promised it was an outstanding jurist.

When I hung up, my mind turned to a thought experiment: What if Hillary Clinton rather than Donald Trump had won the 2016 election? What if voters of faith had joined Never Trumpers and stayed home or wasted their vote on a third-party candidate? Who would President Hillary Clinton have chosen to fill the vacant seat once held by conservative hero Justice Antonin Scalia? No doubt it would have been an ideologically liberal jurist as committed to abortion on demand and restrictions on the First Amendment's protection of freedom of religion as Hillary. It also likely would have been a nominee in their forties or early fifties who would have served thirty or forty years on the court. It was a reminder that elections had consequences, and in this case they were huge.

The next morning, I received an email from a senior White House official informing me that the president had requested my attendance at the announcement of his Supreme Court nominee. I provided the staff with my social security number and other personal information required by the Secret Service.

I arrived at the White House that evening and was greeted by an aide to the president who escorted me at breakneck speed through the West Wing, maneuvering through a labyrinth of hallways and passages until

I lost my bearings. We finally arrived in a room occupied by a group of Republican senators. As I glanced around, it dawned on me that most of them were members of the Senate Judiciary Committee. A staffer from the White House counsel's office briefed them on the president's nominee, and the senators held a stapled memorandum in their hands, some of them flipping through the pages as the staffer went through his briefing points. Somehow, I had ended up in a briefing of U.S. senators who were getting their first word on the identity of the president's choice! I turned to my right and was surprised to see my friend Ted Cruz. His brow was furrowed in deep concentration, and his dark eyes darted over the pages like a supermarket bar-code reader. He glanced up, his facial expression indicating he was as surprised to see me as I was to see him. He held the paper open to reveal the name at the top of the page: Neil Gorsuch.

"Is he good?" I asked quietly.

Ted nodded vigorously. "Outstanding," he said, half whispering. "He's incredible."

I didn't know Gorsuch. But when I came to Washington in the early 1980s, I followed his mother, Anne Gorsuch, who was Ronald Reagan's first administrator at the Environmental Protection Agency (EPA), and later met her when she gave a speech at the Republican National Committee (RNC), where I worked at the time. Anne was a true believer, a Rocky Mountain Reaganite from Colorado, and a solid conservative who downsized the EPA, challenged the radical environmental lobby, and refocused her agency on science-based policy. She later resigned following partisan attacks on her record by the media and congressional Democrats. I hoped her son was a chip off the old block, and I also hoped the mistreatment of his mother might have instilled in him a sober knowledge of how unfair his own treatment by the media would soon be.

Suddenly, the young aide reappeared, apparently realizing she had mistakenly taken me to the wrong room (thank you for that!), and she escorted me to the East Room, where she guided me to a seat behind Donald Trump Jr., the president's eldest son. I had campaigned with Don

Jr. at a rally for his father in Georgia the previous October, and he had impressed me as a natural political talent and a good man. Smart and tough like his father, I thought. My good friend Nick Ayers, the political wunderkind from Georgia who served as an advisor to Vice President Mike Pence, sat down, and we caught up on the Atlanta Braves and the team's prospects in the upcoming baseball season.

Just then, the senators filed in wearing the officious masks of Very Important People, grinning a bit like Cheshire Cats, clearly satisfied with the president's selection. I greeted Chuck Grassley, the chairman of the Senate Judiciary Committee, whose job it would be to guide the nominee to confirmation. As Kellyanne Conway, Jared Kushner, Ivanka Trump, and other senior officials entered the room and took their seats, people in the crowd exchanged hugs, air-kisses, and stage waves. The atmosphere was giddy and anticipatory, filled with cheer.

For all the hysterical hyperbole about Donald Trump as the disrupter of American politics—whose campaign and even his inaugural speech rewrote the accepted rules of politics as interpreted by the so-called "experts," a man whom they claimed had landed in the nation's capital like an unguided human missile—the new president had in fact followed a thoughtful, deliberative, and fairly conventional path to this moment. Trump worked from a list of highly respected conservative jurists, solicited the views of conservative groups like the Federalist Society and the Heritage Foundation, was aided by a team of advisors that included White House counsel Don McGahn and Vice President Pence, and conducted wide-ranging interviews with candidates during the transition. He had treated the pick with all the historical weight it deserved. The finalists were federal appellate court judges William H. Pryor Jr., Neil Gorsuch, and Thomas Hardiman. Few outside the senior White House staff knew upon whom Trump had settled.

Suddenly, a Marine band played "Hail to the Chief." Everyone in the room rose to their feet, their heads turning and necks craning as President Trump entered the room and appeared to practically glide down the red carpet from the formal rooms. Trump moved with purpose and deliberation, a born performer who needed no stage directions, basking in the glow. He stood ramrod straight, his hands grasping the podium as camera flashbulbs exploded, projecting gravitas, savoring the moment.

"When Justice Scalia passed away suddenly last February, I made a promise to the American people: if I were elected president, I would find the very best judge in the country for the Supreme Court," Trump said. "I promised to select someone who respects our laws and who loves our Constitution, and someone who will interpret them as written."[1] Trump stated that it had been perhaps the most transparent judicial selection process in U.S. history because he had released a list of jurists during the presidential campaign and promised to select from that list; millions of people had voted for him based on that issue. He then called Judge Gorsuch and his wife, Louise, to the podium to loud applause.

Trump then turned the podium over to Judge Gorsuch. "Standing here, in a house of history, and acutely aware of my own imperfections, I pledge that if I am confirmed, I will do all my powers permit to be a faithful servant of the Constitution and the laws of this country," Gorsuch pledged. His wife beamed with pride at his side. Gorsuch, with his grey hair, humility, and a touch of humor, seemed straight out of central casting. As the son of an attorney and cabinet officer, a Harvard Law School and Oxford University graduate, and a former clerk to Supreme Court justice Anthony Kennedy, Gorsuch boasted one of the most impressive backgrounds of any recent nominee to the high court. He exuded gravitas, pledging as a judge to be independent, impartial, and courageous. His brief statement took my breath away. *Trump chose well*, I thought. *He will be hard to defeat.*

After the ceremony, I was ushered into the Blue Room for a reception with dignitaries and White House staff. I passed a group of people surrounding Gorsuch's family who were huddled in a quiet prayer, their eyes closed, hands held tight, faces etched with intensity. I had never seen a spontaneous prayer meeting in the formal rooms of the

White House in my career. I passed by discreetly, careful not to disturb them. This certainly wasn't your father's administration, I reflected with some wonderment.

As I made my way through the crowd, I bumped into Chief of Staff Reince Priebus and Steve Bannon, two old friends from past battles. Both of them were beaming like proud family members at a christening. The transition and early days of the Trump administration had been a shakedown cruise, with swirling controversies stoked by the liberal media over the size of the inaugural crowd and the travel ban. They looked relieved; finally, here was an unqualified win!

"Congratulations, guys," I said. "Home run."

Bannon fairly gushed that President Trump had been a profile in presidential leadership, constantly stressing that the intellect, conservative philosophy, and qualifications of the nominee were paramount in his decision. "The president was just amazing," Bannon said. "He knew the stakes, asked all the right questions, stuck to the process." Reince nodded vigorously, smiling broadly. Bannon added that Pence had suggested edits to the formal questionnaire that the finalists filled out that turned out to be important in the president's decision.

I headed for the door, pausing to thank the vice president for all he had done behind the scenes without mentioning what Bannon had just shared with me. I told him we would be honored to have him keynote the gala at the next Faith & Freedom policy conference, which was coming up in a few months.

"Done," Pence replied. He pointed to an aide and told him to work with me to get it on his schedule. I headed down the stairs and out into the cold, brisk January air, my mind racing, a thousand jumbled thoughts spinning in my head.

All the doubts, reservations, even suspicions, and all the accusations hurled by critics of Evangelical voters who backed Trump in 2016 that he would betray us—every one of them had been false. In one of the most consequential elections in our lifetimes—indeed in American history—with control of the Supreme Court hanging in the balance, Trump had not only prevailed on Election Day, but he had also delivered on one of his central campaign promises as president: nominating a conservative, strict constructionist judge. Mike Pence, a stalwart friend of the pro-family movement and a committed Christian, offered his counsel and wisdom to the president during Trump's deliberations. In the months since the election, Pence had become all we had hoped for when Trump selected him.

And there was this reality: Trump had chosen both Pence and Gorsuch. Both selections revealed a conservative governing philosophy that was breathtaking in its aspirations and boldness. Pence and Gorsuch were steeped in the modern conservative movement, their lives and careers stretching back to the Reagan era and reflecting a deep commitment to philosophical conservatism. I had been around long enough to know that such personnel decisions didn't just happen; they required a steady hand and an intentional desire by Trump to surround himself with the best. These choices also dramatically disproved the accusations of his critics that he was a faker and an ideological chameleon who lacked core beliefs. During the Reagan presidency, conservatives were fond of saying that personnel was policy. Indeed—it is. And Trump's selection of Pence and Gorsuch (and most of his cabinet) suggested that he intended to govern as a conservative, despite what the media and Never Trumpers claimed. Every president makes personnel mistakes, and Trump has made a few himself. But on the biggest decisions, like the vice presidency and the Supreme Court, Trump chose battle-tested champions with conservative principles.

As I walked back to my hotel, it occurred to me that Trump as president wasn't such a crazy idea after all, as his (and our) critics incessantly claimed. As a Christian, I believed God was sovereign in the affairs of nations. Could Providence have ordered this moment, contrary to our own ambitions and expectations? I did not know, but I was certain of one thing: there was an angel in the whirlwind and a heavenly hand guiding the affairs of state in what the media insisted multiple times daily was the chaos of the Trump White House.

■   ■   ■

In May 2018, I was privileged to be part of a delegation of former members of the Trump campaign's faith advisory team who attended the official opening of the U.S. Embassy in Jerusalem. It was a celebratory affair, featuring a who's who of the U.S. Christian and Jewish communities. At the opening reception, which was held at the Israeli Foreign Ministry offices in Jerusalem, I saw my friend Jay Sekulow, one of the leading First Amendment attorneys in the nation who was also performing double duty as one of the president's personal lawyers. I also ran into Harvard Law professor Alan Dershowitz, White House advisors Jared Kushner and Ivanka Trump, faith advisor and pastor Paula White, and John Hagee, the founder of Christians United for Israel. In a brief conversation with Senator Lindsey Graham, I asked him why not a single Democratic senator or congressman was in attendance. Lindsey shrugged his shoulders and shook his head in bewilderment, telling me that by State Department protocol, many Democratic elected officials had been invited, but they had all declined. Whatever happened to politics ending at the water's edge? It seemed that anything remotely associated with Donald Trump earned the Democrats' disapproval, even when it was keeping a promise to defend and protect the state of Israel.

The next morning, I attended a breakfast reception at a home overlooking the Old City of Jerusalem that offered breathtaking views of the ancient walls and Temple Mount. Shortly after arriving, I ran into my old friend Daniel Ayalon, a former Israeli ambassador to the United States and former deputy foreign minister. I had worked with Danny during his service in Washington during George W. Bush's presidency, and I was glad to see him again. Married to an American wife, Danny was a keen observer of the U.S. political scene and a player in Israel. Pointing to the Old City beyond us, I remarked, "Can you believe that we are witnessing the recognition of Jerusalem as the eternal, undivided capital of Israel by the United States, and that Donald Trump is the one who made it happen?"

Danny agreed that it was ironic. Turning serious, he pointed out that God had always used imperfect and unlikely figures to serve His purposes and protect the Jewish people.

"I'm not sure what Jewish theology teaches," I replied. "But evangelicals believe that we're all sinners and we all fall short of the mark." I pointed out that some of the best U.S. presidents had also experienced great failures: FDR had an unhappy marriage, Harry Truman had gone bankrupt, and Ronald Reagan went through a painful divorce and the end of his acting career. Perhaps those who had experienced personal failure in their lives made better leaders.

"There's actually a rabbinical teaching about that," Danny told me. "The rabbis teach that if you elevate someone to leadership who thinks they are perfect, they rely on their own self-righteousness. But a leader who has suffered from a failure or personal shortcoming in their past will try to prove their worth by doing righteous deeds."

It was a remarkable statement. A few minutes later, I bumped into a friend who was a rabbi and asked about this teaching; he confirmed what Danny had told me. The truth is that God often chooses the discredited, the dismissed, the disdained, the person who comes from the wrong family or the wrong side of the tracks. They are unworthy and disqualified in the eyes of many; they have made too many mistakes in their lives, they don't have the right background, or they may be rough around the edges. But God chooses what the world rejects in order to confound the worldly wise, humble the self-important, and glorify Himself. Paul observed that there were "not many wise according to the flesh, not many mighty, not many noble" among the early Christians because "God has chosen the foolish things of the world to shame the wise, and God has chosen the weak things of the world to shame the things which are strong, and the base things of the world and the despised God has chosen, so that no man might boast" (1 Corinthians 1:27–29).

I am not a prophet, preacher, or theologian. I do not claim that God chose Donald Trump beyond the larger truth of the Christian faith that God is sovereign and that nothing occurs in human affairs contrary to

His participatory or permissive will. But the American people did choose Trump, and it is fair to ask what they saw in him that so many opinion elites missed and still don't understand. Is it possible that whatever flaws and failures Trump experienced in the past—which some argued disqualified him from being president—are the very things that made him yearn to do what was right as president? Perhaps Trump's desire to redeem an imperfect past instilled in him a yearning to keep his promises to the American people, provide bold leadership at a time of national testing, and reject conventional wisdom.

My mind raced back to the conversation with Ayalon the following year when I returned to Jerusalem to mark the one-year anniversary of the opening of the U.S. Embassy in Israel's capital. I had the opportunity to join Prime Minister Benjamin Netanyahu at a reception marking the occasion, along with American faith leaders, U.S. ambassador David Friedman (Trump's former attorney and a very sharp guy), and members of the Knesset, the Israeli parliament. Netanyahu had just narrowly prevailed in a bitter election and was scrambling to form a government.

One morning, I joined a delegation of faith leaders at the Knesset, which was abuzz with intrigue, rumors swirling by the hour. (In the end, Netanyahu came up a few votes short of a majority, and a new election was called for the fall.) When we met privately with members of the Knesset, most of their comments were *pro forma* and scripted. Then came the turn of Tzachi Hanegbi, a balding, wiry man, his body coiled with energy, a veteran of Israeli politics who had served in several cabinets under Netanyahu.

Hanegbi noted that he had worked with Netanyahu for over two decades. His voice was firm and resonant, his eyes piercing. Like Winston Churchill or Reagan, he said, Bibi was a man animated by core convictions he held with great confidence and was not easily intimidated or plagued by self-doubt. But when the prime minister returned to Israel after his first meeting with Barack Obama, he was shaken. In his storied career, Netanyahu had worked with many U.S. presidents from both parties. After meeting Obama, however, he said that this man was different; he didn't have Israel's back. The prime minister worried that Israel might be on its own.

The room was transfixed. Hanegbi continued, recounting that as the years passed, Netanyahu's warning proved to be prophetic. The Obama administration criticized Israel for defending itself against terrorists in Gaza, blamed the Israeli government for expanding Jewish neighborhoods on the West Bank, intervened through its proxies in Israeli elections, and negotiated a nuclear deal with Iran that would allow it to maintain its ballistic missile program and ultimately obtain weapons of mass destruction that posed an existential threat to Israel. He paused for dramatic effect.

"And then, a miracle occurred: Donald Trump!" Hanegbi exclaimed, throwing his hands in the air for emphasis.

The Evangelical leaders lit up, their faces on high beam. The Knesset members of the Blue and White (the center-left party) sat in stoic silence.

Hanegbi recounted everything that the Trump administration had accomplished that protected Israel's security: the military defeat of ISIS, launching air strikes against Syria, withdrawing from the Iran nuclear deal, crippling the Iranian economy with targeted sanctions, declaring Jerusalem the capital of Israel, moving the U.S. Embassy, and recognizing Israeli sovereignty over the Golan Heights—a critical security buffer against Syria and terrorist networks. In summary, Trump had not only reversed the anti-Israel policies of Obama, but he had also restored the special relationship between the U.S. and the Jewish state and shifted the geopolitics of the entire Middle East in a direction more favorable to Israel and U.S. national security interests.

Hanegbi's dramatic remarks were a reminder of the importance of leadership. As I left the Knesset that day, I marveled at what a difference President Trump had made in the region and the world. He had defended religious freedom for Christians and other religious minorities, defended Israel, taken on terrorism, backed Brexit in the United Kingdom, renegotiated trade agreements, and taken on China for its theft of intellectual property and unfair trade practices. And if Trump's worldview could be summed up with the bumper-sticker slogan "America First," then "Israel Second" came next. For Christians who believe that God gave Israel to the Jews as their homeland and for those who believe they are called to be righteous Gentiles who defend Jews and Israel, Trump was nothing less than an answer to prayer.

If Trump could run for president in Israel and Netanyahu could run for prime minister in America, they would both win in landslides. As it is, both are a little like prophets without honor in their own countries. But if every American could have heard what I did that day at the Knesset, their view of Trump might be very different indeed.

■   ■   ■

The month before my trip to Israel, I was invited to the White House for a criminal justice reform event celebrating the passage of the First Step Act, which had been signed into law by President Trump the previous December. The Faith & Freedom Coalition had made criminal justice reform based on a biblical model of repentance, redemption, and reconciliation one of its top legislative priorities. Under the leadership of Tim Head, our executive director, and Patrick Purtill, our legislative director and a former official in the Justice Department under George W. Bush, we had worked for years to pass historic criminal justice reform that would give offenders a second chance at life. This required Republicans to get out of their comfort zone and transcend political stances that promised to get tough on crime, though often with questionable results and high costs. Some laws passed in the 1990s with bipartisan support that were intended to crack down on drugs and violence resulted in the incarceration of many first-time and nonviolent offenders. They also caused costs to spiral out of control until some states with high incarceration rates were spending more on building prisons than they were on building schools to educate children. These failed policies led to prisons that were little more than warehouses housing the hopeless—where inmates learned how to be better criminals.

As a result, the United States led the world in its incarceration rate with over two million offenders in state and federal prisons or local jails, and 79 percent of the inmates released were rearrested and back in the criminal justice system within six years.[2] At Faith & Freedom, we wanted to change that by offering a high school education, job training, mentoring, and religious faith to more of those languishing in federal prisons. But many Republican elected officials opposed us, and too many Democrats were primarily interested in decriminalizing drugs and criminalizing behavior by corporations and businesses. Despite years of lobbying, we were stymied in our progress until Donald Trump became president. He embraced a bipartisan criminal justice measure that gave prisoners credit toward early release for engaging in life-changing programs like spiritual mentorship and job training while they were incarcerated and lowered the barriers for faith-based organizations to operate programs in federal prisons. After years of coming up short in Congress, Trump's leadership made the difference.

At the White House event, an unusual crowd of liberal activists including Van Jones, a former advisor to Barack Obama, mixed with Evangelical figures on the Right. It was a strange gathering rarely seen in Washington. After remarks by Attorney General William Barr, there was a break in the program, and I ended up chatting with one of the first offenders released under the First Step Act. He had been incarcerated for a drug crime and readily acknowledged that he had gone down the wrong path as a young man. But he said that all he had ever wanted was a second chance at life and that prison didn't provide the help he and other inmates needed to get ready for life on the outside.

"Thanks to Donald Trump, I've now got that second chance," he said, smiling, his hand tightly gripping my shoulder. "And I thank God, I thank President Trump, and I thank you for helping to put him where he is so I could get this chance to redeem myself." He told me he had gotten a job at a furniture factory in Virginia and was taking it one day at a time, putting one foot in front of the other, trying each day to do the right thing.

After this short break, we headed for the East Room, where President Trump, joined on stage by recently released offenders, presided over a ceremony celebrating the passage of the First Step Act—a celebration that had been delayed by an extended government shutdown in a budget dispute between the administration and congressional Democrats. To my surprise, actress Kim Kardashian walked in and sat across the aisle from me. As those in the audience took photos with their smartphones, it occurred to me that this might be the first time the president had been in a room with someone who garnered as much attention as he did in quite a while. In typical fashion, Trump acted as the emcee, turning the podium over to five former offenders who had recently been released.

One releasee bounded to the podium with obvious enthusiasm. "Mine is real short," he said. "Two months ago, I was in a prison cell and [now] I'm in the White House." The crowd laughed. "Let's continue to make America great again!" He and the president hugged, and everyone applauded at the invocation of Trump's signature campaign line.

Yvonne Fountain, also recently released under the First Step Act, came to the microphone. Her words were simple, but her message was powerful—and emotional. "First, I want to thank God because God got me through a lot in prison," she said. "I did my time. I was good the whole time. I worked. I stayed out of trouble." The crowd applauded appreciatively. She turned to the president. "I thank everybody who put their hands in it, all the hard work. And I really thank you for signing that bill. When you signed that, I really could have fell through the floor. Thank you so much."[3]

I departed the White House that day with tears in my eyes. I had to admit that I had never thought I would see the passage of such a bill, or President Trump signing it into law. My heart overflowed with gratitude. In my forty years of political combat and work on public policy, I had rarely seen a bill make such a tangible difference in so many lives. Sixteen thousand people have enrolled in drug treatment programs since the passage of the First Step Act. I was overwhelmed by the testimony of these men and women who only weeks before had been behind bars. They had a new lease on life, and by their own public testimony it had been made possible by the grace of God, the leadership of Donald Trump, and a rare bipartisan coalition in which conservatives and liberals put aside their differences and worked together for the common good. I was struck by the chasm between that reality and the false and misleading portrait of Trump that I saw portrayed in the media every single day.

Needless to say, it was nearly impossible to find a single video clip of one of these moving testimonies about Trump in the liberal news media that day. No surprise there. One recent analysis found that 90 percent of all the coverage of Trump on the network evening news broadcasts in 2018 was negative, the highest share of negative coverage for any president in modern history.[4] A Harvard University study found that NBC's coverage and CNN's coverage of Trump were both 93 percent negative, CBS's coverage was 91 percent negative, the *New York Times'* coverage was 87 percent negative, and the *Washington Post's* coverage was 83 percent negative.[5] No wonder the media have some of the lowest approval ratings of any institution in America.

Trump's leadership on criminal justice reform calls to mind one of the teachings of Jesus about the difference between words and works. When attacked by the Pharisees for violating their traditions, Jesus told his critics, "Though you do not believe Me, believe the works...." (John 10:37–38). Christ's works of healing the sick and feeding the hungry— not his preaching alone—showed God's grace, goodness, and majesty. Rather than acknowledge them, his critics twisted His words, accused him of blasphemy, lied about Him, and claimed He was acting as an agent of Satan.

Words matter, but our deeds speak more to the condition of our hearts than mere words do. In the famous parable of the two sons, Jesus posed the following question: "A man had two sons, and he came to the first and said, 'Son, go work today in the vineyard.' And he answered, 'I will not'; but afterward he regretted it and went. The man came to the second and said the same thing; and he answered, 'I will, sir'; but he did not go. Which of the two did the will of his father?" The Pharisees responded correctly that the first son did. Jesus replied, "Truly I say to you that the tax collectors and prostitutes will get into the kingdom of God before you" (Matthew 21:28–32). What Jesus was saying is that our works, not our words, reveal the true measure of our character. And it is the failure to do God's will—not their sanctimonious words—that will indict the self-righteous on the Day of Judgment.

Trump's media critics parse his tweets like they are studying the Holy Writ and roam the world for his tax returns as though in search of the Holy Grail. Meanwhile, they ignore his works, deeds, and amazing accomplishments: over 7 million new jobs created, a robust economy, the lowest African-American and Hispanic unemployment in recorded history, renegotiated trade agreements with Canada and Mexico, ISIS defeated, Israel defended, Iran challenged, 190 Trump-appointed federal judges at this writing, cuts in funding to Planned Parenthood, restrictions on the taking of unborn human lives, nearly 40 million families receiving an average of $2,200 in tax credits under the Trump tax cut (with 11 million people lifted out of poverty as a result), and thousands of ex-offenders released from federal prison under historic criminal justice reform.

Trump sometimes says (or tweets) things I wish he wouldn't. But as much as I value speech seasoned with God's grace and try to practice it myself, in the end I measure a man more by his actions than by the occasional rash or ill-advised word. Smooth speech and empty eloquence are the special talents of politicians. I have learned to be suspicious of the smooth talker who never delivers. What matters most in the end are one's decisions and deeds, whether they advance good or evil, and whether they produce good or bad outcomes.

How Trump came to occupy the most powerful office in the world to perform such good deeds is a story stranger than fiction. Let us turn to the amazing story of how this most unlikely of conservative and pro-family champions became president—and how Evangelicals made the difference.

CHAPTER 3

THE NERD PROM

I n the weeks after our initial conversation, I stayed in touch with Donald Trump's staff to prepare for his much-anticipated appearance at the annual Faith & Freedom policy conference, which was known as the "Road to Majority." We had invited all the presidential candidates, and most of them would be speaking. Former Massachusetts governor Mitt Romney (the frontrunner), former senator Rick Santorum, former pizza magnate Herman Cain, former Utah governor and ambassador to China Jon Huntsman Jr., firebrand conservative and congresswoman Michele Bachmann, and Texas congressman Ron Paul would be speaking. Trump's inclusion in this lineup generated palpable excitement, causing ticket sales to soar.

In April 2011, I was a guest of the *Washington Post*'s at the White House Correspondents' Dinner, the annual black-tie press confab famous for the socializing between reporters and their sources at endless parties that is often referred to by its nickname: the "Nerd Prom." I had attended the dinner for decades and viewed it as an anthropological slice of elite American political culture: rich, powerful, well-connected, highly educated, ambitious, and often completely disconnected from the real world.

Some prominent journalists had begun to criticize the Nerd Prom as an embarrassment to the Fourth Estate. From where I sat, nothing much could embarrass them. Either way, the show went on with a stand-up comedian serving up personal insults, ribald jokes, and nasty takedowns of various people in the audience. It was all in good fun with a healthy dose of venom and barely disguised contempt for the great unwashed masses in flyover country. The high point of the evening came with remarks by the president, who took good-natured shots at the media and his political foes with a few jokes at his own expense.

When I arrived at the table, to my surprise none other than Donald Trump entered the ballroom accompanied by his beautiful wife, Melania, and it struck me that the excitement he sparked resembled that of a Hollywood film star arriving at Comic-Con. The crowd parted for him like the Red Sea. Starstruck people gawked, grasped for his hand, posed for selfies, and pointed him out to their dinner guests. For some in the press, Trump was the skunk at the garden party, an unwelcome guest crashing their party. Still, the curiosity was undeniable, and the mob around Trump, cameras flashing and arms and legs akimbo, moved like a giant amoeba. People tripped over chairs or scrambled to intercept him. It was controlled pandemonium. Trump passed me like a well-coifed, tuxedoed rugby player caught in a scrum and proceeded to stand ramrod straight in front of a chair at the table next to mine.

I caught the eye of Lally Weymouth, the savvy daughter of the late Katharine Graham, who was the publisher of the *Washington Post*. I gave her a thumbs up. Lally's mouth curled into a knowing smile. She had accomplished her objective: every eye in the ballroom was fixated on Trump sitting next to her—including, as it turned out, President Obama's.

The entrée was filet mignon and salmon, but it soon turned out that Donald Trump would be the main course. Obama took the stage, and everyone sat up in their chairs, leaning forward in anticipation. The Washington press adored Obama. He was all they aspired to be; he was intelligent, articulate, attractive, and liberal. With the help of comedy writers and White House speech mavens, Obama's remarks at the dinner were usually quite funny. Four days earlier, Obama had released his long-form birth certificate proving he was born in Hawaii, apparently in response to Trump's calling for its release. Obama had denounced the "carnival barkers" who put on "sideshows" that distracted from the pressing issues facing the country. Trump, while in New Hampshire testing the presidential campaign waters, held an impromptu airport press conference where he took credit for the release of Obama's birth certificate.

Obama wasted no time in his after-dinner remarks in raising his birth certificate. He opened by announcing the release of his birth video that very night to further document the fact that he was, in fact, a native-born citizen of the United States. The house lights went down, and the scene of the celebration of the birth of Simba from the Disney film *The Lion King* played on the video screens to loud roars and laughter. Obama then went after Trump with undisguised pleasure.

"Now, I know that he's taken some flak lately, but no one is happier, no one is prouder to put this birth certificate matter to rest than the Donald," Obama said. "And that's because he can finally get back to focusing on the issues that matter—like, did we fake the moon landing? What really happened in Roswell? And where are Biggie and Tupac?" Loud laughter and applause greeted his reference to the unsolved killings of the two rappers. Obama clearly enjoyed ridiculing Trump, as did the crowd.

"All kidding aside, we all know about your credentials and breadth of experience." Then Obama twisted the knife. "For example, in an episode of *Celebrity Apprentice*—at the steakhouse, the men's cooking team did not impress the judges from Omaha Steaks. And there was a lot of blame to go around. But you, Mr. Trump, recognized that the real problem was a lack of leadership. And so ultimately, you didn't blame Lil' Jon or Meatloaf. You fired Gary Busey. And these are the kind of decisions that would keep me up at night. Well handled, sir. Well handled."

By now, the tuxedoed and sequin-gowned media mavens in the crowd were doubled over with laughter. Those sitting at the *Washington*

Post's tables were far more subdued. They stifled their laughs or turned to one another, eyes wide and mouths agape. Trump, meanwhile, sat serenely as television cameras recorded his non-reaction.

Comedian and *Saturday Night Live* alumnus Seth Meyers took the podium next, peppering his monologue with his own shots at Trump. "The press speculated whether Donald would run as a Democrat or Republican," he said. "I thought he was just running as a joke." As the pummeling continued, no one was laughing with Trump; they were laughing at him.

Sitting nearby, I never got the feeling that Trump was fazed. In fact, he seemed to enjoy being the center of attention, a place where he was clearly comfortable. In the days to come, the media would proclaim that Trump had been "humiliated" by Obama. When Trump did eventually run for president, the myth emerged from armchair psychiatrists in the pundit class that it had all begun that night, and that Trump's real motivation was settling a score for being so badly mistreated by Obama and the press. This was nonsense. Trump had publicly mulled about running for president for decades, and as I knew from my recent conversation with him, his consideration of a run for the White House had nothing to do with a comedy sketch. The fact that the media thought their dinner played a role in his later decision to run revealed more about their own exalted view of themselves than it did about Trump.

When the evening ended, Trump rose from his chair, shook hands around the table, and waved to the crowd, ever the good sport. He then turned around to me, making a hand gesture simulating a phone, his right hand to his ear. "Call me," he said. As I left the ballroom, it occurred to me that by singling out Trump for such comic needling, Obama had all but dared him to run. Would he? I would soon learn the answer.

■   ■   ■

The next afternoon, I boarded a flight to Paris for a *National Review* river boat cruise down the Seine River, the highlight of which was a visit to Normandy, where U.S., British, and Canadian forces landed on D-Day in 1944. I was scheduled to speak several times during the cruise. After a week of sightseeing with the magazine's subscribers, donors, and staff, we sailed slowly back to Paris. I was sitting in my cabin and watching the outskirts of the city go by when my cell phone unexpectedly rang. When I answered it, I was surprised to hear the voice of Donald Trump.

Trump told me that he had had been forced to wait until the end of the current season of *The Celebrity Apprentice* to announce his candidacy. Otherwise, NBC would have been required to pull the show from the air or give equal time to other candidates.

"I get it," I replied. "Makes perfect sense."

Trump told me that the final episode of the season would air that Sunday night. The next morning, he informed me, he would walk into a hotel ballroom in New York City in front of two thousand reporters and TV cameras and announce his candidacy for president. I knew that moment would be like a bomb going off, shaking the political establishment to its core. To my surprise, Trump asked me if I would manage the campaign.

I was floored. Trump and I had only known each other for a matter of weeks. I was flattered and intrigued, but I had also had a load of other commitments, including my business consulting firm and my public policy organization, Faith & Freedom Coalition, which was barely two years old and needed my help in raising funds and setting strategies. As a condition of their own service, the board of directors had required that I make a long-term commitment at the time of its founding in 2009. "Mr. Trump, I'm honored that you would think me capable of taking on such a major responsibility for you," I said. "But I have an issue."

Trump asked me what the issue was.

"When I started Faith & Freedom two years ago, I went to some of my best donors and grassroots organizers and asked them to come on board," I said. "They agreed to do so, but they had one condition: I couldn't leave to pursue other opportunities. I gave them my word."

Trump didn't seem dissuaded. He said we could discuss a possible solution to the problem. Perhaps if he hired a manager in whom we both had confidence, I could stay in touch with them on a regular basis.

"There's certainly no law against my talking to my friends," I agreed.

Trump asked if I could fly to New York the next day to discuss the matter further. I explained that at that very moment I was in France floating down the Seine River. I told him I would be back in the States in two days. Coincidentally, I was landing in Newark, New Jersey, just a short drive from his office.

Trump asked me to come to his office at nine o'clock on Monday morning, and after a brief meeting, accompany him to his campaign announcement. He generously suggested I bring along my wife and children, if they were available.

I had met a lot of alpha males in my political career, but Trump was a force of nature I had never encountered before. I hung up and stepped out of the bathroom where I had gone to take the call. My wife, Jo Anne, was sitting on the edge of the bed in our cabin. The look of shock on her face told me she had overheard the conversation.

"Donald Trump just asked me to join his campaign," I said.

"I heard," she said. "Are you going to do it?"

"I don't see how I can," I replied. "But I don't think he's someone who takes 'no' for an answer."

I told my wife I would stay in New York when we landed from Europe instead of flying home to Atlanta. I saw no downside to meeting with Trump, especially if he was really going to jump into the race. I had a lot of friends running for president, apparently now including Trump, and I was for my friends. I certainly didn't think it was smart to decline the meeting. I was happy to share my views and offer advice to anyone running for president, and certainly Trump was no exception. The fact that signing on with Trump's presidential campaign would likely resemble being strapped into a roller coaster ride with no brakes was both a little frightening and thoroughly exhilarating at the same time.

■ ■ ■

I spent a good deal of the next two days on my knees praying for God's direction, protection, and wisdom. On Monday morning, I walked from the Trump Hotel to Trump Tower, rehearsing my lines about how I couldn't break my commitment to Faith & Freedom. When I arrived at Trump Tower, Trump's assistant ushered me into his office.

Trump greeted me by telling me he owed me an apology.

I read the expression on his face and knew instantly that he had changed his mind. "You're not running, are you?"

Trump said he was not. But he assured me that he had fully intended to run when we spoke on the phone earlier.

"What happened?" I asked, puzzled.

Trump said that after our call, NBC had called and asked him to re-up with *The Celebrity Apprentice*. He recounted the conversation with a senior NBC executive in which he declined, saying he planned to run for president. Several hours later, he received a call from a senior executive at Comcast, the parent company of NBC, almost begging him to do the show for one more season and asking him to name his price. Trump said that when he did so, he gave the highest number he could imagine, and to his great surprise, they agreed.

The good news was that I didn't have to turn down Donald Trump. Part of me was actually disappointed, as I had grown excited at the prospect of what a rollicking ride Trump's campaign would have been. Trump would have landed in the roiling waters of American politics like a whale in a bathtub. I believed he would have transformed the GOP presidential primaries into must-see TV and turned the debates into a ratings bonanza, drawing millions of new voters into the Republican Party.

Even then, I didn't see him as a liability to the role of Evangelicals in the GOP; I saw him as an invaluable asset and ally. Assuming his conservative and pro-life views were genuine—and I believed they were—he could become an unlikely champion for Evangelicals. He certainly wanted to win their trust.

Besides, Trump had drawn record crowds everywhere as he explored a presidential bid, stoking curiosity and piquing interest like a carnival coming to a small town. His ability to command media attention was legendary. I recalled Ross Perot early in his 1992 campaign for president when he was an ubiquitous presence, booking himself on television as his own press agent, packing arenas with his throwback crew cut, "Aw-shucks" demeanor, and his populist promise as a no-nonsense business-man to go to Washington and "get under the hood and fix it." I had gotten to know Perot fairly well during those years. I found him to be a patriot—brilliant, if quixotic. "Ralph, I'm the white albino monkey of American politics," he once told me. "Everyone has seen the elephant and the zebra. But have you ever laid eyes on a white albino monkey? No. Well, that's me. I can put fannies in the seats and eyeballs on the TV." (Famously suspicious about surveillance, Perot also told me once to have my office swept for listening devices. A conversation with Ross was never boring.)

Could Trump succeed where Perot had failed? I was certainly curious to know the answer.

Politics is a serious business with the highest of stakes, including war, peace, the destiny of nations, and the fate of civilization. But it is also stagecraft, possessing a measure of pageantry and showmanship. Ronald Reagan understood this. His critics dismissed Reagan as a B-grade actor who had once starred opposite a monkey (in *Bedtime for Bonzo*) and lacked the intellectual chops to be president. But Reagan knew how to occupy the stage, how to stand on a tape mark and deliver his lines, how humor could deflect the blow of an opponent, and even how to let another person steal the scene when the moment called for it (as he did when Mikhail Gorbachev came to Washington at Reagan's invitation in 1987). These skills, which were derived from his acting career, were essential to Reagan's success. When asked after a shaky first debate performance against Walter Mondale in 1984 whether his age was an issue, Reagan paused, bowed his head, and delivered the kill line: "Age should not be an issue in this campaign. I will not exploit my opponent's youth and inexperience for political purposes." The joke brought the house down. Reagan won the election at that moment, not by citing facts or relating the details of his latest medical checkup, but because he knew how to deliver a line that totally diffused the issue.

Trump had a similar performer's instinct. Later, after another meeting in his office, I followed him down to the lobby of Trump Tower at his invitation to watch him shoot a scene for *The Celebrity Apprentice*. I observed as Trump and the floor director huddled as they prepared for him to be presented with a custom gold motorcycle by the stars of *American Chopper*, another reality show. One of the stars also happened to be a contestant on Trump's show, so the segment was a clever cross-promotion. The director, holding a rough outline of a script in her hands, briefly walked through the scene with Trump, who nodded his head. He asked her one question, shook hands with the crew, and said he was ready. As the lights came on and the cameras rolled, he played his part perfectly, and they shot the scene in one take. I noted how easy he made it look. Admittedly, Trump was playing himself. But Trump would only have to play himself in a campaign, too, and it was a larger-than-life persona that he had become quite skilled at playing, not only on his own TV show, but for decades as a celebrity.

As long as Trump remained true to the pro-life and pro-family evangelical positions, I saw him as having the potential to appeal far beyond the traditional confines of what was once called the Religious Right. The fact that he didn't act or talk like a typical Evangelical, didn't come from the Bible Belt, and didn't attend a Christian college or quote Scripture also meant he could reach a new—and larger—audience. That did not mean I shared every view he espoused. I supported his call for border security, but probably had a more positive view of (legal) immigration overall. I had supported the Iraq War and believed it was the right decision, and he did not. But I had learned a long time ago that one never agreed with any candidate 100 percent of the time. Reagan was fond of saying that an 80 percent friend was not a 20 percent enemy. I felt that too many in the GOP were treating Trump like an enemy when he was at least an 80 percent (and probably much higher) friend—especially on the core issues of life, marriage, the family, religious freedom, tax cuts, growing the economy, and supporting Israel. Besides that, I found him to be highly approachable, personable, and—contrary to my expectations—he listened more than he talked, a rarity among politicians.

As Trump and I discussed the campaign that did not happen, various and sundry supplicants and secretaries circled in and out of the office. Ivanka appeared to discuss a business matter and Trump reintroduced us. Michael Cohen, Trump's attorney at the time, stuck his head in, and we met for the first time. Trump played the perfect host, making me feel welcome with his staff and children, heaping praise on everyone, and rapid-firing questions about how I saw the presidential race. Seeing Trump in his element was eye-opening. At one point, he took a call on a real estate deal, and to my surprise, he allowed me to stay as he practiced what he had once called the "art of the deal"—cajoling, haggling, and sweet-talking the other party about a building project. It was impressive watching him at work. I wondered if he would be as good at politics and wondered now if I'd ever find out.

He buzzed his secretary and asked her to bring him an article he had seen about the presidential race. Handing it to me, he asked me for my opinion. Kinetic with energy, Trump bounced from topic to topic, sometimes in midsentence. We surveyed the rest of the 2012 GOP presidential field. I told him that with him out of the race, the nomination was probably Mitt Romney's to lose. Newt Gingrich and Rick Santorum had stronger grassroots support but would have a harder time raising money. Romney would have the money (including plenty of his own), lots of endorsements, a good political team, and a solid organization.

Trump asked for my thoughts on Obama's going after him at the White House Correspondents' Dinner. "I thought he overplayed his hand," I said. "It would have been fine for him to needle you or tell a few jokes. But it was over the top. The meanness of it showed a certain smallness on his part. I thought it was petty."

Trump shrugged it off, saying he thought Obama was somewhat funny, but Seth Meyers wasn't funny at all. He took Obama's fire as a compliment, proving that he was a force to be reckoned with in the future. Pointing out that he was leading in the polls for the Republican presidential nomination at the time, Trump noted that politicians don't attack potential opponents if they don't think they can beat them.

As our meeting wrapped up, I encouraged Trump to stay involved, suggesting that he could be a big help to the Republican Party in the future, whatever he decided to do. "You're one of the most famous people in the world, and you've got a common touch, which is rare," I said. "I think you can energize the grassroots and bring new people into the tent." I told him the invitation to speak to the Faith & Freedom policy conference still stood, and I hoped he would still come, despite not being a candidate.

Trump replied without missing a beat that he had said he would be there, and therefore he would be there.

We shook hands, and I left. I took the elevator down to the Trump Tower lobby and walked out on Fifth Avenue to grab a taxi. In the back of the cab on my way to a lunch appointment, my mind raced. Trump was out of the running, but clearly not finished politically. He still had his eye on the prize. Why else would he keep his appointment at our conference? I suspected that in taking a pass on 2012, he was only laying the groundwork for the future.

■   ■   ■

The following month, Trump's jet landed at the Dulles International Airport, and he zipped to the Renaissance Hotel in downtown Washington to address a crowd of a thousand Evangelical pastors, leaders, and activists. He was running a little late, and bumper music played over the loudspeakers in the ballroom as the crowd buzzed with anticipation. I greeted Trump when he arrived and escorted him to a holding room backstage. Michael Cohen was in tow. Trump handed me a photograph of him as a boy with his confirmation class at First Presbyterian Church in the Jamaica neighborhood in Queens, New York. He asked me if we could show it on the jumbotrons when he spoke.

"Sure," I replied, not entirely certain how he intended to use the photo.

Trump stood before a blue curtain with American flags and took pictures with some of our donors and state leaders. Cohen pulled me aside. "Listen," he whispered, "I'm really angry because I wanted you to introduce the boss. But Roger Stone wants S. E. Cupp to introduce him." He grimaced, uncorking some profane words about Stone, whom he considered to be a micromanager and troublemaker. I said nothing in reply. S. E. was an up-and-coming news commentator with a libertarian streak. I was somewhat surprised to find that Stone was so heavily involved.

After the photo opportunity, Trump sat down for a roundtable discussion with about twenty of our top state leaders, pastors, and national board members prior to his speech. I was a little nervous about how they might receive him, but my concerns were unfounded. Thrilled to be in the presence of such a famous businessman and celebrity who was solicitous of their views and values, they asked substantive questions and hung on his every word. Trump used the occasion to make it clear that he viewed the Evangelical community as one of the most important and effective communities in American politics with an influence almost inversely proportional to its numbers. He told them he wanted to help change that. His interaction with these faith leaders confirmed my suspicion that Evangelicals viewed Trump—despite his past foibles and liberal social views—as an ally and, perhaps, a future leader.

S. E. Cupp, resplendent in a white pantsuit, went to the podium to introduce Trump, lavishing radiant praise and superlatives on him. (I would recall her words years later when she would eviscerate Trump on CNN.)

Backstage, Trump paced like a heavyweight prize fighter before a big fight. At one point, he half-crouched like a Golden Gloves boxer and playfully punched me on the arm. I told him to have a good time, and he said he would. He bounded on stage to the thumping strains of "Money, money, money!" from the song "For the Love of Money" by the '70s soul group the O'Jays. The ovation was thunderous, his high-wattage celebrity filling the room. Flashbulbs exploded, television camera crews scampered to get the best shot, and people raised their phones in the air to take photos of The Donald.

Trump had asked that his confirmation photo be displayed, and he referenced the photo, pointing himself out in the crowd and talking about his faith, primarily in the context of his churchgoing mother, an immigrant from Scotland. He seemed unaware that most Evangelicals view their spiritual journey as beginning with a conversion experience, which they describe as being "born again"—not a graduation from confirmation. But no matter. The crowd applauded appreciatively, and the use of the photo showed Trump's longing for a connection with Evangelicals as he sought, however awkwardly, to establish a bond with them. Woody Allen once said that half of life was showing up; in this case, Trump had shown up, and he was richly rewarded.

Trump launched into an extended riff in which he described how Obama flattered him by targeting him with jokes making up "a majority of his speech" at the White House Correspondents' Dinner. Trump described his surprise at receiving such an extended treatment by Obama. "The President is talking about me, this is great, what an honor, what a great honor. I had a great time!" he exclaimed. He said he told Melania that it was a high compliment. "The next day I wake up and about 90 percent of the papers said Trump was humiliated." Trump then turned on the media in remarks foreshadowing a central theme of his 2016 campaign: "And that's part of the problem that the Republicans are going to have," he said. "Nobody is protected by the media like Barack Hussein Obama. I have never seen press that is so protective of a human being." The crowd groaned, laughed, and applauded. I didn't fully grasp it at the time—since complaining about media bias was a common refrain among Republicans—but with the benefit of hindsight, Trump was trying out a message he would later refine as "fake news." In his early forays as a political figure, Trump had clearly concluded that the media had ceased being referees and had instead become combatants on behalf of one political party: the Democratic Party.

The Faith & Freedom activists gave him an "A" for effort and welcomed him with open arms. The ballroom was packed with people lining the walls and the back of the room. Part of Trump's appeal was pure curiosity, like Perot's self-description as a "white albino monkey." But there was more. Trump boasted, for example, that he could use words like "stupid" or "they don't have a clue" because he was not a typical politician. In other words, he vowed to speak the truth—unvarnished, politically incorrect, and unflinching. Some would later underestimate this aspect of his appeal, dismissing his willingness to say what everyone else thought but would never actually say as boorish and low-rent, when many voters were drawn to his brash style because it showed that he was genuine. Much of his message was already fully formed. He criticized the trillions of dollars spent by the United States in Iraq, Afghanistan, and the Middle East without demanding access to oil reserves and while neglecting the needs of our own citizens. He said that Iran was likely to become the dominant power in the region by posing an existential threat to Israel, controlling the Baghdad government and its energy resources, and undermining and destabilizing moderate Arab states. He vowed that the right leadership could "make America great again." These were all prescient comments.[1]

Trump's star power, his performance art, his unapologetic and brash authenticity, his New York state of mind with a heavy dose of Queens, and his willingness to wing it without a script were all riveting. Trump on stage was a high-wire act performing without a net, and no one could avert their gaze.

Over the next several years, I would stop by to see Trump when I was in New York. We spoke on the phone, as well. We remained friends, and he continued to be a featured speaker at the Road to Majority policy conference. He keynoted our gala dinner in 2013. After Obama was reelected, we would sometimes talk about whether or not he planned to run for president, but I never got the feeling that Trump was feeling the strong pull of a candidacy like I did in 2011.

In our conversations, Trump acted like a human sponge, soaking up information. He would ask for my off-the-record opinions of various Republican strategists, pollsters, and media consultants. I was surprised by how many GOP operatives and donors he knew; he obviously talked to a lot of people. Once, he asked me what I thought of Roger Stone. I had known Stone for over a quarter of a century, and while we had different styles, I told him that I thought Roger was brilliant and mercurial, with a dollop of self-promotion. I suggested it might be better to have Roger in the tent spitting out than outside the tent spitting in.

We discussed many issues, most notably abortion, same-sex marriage, and immigration. I never tried to persuade Trump to take any particular viewpoint. I felt I could best serve him by giving him my best and unvarnished advice and let him come to his own conclusions. I never had an agenda beyond trying to build a bridge between him and the faith community, believing that both would be well-served by a strong relationship.

During one of these conversations, Trump told me he had been pro-choice for much of his life. Then, he said, a woman who was a good friend became pregnant. The husband pressed this woman to have an abortion, but she resisted the idea. One day, she called him for advice, and he wasn't really sure what to tell her. In the end, the woman decided to keep the baby. Trump said he had watched the child grow up, and today she is a total star. This young woman obviously does not know that her mother almost aborted her; she certainly does not know that Trump knows. He talked about how she was now an amazing, talented, beautiful young lady. Trump said the episode made him reflect upon how many other wonderful, gifted people are not here because they were lost to abortion.

I had heard a lot of formerly pro-choice candidates explain how they came to their pro-life views in my career, but few had more genuine stories than Trump's. He seemed to have had a true change of heart. Later, when he ran for president in 2016, I recalled our conversation, and while some questioned his commitment to the unborn, I did not. I could not know or judge Trump's heart (for no one can ever know the heart of another person), but I never doubted his sincerity or his commitment to the sanctity of life—not for a moment. And he hasn't let me down.

My conversations with Trump were largely theoretical, but in 2014, we discussed the possibility that he might consider running for governor of New York. The Republican Party in New York lay in shambles, and their leadership hoped Trump could rescue them from oblivion, not to mention self-finance his campaign. Trump told me he was confident he could win. I thought he would make a formidable presidential candidate if he were governor of New York and told him so, pointing out that most recent presidents had first served as governors, including FDR, Carter, Reagan, Clinton, and George W. Bush. But my thinking was conventional. As events would later demonstrate, Trump had his eye on a larger prize, and he didn't run for governor.

Then in the spring of 2015, I began to hear rumblings (again) about Trump running for president, and rumors swirled that he was hiring staff in Iowa and New Hampshire. I still don't know why I didn't just call Trump and ask him about the rumors. Instead, I called my friend Chris Ruddy, the CEO of the conservative news site Newsmax, who lived in Palm Beach and was also a member at Trump's club at Mar-a-Lago. Chris and I had discussed Trump in the past, and I found that he often had good insights. I occasionally would have lunch with Ruddy when I was in Palm Beach, and he could always be counted on to share a Trump nugget. So I called Chris and told him what I was hearing. Was there any truth to the rumors Trump was running for president?

Chris was emphatic that it was not true. "Trump is a negotiator. He's driving up the asking price for another season of *Celebrity Apprentice*. He's going to make noise and he might even hire a small staff. But in the end, he won't run."

Chris's analysis made perfect sense, especially given what had happened in 2011. After all, Trump had been dipping his foot in the presidential waters since the 1980s, but he had never taken the plunge.

I hung up the phone, confident based in part on Chris's insight and in part on my own experience four years earlier that Trump would test the waters but wouldn't run. I could not have been more mistaken. My friend

Chris (a very smart guy), as well as the entire elite media and the political establishments of both parties, would soon learn that they were wrong, too. What happened next would turn the political world upside down.

CHAPTER 4

A WHALE IN A BATHTUB

Contrary to the liberal media's narrative, Evangelicals were not all that enthused about Donald Trump at the beginning of the 2016 presidential campaign. Few knew him, and even fewer trusted him. The marriage between Trump and the Evangelical movement would prove to be a shotgun wedding, with the real estate magnate in avid pursuit and most Evangelicals in love with someone else, at least initially. That changed with the passage of time and a herculean effort by Trump—aided by the horrifying prospect of a Hillary Clinton presidency.

Trump focused on Evangelicals like a laser beam with a discipline and focus that belied the caricature drawn of him by pundits and inside-the-beltway politicos as a novelty candidate who made it all up as he went along. When it came to the faith community, Trump was a man on a mission, and he was someone who was used to getting his way.

As Evangelicals prepared for 2016, they circled the stable of prospective presidential candidates like jockeys in search of Secretariat. Deepening their sense of urgency were two back-to-back landslide defeats at the hands of Barack Obama in 2008 and 2012, when Republicans had nominated John McCain and Mitt Romney, two frontrunners with strong backing from the establishment wing of the party. Another loss in 2016, this time to Hillary Clinton, would mean four (or eight) more years of liberal governance with devastating consequences for the federal judiciary, the permanent bureaucracy, and the causes of life and religious freedom. Convinced that leaving the choice of the next nominee to the establishment meant another certain defeat, Evangelicals hatched a holy conspiracy with an audacious goal: to win the GOP presidential nomination for one of their own. To succeed, they had to unite to prevent their votes and influence from being diluted in a crowded GOP field that would soon swell to seventeen candidates. It required anointing a single candidate as the Evangelical favorite in the hopes that he or she could propel them to the White House. The question was who?

I attended a meeting of Evangelical donors and leaders at a hotel in Times Square in New York City in August 2014 to discuss the midterm election and look ahead to the 2016 presidential race. I had been invited by my friend Tony Perkins, the head of the Family Research Council. I respected Tony's leadership and political skills, first honed as a state legislator in Louisiana, where I watched him move legislation by being philosophically solid but also pragmatic. He had demonstrated an ability to build coalitions with unlikely allies in Louisiana. I was honest with Tony and told him I wasn't sure it was possible to herd the leaders of the entire pro-family movement—and even if one could, there was no guarantee the voters would follow. Since those were my views, I told him I wasn't sure he wanted me at the meeting. Tony's reply impressed me: I want you at the meeting precisely because those are your views. He only asked that I keep the proceedings of the meeting confidential, which I did.

Mike Huckabee spoke first, which I took as a sign that he had the inside track among many of the leaders, and for good reason. As a former pastor and religious broadcaster, as governor of Arkansas, as a presidential candidate, and as a popular Fox News host and contributor, Mike had been one of our best leaders. Mike said that when he ran for president in 2008, many potential wealthy donors told them they liked him, respected him, and could get behind him, but they wanted to hold off until they saw how he performed in the early primaries. Mike said he tried to tell these donors he couldn't get a lift-off if they didn't support him then. It was a circular argument: Money conferred credibility, which led to more money, which funded television and a ground game. It was a chicken and egg problem, Mike explained. Heads nodded throughout the room. He urged us to get behind a candidate early and put our money where our mouth was. Oh, and by the way, I hope it's me, he said, flashing a grin. Mike had the top-rated weekend program on Fox News and was writing bestselling books and giving paid speeches. But it seemed clear that he would soon walk away from all of it for one more shot at the ultimate prize of American politics.

I had great respect for Mike and other Evangelical leaders who were intent on backing one candidate. But I also had my doubts, in part because of a similar effort in 2012. Many Evangelical leaders were wary of Mitt Romney, some because of his past liberal social views and others because of his Mormon faith. These suspicions ran deep in the Evangelical psyche. I was on a flight with some prominent Southern Baptist preachers in May 2007 en route to the funeral of Jerry Falwell Sr. in Lynchburg, Virginia. The 2008 Republican primary campaign was already underway, and I used the opportunity to conduct an impromptu focus group of Evangelical leaders. I wondered how they compared Rudy Giuliani (then the frontrunner in the polls) to Romney. "Which is worse in your mind?" I asked. "Being married three times and being pro-choice and pro-gay rights (which were Rudy's vulnerabilities), or being a Mormon?" One of the Baptist preachers, a battle-seasoned war horse of many denominational and political battles, thought for a few seconds. "About the same," he answered.

That told me Romney was in trouble with Evangelical voters (and so was Giuliani). I had met with Romney on several occasions and discussed his views on abortion and other issues, and I did not share the same level of concern. Nor did I think it wise to oppose anyone based on their religious beliefs or theology. Finally, after numerous fits and starts, in February 2012, a group of faith leaders gathered at a Texas ranch and formally endorsed Rick Santorum for president.[1] It was a last-ditch effort to stop Romney just days before the South Carolina primary.

That same day, by coincidence, the Faith & Freedom Coalition was holding a candidate forum in Myrtle Beach, South Carolina, hours before a televised primary debate on CNN. Almost all of the candidates still in the race came to make their final pitch to Evangelicals in a state where they made up over half of the primary voters. Over five hundred grassroots activists packed into a white tent on the grounds of the Myrtle Beach convention center to hear from the candidates, with dozens of television cameras ready to record their pitches to this critical constituency.

Rick Santorum showed up backstage, and I asked him if his anointing by faith leaders in Texas would turbocharge his campaign. Rick shook his head. "They waited too long," he said. Shortly before Mitt Romney's arrival, one of his campaign advisers called to check in. I asked if he was worried about the Evangelical leaders endorsing Santorum? The strategist laughed, saying that delivering a presidential nomination is not like delivering a pizza. It takes tens of millions of dollars and an organization in forty states, not endorsements and press releases. I was taken aback by his level of confidence.

Romney showed up looking a little like a movie star, jet-black hair combed back, perfect tan, his prominent jaw set, flashing a Pepsodent smile. I greeted him warmly. "Well, Mitt, you didn't get the evangelical leaders, but you got Jon Huntsman," I joked. (Huntsman had announced he was dropping out of the race hours earlier and endorsing Romney. The relationship between the two men was famously strained.) Romney broke down laughing, telling me he had no idea that Huntsman was getting out and that Huntsman had called him only moments before his announcement to tell him.

That evening, my wife and I attended the South Carolina primary debate at the convention center. With Santorum, Romney, and Gingrich bombarding one another with negative television ads with the primary just days away, the massive crowd packed into the convention center buzzed with energy, ready for the fireworks. No one knew that the first explosive would be lit by the press. John King of CNN opened the debate by firing a question at Newt Gingrich that landed like a howitzer. He asked about claims made by his ex-wife that he had once requested an open marriage. Newt waited patiently while King methodically went through the dirty laundry, and then he proceeded to tear into him with a vengeance. "I think the destructive, vicious, negative nature of much of the news media makes it harder to govern this country, harder to attract decent people to run for public office," he said, eyes shooting daggers. "And I am appalled that you would begin a presidential debate on a topic like that." King tried to backtrack, shifting the blame to ABC News (which had aired the interview with Newt's ex-wife), but Newt was having none of it. "Every person in here has had someone close to them go through painful things. To take an ex-wife and make it, two days before the primary, a significant question for a presidential campaign is as close to despicable as anything I can imagine...I am frankly astounded that CNN would take trash like that and use it to open a presidential debate."

The crowd erupted in a standing ovation, the hall echoing with the guttural roar of resentment directed at the liberal media. It is difficult to fully describe the level of anger felt towards the elite media among grass-roots conservatives. Newt had touched a raw nerve with a blowtorch, a move that prefigured Trump's tactic in 2016 of denouncing what he called "fake news." Some people stood on chairs pumping their fists, screaming at the top of their lungs. Others twirled handkerchiefs or waved Newt campaign signs. The debate was over after only one question. I whispered to my wife, "Newt may have just won the primary."

And win Newt did, with 40 percent of the vote in a four-man contest. According to exit polls, self-identified Evangelicals cast 44 percent of their ballots for Newt, 22 percent for Romney, and 21 percent for Santorum. The candidate endorsed by Evangelical leaders just days before the primary came in third among Evangelical voters—trailing a lifelong member of the Mormon Church. But Santorum did emerge as a stiff challenger to Romney, winning thirteen primaries and caucuses while narrowly losing the Ohio and Michigan primaries. Had he won those two primaries, Santorum might well have gone all the way to the convention. Still, the CNN debate underscored that what the famed GOP strategist Lee Atwater once called "defining moments" in campaigns mattered a lot. There was no way to know how a candidate might perform when the spotlight hit them, and it was almost impossible to script such moments. (A similar moment unfolded in the first Democratic primary debate in 2019 when Senator Kamala Harris dressed down Joe Biden for his past praise for segregationist senators and his previous opposition to bussing. Biden so badly fumbled his response that he dropped in the polls, foreshadowing his weaknesses as a candidate.) Because of this, I was wary about any attempt to mobilize Evangelical voters behind a single candidate.

By the time of the second "unity" meeting in Washington in December 2014, the momentum had shifted to Ted Cruz. Someone presented a report on the field of potential candidates, detailing their fundraising, name identification, polling, and organization. When it was my turn to speak, I suggested that they consider whether anointing a candidate was wise. There were many pro-family champions in the Republican field, including Huckabee, Cruz, and Santorum. Even more centrist candidates like Marco Rubio, Scott Walker, and Jeb Bush were strongly pro-life and were deeply committed in their Christian faith. Why choose among our friends and risk alienating the others, not to mention their supporters? I also worried that a public endorsement could hobble the eventual nominee in the general election, making them look beholden to an interest group. I pointed to the American Federation of Labor and Congress of Industrial Organizations' (AFL-CIO) endorsement of Walter Mondale in the 1984 Democratic contest, which had allowed the Reagan campaign to portray Mondale as being in the pocket of union bosses. Did we want to allow the media and the Democrats to portray the GOP presidential nominee as somehow beholden to us? We were popular among a certain segment of the electorate, but we were not necessarily helpful among others.

I argued that although Evangelicals were a significant constituency (roughly one-fourth to one-third of the electorate, depending upon how one did the math), we were not a majority of all voters. It was better, I suggested, to think and act as a minority. The Jewish and pro-Israel community understood this. As a general rule, the Jewish community worked to ensure that it had someone influential in the camp of every candidate. That way no matter who emerged as the victor, the Jewish community would have a friend in the White House, and hopefully one of their own close to the president. I suggested that we identify leading pastors or faith leaders who were close friends with each candidate, and make sure one of them was involved in the campaign of every candidate. In other words, back them all. "That way," I said, "no matter who wins, we win."

One glance around the table told me that my argument was not likely to prevail. They felt strongly that allowing the process to unfold on its own would lead to a repeat of an establishment candidate winning the nomination, only to go down in defeat in the general election. I was sympathetic to this view. But how could we really decide the outcome of a pitched battle among seventeen candidates, fought over forty or more primaries and caucuses, with an estimated thirty million votes cast, at a cost of over one billion dollars? Ironically, in the meetings I attended, I don't recall Donald Trump's name coming up. But it was Trump—not the favored candidate of conservative and faith leaders—who would go on to win the Evangelical vote in the primaries, a phenomenon to which we will turn next.

In an early warning sign, Jeb Bush—the putative frontrunner for the nomination, at least in terms of fundraising ability—had the support of only one faith leader who was in the room. I had known Jeb since his first run for governor in 1994, when as executive director of the Christian Coalition, I helped mobilize Evangelical voters to support him when he ran as a "head banging conservative" (his description) against the popular incumbent governor, Democrat Lawton Chiles. Back then, Jeb had campaigned as an unflinching social conservative: pro-life, pro-family, pro-religious freedom. I was deeply impressed. When he narrowly lost that race (after some low-down politics by Lawton Chiles's campaign in the form of push-polls the weekend before the election) while his brother George W. easily won the gubernatorial race in Texas, Jeb went through a period of deep personal and professional introspection that led to his conversion to Roman Catholicism. In 1998, Jeb ran again and won easily. I went to his inaugural in Tallahassee in January 1999 and spent time with him and George W. Bush (who would soon announce his candidacy for president). I walked away impressed by Jeb's humility, persistence, and sharp political instincts. During George W. Bush's presidential runs in 2000 and 2004, when I served as a campaign advisor, I worked closely with Jeb and his very able political team and found him to be incredibly sharp. He knew every inch of the state of Florida, every region, every media market, every constituency, and every issue. In his two terms as governor, Jeb transformed Florida into a reliably Republican—if competitive—state as the GOP controlled the legislature and held every statewide constitutional office. Jeb was a rare political talent and a good man. I filed away in my mind to keep an eye on him in the future, whatever it might hold.

In early 2011, I flew to Miami and met with Jeb in his office at the Biltmore Hotel in Coral Gables and urged him to seriously consider a run for president. Since he left the governorship in 2007, he had built a business and sat on some corporate boards. After a long and wide-ranging conversation in which he shared book recommendations and we discussed everything from hurricane response to education reform, he stood up and shook my hand firmly, but remained noncommittal. Jeb pointed to an American flag hanging on the wall and said that if he did run, he would do it because of the country it represented. But like Trump and Huckabee, he took a pass.

I was close to many of the other candidates. I had known Mike Huckabee since he ran for the U.S. Senate in 1992, and I considered him to be one of the finest representatives of the Christian faith and conservative values in American politics. Rick Santorum had been a friend since he came to Congress in 1991, and he was our leading champion in the Senate on welfare reform and the partial-birth abortion ban, as well as an early and prophetic voice warning about the dangers of radical Islam. I got to know John Kasich in the early 1990s when, as the ranking Republican on the House Budget Committee, he drafted the GOP budget that first included the $500 child tax credit, one of the top legislative priorities of the Christian Coalition. (The famously irascible Kasich would yell at me about seeking favors for my special interest, but no one was a fiercer advocate for the child tax credit once he came on board. It was later included in the Contract with America and signed into law by Bill Clinton.) Ted Cruz and I worked together on George W. Bush's 2000 presidential campaign, and I had once asked him to head Faith & Freedom in Texas. (He chose to run for the U.S. Senate instead.) Marco Rubio and I had become friends when, as the darling of the Tea Party, he challenged Governor Charlie Crist for the U.S. Senate in 2010, drove Crist from the party, and won a three-way general election. Scott Walker had attended the organizational meeting of Faith & Freedom in Wisconsin in 2010, and we later built a strong grassroots network in the churches with his help.

Finally, there was Donald Trump. He had become a good friend and frequently spoke at Faith & Freedom Coalition events. If he ran, he would land in the race like a whale in a bathtub. In such a crowded field, I didn't see how I could back one of them against the others. Not long after the December meeting in Washington with faith leaders, I convened a meeting of the Faith & Freedom board of directors in Atlanta. Over steaks at a local restaurant the night before the meeting, the board members surveyed the field and speculated as to who might emerge as the nominee. Steve Scheffler, our Iowa state leader and the Republican National Committeeman from the Hawkeye State, informed us that the entire membership of the Iowa GOP central committee had agreed to remain neutral in the Iowa caucus. This policy had been adopted after the 2012 caucuses, when various committee members had signed on to different campaigns, with some endorsements accompanied by consulting contracts, which sparked charges of corruption. When the state party declared Mitt Romney the winner on caucus night, only to correct the result and announce that Rick Santorum had won, cries of favoritism filled the air. In response, Iowa party leaders decided on a policy of neutrality.

Since Steve was bound by the Iowa central committee in 2016, the board decided we should all do the same and refrain from endorsing, contributing, or publicly supporting any presidential candidate prior to someone becoming the official Republican nominee. The board felt that given the abundance of acceptable candidates on our key issues, there was no reason for us to seek to impose our views on our Evangelical members. We would leave it to the voters, even as we did all we could to highlight our issues and turn out Evangelical and pro-life voters in the primaries.

Candidates began to announce their campaigns as soon as the calendar turned to 2015, and most made no bones about targeting the Evangelical community. Ted Cruz announced his candidacy in March 2015 at a Liberty University student convocation, making it clear he would build his campaign around a full-throated appeal to Evangelicals. Jeb announced at a raucous rally in Miami in early June. The next morning, Donald Trump rode the escalator down to the lobby of Trump Tower. Although almost no one understood it at the time, the world would never be the same—either for American politics or the faith community.

Trump announced his candidacy two days before Faith & Freedom Coalition's Road to Majority policy conference in Washington, where over two thousand grassroots activists would hear speeches from fourteen announced presidential candidates. Ted Cruz, Marco Rubio, Rick Santorum, Mike Huckabee, Jeb Bush, Scott Walker, Rand Paul, Chris Christie, Lindsey Graham, and even moderate former New York governor George Pataki were all coming. (In what proved to be a disturbing omen, a bomb threat forced the evacuation of the ballroom for Pataki's speech.) But like much of the political world, we were caught flat-footed by Trump's announcement. I texted Corey Lewandowski, his campaign manager, and told him we'd be happy to have Trump address the conference again. "We would love to have Mr. Trump, and I can guarantee a hero's welcome," I promised Corey.

Corey called me back right away. He said he had talked to Trump, who wanted to come, but events already scheduled in Iowa and New Hampshire would make it nearly impossible to get there. I told Corey to come if they could and said we would clear the schedule for him. I also said there would be numerous other opportunities at our candidate forums during the primary. We hung up after agreeing to stay in touch.

Based on the unscientific crowd reaction at the conference, Ted Cruz was the early favorite. He spoke at a luncheon moderated by my good friend Kellyanne Conway (who did a spectacular job as always), delivered a stem-winder speech, and was mobbed by activists after his speech. Walker, Huckabee, Santorum, and Rubio also received strong responses.

Two months later, I swung by the RedState Gathering in Atlanta, a right-wing confab hosted by my friend and radio talk show host Erick Erickson, where many of the candidates were scheduled to speak. As it happened, a few days earlier at the first televised Republican presidential debate, Fox News host Megyn Kelly had hurled a fastball at Trump about his past alleged comments about women, referring to some as "fat pigs," which Trump had waved off as directed at Rosie O'Donnell during a New York tabloid spat. After the debate, Trump took a swipe at Kelly during a CNN interview, referring to "blood coming out of her eyes, or blood coming out of her wherever," which the elite media claimed referred to her menstrual cycle. Trump denied the charge.

Walking into the lobby of the Renaissance Hotel in Buckhead in Atlanta, I ran into *Washington Post* political reporter Robert Costa, his face beaming as if to say, "How did I get this lucky? Donald Trump is running for president and I get to cover it!" He asked me if I had heard about the comments by Trump about Megyn Kelly. I had not. Costa proceeded to describe them in all their explicit detail.

"Care to comment?" he asked, a wicked grin spreading on his face.

I laughed. "Not a chance."

"Can't blame me for trying," he said.

"Is he imploding?" I asked.

"I think he may be," he replied.

"You better hope not," I volleyed back. "You'll lose half your readers!"

I had been invited to an informal meeting with Jeb Bush and some local pastors and faith leaders, so I departed the lobby and rode the elevator up to the meeting room. Atlanta is a celebrated mecca for Evangelicals with its sprawling suburbs dotted with the soaring spires and cavernous auditoriums of megachurches, so there were some Evangelical heavy hitters in the room. Among them were Mark DeMoss, a public relations executive with deep roots in the Evangelical world, and Jay Sekulow, head of the American Center for Law & Justice, who was then advising Bush on judicial nominations, but would later become one of Trump's personal attorneys. The pastors listened and asked friendly questions. They were polite and respectful, but I did not sense the enthusiasm I had seen for his brother George W. Bush. Was it Jeb's Catholicism or his more cerebral, intellectual approach to public policy? I couldn't put my finger on it.

After the meeting, I headed downstairs to watch Jeb and await Trump's arrival. I thought that perhaps watching the two men back-to-back in front of a grassroots conservative audience would prove instructive. But when I arrived at the ballroom, Erickson was at the podium announcing that he had contacted Trump's campaign and disinvited the candidate over his comments about Megyn Kelly. Erickson said that as a father and a man of faith he could not countenance having Trump at the event after such crude remarks. Personally, I would have handled the situation differently. At Road to Majority, we had invited all the candidates, even those who were pro-choice. That didn't mean we endorsed their views; we were only providing a fair and neutral forum for each candidate to make their case.

A few minutes later, my cell phone rang. It was a good friend who was a huge fan of Donald Trump's. He had asked me for a ticket to the RedState event, which I had arranged by calling in a few favors, since the event was sold out. He said he was on his way but had just heard on the radio that Trump had been disinvited. Was that true? I told him that it was. My friend thanked me for the trouble of getting him a ticket, but he said he was no longer interested in attending. He told me he had gotten off the highway, turned his car around, and was driving home. I was stunned. For him, it was Trump or no one.

What was Trump's effect on voters like my friend if they wouldn't even attend a star-studded event unless Trump was there? For him, there was no second choice in the field. I had never seen anything quite like it.

For his part, Trump responded to his exclusion with a counterpunch. His campaign spokesperson called Erickson a "total loser" who "has a history of supporting establishment losers in failed campaigns." Trump's comment referred to a nosebleed, and "only a deviant would think anything else."

Erickson returned to the podium to recount the attacks he was receiving via email and text, reading a few that were littered with profanity and racist insults. The media lapped it up, always loving a food fight about Republicans. Some in the crowd stood to their feet applauding, while others (I gathered who were Trump supporters) remained seated, their arms crossed. The term "deplorable" had not yet entered the political lexicon. But the implication that Trump supporters included racists, haters, and cranks would become a common theme.

I thought about my friend the Trump supporter, a successful businessman, a patriot, and a family man. He and I would occasionally discuss the presidential race, and he would listen politely as I analyzed poll numbers, fundraising, favorable and unfavorable ratings, and grassroots organization. Then he would wave it all off. "It's Trump all the way, baby," he told me with great bravado. "Take it to the bank!"

I wondered how many people like my friend would vote in the GOP primaries. It struck me that not only the elites in the liberal media, but even many conservative journalists and commentators seemed to be missing the Trump phenomenon. Something was happening that was real and powerful—a deep yearning to shake up a sclerotic political system and bring dramatic change to Washington, a hunger for a champion and a fighter—and it seemed that no attack on Trump or insults directed at his supporters could stop it.

CHAPTER 5

CRUZ CONTROL

By the time Trump rolled up in an SUV behind the Knapp Conference Center on the Iowa State Fairgrounds in Des Moines for the Iowa Faith & Freedom Fall Kick-Off in October 2015, he was the frontrunner for the nomination, leading in every national poll and most state polls. Iowa, however, had so far resisted his charms. The Hawkeye State was slowly turning to Cruz, and the Trump campaign had decided to make a forceful play for Evangelical voters, who represented 60 percent of caucus attenders. Trump shot out of the vehicle as though fired from a cannon, a blue-suited bundle of kinetic energy, his towering physical presence a force of nature, with a thicket of television cameras and boom mikes following him like a mechanical spider. Once backstage, Trump took pictures with local elected officials and Faith & Freedom donors. A famous germophobe, Trump replaced the requisite handshake with his trademark thumbs up. He carried his mother's Bible and a stack of papers that I assumed were his notes, but they turned out to be copies of national and state polls showing that he was leading the race. He pulled me and Tim Head, our executive director, into a power clutch and pointed out all the primary states where he was ahead. Flipping through the pages, he pointed out that he was leading all his opponents every-where. He seemed to be saying, *sotto voce*, "Guys, this thing is over. Get on the team."

Trump towered over us with deliberate, practiced physicality, his presence imposing. Other candidates charmed, leaned in, whispered, flattered, cajoled, touched an arm, or patted a shoulder. Not Trump. He was not the subtle type; he just bowled you over. He owned every room he entered.

And yet this room, packed with Evangelical activists, proved to be a hard one to win over. A July NBC/Marist poll of GOP caucus attendees showed Scott Walker with a narrow lead of 19 percent, Trump at 17 percent, Jeb Bush at 12 percent, Ben Carson at 8 percent, and Huckabee at 7 percent. Among self-identified Evangelicals, however, Trump's support was 13 percent.[1] Trump knew he needed to increase that number.

Trump's speech was warmly received by the crowd at the Faith & Freedom event; some in the audience stood and cheered, but the majority remaining seated, still surveying the field before making a final decision. Iowa caucus attenders were notoriously stingy with their support. Trump wowed the crowd by waving the polls that pointed to his inevitability. His circuitous speech cited his mother's Bible, a talisman of her devout Presbyterian faith and his family's spiritual heritage, and his proven applause lines about cracking down on China's unfair trade practices, building the wall on the southern border, and saying "Merry Christmas" in America again when he became president. But the room remained reserved, its wait-and-see posture clearly on display.

As a veteran of the Iowa caucuses, I knew Trump would have an uphill battle in the Hawkeye State. Evangelicals may dominate the GOP caucuses, but that didn't make the contest a prayer meeting. The politics was cutthroat, a quadrennial take-no-prisoners death match that seemed strangely incongruous playing out across a serene landscape dotted with soybean and cornfields, coffee shops, small town diners, and white clap-board churches. Iowans had come to expect quadrennial VIP treat-ment—meeting candidates multiple times, with the professional activists flattered and cajoled in one-on-one meetings over pie and coffee in their homes. Cruz, Carson, and Huckabee battled it out for the Evangelical vote, a fierce scrum where sharp elbows and high knees determined the outcome. As previous winners of the Iowa caucuses in 2008 and 2012, Huckabee and Santorum had a special claim to the hearts of Evangelicals. But they would find that voters are fickle with inconstant loyalties and a hunger for the shiny new object. Cruz and Carson filled this desire.

To his credit, Trump refused to concede the Evangelical vote to anyone. It was a strategy that would pay huge dividends down the line. "They love me, and I love them," he said. At an Evangelical confab in Iowa earlier in the year in which Trump made headlines because of his criticism of Senator John McCain, he had insisted he was their coreligionist. "People are so shocked when they find…out I am Protestant. I am Presbyterian," he said. "I go to church and I love God and I love my church." This was a familiar refrain—one he had continually made since he had spoken to Faith & Freedom back in 2011.

At the 2015 event hosted by the Family Leader organization, moderator Frank Luntz asked Trump if he ever asked God for forgiveness for his misdeeds.

"I am not sure I have," Trump said. "I just go on and try to do a better job from there. I don't think so. I think if I do something wrong, I think, I just try and make it right. I don't bring God into that picture. I don't."

Trump's statement appeared to run counter to one of the core Evangelical beliefs: that forgiveness for sins comes from confession and repentance—not from doing good deeds. Trump also said he regularly participated in Holy Communion.

"When I drink my little wine—which is about the only wine I drink—and have my little cracker, I guess that is a form of asking for forgiveness, and I do that as often as possible because I feel cleansed," he said. "I think in terms of 'let's go on and let's make it right.'"[2]

The liberal media slammed Trump for the "little cracker" line. But in fact, Trump had correctly stated that communion offered believers the grace to ask for God's forgiveness and seek His cleansing from sin. In Protestant teaching, Holy Communion recalls the sacrifice of Christ on the cross, the breaking of His body (bread), and shedding of His blood (wine). Despite the media's fixation on Trump's checkered past and occasionally awkward phrases, Evangelicals were driven far less by identity politics than they were by the issues. They also extended far more grace to Trump than the media ever did. Evangelicals accepted Trump for who and where he was spiritually, believing that by loving him and showing him kindness and mercy they might have a sublime influence on him. That mission was made easier by the fact that on the issues that mattered most—such as abortion, marriage, religious freedom, and repealing Obamacare—Trump was rock solid. The chattering class misunderstood the Trump-Evangelical connection as purely transactional or the product of rank hypocrisy. In truth, it was based on shared values and his enthusiasm for championing them and the issues that animated Evangelicals. This resonated at the grassroots level, where many believed the GOP establishment had long promised to advance their issues, only to then pay lip service once in office.

Martin Luther is reported to have said that he would rather be operated on by a Turkish surgeon than a Christian butcher. Evangelicals have the same attitude about political leaders. They might prefer a politician of their own faith and theology, but they are most concerned with whether a politician is a gifted and capable leader. Trump's candidacy involved a measure of calculation by Evangelicals (as well as other voters) as to what kind of leader the moment required. They preferred someone who had the guts to shake up Washington and drain the swamp to a fellow believer who couldn't take or throw a punch. Politics is a contact sport, and few Evangelicals have illusions any longer about what is required to prevail in the arena. They needed a nominee who could take on the Clinton attack machine and prevail. Trump, warts and all, was a formidable competitor, and he had the hide of a rhinoceros.

Nor were Evangelicals immune from the deep discontent roiling the GOP grassroots about candidates who sought their support at election time, only to give short shrift to their policy (and personnel) issues once elected. Long the red-headed stepchild of American politics, conservative Christians had grown weary of being stiff-armed by the party establishment, tired of paint-by-the-numbers candidates offering up pro-life rhetoric during the primaries, only to be pushed aside and ignored like lepers after the election. They had relied on the promises of GOP presidential candidates for decades to appoint strict constructionists to the Supreme Court, then watched as Republican presidents appointed Sandra Day O'Connor, Anthony Kennedy, and David Souter, who cast deciding votes to uphold *Roe v. Wade* or overturn the marriage laws of dozens of states by imposing same-sex marriage on the entire country by judicial dictate. By 2015, the faith community resembled a jilted lover—no longer trusting and a little righteously indignant. If the definition of insanity was doing the same thing over and over and expecting a different result, then Evangelicals were willing to try something—and someone—new and different. With his celebrity and unconventional style, this is what gave Trump a huge opening in a field filled with conventional politicians. Therefore, Trump got a fair hearing—including from Evangelicals—but he still had to close the deal.

For conservative Christians, the dilemma presented by Trump's candidacy was not about whether he was part of the elect. It was about whether he would govern as a pro-life, pro-family conservative and would keep his word to appoint strict constructionists to the federal courts—especially the U.S. Supreme Court. One complicating factor was this: Trump had previously floated his sister, first appointed by Ronald Reagan in 1983 and then elevated to the appellate court by Bill Clinton (she was reportedly a moderate and pro-choice), as a possible Supreme Court pick. "Oh, my sister's great," Trump told Bloomberg. "I think she would be phenomenal. I think she would be one of the best." Then he seemed to catch himself. "But frankly—we'll have to rule that out now, at least temporarily."

When I attended a Council for National Policy (CNP) meeting in October 2015 within days of the Iowa Faith & Freedom event, Trump was consolidating his lead, and most of the people in the audience of Evangelical and conservative leaders were flabbergasted. The Council for National Policy had been founded in 1981 by the leaders of the conservative movement with backing from business magnates and GOP mega donors Nelson Bunker Hunt and Joseph Coors. In the years since, it had become a critical nexus of donors and doers, conservative and Christian philanthropists who mingled with the grassroots leaders who built the conservative infrastructure in the states and Washington, D.C. Trump was scheduled to address the group, which offered a critical opportunity for him to make his case and find common ground with the leaders of modern conservatism.

As the crowd filed into the ballroom, I ran into a good friend who served as the president of a Christian college.

"Who are you for?" I asked my friend.

"Rubio and Cruz in that order. After that, anybody but Trump," he said, smiling.

He was not alone. While Evangelical and Catholic leaders would later be pilloried for supporting Trump, the reality was that most of them supported someone else during the primaries. For some, Trump was their seventeenth choice. Their reaction to Trump and the phenomenon he had come to represent was a strange mixture of bewilderment, disbelief, and denial. After Trump spoke to the group (as usual there was not an empty seat in the room), Marjorie Dannenfelser, the president of the Susan B. Anthony (SBA) List, a leading pro-life organization, asked him a pointed question about his sister as a potential Supreme Court justice. Trump took it in stride, saying that while she was qualified, he would not likely select his sister.

After the speech, Trump agreed to take a photo with anyone who wanted it. This gave him the chance to personally greet every leader and work them with his famed charm and celebrity. To my surprise (given the fact that most were for Cruz, Huckabee, or Rubio), the photo line snaked out of the main ballroom, through the lobby, and then back into a second ballroom where Trump stood patiently in front of a blue curtain and an American flag. The excitement among those in the line waiting to meet Trump was palpable. As I headed backstage to say hello to him, I passed a couple I knew to be die-hard Cruz supporters. They stood near the back of the line, waiting for their photo.

"You're getting a picture with Trump?" I asked. "I thought you were for Cruz."

"We are, but why turn down a photo with Trump?" the woman asked brightly. "Who knows? He could become president!"

The husband unbuttoned his jacket, revealing a Cruz lapel sticker affixed to his coat lining.

"You better hope Trump doesn't see that!" I warned. They laughed.

The Trump train kept rolling, and Evangelical leaders were either going to have to get on board or get out of the way.

■   ▩   ▩

The same month as Trump's successful appearance at CNP, Faith & Freedom held a candidate forum at Prestonwood Baptist Church in the suburbs of Dallas, Texas. Each candidate was given an opportunity to address a crowd of several thousand Evangelical activists and then be interviewed by my good friend Jack Graham, the church's pastor and a former president of the Southern Baptist Convention. Jeb Bush, Ben Carson, Rick Santorum, Mike Huckabee, and Carly Fiorina all spoke. But Texas was Cruz Country, and there were numerous prominent Cruz supporters and donors in attendance.

Backstage, I greeted Ted and his wife, Heidi, both of whom I had worked with on George W. Bush's campaign in 2000. We discussed their campaign strategy in the green room while standing and eating plates of deviled eggs and finger sandwiches. Both expressed total confidence in their chief strategist, Jeff Roe, their data analytics, and a digital strategy that allowed the campaign to identify and target every single potential Cruz supporter in the early primary states and their key issues: abortion, guns, taxes, or the economy. Ted exuded confidence, predicting that he would win in Iowa, and a victory there would propel him past the other candidates as the conservative alternative to Trump. Once the race became a binary choice between him and Trump, Cruz argued, he would win. While other candidates like Bobby Jindal and Rick Perry had taken Trump on, Ted had treated Trump with kid gloves, occasionally throwing him a compliment, part of his wily strategy to avoid the furnace blast of Trump's wrath until he found himself in a two-man elimination match that he believed the Manhattan billionaire could not win. South Carolina and the Super Tuesday states, Ted observed, boasted a disproportionately Evangelical electorate—a group he would carry big.

Ted's theory of the case made a lot of sense, but it assumed that both Evangelical voters and his vanquished rivals felt the same. Eight years earlier, Rudy Giuliani had planned on becoming the alternative to John McCain and obtained a commitment from then-governor Charlie Crist of Florida to endorse him before the state's primary. However, when Rudy then failed to win a primary prior to Florida, Crist reneged and endorsed McCain instead, dealing a death blow to Rudy's hopes for the nomination. Presidential politics had a way of frustrating the best-laid plans. But one thing was certain: Ted had a strong base among Evangelicals, and that meant he would have staying power.

I ambled out from backstage and watched Ted's speech from the congregation to gauge the crowd's reaction—a tactic I had learned from years of campaigning. Ted was a luminous orator who thrived in this setting, prowling the stage like a lion hunting its prey. He spoke without notes, pacing the stage while wearing his footwear of choice: shiny black ostrich-skin boots, which testified to his Texas roots. He chopped the air with hand gestures, quoted Scripture and Supreme Court decisions from memory with ease, and punctuated his sales pitch with jokes needling Hillary Clinton. The crowd lapped it up, rising to its feet in multiple standing ovations. Ted would prove to be a formidable opponent, perhaps the only man standing between Donald Trump and the prize of the Republican nomination.

■   ■   ■

Contrary to the stereotype later put forward by the liberal media, Evangelicals gravitated to Trump with ambivalence and more than a little reluctance. Some were dragged kicking and screaming to the voting booths. In early December 2015, after fits and starts and jockeying by multiple campaigns, the faith leaders seeking to coalesce the pro-family movement behind a single candidate finally voted in a straw poll to back Ted Cruz. It was a major public relations coup for Cruz, who had been tireless in courting the Evangelical leaders, banking on an avalanche of public endorsements giving him momentum heading into Iowa and other early primary states.

Within days, direct mail guru Richard Viguerie, Brian Brown of the National Organization for Marriage, and Bob Vander Plaats, a social conservative leader in Iowa, all quickly endorsed Cruz. Focus on the Family founder Jim Dobson, an iconic figure on the Evangelical right, traveled to Iowa to stump with Cruz. "Ted Cruz's record on religious liberty, life, and marriage is second to none in this Republican field," Dobson said. "Shirley and I have been praying for a leader such as this, and we are confident that Ted Cruz has the moral and spiritual foundations to lead our nation with excellence." He urged "people of faith to join us in supporting his race for the presidency." With Dobson at his side at a campaign event in the town of Winterset, Cruz vowed, "We have a federal government that is waging a war on life, a war on marriage, a war on religious liberty." He warned that "if we allow non-believers to elect our leaders, we shouldn't be surprised when our government doesn't reflect our values."[3]

These endorsements by faith leaders had the desired effect in Iowa, though it wasn't entirely clear whether those endorsing were running in front of the parade or genuinely causing the Cruz groundswell. Either way, the results were decidedly mixed. Trump remained the top candidate in the Republican primary race, consistently leading in the polls. A

December Quinnipiac University poll showed Trump leading with 27 percent among Republican primary voters, 17 percent for Rubio, 16 percent each for Cruz and Carson, and 5 percent for Jeb Bush.[4] Trump remained on top, and everyone else fought for second place. Seemingly no gaffe, controversy, media attack, or negative ad slowed him down. Indeed, Trump dominated the race like a modern-day Prometheus, a culture warrior who packed the masses into basketball arenas even as he repelled conservative and liberal media elites, a master of social media who flung tweets like heat-seeking missiles, a counter-puncher who took the force of his critics' blows and threw their energy back into their faces, and a man whose every utterance and refusal to pay abeyance to political correctness reduced his primary opponents' candidacies to a joyless exercise in either assent or opposition to all things Trump. In conservative salons, a slow and astounding realization took hold: Trump might actually win the Republican presidential nomination.

For many, this was a terrifying prospect. Rich Lowry, editor of *National Review*, determined that principled conservatives needed to take a united stand against Trump before it was too late. So on January 21, 2016, *National Review* published an issue that landed like a thunderclap with the title "Against Trump" emblazoned across the cover. Lowry described the purpose of the issue in no uncertain terms: "The most important thing is putting a marker down and saying, 'He's not one of us. He's not a conservative, and he's not what conservatism is.'"

"All along, there have been principled conservatives opposing him," Lowry explained. "So we wanted to gather together a group to make that point quite dramatically."[5]

The "Against Trump" issue certainly succeeded in making a dramatic point. Lowry rallied over twenty conservative leaders, writers, commentators, and activists to the cause, and the issue featured a slew of essays criticizing Trump from nearly every possible angle. Some warned that he would support the expansion of big government, while others cited his authoritarian-style rhetoric. Many pointed out that he had in the past been pro-choice and supported Planned Parenthood. They saw his conversion to the pro-life cause as political calculation, not a genuine change of heart. Although his status as a political outsider and his scorn for the Republican establishment made him attractive to a cynical, disaffected voter base, *National Review* contributors begged their readers not to be taken in by the show. They predicted that Trump would turn out to be a "political opportunist," "a menace to American conservatism," a pure "huckster," and "the greatest charlatan of them all."

Among the essays were several penned by Evangelical leaders. Southern Baptist leader Russell Moore warned that though "Trump says he is pro-life now," his "supposed pro-life conversion is rooted in Nietzschean, social Darwinist terms."[6] He attacked Trump's personal life in withering terms, pointing out that he "has abandoned one wife after another," bragged about "having sex with some of the top women of the world," and "after all that, that he has no need to seek forgiveness." After generations of claiming that "virtue matters in the citizenry and in the nation's leaders," if social conservatives joined Trump's "celebrity focused mobocracy" where "a narcissistic pursuit of power" replaced "sound moral judgments," they would surrender to decadence and deviance and thereby "lose their soul."

This was strong stuff. One essayist called Trump an "explosive, know-nothing demagogue" whose ignorance would surely derail the country.[7] Andrew McCarthy and former attorney general Michael Mukasey, two of the foremost experts on the war on terror, argued that his ignorance of Islamic terrorist leaders and tactics would make him a danger to national security.[8] Michael Medved, an orthodox Jewish talk show host on the Christian-owned Salem Radio Network with a large Evangelical audience, bemoaned his "brawling, blustery, mean-spirited public persona," which seemed to confirm all the liberal stereotypes about intolerant, privileged conservatives.[9] Others compared Trump's "crowd-pleasing" campaign style to the populist rise of European dictators and South American demagogues.[10]

The Republican National Committee cut off the partnership it had held with *National Review* for the GOP debates. But Lowry and the rest of the staff had planned for such a reaction. According to Jack Fowler, the publisher and vice president of *National Review*, the loss of the sponsorship was a "Small price to pay for speaking the truth about The Donald."[11]

I called Lowry, who happened to be a good friend of mine. I had been a fan and avid reader of the magazine since college. "You didn't leave yourself much of an exit sign in the burning theater, did you?" I joked.

"Not so much," Rich replied, chuckling.

"What do you do if Trump is the nominee? He's leading almost everywhere except Iowa. How do you walk this back?"

"We can figure out a way if necessary," Rich said, unconcerned. He said his primary motive was a defense of conservatism. If Trump emerged as the Republican presidential nominee, the magazine might not actively support him, but it probably wouldn't oppose him either.

The term "Never Trumper" had not yet entered the political lexicon, but that didn't appear to be the posture of *National Review*. Despite the ferocity of its blast, it sounded more like, "Against Trump...for now."

Five days after *National Review*'s broadside and less than a week before the Iowa caucuses, a group of prominent pro-life women leaders fired their own salvo. In an open letter to social conservative voters in Iowa, they urged them "to support anyone but Donald Trump."[12] Arguing that the "next president will be responsible for as many as four nominations to the Supreme Court," it faulted Trump for citing his sister as a potential nominee to the highest court and for praising pro-choice former U.S. senator Scott Brown of Massachusetts as a possible vice president. "Moreover, as women, we are disgusted by Mr. Trump's treatment of individuals, women, in particular," the signers said, claiming he had "impugned the dignity of women," in his comments about Megyn Kelly and Carly Fiorina (whose appearance he had disparaged in an interview), "and has through the years made disparaging public comments to and about many women." When it came to "defending unborn children and protecting women from the violence of abortion," the signers concluded that "Mr. Trump cannot be trusted." The pro-life leaders stated that America needed "leaders of strong character who will defend both unborn children and the dignity of women," concluding, "We cannot trust Donald Trump to do either. Therefore we urge our fellow citizens to support an alternative candidate."

Trump, meanwhile, penned an op-ed for the *Washington Examiner* in which he vouched for his pro-life credentials. "Let me be clear—I am pro-life," he insisted, acknowledging he had not always held this position. He expressed alarm that "our culture of life in this country has started sliding toward a culture of death." The millions of unborn who had lost their lives to abortion "never had the chance to enrich the culture of this nation or to bring their skills, lives, loves or passions into the fabric of this country." They "are missing, and they are missed." Trump pledged to appoint conservative judges, to defund Planned Parenthood, and to oppose abortion except in the cases of rape, incest, and if the mother's life was endangered—the identical position taken by every Republican presidential nominee since 1980. He called federal funding of Planned Parenthood "an insult to people of conscience at the least and an affront to good government at best." The op-ed could have been written by the pope himself, yet Trump's remarkable pro-life statements weren't enough for many Evangelical and pro-life leaders.[13]

My good friend Penny Nance, CEO of Concerned Women for America and a respected pro-family leader, called me to seek my advice about signing the letter. I recommended against it. First, Trump had converted to the pro-life cause, and I argued that as pro-life leaders, we should welcome converts to our cause. Second, the letter was not advocating on behalf of anyone; it was merely an attack on Trump. This might peel off some social conservative voters, but those votes would ricochet like billiard balls on a pool table, scattering them to various candidates on caucus night without benefiting any single Trump opponent. Negative attacks in a crowded field rarely work. Finally, I argued that Trump might well win the nomination, and to have pro-life leaders question his pro-life convictions (which I believed were genuine) might make it difficult to rebuild the bridge to Trump later.

Penny heard me out but decided to sign the letter. She was joined by Marjorie Dannenfelser of the Susan B. Anthony List, Concerned Women of America founder Beverly LaHaye, former pro-life congresswoman Marilyn Musgrave, and the president of Iowa Right to Life. (After Trump had been elected and had proven to be reliably and solidly pro-life, I would good-naturedly remind Penny of our conversation; she readily admitted she had been wrong about Trump and was glad and relieved to be wrong.)

The same day that the pro-life letter landed in Iowa, Family Research Council president Tony Perkins endorsed Ted Cruz during an appearance on Fox News. Although Tony wisely declined to attack Trump, others were less reticent. Appalled by Trump's personal past and unconvinced by his pro-life promises, some Evangelical leaders unloaded on the real estate magnate. Al Mohler of the Southern Baptist Theological Seminary sounded the alarm:

> The candidacy of Donald Trump now presents American evangelicals with some unavoidable questions that are simply going to have to be answered. What exactly do we expect of a candidate? In someone who identifies as a Presbyterian, but has made his fortune largely by building industry such as casinos…someone who has held to moral positions that are far outside moral traditionalism…and someone who has held to public policy positions on an issue like abortion that has been at one point and then the other, raises a host of questions. This is where evangelical Christians need to think very, very carefully.[14]

Other Christian activists and writers called for not only thought, but action. They pleaded with their fellow believers not to vote for Trump in the primaries. As David French proclaimed in a March 2016 article in *National Review*, "[H]ow can I responsibly cast a vote to give one of the nation's foremost cultural platforms to a man who has openly, loudly, and unrepentantly bragged of his adulterous sexual conquests? How can I support a man who demonstrates such a breathtaking level of malice and cruelty in his treatment of his fellow citizens? Our nation can survive lost elections, but over the long term it cannot survive a decayed culture.

And by God I won't vote for a man who takes a wrecking ball to the core values I hold dear."[15]

Mark DeMoss, a board member at Liberty University, concurred: "Donald Trump is the only candidate who has dealt almost exclusively in the politics of personal insult. The bullying tactics of personal insult have no defense—and certainly not for anyone who claims to be a follower of Christ. That's what's disturbing to so many people."[16]

Other Christians denounced the party for even considering Trump as its nominee. In a scathing post on The Resurgent, Erick Erickson vowed to withdraw his support from the Republican Party "if it chooses to nominate a pro-abortion liberal masquerading as a conservative, who preys on nationalistic, tribal tendencies and has an army of white supremacists online as his loudest cheerleaders."[17]

Still other Christian reporters highlighted Trump's lack of past personal virtue, as well as the unsavory sources of his wealth. Rebecca Hagelin, former vice president of the Heritage Foundation, called him the "King of Sleaze," pointing out that he had built casinos that featured strip clubs and soft pornography: "It is beyond tragic that so many of my Republican and Christian brothers and sisters have forgotten that it is the moral fiber of a country that determines its ultimate destiny. If the GOP disregards moral, principled leaders in favor of one who promises only great riches, then we deserve neither."[18]

A group of Catholic academics, headed by Princeton professor Robert George, joined in the chorus of condemnation. George co-authored an open letter in March that firmly stated:

> Donald Trump is manifestly unfit to be president of the United States. His campaign has already driven our politics down to new levels of vulgarity. His appeals to racial and ethnic fears and prejudice are offensive to any genuinely Catholic sensibility.... And there is nothing in his campaign or his previous record that gives us grounds for confidence that he genuinely shares our commitments to the right to life, to

religious freedom and the rights of conscience, to rebuilding
the marriage culture, or to subsidiarity and the principle of
limited constitutional government.[19]

I had an accidental (or divinely ordered, depending on one's perspective) advantage over some of these leaders, having gotten to know Trump
years before. He and I had many frank and candid conversations about
his views on the issues, including those dear to Evangelicals. I had found
Trump to be highly intelligent, well-informed, and a straight shooter. One
thing that struck me about Trump was that he seemed to know everyone
in the worlds of business, finance, media, and politics. And when Trump
gave his word, in my experience, he kept it. When I read some of the
harsher descriptions of him by other prominent Christians, the portrait
they painted bore no resemblance to the man I knew. I wondered: Had
they ever had one conversation with the man? And although I remained
neutral in the campaign according to Faith & Freedom's board policy, I
never hesitated to share my estimation of Trump in private with others.

Not everyone in Trump's world was thrilled that I stayed on the
sidelines, including my friend Michael Cohen, who would call occasionally, pressing me to endorse his boss, promising to line up high-profile
media coverage and implying he was calling at Trump's request. I liked
Michael and I found his persistence endearing in its New Yorker aggres-
siveness. Still, I politely declined. Later, after he was elected president,
Trump greeted me in a receiving line, stepping back and pointing a finger
at me, reminding me that I had not supported him early on, had apparently taken a while to figure it out, but eventually got it. "Actually, Mr.
President, I figured it out pretty early on," I said, laughing. He flashed a
knowing smile and nodded.

Trump did snag some valuable Evangelical endorsements. Jerry Falwell
Jr., president of Liberty University, stepped out in a major way, urging voters
to back Trump as a proven leader and solid conservative, praising his business acumen as what the country most needed. Robert Jeffress, pastor of
First Baptist Church of Dallas, traveled with Trump to Iowa and delivered

a stem-winder of a speech at Dordt University in Sioux Center. "Most Americans know we are in a mess, and as they look at Donald Trump, they believe he is the one leader who can reverse the downward death spiral of this nation we love so dearly," Jeffress vouchsafed. Pastor and religious broadcaster Paula White, who had been close to Trump and his family for years, played a pivotal role behind the scenes, bringing Evangelical leaders to meet with Trump privately, most of whom came away impressed and pleasantly surprised by what they heard while remaining publicly neutral. For Trump, these meetings were critical in the embryonic stages of his relationship with the faith community; any Evangelical leader who remained neutral was a win because it kept them out of the camp of a rival.

Trump got another boost when Sarah Palin flew to Iowa before the caucuses to endorse him. Palin's endorsement became a sort of Holy Grail in Republican Party politics in the aftermath of the 2008 presidential race, when her star turn as John McCain's running mate electrified the party base. Despite McCain's crushing defeat, her star soared, and her endorsement became the most coveted prize in the GOP. Palin's backing helped elect Nikki Haley as governor of South Carolina and elect Marco Rubio of Florida, Deb Fischer of Nebraska, and Kelly Ayotte of New Hampshire to the U.S. Senate. Her embrace of Trump was a blow to Cruz, as she had endorsed him for the U.S. Senate in Texas in 2012.

Maggie Haberman, the whip-smart and tough political reporter for the *New York Times*, called to ask: Would Palin's endorsement have the same effect for Trump? Without predicting any outcome, I observed that Palin's endorsement had catapulted many GOP candidates from asterisks in the polls to landslide wins. "Palin's brand among evangelicals is as gold as the faucets in Trump Tower," I added. "Endorsements alone don't guarantee victory, but Palin's embrace of Trump may turn the fight over the evangelical vote into a war for the soul of the party."

Maggie said that sounded right to her. She asked if I would give her permission to use the quote in her story.

I was reluctant. Still neutral, I was wary of praising endorsements for any candidate. But why not show Palin some love after she had been treated so shabbily by the party establishment? (This included the McCain campaign, which had chosen her, benefited from her star power, and then threw her overboard with damaging leaks to the press.) I told Maggie she could quote me. The next day, I was pulling up to a meeting in Atlanta when my cell phone rang. It was Corey Lewandowski on Trump Force One. He told me that Trump had asked him to call and thank me for my nice comment. I told Corey to convey to his boss that I meant every word of it. Not for the first (or last) time was I amazed at Trump's ability to take note of every public utterance about him. He seemed to miss nothing.

The nomination fight was far from over. But one thing I knew: win, lose, or draw, I wanted to keep Donald Trump close. With tens of millions of social media followers and a Twitter feed he wielded like a Jedi lightsaber, Trump was a formidable foe. A famous counter-puncher, Trump had what Hedrick Smith, a *New York Times* reporter and author of the renowned book *The Power Game*, once referred to as "porcupine power." Smith defined porcupine power as the ability to stick one's opponents so many times that it just wasn't worth the trouble to go after you. Trump had raised porcupine power to a new level. It seemed everyone who went after him died politically or was diminished by the contest. This largely misunderstood element of the Trump dynamic enabled him to walk into a political party he had only recently joined—a party whose heritage stretched back to before the Civil War and the abolition of slavery, producing leaders like Abraham Lincoln, Teddy Roosevelt, Dwight D. Eisenhower, and Ronald Reagan. As a first-time candidate and a political neophyte, Trump was well on his way to taking control of the GOP as if he were buying a golf resort out of bankruptcy.

I didn't know what the future held for either Trump or Evangelicals, but as a trained historian, I knew Trump was a phenomenon that came along once a generation, if not once a century. Whatever the final fate of his candidacy, I hoped his campaign could be utilized to advance the pro-life, pro-family issues agenda and build the faith-based grassroots of the country. I certainly wasn't his foe, and I hoped to be his friend.

CHAPTER 6

"YOU CAN'T ALWAYS GET WHAT YOU WANT"

Cruz won the Iowa caucuses as expected while Trump won big in New Hampshire, which set up a showdown between the two in South Carolina. No Republican had been elected president since 1980 without first winning the Palmetto State's brutal and bloody primary. When I worked for George W. Bush in 2000, Bush and John McCain had also traded victories in Iowa and New Hampshire, turning South Carolina into a high-stakes elimination match, with the Bush campaign hammering McCain for his liberal voting record and McCain (falsely) accusing Bush operatives of engaging in a racist whisper campaign. For Cruz, South Carolina was home cooking. As the shiny buckle of the Bible Belt with an astonishing 72 percent of the primary electorate comprised of self-identified Evangelicals, it was friendly terrain for Cruz, who was anything but reticent about invoking his Evangelical faith and conservative bona fides. For Trump, it was a chance to prove once and for all that he could compete for—and win—conservative Christian votes. For most of the other candidates, it would be a final stand.

The weekend before the primary, Faith & Freedom held a candidate forum at a Baptist megachurch in Spartanburg that was attended by over three thousand Evangelical activists. Jeb Bush, Cruz, and Rubio all spoke. Trump was invited, but he had a statewide college tour scheduled that day. In the end, it didn't matter. Trump won South Carolina with 33 percent of the vote, including 33 percent of the Evangelical vote to Cruz's 27 percent. Jeb Bush dropped out that night, and Ben Carson would soon follow.

As we worked on the South Carolina candidate forum, I was attending a Christian ministry conference in California with Jo Anne. In the midst of firing off text messages to campaigns and making calls to candidates inviting them to attend the forum, I received a news alert on my mobile phone: Supreme Court justice Antonin Scalia had died while on a hunting trip in Texas. It was shocking news. The conservative majority on the high court had lost its intellectual leader, and it was even worse that Barack Obama would appoint his successor. I almost felt physically ill as I absorbed the news. My first reaction was a desperate prayer: Why had God allowed this to happen? Losing the Scalia seat on the court would set back the causes of life and religious freedom for years, possibly decades. Republicans controlled the Senate after Obama and the Democrats suffered a shellacking in the 2014 elections, but Republicans historically had deferred to incumbent presidents when it came to Supreme Court nominees. Unlike the Democrats, Republican senators tended to focus singularly on a nominee's qualifications—not their ideology. As a result, they generally supported the nominees of Democratic presidents. (For example, Stephen Breyer, appointed by Bill Clinton, had been confirmed by a vote of eighty-seven to nine.) When it came to judicial nominations, Democrats played hardball while Republicans played patty-cake.

Just hours after Scalia's death rocketed across the news websites, I received an email from Senate Majority Leader Mitch McConnell's office. Senator McConnell released a statement (I later learned without consulting with his colleagues) announcing that the U.S. Senate would not take up the Supreme Court vacancy until after the 2016 elections, thus allowing Obama's successor to make the selection. "The American people should have a voice in the selection of their next Supreme Court Justice. Therefore, this vacancy should not be filled until we have a new president," McConnell said. My eyes widened as I read the email. Frankly, I could not believe McConnell's moxie. I held my phone up to show the statement to my wife. She smiled. "This guy has got guts," I commented. The White House put it differently. "It was a real shocker," a senior Obama aide said of McConnell's move.[1] It wouldn't be the last time liberals or the media underestimated McConnell. (I later learned from Senator Ben Sasse that he was attending a security conference in Moscow with a group of senators who received a call from McConnell letting them know of his decision. It was a brilliant stroke by McConnell, and it won him the fierce loyalty of his colleagues.)

Scalia's death and McConnell's decision to hold the seat open would have far-reaching implications for the 2016 elections. The last time a Supreme Court confirmation had figured so prominently in a presidential election was in 1968, when Lyndon Johnson attempted to elevate his former personal attorney, liberal justice Abe Fortas (whom Johnson had appointed to the court in 1965) to be chief justice at the retirement of liberal icon Earl Warren. But the Senate rejected Fortas because of ethical issues, so Warren never resigned, and the vacancy technically never happened. One had to go back to 1860 to find a time when the American people went to the polls on Election Day to select not only a new president, but also decide the ideological balance of the U.S. Supreme Court. The anomaly occurred because Justice Peter Daniel died in May 1860. Daniel, a pro-slavery Jacksonian Democrat from Virginia who had once killed a man in a duel, was one of the most fervent defenders of slavery on the court. His death left the high court divided between four northerners and four southerners.[2]

President James Buchanan delayed naming a replacement for Daniel, perhaps fearing that a Supreme Court nominee put forward during a heated presidential campaign would further inflame sectional passions. Buchanan was also the subject of an impeachment inquiry that left him hobbled and politically hamstrung. For anti-slavery voters in the 1860 presidential race, the Supreme Court loomed large. Not only was the North insulted by the recent *Dred Scott* decision, which essentially defined slaves as property, but an obscure case out of New York involving the transit of slaves was on its way to the high court with potentially sweeping ramifications. If the justices ruled (as seemed likely based on the *Dred Scott* precedent) that southerners could take their slaves anywhere in the country, then slavery would spread everywhere—and there was nothing the fire-breathing, Evangelical opponents of slavery in the North could do about it.

After Lincoln won the 1860 election, Buchanan moved quickly to try and block him from naming Daniel's replacement. Hoping to get a nominee confirmed during the lame-duck Congress, Buchanan nominated Jeremiah Black, a former attorney general, the current secretary of state, and moderate Union Democrat. This was a compromise pick designed to straddle sectional divisions over slavery. But Buchanan's delay proved costly. Republicans in the Senate strongly opposed the nomination, hoping to hold the seat open for Lincoln, while many Southern Democrats had abandoned Washington to join their states in secession. Making matters worse, Stephen A. Douglas, the recently defeated Democratic presidential nominee, opposed Black. As a result, Black's nomination failed by a single vote.[3] Whether the Supreme Court vacancy made a difference in Lincoln's election is a matter of conjecture, but it certainly didn't hurt. When two other southerners left the high court to join their states in rebellion, Lincoln ended up with three seats to fill. For Trump in 2016, the Scalia vacancy meant that for the first time in 156 years the presidency and control of the Supreme Court hung in the balance while a critical seat sat vacant. This would play a significant role in encouraging Evangelicals and other conservative Christians to put aside their reservations about Trump and strongly support him in the general election.

■   ■   ■

By the time the primary campaign shifted to Georgia, the only candidates still standing were Trump, Cruz, Rubio, and Ohio governor John

Kasich. I swung by events for all the remaining candidates to underscore our neutrality in the contest. At a rally attended by thousands in downtown Atlanta, Cruz offered up a diet of pure red meat: He promised that if he were elected president, he would defund Planned Parenthood, end the persecution of Christians at the hands of the IRS and Justice Department, "tear to shreds" the Iran nuclear deal, and move the U.S. Embassy in Israel to Jerusalem. (Ironically, every one of these policies was later implemented by Trump after he became president.)

I joined a roundtable of faith leaders with Rubio before he spoke to a huge crowd of over 5,000 people in a football stadium at a Christian high school in Cobb County, where he vowed to "save the Republican Party from being taken over by a con-artist" and pledged to stay in the race "for as long as it takes."[4] I stopped by to pay my respects to John Kasich at a GOP luncheon in Fulton County, where he ribbed me for staying neutral. We had been close when he served in the House of Representatives, but John now complained that my "right-wing Christian friends" were criticizing him for expanding Medicaid in Ohio. Holding nothing back, John said that providing health care to the poor was consistent with the Gospel, and these believers would have some explaining to do to Saint Peter when they arrived at the pearly gates of Heaven. I patiently explained that Evangelicals had long supported Medicaid expansion (Mike Huckabee, for example, had added 175,000 additional children to Medicaid in Arkansas as governor). Doing so as part of Obamacare, however, also required participation by states in the program's high taxes, skyrocketing premiums, coverage mandates, and conscience mandates (including abortion-inducing medication) that offended many Christians. I didn't change Kasich's mind, but as always, we remained friends and enjoyed the verbal swordplay.

Trump's final rally prior to Super Tuesday was on Monday night at Valdosta State University in southern Georgia. The stakes were high. The following day, 12 states would award 595 delegates, which amounted to one-fifth of the total number of GOP delegates and 40 percent of the delegates needed to win the nomination. I had not yet attended a Trump campaign rally, so I called a friend who owned a plane and asked him if he wanted to go. I then texted Corey to tell him I was coming, and I flew to Valdosta with Tim Head, my executive director. After we landed at the airport, we headed to the city limits in our rental car, and to our surprise saw a massive crowd snaking down the sidewalk and stretching a mile from the campus. They wore red, white, and blue attire, waved American flags, held Trump campaign signs aloft, and wore red "Make America Great Again" hats. I had worked on almost every campaign in Georgia for forty years, including presidential campaigns, and I had never seen a crowd this size.

We pulled up to the basketball arena to find pandemonium. The arena was already packed to the rafters and the doors had been shut by order of the fire marshal. A picket line of security guards and harried campaign volunteers struggled to contain a surging mass of humanity, holding up their hands and gesticulating wildly, trying to assuage thousands of crestfallen Trump supporters who couldn't get in. A sea of cars and pickup trucks, their bumpers covered with Trump stickers and rear windows displaying hunting rifles, lined every side street and filled every patch of grass. Mobs of men and women roamed the plaza outside the arena. I saw at least one person who wore a "Don't Mess with the U.S.A." T-shirt griping about not being able to get in. A crowd gathered in front of a jumbotron to watch the show on the grass. There didn't appear to be a place to park anywhere. For a moment, we were transfixed by the chaos. The scene resembled a European soccer match more than a political rally in the U.S. Fearing that we might have come all the way to southern Georgia for naught, Tim dropped me off at the arena so I could try to talk my way in, and he drove away to find a place to park the car.

When I arrived at the arena entrance, I bumped into Brandon Phillips, a Georgia political operative who had worked for me ten years earlier. He looked slightly harried in the midst of the mayhem. I asked him what he was doing there, assuming he was a volunteer.

"I'm Trump's campaign director in Georgia!" he exclaimed, his face beaming, brow glistening with sweat.

"You're kidding?" I replied. "Why didn't you call me?"

"No time," he said as the crowd pressed in around him. "I started three weeks ago, and I'm working 20-hour days. It's like drinking water from a fire hose. I've been organizing bus tours and holding the biggest rallies in Georgia history." He laughed. "The campaign leaves me alone and lets me make the calls. I suggested we come to Valdosta, and they signed off on it." He looked around at the mob, his eyes sparkling.

It was one more example of the chaos of the Trump campaign working to the candidate's advantage. The buttoned-up, paint-by-the-numbers, hierarchical political organizations in which I had spent most of my career tended to be lethargic, lumbering giants. By contrast, the Trump campaign turned on a dime, sometimes apparently at a whim. But there was a method to the madness. In this case, Trump was the first GOP presidential candidate to visit Valdosta since Ronald Reagan. By venturing below the "gnat line," as Georgia politicos referred to southern Georgia, Trump was sending a message to rural and exurban voters that he knew who they were and wanted their votes. It was a brilliant move.

"Come with me," the state director said, guiding me through the maze of bodies and security. "Let's find Mr. Trump."

I grabbed Tim, and we stumbled through the darkness, using the flashlights on our phones to illuminate the pathway through the bowels of the arena. The deafening noise of the crowd could already be heard, intermittent chanting and cheering to undercard speakers and bumper music preceding Trump's arrival. The concrete floor shook with vibrations. It was as if a seventies band reunion tour had met a NASCAR race—all for the enjoyment of the great unwashed of the American heartland, the forsaken and forgotten, the rejected and looked-down-upon, the lepers and castaways of American politics. No one else seemed to want them or paid them much mind. But these voters had found their Pied Piper, and his name was Donald J. Trump.

We entered a VIP holding area where Trump held court, a figure of remarkable calm in a sea of chaos. He seemed to be thoroughly enjoying himself, relaxed and confident, posing for photos with local dignitaries and donors, his famous hair perfectly in place, his trademark blue suit, crisp white shirt, and fire-engine red tie resplendent. He asked me what

I was hearing on the ground, ever the sponge for political intelligence. I told him he would win the Georgia primary with relative ease, with Cruz nipping at his heels and likely coming in second, while Kasich and Rubio duked it out in the suburbs. By dividing the suburban moderate vote, Rubio and Kasich all but assured Trump's victory. He nodded, listening. Then he corrected me, predicting not only a victory in Georgia, but in every Super Tuesday state. He said it would be a blowout. (He wasn't far off the mark; he won Tennessee, Arkansas, Alabama, and Georgia, while Cruz carried Texas and Oklahoma.)

We headed to our seats, where I ran into my good friend Cecil Staton, a former state legislator who happened to be the interim president of the college. The look of satisfaction on Cecil's face told me he was pleased to have the college as the center of the political universe, if only for a few hours. As I gazed out across teeming crowd, I asked, "How many does this arena hold?"

Cecil told me the arena held eight thousand people and had been full for two hours. The head of campus security had informed him that the line to get in had roughly ten thousand people in it. This was truly staggering. The entire population of Valdosta was only fifty-five thousand people.

Trump came on stage to an ovation that rolled from the back of the arena like a wave, bathing him in adoration. He paced the stage like a gladiator, his shoulders back, chin and chest jutting, unreeling his greatest hits to uproarious applause and cheering. He vowed to build the border wall ("Who's going to pay for it?" "Mexico!"), appoint conservative judges, move the U.S. Embassy to Jerusalem, renegotiate the Iran nuclear deal ("the worst deal ever made in the history of our country"), and make sure Americans said "Merry Christmas" again. The Christmas line elicited a standing ovation that seemed to last two minutes. When the crowd chanted "U.S.A., U.S.A., U.S.A." or "Trump! Trump! Trump!" he would step away from the podium, slow-clapping or patting his heart to show his gratitude. On a purely anthropological level, it was amazing to witness, unlike anything I had seen in my forty years of political campaigns, and the bond between Trump and his audience was undeniable and almost without precedent. Trump had tapped into a profound sense of grievance and alienation among people of faith about the marginalization of their faith that had been brought about by liberal judges and a media that trafficked in anti-Christian bigotry. He checked every box on the issues: life, religious freedom, Israel, Iran, and judges. But Trump's transcendent and effervescent appeal lay elsewhere—in his willingness to assert the central role of faith in the life of the nation after decades of assault by the legal culture, the media, and Hollywood.

With hindsight, what is most striking is not that Trump tapped into these eddies of voter sentiment, but why no one else did before him. My eyes scanned the audience to read the faces and gauge the crowd reaction. On the floor of the arena, I noticed a bleached-blond woman wearing a white cowboy hat and cowboy boots, blue jeans, and a sleeveless blouse revealing truck-stop tattoos emblazoned on her deeply tanned back and arms. She pressed her body against the bicycle racks ringing the stage, jumping up and down nonstop throughout the entire rally, alternately cheering, screaming, and laughing at Trump's best lines. This woman, so fired up for Trump that she did not stop jumping in place for an hour, was not a regular at Republican campaign fundraisers or events. I surmised that she had probably never even voted in a GOP primary. It was evident that Trump was drawing millions of people into the Republican party who had never before felt welcome in its ranks. As this new wine rushed into the old wineskins of the establishment GOP, the skins rattled and even threatened to explode. Trump as a candidate offered both a threat and a promise to the Republican Party: grow to accommodate me and my supporters, or potentially die. This explained the ferocity of both his supporters and detractors. He was more than just a change agent; he was a human missile aimed at the heart of one of the great political parties in the history of the West.

After the rally, Tim and I headed back to the airport where we waited for Trump to depart. (His jumbo jet apparently took priority over our turboprop in the queue for departure.) But Trump's plane sat on the tarmac for a long period of time, unmoving. I wondered what the delay was and asked an airport staffer what was going on. The campaign plane was waiting for the delivery of food, came the reply. Soon a van drove down the runway and pulled up alongside the Trump plane; someone clambered up the stairs carrying plastic bags bearing the likeness of Colonel Sanders. I pictured Trump and his team ensconced in the leather-and-gold interior of his jet, watching Fox News on a big-screen TV while eating Kentucky Fried Chicken.

"If he's courting the Evangelical vote, shouldn't it be Chick-fil-A?" I asked, laughing.

Fully stocked with catering, Trump's blue-and-white plane taxied down the runway, strangely resembling a space shuttle as it rapidly accelerated against the dark and desolate landscape, its nose edging skyward into the black night.

"No one is going to stop him," I said to no one in particular as we watched the plane depart.

■   ■   ■

Despite the fierce opposition of the Never Trump movement, including a small but vocal caucus of Evangelical leaders, Trump continued to gain favor as the primaries progressed. The possibility of a November election in which Christians would have to choose between Hillary Clinton and Donald Trump became a reality. Some conservatives swallowed their distaste for Trump. Others, like Michael Farris, an advocate for homeschooling and the founder of Patrick Henry College, remained convinced that "neither candidate qualifies as the lesser of the two evils." Never Trumpers stuck to their guns, keeping up a steady barrage of attacks and criticism even after Trump became the presumptive nominee.

Around this time, I called Mike Huckabee, who had recently dropped out of the race. I congratulated him on a race well run, and in a refrain I had heard from all the other candidates, he reflected upon how thoroughly Trump had dominated the race, forcing everyone else into a reactive posture. Was he planning to make an endorsement later? Mike told me he had no plans to do so, but he said if he changed his mind, it would probably be Trump. I asked him why. Mike said that Trump had been more upfront in his dealings with him, and he trusted him to do the right thing if he made it. This was quite a statement coming from one of the leading Evangelical figures in the country.

Conservative icon Phyllis Schlafly endorsed Trump just before the Missouri primary in March, reportedly after he committed to supporting the pro-life plank in the Republican Party platform. The pro-life platform had been Phyllis's *cause célèbre* since she had helped insert the pro-life plank in the platform in 1976 as a Ronald Reagan delegate in Kansas City. Trump was deeply gratified by the imprimatur that Phyllis's endorsement afforded him, but her Eagle Forum organization, with many of its activists strongly supporting Cruz, exploded in protest. Several Eagle Forum state leaders publicly rebuked Phyllis, and a coup attempt ensued in which some board members sought to remove Phyllis as their leader. When they failed, they set up a rival organization, filing a lawsuit over control of the group's name and assets. I watched the unfolding drama with sadness. I called Phyllis to offer my support. Was it worth this much trouble and strife to back Trump? I asked.

"Absolutely," Phyllis said without hesitation. "He's the closest thing I've seen to Ronald Reagan since Reagan left the scene."

I was taken aback by Phyllis's statement. She had first attended a Republican national convention as a delegate in 1952 and had seen it all.

"How so?" I asked.

"Trump doesn't know all the issues entirely. He hasn't spent his life in politics. That's fine. But he's teachable," she explained. "So was Reagan. When those of us who were fighting the feminists first met with Reagan, he understood Communism and capitalism, but we had to educate him about other issues. Reagan and Trump are both outsiders. They ran against the party establishment, and the establishment opposed them." She saw in Trump the possibility for greatness. "More than ideology or issues, which can be taught, that's the main thing. It's all about the grassroots versus the establishment, and Trump is with us, not the establishment. If he wins, he'll listen to us, not them."

Phyllis was a warhorse who had spent six decades battling for conservative principles in the Republican Party, a veteran of the Barry Goldwater and Reagan campaigns, and someone who was present at the creation of the modern conservative movement. She had almost singlehandedly defeated the Equal Rights Amendment in the 1970s. By her own testimony, she saw Reaganesque qualities in a man that many conservative thought leaders denounced as a boob, a libertine, and a demagogue. What did she see in Trump that others were missing? Whatever it was, it seemed that millions of voters saw it, too.

▪   ▪   ▪

By the time Trump arrived at Faith & Freedom Coalition's Road to Majority policy conference in Washington in June, he was the presumptive Republican presidential nominee, intent on uniting the party and consolidating his support among its Evangelical base.

The previous month, he had released a list of twelve conservative judges, promising to fill the vacancy created by the death of Antonin Scalia with one of them. The list was a who's who of the conservative legal community, the product of a collaboration between the Trump campaign's legal counsel, Don McGahn, the Heritage Foundation, and the Federalist Society. (Later on, the list would be expanded to twenty-one names.) But Trump's critics remained unmoved. Radio talk show host Erick Erickson dismissed the list as "subject to change." He predicted "the moment a reporter or a Clinton highlights something potentially controversial" about one of his nominees, "Trump will run from the person he has named. He will waffle, he will backtrack, and he simply cannot be believed."[5] A biblical studies professor called Trump's list the worthless promise of "a pathological liar." It was more evidence of "why character matters.... On what grounds could we possibly trust him to do as president what he promises to do as a candidate?"[6] Wisconsin conservative radio host Charlie Sykes concluded, "I simply don't believe Trump."[7] This was rather ironic, given the fact that Sykes's ex-wife, a former Wisconsin Supreme Court justice and federal appellate court judge, was on the list.

The Trump campaign hoped his appearance at the Faith & Freedom conference would allay the stubborn reservations about the candidate that lingered among conservatives and Evangelicals. Without a long track record in politics or a voting record as an elected official, many wondered if Trump was a liberal in sheep's clothing, a conservative convert, or an ideological chameleon. On a certain level, this was understandable. Not since Dwight D. Eisenhower won the GOP nomination in 1952 against rock-ribbed conservative Ohio senator Robert Taft, known as "Mr. Republican," had the party chosen as its leader a man with such a scant record on many public policy issues. In Eisenhower's case, the GOP turned to a military hero after losing five presidential elections in succession, desperate for anyone who could lead them out of the wilderness. The conservative movement's infrastructure was almost nonexistent in the early 1950s. In the case of Trump, the skepticism went deeper, and the leadership was more seasoned.

For all these reasons, the Trump high command welcomed the opportunity for the candidate to make his case before an influential audience of Evangelicals. The Faith & Freedom policy conference was a friendly setting where he had spoken many times before. The campaign was still editing the speech as Trump's motorcade headed from the airport to the Omni Shoreham Hotel in Washington, where a crowd of over two thousand activists awaited his arrival. Coincidentally, Hillary Clinton was addressing Planned Parenthood across town at the same time, creating a made-for-TV split-screen moment that brought into stark relief the sharp ideological contrast between the two major party candidates and their supporters.

While I waited backstage for Trump's arrival, I received a text from Paul Manafort, Trump's campaign chairman, asking me to call him immediately. Paul, a friend of over two decades and a veteran of numerous GOP presidential campaigns, was a consummate professional, a skilled operator, and the ultimate party insider. In a campaign known for its improvisational style and propensity to wing it, Paul had brought stability and discipline. When I called him, he asked if there were any prominent faith leaders in the audience that Trump should mention from the podium. I promised to text them to him, which he asked me to do quickly so they could get it on the teleprompter. He told me Trump would tout the list of judges he had released and reiterate his pledge to appoint one of them to the Supreme Court. Paul asked if I recommended anything else. I suggested a line about supporting Israel. Paul said it was a good idea and that he would get it into the speech. I hung up the phone in wonderment at the Trump campaign's ability to finish a major speech as the candidate literally arrived at the venue in his motorcade.

Suddenly, Trump appeared in the hallway surrounded by an entourage of Secret Service agents and campaign staff. He greeted me warmly and then ducked into a holding room for a few quick photos with donors and faith leaders.

When he walked on stage to an extended standing ovation and camera flashes, Trump displayed an ease and familiarity with the Evangelical crowd that reflected his remarkable evolution as a politician. "I'm a Presbyterian," he said. "There are about three of you out there, I think," he added to appreciative laughter. Trump, it seemed, had broken the code of the Evangelical vote. He didn't need to quote the Bible or pretend to be something he wasn't; he only had to demonstrate that he shared their values and would fight for their issues. He thanked Evangelical luminaries like Jerry Falwell Jr., Paula White, and Robert Jeffress for their early support. He pointed out that he had carried the Evangelical vote in the primaries, a clear point of personal pride for him. We had arranged for numerous faith leaders to be seated in the front row so Trump could point them out and say nice things about them.

Trump then dove into the major goals of his presidency, should he be elected. He said he had written them himself specifically for this meeting. "We must uphold the dignity and sanctity of human life," he promised to applause and cheers. He ticked through a list of policy priorities that included strengthening marriage and the traditional family, religious freedom, racial reconciliation and equality, opposition to radical Islam, and support for the state of Israel. Trump said "crooked Hillary" was unfit to be president because of her refusal to call radical Islam by its name and her support for open borders. He hammered Hillary for her support for higher taxes and increased funding for Planned Parenthood and late-term abortions—including up to the moment of birth. He pledged to appoint judges who "will uphold our laws, protect our Constitution, and protect the rights of all Americans. As you know, I've put together a list of highly respected judges." Veering off script, he added, "And by the way, these judges are all pro-life." The room erupted in applause. The crowd broke into a chant: "Trump! Trump! Trump! Trump!" To my amazement, among the hundreds of reporters in the back of the room, not a single story appeared in the media pointing out that Trump had promised to appoint pro-life judges to the federal bench.[8]

After working the crowd, Trump left the stage, and I walked with him as he headed back to his car, the hall lined with staff and donors applauding and flashing grins. He turned to me, unprompted, saying, "Ralph, I'm not going to forget the people who were with me." He paused, standing still for a moment, and said with emphasis, "I won't forget the Evangelicals."

"If that's the case, and I believe it is," I replied, "then it will be one of the first times."

Trump nodded and chuckled slightly, and said I was probably right. With that, he was gone, on his way to Florida for yet another campaign rally.

Afterwards, I did a handful of media interviews in which I predicted the speech would help consolidate his support among Evangelicals. The release of the Supreme Court list had been critical, and Trump had doubled down on his public pledge to choose his nominee from its ranks. This would become a major factor in the voting decisions of many people of faith. A handful of Evangelical Never Trumpers criticized us for hosting the presumptive Republican nominee. I saw their criticism as misplaced, reflecting political naiveté and perhaps even some spiritual immaturity, rejecting someone (in this case Trump) who could do much good because he was not perfect. But small and shrinking ranks of

Christian Never Trumpers did not represent the vast majority of Evangelical voters who quaked in fear at the prospect of a Hillary Clinton presidency, with its liberal Supreme Court appointments, IRS harassment of churches, and pro-abortion policies.

Ten days later, Trump continued his aggressive play for the faith vote, convening the inaugural meeting of a formal faith advisory board for his campaign in Trump Tower, to be followed by a gathering of a thousand faith leaders, pastors, evangelists, and Christian college presidents. Chaired by longtime Trump spiritual advisor Paula White, the board included Franklin Graham, Jim Dobson, religious broadcaster James Robison, First Baptist Church of Dallas pastor Robert Jeffress, former Southern Baptist Convention president Jack Graham, former congresswoman Michele Bachmann, evangelist Jay Strack, and Jerry Falwell Jr., the president of Liberty University. Trump came into the room and sat at the head of the table, clearly at ease and showing a familiarity with everyone in the room. He referenced phone conversations with several of the attendees, and asked Franklin about the health of his father, Billy, recalling a meeting he had earlier with the famed evangelist at his home in North Carolina. Trump again highlighted his promise to repeal the Johnson Amendment, a provision of the Internal Revenue Code that restricted the freedom of speech of churches and ministries on public policy and political matters, which he argued correctly had muffled or silenced the voice of the Church in society. He listened intently as the leaders shared their thoughts on the coming fall campaign, pointing to staffers to follow up on specific ideas and suggestions. For someone who had been involved in politics for only a year, Trump's performance was remarkable, showing a skill and aplomb in interacting with faith leaders that was among the best I had seen in my career.

When it was my turn to speak, I thanked Trump for his bold speech to Faith & Freedom, telling him that if he just stuck to that message, he would surprise many with how well he did among Evangelicals. Some of those around the table—like Franklin Graham—made it clear that their membership on the advisory board did not imply a political endorsement. Graham said he would share his spiritual and policy views with any candidate who sought them. Trump took it all in stride, telling the group that they had his ear and a place at the head of the table in his campaign. I had never attended a meeting quite like it. Trump wasn't just asking for support; he was telegraphing his desire that we provide ongoing advice to him and the campaign high command on issues and strategy. We closed the meeting in prayer and then rode the elevators to the lobby, where we got into sports utility vehicles that whisked us down Fifth Avenue towards the Evangelical Trumpalooza that awaited us at a Times Square Hotel.

As we pulled up to the hotel, we ran into a rent-a-riot of protesters shouting slogans and brandishing printed signs bearing anti-Trump slogans: "Faith Over Fear" (with a drawing of a Cross, a Star of David, and a Muslim crescent), "Jesus Doesn't Build Walls," and "We Love Our Muslim Brothers and Sisters" (so do we, I thought.) As we plowed through the crowd to enter the JW Marriott hotel, a phalanx of television cameras and a knot of protesters surrounded us, creating a blur of bright lights, raised voices, and gyrating bodies. Out of the corner of my eye, I caught a glimpse of Eric Teetsel, the one-time faith outreach director for Marco Rubio, wearing a sandwich board that read, "Torture is not pro-life. Racism is not pro-life. Misogyny is not pro-life. Murdering the children of terrorists is not pro-life." Apparently, it was a bipartisan protest.

Before Trump arrived, we heard from Ben Carson, a crowd favorite who had dropped out of the race and endorsed Trump right before the Florida primary. In remarks laced with humor, Carson likened America under a Hillary Clinton presidency to a boat full of innocent passengers plunging over Niagara Falls, insisting that the only way to stop the boat and save the innocent lives was to back Trump, and quickly. Franklin Graham then took the podium and delivered a Bible lesson on the flaws of many great leaders from the Bible, including the disciples who forsook Jesus on the night before his crucifixion, reminding them that all people sin, and no perfect man has ever existed "except our Lord Jesus Christ. And he's not running for president this year." Franklin's unmistakable point was that Trump may not have been the first choice of many faith leaders and he may not be a perfect man, but the time had come to choose a president from among the candidates on the ballot, not pine for a perfect candidate who wasn't on the ballot.

The room buzzed with anticipation when Falwell finally stepped to the podium to introduce Trump. Some of the most influential Evangelical pastors, college presidents, religious broadcasters, denominational leaders, authors, bloggers, and their spouses filled the cavernous ballroom. Outside the hotel, protesters picketed. Television cameras and reporters filled the lobby, hoping to glean a quote from someone expressing skepticism about the candidate. Trump came on stage to a standing ovation. Mike Huckabee, the moderator of the program, opened by reminding everyone in the room that they were electing a commander-in-chief, not choosing a pastor. "This is not a pastoral search committee," he said to laughter. Huckabee conducted an interview that pulled no punches but also contained no "gotcha" questions designed to embarrass or insult the candidate, promising no questions about theology. He first asked about Trump's children and his own spiritual journey.

"I've been a Christian and I love Christianity," Trump said emphatically. "And the Evangelicals have been so incredibly supportive." Trump leaned forward in his chair like a lineman about to charge the line of scrimmage, his arms resting on his knees, his body language projecting intensity. Ever the negotiator, he politely but firmly reminded his audience that he had won heavily Evangelical primary states like South Carolina and Georgia. "Trump won't win this state because it's heavily evangelical," he said, quoting his critics (some of whom sat in the audience). "Not only did I win, I won by landslide." The Evangelicals "really get me. They understand." (His not-so-subtle message was this: join the parade, or you may get left behind.)

Trump turned on the charm, displaying an earnestness and humility that few had expected. To applause, he restated his pledge to repeal the Johnson Amendment. After about twenty minutes, Huckabee threw open the floor for questions. The first came from Jim Dobson, who asked him what he would do to defend religious freedom.

Trump deftly turned the question back to the Supreme Court, and the multiple appointments that would fall to the next president. He promised his picks "will be great intellects, they will be talented men and women, but also pro-life." He acknowledged that as a newcomer to politics "there's always skepticism of someone who hasn't been speaking to the public for 25 years and you know exactly what their views are," and explained that the reticence of many conservatives encouraged him to release his list of jurists. Trump reminded his audience that the next president could appoint as many as five Supreme Court justices. "If Hillary gets in, we know who she's going to be putting" on the federal courts, Trump warned. "We know exactly what's going to happen. We're going to end up being a different world, a different country. We're going to end up being a Venezuela if she gets in, for a lot of different reasons."

Surprisingly, no one asked Trump about abortion, perhaps because he had already stated his pro-life views with such frequency during the primary campaign. But Trump did take questions on Israel, immigration, and another question on religious liberty. Knowing his audience, he again pivoted to the topic of judges. That issue and ultimately all others will be decided by the Supreme Court, he told the Evangelical leaders. He then turned to the manner in which the Obama administration and the courts had marginalized the faith community's voice in the larger culture. The nation's Christian heritage and foundations were in danger of being lost. "But just remember this," he said. "You are the most powerful group in this country. But you have to realize that. You have to band together. If you don't band together, you're really not powerful." Trump gave them hope. "You have a powerful church. I see it. I see some of these incredible pastors and ministers and people that speak so brilliantly," he said. "They're great within their audience but then outside they don't have it. You have to band together as a group. And if you do that, you will bring it back like nothing has ever been brought back."[9]

Trump had gone way over his allotted time, seemingly not wanting to leave. Finally, Huckabee closed the interview, saying, "I'm sure your staff is upset because we have extended your schedule."

Trump replied without missing a beat: "Mike, there's nothing more important than this group of people to me." It was a smart thing to say, and it expressed his true feelings. After spending half the day with his newly minted faith advisory board and the Evangelical leaders, Trump departed. My assessment was that he had done himself a lot of good, appealing to the Evangelicals on judges, religious freedom, Israel, and perhaps most important of all, their anxiety at the assault on religion by the federal government and the marginalization of faith in the larger culture. Issues came and went, and politicians occupied the national stage for only a brief period of time. But if the voice and role of faith were relegated to the sidelines by hostile federal courts and the enforcement power of the federal government, what then could the faithful do? Trump had tapped into their concerns.

After Trump left, I headed to the lunch buffet line and encountered numerous pastors and ministry leaders from around the country who ranged from pleasantly surprised to completely blown away. "No Republican presidential candidate in my lifetime has ever met with so many of our leaders and said what he just said," one of them gushed.

Still, not everyone was ready to board the Trump train. At a news conference after the event, several faith leaders expressed gratitude that Trump had been so generous in his remarks but said they needed rock-solid policy commitments. "There are some very concrete things that have to take place," said Tony Perkins, president of the Family Research Council. "Trump does not have a track record when it comes to public office. The best indicator of future performance is past performance."

"I don't think he hurt himself, but there was a general lack of specificity on some of these issues," said Penny Nance. "I don't know that he did anything to bring new people over to his side." Marjorie Dannenfelser echoed these sentiments. "I will be the first to say he was not my first choice. We were very vocally opposed to his nomination."[10]

When a reporter asked the faith leaders at the press conference to raise their hands if they were prepared to endorse Trump that day, not a single leader raised his or her hand. With a little over four months before the election and Hillary Clinton coming around the corner, not all Evangelical leaders were on board with the Republican Party's nominee for president. But Donald Trump was about to take a major step that would change their view of him, and in the process change the course of history.

CHAPTER 7

A MATCH
MADE IN HEAVEN

When the dust had settled and the Republican presidential primaries were over, Trump had beaten sixteen other candidates and
emerged as the unlikely nominee. But the GOP establishment and some
faith leaders still resisted his charms. Complicating matters even further,
a loud chorus of Never Trumpers and some die-hard Cruz supporters
launched a quixotic campaign for a brokered convention in the hopes of
denying Trump the nomination.

But the primary voters had rendered their verdict, and it was
unequivocal. A record 31 million voters had cast ballots in the Republican presidential primaries, representing an astonishing 63 percent
increase in turnout from the GOP primaries in 2012. Trump had won
37 primaries and caucuses and nearly 45 percent of the vote in a crowded
field. He defeated Marco Rubio two-to-one in his home state of Florida,
trounced Ted Cruz in Indiana despite the endorsement of Cruz by Governor Mike Pence, and defeated John Kasich in his home state of Ohio
by a landslide. The Evangelical vote in the primaries totaled over half
the total vote (52 percent, or 16.2 million voters), an increase of 6.6 million Evangelical voters over the 2012 primaries. Roughly one-third of

these voters had never cast a ballot in a Republican primary before. Trump had acted like a magnet drawing these voters into the party, and these voters were likely to go back to the polls in November.[1]

As the primaries wrapped up, I called my old friend Paul Manafort, who I had worked with on previous presidential campaigns, most especially the 1996 Bob Dole campaign. Manafort had become a frenemy after Dole insisted that a "tolerance plank" be inserted into the Republican platform stating that while the party remained pro-life, it tolerated those of different views. As executive director of the Christian Coalition at the time, I felt such a statement was self-evident, but we opposed anything that appeared to weaken the GOP's commitment to the right to life. We also worried about any language that implied that pro-life Americans were somehow intolerant. Working with Phyllis Schlafly and the pro-lifers on the platform committee, we corralled the votes to defeat the tolerance plank and conveyed our intention to the Dole campaign. Manafort, one of the best vote counters in the business, could do the math. After I huddled with him in a small office in the bowels of the San Diego convention center that resembled a concrete bunker, it fell to Paul to call Dole and deliver the bad news. I stood outside while Manafort made the call and could hear Dole screaming on the speakerphone through the concrete walls and metal door. A few minutes later, Manafort came out, looking a bit shaken. Dole didn't like it, he told us, but he gets it.

Twenty years later, I was on the phone with Manafort again, this time to run through a checklist of items on Evangelical voter outreach. Manafort had come on board to assist with convention strategy, and he gradually assumed leadership of the campaign. He mentioned a request for Trump to hold a meeting with Evangelical leaders, and I strongly recommended that Trump should go. We discussed the platform, and Manafort assured me that Trump supported the platform without a single word change. Finally, I asked for Trump to return to Faith & Freedom's Road to Majority policy conference. Manafort asked for the dates and times and told me to count on Trump being there.

One thing we didn't discuss was Trump's search for a running mate. I knew from previous presidential campaigns that trying to divine the running mate of a presidential nominee was like reading the stars on an LSD trip. Most of the picks in my career had been complete shockers: Dan Quayle in 1988, Jack Kemp in 1996, Dick Cheney in 2000, and Sarah Palin in 2008. The vice-presidential search process is less like a beauty pageant and more like the reality TV show *Survivor.* Some candidates who look great on paper fall by the wayside because of financial or personal issues. Sometimes the list narrows to only one person still standing after a full vetting and FBI background check. This time would be different.

Trump's shortlist was narrowed down to Pence, former Speaker of the House Newt Gingrich, and New Jersey governor Chris Christie. As a Georgia Republican, I had been a friend and collaborator with Newt for almost thirty years. I found Newt to be one of the most brilliant and visionary politicians I had ever encountered. But he also had a strong personality, and I wondered if two alpha males could coexist on the same ticket. One thing was for sure: if Trump chose Newt, he wouldn't be reticent about playing the role of attack dog and savaging Hillary for her ethical challenges and liberal views. Christie, though hobbled by the Bridgegate scandal, had been a loyal and fierce defender of Trump's. I kept my views to myself and did not seek to lobby Trump or his campaign.

I was walking off a golf course outside Cleveland, Ohio, with some donors just days before the start of the Republican convention when I received a phone call telling me that Trump was about to name Mike Pence as his running mate. "Holy smoke!" I exclaimed to no one in particular. "This is almost too good to be true!"

Pence later told me the amazing story of how he and Trump (and his children) had bonded during the process. Trump had decided to campaign with both Christie and Pence to test his compatibility with the two finalists and see how they each performed on stage. On July 12, the day after campaigning with Christie in New Jersey, Trump appeared at a rally in Indiana with the governor, a kind of public audition for Pence, which he passed with flying colors. The original plan had called for

Trump to fly back to New York that evening. But at dinner with the Pences after the event, Trump and his son Eric, who had accompanied him on the trip, learned that their plane had a flat tire and there were no spares available at the airport; a fresh tire would have to be flown in the next morning. They were stranded for the night. During their conversation over dinner, they arranged for the other Trump children to fly in and meet the Pence family, and Mike and his wife, Karen, suggested that they host both families for breakfast the next morning.

There was only one problem: the next morning was Sunday, and the mansion staff had the day off. So at ten o'clock that night, the governor and first lady of Indiana found themselves arranging for breakfast the next morning. When they returned to the mansion, Mike and Karen went out into the backyard and got down on their hands and knees, picking flowers for an arrangement for the dining room table, illuminating the darkness with the flashlights on their cell phones. Mike joked to Karen that if he did end up on the ticket, no one was ever going to believe this story. The next morning, the Trump children and the candidate arrived at the mansion for a breakfast prepared by their hosts. According to Pence, contrary to the stereotype of the Trumps living in gold-encrusted luxury in Manhattan, they are actually very down-to-earth, and they loved the fact that the Pences had prepared such a casual breakfast rather than something fancy prepared by staff. As they talked and got to know one another, it became clear that Mike and Karen were genuine people. Beyond the obvious political compatibility, the Trumps and the Pences liked each other a lot.

Was the flat tire on Trump's plane a simple accident, or was it in some strange way ordered by Providence? Cynics in the media have suggested it was all a ruse by the Trump campaign to strand the candidate for the night so he could grow more comfortable with selecting Pence. We will never know, but I am dubious. The episode was one more example of the seemingly inexplicable taking place and paving the way for Trump to achieve what seemed impossible and which had never occurred in the history of America—the election of a president who had never held elective office, never been involved in politics in a significant way in his life, and never gained prominence as a military hero. The chemistry between Trump and Pence was evident to all who dealt with both men. I have seen it up close on the campaign trail and in the White House, and I believe there is a deep, personal, and spiritual bond between the two men that transcends their political partnership. They love one another and they complement one another beautifully. I've been around a lot of White Houses in my career, and I've seen the staff rivalry, personal ambition, and strange awkwardness that often prevails among presidents and their vice presidents. In Pence, Trump gained what all presidents want, but few get: an effective, loyal advocate who has no agenda other than to advance and protect a single client—namely the president.

Trump is a relatively recent arrival to the Republican Party and the conservative movement; Pence is a Reaganite and full-spectrum conservative who came up through the ranks of the conservative movement. Trump is an instinctive politician not known for studying briefing books; Pence headed a public policy think tank and the policy arm of the House Republican Conference. Trump was a stranger to Washington; Pence spent a dozen years there, rose to leadership in the House, and enjoyed a large fraternity of D.C. friends—not only among former colleagues in the House (some of whom now served in the Senate), but also among former Hill staffers, conservative leaders, and strategists in the center-right policy community. Trump was from Manhattan and Queens; Pence hailed from the heartland. Trump's personal past made him (unfairly, in my view) suspect to some Evangelicals; Pence bolstered their faith in the ticket because of his ability to speak their language and because he had lived out his own Christian faith with sincerity and humility—two qualities in rare supply in the political arena. Finally, Trump was a Queens brawler who had triumphed in the world of real estate in Manhattan; Pence was a reserved gentleman from the Midwest. In his selection of a running mate, as in so many other aspects of his campaign, Trump seemed to defy convention, as it appeared that the attack dog would be at the top rather than the bottom of the ticket.

By selecting Pence, Trump had revealed much about his own govern-ing priorities. Flying in the face of claims by the liberal media and Never Trumpers that Trump was a closet Democrat, he had chosen as his partner a man of impeccable and unquestionable conservative convic-tions. As a congressman, Pence had voted against No Child Left Behind, the prescription drug benefit under Medicare, and the bailout of financial institutions during the 2008 financial crisis. As someone who was in D.C. at the time, I knew he had done so under enormous pressure from Republican leadership and the White House. Why would Trump select Pence if his ambition was to sell out conservatives and cut deals with Democrats? It made no sense. Second, if Trump was only paying lip service to the faith community and his commitment to the pro-life agenda was so suspect, why would he choose a man of such deep faith whose pro-life credentials were as solid as granite? One would have thought that Pence's selection would have ended all further debate on whether Trump was a conservative or a con artist and an interloper.

But the capacity of die-hard Never Trumpers to question anything the New York billionaire did was apparently limitless. Bill Kristol, one of the leaders of the Stop Trump caucus, dismissed Pence as the product of machinations by campaign strategists Kellyanne Conway and Paul Manafort, and he urged Trump to "dispense with Pence."[2] A Colorado delegate who had previously backed Cruz dismissed Pence as mere win-dow dressing: "The red meat Trump just tossed to conservatives has the markings of 'front man for the con man' on the label."[3] Iowa radio firebrand Steve Deace went further, saying, "It was the worst we've ever been stabbed in the back by a Republican."[4]

Some of this grousing could be dismissed as pot-stirring by the liberal media or the bitterness of Never Trump dead-enders, but I was floored by the skepticism. In my view, Trump and Pence were a match made in heaven—not only for the faith community, but for the country. I firmly believed that if Trump were fortunate enough to be elected, he would need a steady, substantive, and discreet partner to help him navigate the tortuous terrain of Washington—someone whose advice and friendship he trusted entirely. Beyond Pence's street cred among Evangelicals and conservatives, that described him perfectly. Leaving politics aside, it was best for the country to have someone who so thoroughly complemented the president's own strengths and weaknesses and who was well-known and trusted on Capitol Hill.

The campaign asked if I would do some television interviews about Pence. I was happy to do so. The afternoon of his selection, I went on Fox News, holding nothing back.

Defending Pence was easy. I had gotten to know him shortly after he arrived in Congress in 2001, and over the years I began to hear a persistent buzz about him from other conservatives that he was a real comer, and I had made a note to keep an eye on him. I knew Pence as a patient but persistent climber. He had suffered a bitter defeat for Congress in 1990, then rehabilitated himself politically by running a conservative think tank in Indiana and hosting a radio talk show ("Rush Limbaugh on decaf," he said), before eventually winning a House seat in 2000 that was previously held by former Dan Quayle aide and conservative champion Dave McIntosh. From the day he arrived in Washington, the frosty-haired Pence impressed everyone with his Boy Scout demeanor, a wholesomeness that seemed right out of a Norman Rockwell painting, and rock-ribbed, Reaganesque conservativism leavened with a genial disposition.

One day, I dropped by his office to size him up, and after our get-acquainted session I departed, impressed by his policy chops and luminescent ambition. Years later, I began to hear rumors that he was thinking about running for president in 2012. When our Iowa Faith & Freedom chapter was looking for a speaker for its annual fall "Friends and Family" banquet in October 2010, just weeks before the GOP regained the House in a sixty-three-seat landslide, I suggested Pence.

I flew to Des Moines for the event, one of the most anticipated dates on the Iowa political calendar, which was attended by nearly a thousand grassroots faith-based activists and dozens of officeholders and candidates. Pence clearly knew the importance of this stage and had prepared thoroughly. I greeted him backstage and then sat in the front row to watch him. I had seen a lot of politicians address Evangelical audiences in my career, but I had seen few own a room like Pence did that evening. Displaying the skills that he had once honed behind a radio microphone, Pence was alternately tough, Midwestern nice, self-deprecating, funny, and serious.

Pence won the crowd with his opening line: "I'm a Christian, a conservative, and a Republican in that order." It was music to the ears of pro-family activists who had poured out of the pews and into the precincts in recent decades, backing the GOP because it represented pro-life and conservative values, but who would leave just as quickly if it did not. Pence blamed Obama's 2008 election on Republicans' losing their ideological and moral compass. "Truth is, our party in Congress walked away from the principles that minted our national governing majority and the American people walked away from us." This was strong medicine, but to the conservative grassroots of the heartland it was the gospel truth. Pence reminded them that he had remained true to his conservative principles, voting against No Child Left Behind, the Medicare prescription drug benefit, and the Wall Street bailout.

Pence had a unique talent for serving up red meat without engaging in the dark arts of a demagogue. He may have been nice, but he was not weak—not in the least. He faulted President Obama for withdrawing U.S. troops from Iraq; vowed to repeal Obamacare, which was a disaster for patients; decried the failed economic stimulus; and lacerated the Obama administration for criticizing Israel for defending itself against Islamic radical terrorists in Gaza. "The American people support Israel's right to defend her borders and expect their president to do the same. Let the world know this, if nothing else: America stands with Israel," Pence said, leaning onto the podium. The crowd leapt to its feet in a standing ovation.

When it came to moral issues, Pence insisted that the GOP could walk and chew gum at the same time. Without naming him, he took issue with former Indiana governor Mitch Daniels, a fellow Hoosier also considering a presidential bid, who had recently made headlines and won media plaudits by urging a "time out" on social issues while the government focused on the economy and jobs in the aftermath of the recent recession. "We must not remain silent when great moral battles are being waged," Pence insisted to enthusiastic applause. "Those who would have us ignore the battle being fought over life, marriage, and religious liberty have forgotten the lessons of history. America's darkest moments have come when economic arguments trumped moral principles." He urged an unapologetic defense of innocent life, traditional marriage, and religious liberty. In the closing moments of his speech, he urged the Iowa activists to take a stand. "We must not be afraid, and we must fight for what has always been the source of American greatness: our faith in God and our freedom." He vowed that conservatives would retake Congress in 2010 and then America in 2012, "so help us God."[5]

As I watched Pence depart, I thought he could do very well in the presidential primaries. His performance in Iowa revealed a seasoning, preparation, and talent far beyond the typical member of Congress. When future presidential aspirants went to Iowa for the first time or their staff asked for talking points, I would email them a transcript of Pence's speech. Put this in your own words, I advised, and you'll hit a home run. At the time, of course, I never contemplated Pence on the same ticket with Donald Trump.

In 2011, Pence came through Atlanta—I presumed on a fundraising foray—and asked to meet. We met at a lunch club in the Buckhead area late in the afternoon, when the popular spot for power lunches by Atlanta business leaders was empty. We sat at a bar table and drank iced water, which somehow seemed fitting for a meeting to discuss a presidential bid by an Evangelical candidate. Pence got right down to business, explaining that he was thinking about running in 2012 and asking pointed and specific questions about what it might take to be competitive. I didn't try to influence his decision one way or the other, but observed that no sitting member of the House of Representatives had been elected president since James Garfield in 1880. (Even Garfield comes with an asterisk; he had been elected to the U.S. Senate in 1880 by the Ohio legislature, but did not serve after his election as president.)

No member of Congress elected to the White House in over 120 years, I said with a chuckle, "constitutes a pattern." Pence smiled as his dark eyes bored into me with a remarkable intensity. I laid out other obstacles to running as a member of the House, such as lacking name recognition or a national financial network and being forced to miss critical votes in order to raise money and campaign in early states. I pointed to John Kasich, who had chaired the House Budget Committee and helped balance the budget, but still struggled to raise funds when he ran for president in 2000.

Pence wondered aloud if he could assemble a national finance network of conservative and faith-based donors. He took my fairly conventional advice in stride and was not in the least discouraged. I liked that; he would need an unshakeable confidence in himself (and in God) for whatever came next. As the meeting wrapped up, I told him I thought the most viable path for him to the presidency was to go back to Indiana and run for governor. When we parted ways in the lobby, he shook my hand firmly, eyes locked on mine, and said he would stay in touch.

My impression of Pence was that he was personable, engaging, bright, and ambitious in the best sense of the word, possessing a godly ambition and a yearning to serve a cause larger than himself. Whether based on advice similar to mine or his own instincts, Pence did decide to run for governor of Indiana in 2012, winning handily. As governor, he cut taxes, reformed education, and established a solid conservative record.

The next time our paths crossed came in 2015, when he had signed a Religious Freedom Restoration Act (RFRA) that had passed the legislature—apparently without much involvement by him or his office. The bill had passed the state House with only ten dissenting votes. If the bill had hewn entirely to the federal statute passed by Congress in 1993 that was signed into law by Bill Clinton, it might have raised fewer hackles. But because of additional protections for faith-based business owners inserted by legislators, the Indiana law was slightly different than the federal law upon which it was based. Pence signed the bill flanked by Evangelical, Jewish, Roman Catholic, and pro-family leaders. Before the ink was dry, gay advocacy organizations exploded in protest, falsely claiming that the bill gave Christian business owners the right to deny services to gay and lesbian customers. (It did no such thing.)

As the controversy swirled, the facts seemed irrelevant. The Republican mayor of Indianapolis blasted the bill, as did former Republican governor and Purdue University president Mitch Daniels. Indiana corporate chieftains, led by the CEO of Eli Lilly, condemned the legislation. Salesforce, a customer relations software provider based in San Francisco, threatened to cancel a planned expansion in Indiana. Making matters even worse, Indianapolis was preparing to host the NCAA Final Four. The NCAA, whose national headquarters were in the state, issued a statement expressing "concerns" about the bill, joined by top players and coaches like Duke University head coach Mike Krzyzewski, threatening to turn the Final Four into a platform to criticize Indiana for alleged anti-gay bigotry. In basketball-crazy Indiana, this was damaging to Pence. The *Indianapolis Star*, not wishing to let the truth get in the way of virtue-signaling, ran a front page editorial titled "Fix This Now." Events soon descended to the theater of the absurd. A pizza place in rural Indiana announced that it would decline to host wedding receptions for gay couples.

One day as I sat in my office, my phone rang, and on the line was my good friend Nick Ayers, one of Pence's top strategists and a veteran of Georgia politics. Nick got straight to the point. Pence and the legislature were under tremendous pressure from the business community; the political heat was almost unbearable. Some were advising Pence to sign an amendment to the bill that protected gays and lesbians. What did I think?

I told Nick the time to fix the bill had been before it was passed. The original legislation should have been a state version of the federal law without a jot or tittle changed. But that ship had now sailed. My advice was to hang tough because I feared a retreat would damage Pence's standing among Evangelicals in the party. Accepting the proposed amendment would effectively turn a religious freedom bill into a gay rights law. But I acknowledged the backdrop of the pending NCAA Final Four, and the reaction of the business community put Pence in a terrible bind. Nick thanked me for the input and said Pence might call me later.

The call never came, however, and I soon found out why. Within days, Pence signed the amendment passed by the legislature that made clear the religious freedom bill did not authorize discrimination against gays and lesbians. The entire flap guaranteed a stiff challenge by the Democrats and the organized Left, softened support in the business community, and demoralized Pence's natural base among Evangelicals. A man deeply committed to his own Christian faith and dedicated to religious freedom now stood accused of having failed to defend them. In addition, the controversy threatened to overshadow Pence's other achievements as governor, including creating new jobs, growing the economy, rolling back regulations, and improving schools.

To his credit, Pence kept his head down and kept doing his job. By the time Trump selected him to be his running mate and we arrived at the Cleveland convention, the religious freedom flap had largely faded. I arrived at the Cleveland Cavaliers basketball arena that normally spotlighted the talents of NBA star LeBron James and bumped into Nick in the hall. He took me into the Trump family box to say hello to Pence. Pence wore a blue blazer, a white cotton shirt with a red tie, and pressed khaki slacks. He seemed cool and confident, an island of calm in the eye of a storm.

We embraced, and I congratulated him, telling him I looked forward to doing anything I could to help in the days to come. I reflected on what an amazing wrinkle of fate Pence's selection had turned out to be for both men. Trump had rescued Pence from a gubernatorial reelection campaign in which victory was anything but guaranteed. Pence provided the moral Teflon that Trump needed to close the deal with the Evangelical wing of the party and would soon act as an emissary to the voters of the upper Midwest who would decide the outcome of the election.

"You're either incredibly lucky or you've got a guardian angel," I joked to Pence.

He smiled and said nothing in reply, his eyes dancing.

CHAPTER 8

CROOKED HILLARY

With his new running mate, Trump had united the party, soothed the Evangelical right, and salved the festering wounds of the primaries by applying Mike Pence like a healing balm of Gilead. One poll showed Trump winning 68 percent of the Evangelical vote going into the Cleveland convention, a solid foundation upon which to build for the general election.

Still, questions lingered about the intensity of his Evangelical support. Cruz delegates planned a series of parliamentary maneuvers they hoped would lead to a brokered convention. Were Evangelicals fully on board the Trump train? To answer the question, the news website *Politico* convened an on-the-record roundtable discussion at a downtown Cleveland steakhouse during the Republican National Convention. I joined Tony Perkins of the Family Research Council, Penny Nance with Concerned Women for America, Marjorie Dannenfelser of SBA List, and Gary Bauer of American Values to discuss the state of the presidential race. The question on the table was this: Were we now going to enthusiastically back Trump? Everyone at the table except me had either opposed Trump publicly or endorsed Ted Cruz in the primary, but one by one they lined up behind the Manhattan billionaire. I was impressed by their answers to pointed questions from Katie Glueck, the reporter who moderated the discussion.

"I really do think [Trump] speaks with the zeal of a fresh convert," said Dannenfelser. "I cannot speak to his soul, but I can say he understands the consequences of a position he has taken. So he'll say things like 'pro-life Supreme Court justices,' which no candidate has ever said." I was struck by the fact that Marjorie had noticed the same thing I did when Trump spoke to Faith & Freedom the previous month.

After Trump became president, Marjorie would work very closely with the administration on pro-life policies and judicial nominations. Getting there during the campaign had proven difficult. "Trump was my last choice until he was my first," she recalled. "But I've never been so happy to be so completely wrong." She called Trump "the most pro-life president the pro-life movement has ever known. He's leading us to save millions of lives of boys and girls intended for this world."[1]

"I would say Mike Pence does bring some confidence for me on what the commitment is for a Trump administration to the pro-life community," Nance said. "We can't just stand by and allow Hillary Clinton to be our next president. I look forward to having a woman president someday, but not that one."

For Perkins, it boiled down to a binary choice. "We have a choice. Hillary Clinton or Donald Trump," he said. Taking a veiled shot at Evangelical Never Trumpers, he called it "irresponsible" to complain from the sidelines without taking sides. Perkins said, "I want him to be successful, because if he's successful, America survives. That's the bottom line."[2]

Gary Bauer said he had no reservations at all about Trump. I happened to run into Gary's son, who had the build of an NFL linebacker, in the hotel gym that morning. Towering over me, he introduced himself and informed me he was Pence's body man and personal aide. When I sat down, I asked the diminutive Gary if he was certain he was the father. Penny's eyes widened in shock. Gary laughed, explaining that his son was so tall that people were often surprised he was his son. After such a contentious primary process, it was fun to enjoy a little levity. We would need it as we braced for one of the ugliest general election campaigns on record.

As it turned out, the convention was anything but a laughing matter. There remained the stubborn resistance of hundreds of Cruz delegates, and a question hung over the proceedings: Would Ted endorse Trump? Cruz had run an impressive campaign, winning nine primaries and caucuses, placing second to Trump, and arriving in Cleveland with 552 delegates. When Cruz addressed the convention on Tuesday night, the delegates, ten thousand journalists, and a national television audience waited in anticipation to see if (as expected) he would endorse Trump. Some of his delegates remained hopping mad at what they saw as the hardball tactics of the Trump campaign. Initially succeeding in recruiting seven states to force a floor vote on the nomination, Cruz delegates were livid when one of the states dropped off the petition and the convention chair declined to recognize them from the floor. I began to hear rumblings from friends in the Cruz camp that some of his advisors were recommending that he emulate Reagan at the 1976 convention in Kansas City, when he declined to endorse Gerald Ford. Would Cruz do the same?

I was in a suite with an old friend from past battles, former senator Bob Dole, and my good friends Jerry Falwell Jr. and his wife, Becki. I had worked closely with Dole when he was Senate Majority Leader and had labored tirelessly to help elect him president in 1996. At ninety-three years old, Dole was sharp as a tack and remained ever the Republican war horse, as well as a big Trump fan. After chatting for a while with Dole and the Falwells, I suddenly realized I had not yet been on the floor of the convention. I left the suite and headed for the floor, oblivious of the convention proceedings. When I arrived, Ted Cruz was beginning his speech right in front of me. I was beside Phyllis Schlafly, who sat in a wheelchair. Though I didn't know it at the time, it was the last time I would see Phyllis alive. (She would pass away in September, and Trump left the campaign trail to attend her funeral.)

As Cruz reached his peroration, he pointedly failed to mention Trump by name or endorse him. Instead, he urged supporters to "vote their conscience." At that point, members of the New York delegation, seated directly in front of the stage, began to jeer and boo with gusto. Some of the Trump delegates around me began to hurl invective and shout obscenities at Cruz, denouncing him as a turncoat and traitor.

"Get off the stage, Ted!" screamed a woman delegate to my right, the blue veins in her neck popping through her skin. "You're a sore loser!"

As Ted finished, a smattering of applause mixed with loud boos echoed in the convention hall. As the venom cascaded within the hall, I worried things might careen out of control. Had Ted ventured on to the floor, I feared he might be torn limb from limb.

Heading to the elevators, I rode back up to the suite level and headed to our box. Rounding a corner, I ran smack into Ted and Heidi. I did not see the point in raising the hostile crowd reaction. To say the horse was already out of the barn was an understatement.

"You handled that just right," I said, fibbing just a little.

"I thought so," Ted replied.

"You urged your supporters to vote their conscience, correct?" I vouchsafed, making Ted's case. "What pro-life voter can examine their conscience and come to any conclusion other than to vote for Trump? Especially when the alternative is Hillary."

"That was my thinking precisely," said Ted, nodding vigorously.

To this day, I believe Ted intended to telegraph his support for Trump without a full-throated endorsement, hoping to let his most hardcore supporters down gently. As it happened, we were standing outside the suite of Sheldon Adelson, one of the biggest Republican donors in the country. Ted turned to an aide and said he wanted to stop in and pay his respects to Sheldon. At that point, I said my farewells and headed back to my seat. I later heard that Sheldon was so upset that he declined. It was just one more indication of how heated the emotions roiling the party were and how strongly people felt on both sides of the divide. Like new wine poured into old wineskins, Trump and his movement had rushed into the GOP, upending the existing power structure and reshaping its ideological contours in ways that caused tremors throughout the party.

As events would soon demonstrate, these were the growing pains of the party as it expanded. Under Trump, the GOP would soon win the support of blue-collar and non–college educated voters in Pennsylvania, Ohio, and Michigan with his unique brand of populist conservatism.

Adelson and other leading GOP donors had boarded the Trump train, but not everyone in the Republican establishment was thrilled with Trump. After the convention, I called one of the top Republican business leaders in the country, a CEO of a Fortune 100 company and an innovative leader in his industry. He took my call to discuss what Faith & Freedom would be doing to turn out voters of faith in 2016. I gave him about a five-minute briefing and asked him to support our efforts with a contribution.

"Ralph, I believe in you and what you're doing. But I can't help you if you're doing anything to help Trump," he replied.

I was thunderstruck. I patiently explained that we were contacting tens of millions of voters in churches and neighborhoods. We could not distribute voter education literature that included state senate, congressional, and U.S. Senate races and leave the presidential race blank. To do so would undermine our credibility with Evangelical voters.

"Well, if Trump is on your material, I can't help you," the CEO said. "I'm focusing all my giving on Senate candidates to try to build a backstop in the Senate in case Hillary wins. My wife and I make all such giving decisions together." Then he said with a chuckle, "If I do anything to help Trump, I'll be sleeping on the couch."

I heard the same story from other donors. According to press accounts, the influential Koch network and its organization Freedom Partners had adopted a similar posture and chose to focus on key Senate races. But in my view, abandoning the top of the ticket was counterproductive, decapitating the party during one of the most consequential elections in modern political history. Adding a senator or two wouldn't stop Hillary from filling the Scalia vacancy on the Supreme Court. I was stunned how far removed the donor class was from the grassroots of the party. I had a foot in both camps, having served on the national finance committee for President George W. Bush and raised millions for the party and its candidates. If Trump lost, he would take other candidates down with him. Politics is a team sport. Giving Hillary a pass was not something I could do in good conscience. President Hillary Clinton was not an outcome I could countenance. Neither could millions of Evangelicals and faithful Roman Catholics.

Fortunately, faith leaders who had done all they could to stop Trump in the primaries by backing candidates closer to their philosophical or spiritual convictions were now doing all they could to elect him. Penny Nance of Concerned Women for America recalled that she "actively worked against [Trump] because I was worried about his sincerity on the pro-life issue. All the other candidates running against him had solid records, but his was mixed at best." Pence was a turning point for Nance. After Trump took office and began to implement his pro-life promises and appointed Neil Gorsuch to the Supreme Court, Nance went on Fox News to admit, "I have never been so happy to be wrong about anything in my entire life." She celebrated the fact that Trump's appointees to the federal bench "will be a safety net for Christians in what I believe will be very difficult times ahead for us on matters of conscience."[3]

Rebecca Hagelin, former vice president of communications and marketing at the Heritage Foundation and co-chair of Women for Cruz, observed, "We hoped against hope that [Trump] would be true to his campaign promises.... We wanted to believe. We prayed we could believe." For Hagelin, it came down to Trump or Hillary, and Trump "did not make us wait long for solid proof of his intentions—he named Governor Mike Pence to be his partner." After the election, many were thrilled that Trump turned out better than their greatest hopes. "While I left blood on the field in an attempt to defeat him in the primary," confessed Hagelin, "I now fall to my knees and thank God that Donald Trump is my president."[4]

As we pivoted to the general election, Faith & Freedom Coalition undertook the most ambitious and comprehensive voter education effort directed at voters of faith in modern American political history. We built a massive database of 41.6 million Evangelicals and pro-life Roman Catholics based on the most advanced data analytics and microtargeting technology available in the industry. Approximately 21.6 million of these voters were in the key states of Florida, Ohio, Iowa, North Carolina, Michigan, Wisconsin, Arizona, and Pennsylvania. Our voter education team mailed 22 million pieces of mail to these pro-family voters, made 10 million phone calls, distributed tens of millions of voter guides in 117,000 churches, sent 15 million emails and text messages, and placed 18 million digital ads on Facebook and other social media platforms. In addition, volunteers knocked on over one million doors in key states by Election Day.

Our voter materials did not advocate the election of Donald Trump or any other candidate. But we did tell voters where Trump, Hillary, and the other candidates stood on the key issues affecting them and their families. While the media chased the latest flap, gaffe, or pseudo-scandal of the day, we provided factual information on the records and positions of the candidates. For Hillary Clinton, the truth about her record was devastating. We didn't have to exaggerate or attack her personally; all we did was give the voters the facts—something the media deliberately failed to do. Hillary was the first candidate ever endorsed in the Democratic primaries by Planned Parenthood, the largest abortion provider in the world. She opposed any restrictions on abortion, even for late-term or sex-selective abortion. She was the first presidential candidate who promised to repeal the Hyde Amendment, which prevented tax dollars from being used to pay for abortions under Medicaid. She not only supported the Iran nuclear deal, which allowed a terrorist state dedicated to the destruction of Israel to maintain its long-range ballistic missile program, but she had helped to negotiate it as secretary of state. She had publicly promised not to consider anyone for appointment to the U.S. Supreme Court who did not pledge in advance to vote to uphold *Roe v. Wade*. This kind of extremism may have been intended to check all the ideological boxes of the Far Left, but it had the unintended effect of alienating and energizing millions of voters of faith who came to see Hillary as unacceptable.

Ironically, Hillary professed to be a committed Christian steeped in her Methodist faith. As first lady, she had spoken often about seeking a "politics of meaning" that embraced morality and faith, forming a spiritual and intellectual partnership with Michael Lerner, a liberal activist, rabbi, and founder and editor of the progressive journal *Tikkun*. But Hillary was so ridiculed and lampooned (unfairly, in my view) by the media and her critics who portrayed her as in the thrall of a New Age Rasputin that she backed off completely and almost never spoke about her faith again. As a presidential candidate, Hillary began every day with a Bible reading and devotional emailed to her each morning by spiritual advisor Bill Shillady, a Methodist minister. Clinton had first met Shillady in 2002 when he pastored a church in New York City, and over the years their relationship grew into a trusted spiritual friendship. But while this may have been the private Hillary, on the campaign trail she rarely if ever mentioned her faith, and when she did, it took the form of the same scripted, self-protective armor that characterized her entire candidacy. This failure to make herself relatable to voters of faith would prove to be a fatal strategic error.

Hillary compounded this mistake when she spoke at a fundraiser for the Human Rights Campaign Fund in New York City on September 9, 2016. While the rest of the speech was anodyne, in what appeared to be an attempt at humor, she unforgettably referred to Trump's supporters as a "basket of deplorables." In Hillary's description, "deplorables" were "racist, sexist, homophobic, xenophobic, Islamophobic—you name it. And unfortunately, there are people like that. And [Trump] has lifted them up." Now deep in a hole, Hillary kept digging. "Now, some of those folks—they are irredeemable, but thankfully they are not America." For any Bible-believing Protestant or faithful Catholic, to accuse someone of being "irredeemable" was over the line. The Christian faith teaches that no one is beyond redemption because salvation through faith in Christ is available to all. When a thief under sentence of death asked Jesus to remember him as he hung on the cross, Jesus told him that because of his profession of faith, "Truly I tell you, today you will be with Me in paradise" (Luke 23:43). The Gospel teaches that all of us are under a sentence of death for our sins, but through faith in Christ we can all be redeemed. Hillary seemed to be saying the opposite—that some people were "deplorable" and could not be redeemed. Hillary's "irredeemable" comment insulted tens of millions of Christians, and the fact that she and her campaign were oblivious to the consequences and did nothing to correct them was political malpractice.

The Trump campaign understood immediately that Hillary had committed a catastrophic gaffe. "Wow, Hillary Clinton was SO INSULTING to my supporters, millions of amazing, hardworking people. I think it will cost her at the polls!" Trump wrote on Twitter to his millions of followers. It wasn't the first time that Trump's much-maligned Twitter feed would prove prophetic. Appearing at a major Evangelical gathering in Washington, D.C., Mike Pence laid the lumber on the Democratic nominee for president. "Hillary, they are not a basket of anything," Pence said to cheers and applause. "They are Americans and they deserve your respect." Sarah Huckabee Sanders, a senior Trump campaign advisor at the time, tweeted, "Hillary calling tens of millions of American men and women 'deplorable' is inexcusable and disqualifying." People soon showed up at Trump's rallies holding handmade signs that read, "One of the Deplorables." Trump began to highlight the "irredeemable" remark in speeches at campaign rallies, which got less media coverage than "deplorables" but was in many respects the far more insulting comment. In typical fashion, Hillary backpedaled halfway, saying she had engaged in "gross generalization," admitting it had been a mistake to characterize "half" of Trump supporters as haters and bigots. But she refused to retract the remark. By then, the damage was done.[5]

＊　　＊　　＊

Trump's own brush with political death came the following month on Friday, October 7, when the *Washington Post* posted a video clip on its website of Billy Bush interviewing Trump on a bus for an *Access*

Hollywood episode in 2005. At the time, Trump was a private citizen and star of his own television series. The video contained outtakes never before aired in which Trump and Bush, apparently not realizing they were being recorded, engaged in a crass conversation about women he had dated, with Trump bragging about past romantic exploits and Bush giggling and egging him on.

When the video went live on the website, I was sitting in a movie theater in Atlanta watching the Tom Hanks film *Sully*. I had spoken to a major donor earlier that afternoon who made the final contribution needed to complete the funding of the Faith & Freedom voter education "ground game" to educate and turn out faith-based voters, a program already well underway in key states. The donor promised to wire his contribution the following Tuesday, since it was too late to get the wire out that day, and the following Monday, Columbus Day, was a bank holiday. Relieved, I decided to celebrate reaching our financial goal by unplugging and catching a movie. About halfway through the film, my phone began to buzz, first intermittently, then incessantly. This was unusual for late on a Friday afternoon. After ten minutes of near-constant buzzing and vibrating, I wondered, *What is going on? Has someone died?* I pulled my phone out of my pocket to discreetly check my messages only to discover that the world had turned upside down with the release of the *Access Hollywood* video. I was getting emails, text messages, and calls requesting comment from nearly every major media outlet in the country.

I could hardly comment on the video without watching it. So I hunched over in my seat and pulled up the website on my phone, putting the phone up to my ear to hear the audio so that I wouldn't disturb others. Just to be sure, I watched it a second time. I did not appreciate the things that Trump said about women when he and Bush did not seem to know they were being recorded. The Bible teaches that we are to treat younger women as sisters and older women as mothers, in all purity and with dignity and respect (1 Timothy 5:2). But I noticed two things in the video. First, Trump had stepped off the bus and extended his arm to shake the hand of the attractive young actress who greeted him. Billy Bush then asked her, "Aren't you going to give the Donald a hug?" When she leaned in to hug him, Trump quickly said, "Melania says this is okay." Every married man knows that mentioning his wife in the presence of another woman creates a boundary. Marriage counselors teach this technique to married men and women to use in social situations involving the opposite sex. So while Trump's language was offensive, his actual conduct toward the woman was not.

I pecked out a statement on the fly on my mobile phone and quickly forwarded it to the reporters who had contacted me. "As the father of two daughters, I was deeply disappointed by Donald Trump's comments," the statement read. "But people of faith are voting on issues like who will protect unborn life, defend religious freedom, grow the economy, appoint conservative judges, and oppose the Iran nuclear deal. I think an 11-year old tape of a private conversation with a television talk show host ranks pretty low on their hierarchy of concerns." I contrasted Trump's inappropriate comments with the criminal conduct of Hillary Clinton, which had been under active investigation by the FBI for most of the campaign (an FBI investigation that would soon be reopened just days prior to the election). Hillary's "corrupt use of her office to raise funds from foreign governments and corporations and her reckless and irresponsible handling of classified material on her home-brewed email server, endangering US national security, will drive the evangelical base." While I could not imagine any voter, regardless of their faith or lack thereof, being happy with Trump's comments, I thought it highly unlikely that Evangelicals and conservative Christians would stay home or support Hillary because of them, especially given the stakes in the election.

This was not what the media wanted to hear. Liberal reporters rushed to find other faith leaders to renounce Trump in what I believed was a calculated and systematic campaign to suppress Evangelical turnout. Such leaders were not hard to find. Beth Moore, the very popular Evangelical Bible teacher, wrote in a tweet to her nine hundred thousand followers: "Trying to absorb how unacceptable the disesteem and objectifying of women has been when some Christian leaders don't think it's a big deal." I had great respect for Beth, and her ministry was enormously influential, especially among women. I worried her stance would negatively impact the turnout of Christian women who were already wrestling with reservations about the Manhattan billionaire. "Trump's horrifying statements, heard in his own proud voice," argued Southern Baptist seminary president Al Mohler in an op-ed in the *Washington Post*, "revealed an objectification of women and a sexual predation that must make continued support for Trump impossible for any evangelical leader." Mohler contended that "continued public arguments that offer cover for Donald Trump are now not only implausible but excruciating."[6]

No one could or should have defended Trump's remarks. But some faith leaders echoed my point that issues mattered more than a private conversation caught on videotape eleven years earlier. "While the comments are lewd, offensive, and indefensible...they are not enough to make me vote for Hillary Clinton," said Robert Jeffress, pastor of First Baptist Church of Dallas. Jeffress's words were echoed by Franklin Graham, who had endorsed no candidate. "The crude comments made by Donald Trump more than 11 years ago cannot be defended," wrote Graham on his Facebook page. "But the godless progressive agenda of Barack Obama and Hillary Clinton likewise cannot be defended." In case there were any doubts about where he stood, Graham added, "The most important issue of this election is the Supreme Court."

The *Access Hollywood* video sparked a feeding frenzy. My phone blew up all weekend with texts and calls from folks inside the campaign, journalists, and grassroots activists, and it became clear that the video threatened the survival of Trump's candidacy. Most people with whom I spoke were disconsolate, many of them reconciled to Trump's defeat. Their only question was this: Do we abandon ship or just stick it out? Speaker of the House Paul Ryan canceled an appearance with Trump in Wisconsin and said in a conference call with GOP House members that he would no longer defend the nominee of his party. It was the political equivalent of a public divorce.

Under siege by the press, a cascade of Republican elected officials threw Trump to the curb and said they would no longer vote for him, including Senator John McCain, Senator Rob Portman of Ohio, Congressman Jason Chaffetz of Utah, Governor Robert Bentley of Alabama, and Senator Mike Crapo of Idaho. Senator John Thune of South Dakota called on Trump to step aside and allow Mike Pence to be the Republican presidential nominee. Governor Bill Haslam of Tennessee urged Trump to do the same, announced he would not vote for him, and said he would write in another name if Trump remained on the ballot in his state. Senator Kelly Ayotte, locked in a razor-thin reelection race in New Hampshire, announced she would be writing in Pence's name. "I'm a mom and an American first, and I cannot and will not support a candidate for president who brags about degrading and assaulting women," she vowed. Sadly, Ayotte likely sealed her own defeat with the statement.

The Trump campaign tried to stem the bleeding by swinging into damage control mode. Trump released a video that evening apologizing for the comments, confessing that they were "foolish" and "offensive" and promising to "be a better man tomorrow." Based on the man I knew, Trump's words rang true: "Anyone who knows me knows these words don't reflect who I am. I said it, I was wrong, and I apologize." I had been with Trump many times in his office in Trump Tower, backstage at political events, and in private meetings with others, often in the presence of women. I had never seen him act in an inappropriate manner and had seen him behave on every occasion, including in the presence of attractive young women, as a professional and a gentleman. This included Trump's interacting at multiple events with both my daughters. Whatever one thought of the inappropriate remarks he had made in the *Access Hollywood* tape—and I certainly found them offensive—they were totally at odds with the man I knew and had seen up close for years.

Rats scrambled from what they thought was a sinking ship. Their pessimism appeared to be backed up by at least some polls. An NBC/

Wall Street Journal poll taken as the *Access Hollywood* firestorm raged found that Hillary Clinton led Trump by fourteen points at 52 to 38 percent. Many feared Trump would lose in a landslide. Some reports circulated over that dreaded weekend of internal polling by both parties showing an implosion of support for Trump among women, moderates, and independents. Reviewing the wreckage, *The Atlantic* predicted, "Democrats—who lead a generic ballot question 49 to 42—could retake both the House and Senate."[7]

By Sunday evening, as Trump and Clinton prepared to square off in the second presidential debate, the situation had grown so dire that the campaign put together a conference call of its faith advisory board, some of whom were in danger of jumping ship. As the call proceeded, it became evident that some were shell-shocked. Many were new to presidential politics and had never been through a firestorm of this magnitude. Several pleaded that we deliver a collective message to Trump: withdraw and allow Pence to be the standard-bearer. To me, this so-called solution only insured that rather than end just one political career (Trump's), we would end two, killing Pence off in the process.

After listening for about ten minutes, I requested permission to speak. "I realize this is a difficult and painful moment, but even if Donald Trump were to withdraw, and I don't think he ever would, the ballot access laws in many states would prevent the Republican Party from replacing him on the ballot," I pointed out. "Voters in those states would have to either waste their vote by voting for Trump or write in someone's name. In addition, early voting is already underway in Florida. There are already tens of thousands of votes already cast for Trump in Florida. There are another million or more absentee ballots that have been mailed in nationwide. If Trump drops out, all those votes will likely be thrown out. So at a minimum Hillary will win Florida by default, and with it, she would win the election." There was a long silence. "This ship is either going to sail into the harbor safely, or it is going down. But either way, I am strapped to the mast. Frankly, we all are."

Paula White and I texted during the call, and she thanked me for being so bold. To me, it was a matter of facing reality, however unpleasant. With the election fewer than thirty days away and early and absentee voting already underway, the die was cast. Once again, Evangelical voters and leaders alike faced a dilemma: Trump (an imperfect man) or Hillary, whose personal and policy agendas advanced grave moral evils. It was not an easy choice, but it was a simple one, and it was a choice we could not avoid.

That morning, I was interviewed on National Public Radio, which was not exactly friendly territory. Once the interview commenced, the host went straight for my jugular vein, asking about Trump's "predatory behavior" and how he "covets another man's wife," likely marking the first time ever that the Ten Commandments were invoked as authoritative on NPR. I replied that the comments "were offensive and inappropriate. As the father of two daughters myself, I did not appreciate them." But I pointed out that Trump had already apologized and released a video expressing his regret and making it clear that this was not the man he was today. I underscored the vital issues that would decide how people of faith cast their votes: protection of unborn life, judicial appointments, support for the state of Israel, religious freedom, creating jobs and growing the economy, and opposition to the Iran nuclear deal, which in my view posed an existential threat to the Jewish state. Given these stakes, I didn't think "a tape of an 11-year-old private conversation with an entertainment talk show host on a tour bus, for which the candidate has profusely apologized, is likely to rank high on the hierarchy of concerns of these faith-based voters."

The host ended the interview with one more fastball at my head: If one of my two daughters took a job on the campaign that required them to travel with Trump, would I feel the need to warn them?

"No," I fired back. "These comments—they were highly inappropriate and deeply offensive," but I knew they were not "reflective of who the man is, his attitudes and behaviors, today. If I did, I wouldn't be supporting him."

As the campaign seemed to spin out of control that fateful weekend, none of us knew that Trump would soon be bailed out and that his unlikely savior would be Hillary Clinton. The second presidential debate loomed on

Monday evening with an audience estimated to approach one hundred million viewers, and the stakes could not have been higher. Trump needed a big night, or he faced the very real prospect of the prominent defections from his campaign turning into an avalanche. Hillary's mission was to avoid committing a fatal mistake that would snatch defeat from the jaws of victory. In a fairly pedestrian performance, Hillary failed to deliver a knock-out punch and let Trump back into the race.

Trump's campaign, anticipating that Hillary would attack him for alleged sexual misconduct and misogyny, scrambled to arrange for a delegation of Bill Clinton's accusers, including Juanita Broaddrick and Paula Jones, to fly to Las Vegas, where the campaign announced they would be in the audience. It was a shot across Hillary's bow: if you wave our dirty laundry, we're going to point out that your husband stands credibly accused of sexual harassment and rape and that you encouraged his goons to smear these women and call them crazy and slutty—destroying many lives and reputations. Trump called reporters into a conference room a few hours before the debate so the accusers could share their stories of Bill Clinton's predations and Hillary's personal attacks. It all contributed to a distinctly circus-like atmosphere only hours before the debate. Everyone braced for what promised to be a night of fireworks.

Not surprisingly, the *Access Hollywood* tape came up frequently, and Trump went on the offense. First, he repeated his apology. "This was locker-room talk. I'm not proud of it. I apologized to my family. I apologized to the American people," he said with emphasis. Then he turned to Bill Clinton, calling him the worst sexual predator who ever served in the White House, and pointed out that he had been impeached by Congress, disbarred by the state of Arkansas and the American Bar Association, and paid $850,000 to Paula Jones, who was present that night. He called Hillary a hypocrite for saying accusers "should be believed" while previously calling her husband's victims liars and frauds, part of a "vast right wing conspiracy." Trump also pointed to an audiotape of Hillary laughingly recounting that as a public defender in the

1970s she had maneuvered to win a reduced sentence for a rapist. The victim, Kathy Shelton, who was twelve years old at the time she was raped, was also in the audience. These exchanges about character and charges of sexual misconduct did not seem to knock Trump out of the box. As Hillary faced persistent questioning about her private email server, Trump hammered away relentlessly, pointing out that she had deleted 33,000 emails that were under congressional subpoena and saying that if the justice system were fair, "You'd be in jail." Trump had come into the debate with his campaign seemingly imploding and had lived to fight another day.

The third and final debate took place on October 19, and the pivotal moment of the evening (and perhaps the campaign) came with the opening question, which was about the future of the Supreme Court. Moderator Chris Wallace of Fox News asked about two specific issues in which the high court's rulings had been decisive: the right to keep and bear arms and abortion.

Wallace gave Trump the first shot at the abortion question, and it was one fraught with hazard. "I want to ask you specifically," Wallace said. "Do you want the court, including the justices that you will name, to overturn *Roe v. Wade*, which includes—in fact, states—a woman's right to abortion?"

Trump said "that would happen because I am pro-life, and I will be appointing pro-life judges, I would think that will go back to the individual states."

Perhaps expecting Trump to dodge the question or decline to make a prediction, Wallace seemed slightly stunned. It was as if he could not believe a presidential candidate had just said on live television that he expected *Roe v. Wade* to be overturned if he became president. Wallace plowed ahead, repeating the question.

Trump stood his ground. He suggested that if he appointed two or three Supreme Court justices, *Roe* would be overturned in a manner "that'll happen automatically in my opinion, because I am putting pro-life justices on the court." If *Roe* were overturned, then abortion as an issue would "go back to the states, and the states will then make the determination."

Turning to Hillary, Wallace asked Hillary about her previous statement that an unborn child has no rights and about her vote as a U.S. senator against a ban on late-term abortion. Hillary ignored the first part of Wallace's question. On late-term abortion, she said that while "cases that fall at the end of pregnancy are often the most heartbreaking," she would not support a ban on them without broad exceptions for the mental and physical health of the mother, which would render the ban nearly unenforceable. "I do not think the United States government should be stepping in and making those most personal of decisions," she said.

This was Trump's opening, and he seized it. "In the ninth month," he said, "you can take the baby and rip the baby out of the womb of the mother just prior to the birth of the baby. Now you can say that that's OK and Hillary can say that that's OK." He pointed at her, then pivoted to face the audience. "But it's not OK with me, because based on what she's saying, and based on where she's going, and where she's been, you can take the baby and rip the baby out of the womb in the ninth month on the final day. And that's not acceptable."

Jo Anne turned to me and said, "I think Trump just won the election."

I began to receive texts and emails from pro-life friends who had sat on their hands for the entire campaign, many with deep personal reservations about Trump's character or his pro-choice past. One wrote in an email, "That is the most strongly pro-life statement I have heard from a presidential candidate in my life. He's got my vote."

Going into the third debate, Trump was winning 69 percent of the Evangelical vote, according to a CNN poll, compared to 78 percent among these same voters for George W. Bush in 2004. Trump was about where Bush was in 2000 and where McCain was in 2008 at that moment. I was confident that his answer on abortion in the debate would push his support into the mid-70s. I also felt it likely that it would move many pro-life Roman Catholic voters, with whom Trump had previously underperformed. As the swing vote in American politics, the Catholic vote was critical, especially in the upper Midwest. With less than three weeks to go before the election, Trump had finally sealed the deal with voters of faith.

After the campaign was over, I asked Kellyanne Conway about this moment. She told me the campaign had prepared for the abortion question and had included the issue in their debate prep. But she told me Trump's answer had never been part of those prep sessions. "That came directly from his heart," she said.

As the campaign entered its final days, I flew to Ohio to appear at an Evangelical event at Ohio Christian University with Mike Pence. The event was in Circleville, about thirty minutes outside Columbus, which unbeknownst to me was hosting a pumpkin festival that attracted tens of thousands of people. I asked a campaign aide to drive me over to the pumpkin festival so I could mingle with some voters before the event. The festival resembled a scene out of a Rodgers and Hammerstein Broadway musical. There were stands offering pumpkin pies, pumpkin coffee, pumpkin donuts, and pumpkin pretzels. As I stood in line to get a bag of pumpkin donuts, gazing through a store window at what the owners claimed was "the Largest Pumpkin Pie in the World," I chatted up a couple of people who told me they were voting for Trump because he was going to be tough on China and build the wall. Their dislike of Hillary was palpable. As we drove west to the college, the landscape gradually shifted from suburban to rural. To my surprise, there were dozens of homemade Trump signs on the side of the highway. A barn had been painted with "Trump for President" on its side. These were not official Trump campaign yard signs; they had been made by folks to express their avid support. I wondered how a state that had been such a fierce battleground for decades could be so strongly in Trump's thrall. His lead in most polls fluctuated between 5 and 7 percentage points. I said to the aide, "It looks like it's over in Ohio."

When I arrived at the church, I met Mike and Karen Pence, and we took a few pictures together. The church was packed. I introduced Pence, who gave a version of his stump speech, alternating between slashing attacks on Hillary's agenda, a full-throated defense of Trump, and an impassioned plea for voters of faith to go to the polls and encourage their friends and family members to vote. Most of the crowd sat ramrod straight in the pews with rapt attention. As I stood in the back of the room watching Pence and surveying the crowd, I was struck by what a soothing and reassuring presence Pence was for many of these voters in the heartland. The general election still looked dicey from where I sat, but one thing was certain: Pence had proven to be an outstanding pick, and he had left it all on the field for Trump and the Grand Old Party.

After the event, Pence met privately with a group of pastors and pro-family leaders. I excused myself to jump on a plane and fly to Virginia Beach for a Trump rally on the campus of Regent University. Founded by my old boss Pat Robertson, Regent provided a symbolic backdrop for Trump's closing appeal to Evangelical voters. After a short flight, I pulled up behind the library building, where a crowd of over five thousand had already spilled out across the campus. I delivered brief remarks as part of the undercard to Trump, then headed into the library to say hello to the candidate and his campaign team. They had just landed from a major speech in Gettysburg, Pennsylvania, where Trump had laid out a "Contract with the American Voters," the twenty-point policy agenda for the first one hundred days of his administration. It offered a solid set of policies, including repealing and replacing Obamacare, rolling back job-killing regulations, and enacting ethics reform.

I bumped into Kellyanne, who was as cool and unflappable as always. "Don't get me wrong, I'm glad you're here," I said. "But what are you guys doing in Virginia? It's not exactly a battleground state at this point. Shouldn't you be in Florida?"

Kellyanne said Trump had given his word to Pat Robertson that he would do a rally at Regent, and he was not going to break it. This is all about Trump and Pat, she said.

Whether or not it made sense in terms of the political map or calendar, one had to admire Trump for keeping his word. It wasn't the first or the last time I saw Trump do so.

I went to greet Trump backstage, where he proceeded to pepper me with questions, asking how I thought it was going. I told him if he closed strong, he had more than a fifty-fifty shot at winning. He looked up at the ceiling reflectively for a moment and nodded. I told him I had just left the event with Pence in Circleville, and the folks I had talked to thought Ohio was in the bag. Trump asked how he was doing with Evangelical voters. I told him that George W. Bush had carried 78 percent of the Evangelical vote in 2004, and I felt confident that he would do as well and maybe better. "If that happens, you're probably going to be elected president," I said.

Trump replied that the answer wasn't probably, but definitely. And he said his share of the Evangelical vote would be even higher. As events would soon prove, he was right.

I ran into Rudy Giuliani and asked him how he was feeling. He told me that if Trump stayed on message—always a question—he could win. He then lit into FBI director James Comey, a former colleague who he had once considered a friend, saying that he no longer recognized him and wondered if he was the same man he once knew. Within days, Comey would reopen the FBI investigation into Hillary's private email server after a search of former congressman Anthony Weiner's computer (for soliciting underage girls online) revealed some of Hillary's emails. When Comey's action leaked, it stalled Hillary's momentum heading into the final days of the campaign.

When Trump took the stage, he used the backdrop of a university founded by one of the nation's most influential religious broadcasters to make a full-throated appeal to Evangelical voters. "One of the greatest privileges of my journey has been the time I've spent with the Evangelical community and the people of faith across our nation," Trump said, speaking from the heart in unusually personal terms. Invoking his Presbyterian faith, he added, "There are no more decent, devoted, and selfless people than our Christian brothers and sisters here in the United States." Trump ticked through a wish list of Evangelical policies, promising that if he were elected, he would repeal the Johnson Amendment that prohibited political activity by Christian ministries or churches, defund Planned Parenthood, and appoint conservative judges. As president, he pledged to unite all Americans "under one God" again.

As Trump reached the end of his speech, I slipped out the back and jumped in a car that whisked me to a nearby airport, where I hopped on another flight—this one to Charlotte, North Carolina, to attend a religious liberty rally organized by our state Faith & Freedom chapter. When I arrived at the rally in a downtown plaza, a Christian rock band was playing and a crowd had formed near the stage. Before I spoke, I learned from Virginia Galloway, the field organizer heading up the North Carolina voter education effort, that our volunteers had knocked on 160,000 doors in the Tarheel State. She introduced me to the top volunteer, an elderly woman who had personally knocked on over 5,000 doors. Thanking the woman for her hard work, I asked her how it was going.

"Fantastic," she replied. "Everyone wants our voter guides. Everyone is grateful. So far I haven't talked to a single person who says they are planning to vote for Hillary."

"Really?" I asked. "Not one?"

"Not one," she repeated.

As I flew home to Atlanta that night, I made an educated guess based on what I had seen on the ground that day that Trump would carry Ohio and North Carolina while narrowly losing Virginia. If that were the case, the election was going to be a lot closer than anyone thought.

In the closing days, our field team worked overtime to make sure the final get-out-the-vote emails, text messages, Facebook ads, and phone calls went out, and our volunteers continued to flood the precincts, visiting every home they could. By Election Day, we would knock on over one million doors in the key states. Each night as each Evangelical or pro-life Roman Catholic voter in our database cast an early vote or sent in an absentee ballot, we removed them from our turnout universe and redirected our resources at those who had not voted yet.

The media continued to predict an overwhelming victory for Hillary Clinton. CNN's final poll showed Hillary leading 46 percent to Trump's 42 percent among likely voters, a bigger lead than Obama had in 2012 or George W. Bush had in 2004. CNN predicted that Clinton had a 91 percent chance of winning the election while Trump had only a 9 percent chance.

I was less interested in polling, which seemed all over the map and largely within the margin of error, and more interested in actual votes. For that reason, Faith & Freedom's data team followed the early vote in Florida closely and concluded that Trump was running about one hundred thousand early votes ahead of Romney in 2012. On the Saturday before the election, Tim Head called to tell me that 47 percent of our entire database in the Sunshine State (totaling over four million faith-based voters) had already cast their ballots early. That number was about 7 percent ahead of the pace in 2012. With Evangelicals representing about one-fourth of the Florida electorate, it translated into a 1.8 percent bump for Trump on the general election ballot. That was more than enough to wipe out the seventy-eight-thousand vote margin by which Obama had carried Florida four years earlier.

As Tim and I reviewed the map, we agreed that based on our tracking of the early vote and other data points, Trump would likely carry Iowa, Ohio, Arizona, Florida, North Carolina, and win one electoral vote from Maine (which awarded its electoral votes by congressional district). These states, along with all the red states carried by McCain and Romney, put Trump safely in our calculus at 264 electoral votes. If we were right, he was only six electoral votes short of winning the White House and only five electoral votes short of throwing the election into the House of Representatives, where Republicans had the majority and he would likely win. As we went down the roster of other battleground states—New Hampshire, Pennsylvania, Wisconsin, Michigan, Colorado, New Mexico—we drew a blank. We thought Trump would narrowly lose New Hampshire and Colorado. I viewed Pennsylvania as fool's gold—a tantalizing prize that Republican presidential candidates had chased for decades, but to no avail. We ended the call speculating that his best shot might be Michigan, where polls showed he was closing fast and where the Clinton campaign had dispatched Barack Obama to

Detroit to help turn out African-American voters. I thought Trump had a shot there.

On Election Day, the exit polls looked bad for Trump. But I recalled what happened in 2004 when the exit polls predicted a victory for John Kerry over George W. Bush. Whether because of the rise of cell phones or the number of voters lying to pollsters, I questioned whether they were reliable anymore, or ever had been.

As the election night wore on, Trump opened up a healthy lead in Florida, as we expected. Liberal commentators breathlessly predicted that Broward County would put Hillary over the top, but we knew better. On my laptop, I jumped around the country pulling up returns on the websites of county boards of elections, and the results were surprising—in some cases shocking. In Hillsborough County in Tampa, Florida, Hillary had a narrow lead at nine o'clock in the evening, but it was being swamped by large Trump margins in surrounding exurban counties. Hillsborough was a swing county that Bush had carried handily in 2004 and Romney had lost big in 2012. As with Hillary's wins in Broward and Dade in southern Florida, they were buried beneath a huge Trump vote everywhere else in the state. Tampa, Orlando, and Miami looked like islands of blue in a sea of red.

At 10:53 p.m., Fox News called the Senate race in Wisconsin, projecting that GOP senator Ron Johnson would win reelection. At that moment, Johnson was ahead by about seventy thousand votes. In general, Trump was trailing Republican Senate candidates slightly in the battleground states, but seventy thousand votes offered a nice cushion in a state the size of Wisconsin. I turned to Jo Anne and announced, "Honey, Trump is going to carry Wisconsin. He's going to win." It was the first time a Republican presidential candidate had carried Wisconsin since Ronald Reagan in 1984. Even Michael Dukakis had carried Wisconsin when he lost in a landslide to George H. W. Bush. As the evening wore on, Trump also carried Michigan and Pennsylvania, also representing the first victories in those states by a GOP presidential nominee in roughly thirty years.

The only thing more fun than Trump's winning was watching the shell-shocked faces of news anchors as the reality dawned on them and they were forced to announce the results to their viewers. Martha Raddatz of ABC News actually cried on the air. A stunned Rachel Maddow of MSNBC told her viewers, "You're awake, by the way. You're not having a terrible dream. Also, you're not dead and you haven't gone to hell. This is your life now. This is us, this is our country. This is real." Van Jones called Trump's victory a "whitelash" against Barack Obama, seemingly oblivious to the fact that Trump had defeated Hillary, not Obama.

Soon the media would realize that voters of faith—led by a record turnout of Evangelicals—had provided the margin of victory on an historic night when Trump and down-the-ballot Republican Senate and House candidates won all over the country. According to network exit polls, self-identified Evangelicals comprised a record 26 percent of the electorate and voted 81 percent for Trump, with only 16 percent voting for Hillary Clinton. This was the lowest share of the self-identified white Evangelical vote ever received by a Democratic presidential nominee. A separate post-election survey commissioned by Faith & Freedom Coalition, conducted by the Public Opinion Strategies firm, found that 33 percent of the electorate self-identified as conservative Christians, and these voters cast 79 percent of their ballots for Trump and only 15 percent for Clinton. This was the highest share of the electorate made up of conservative Christians in a presidential election in the modern era.

Faithful, pro-life Roman Catholic voters also contributed mightily to the faith vote. White Catholics comprised one out of every six voters and voted 54 percent for Trump and 36 percent for Clinton, swinging Rust Belt states like Ohio, Iowa, Pennsylvania, and Wisconsin to the GOP column. Catholic voters who regularly attended mass broke for Trump two to one. Trump even won the entire Catholic vote, which for decades was the swing vote in American politics, by a margin of 50 to 46 percent, contrary to almost all expectations and pre-election polling.

Even this understated the significance of the faith vote in Trump's victory. A number of state exit polls showed astonishing margins for

Trump among Evangelicals in the key battleground states that decided the outcome of the election. In Florida, Trump won self-identified Evangelicals by 85 percent to 13 percent. In Georgia, Evangelicals voted 88 percent for Trump and 6 percent for Clinton. In Michigan, Trump won 81 percent of the Evangelical vote to only 14 percent for Clinton. In Wisconsin, the Evangelical vote broke 71 percent for Trump and 24 percent for Clinton. Voters of faith turned out in historic numbers and gave Trump the margin he needed to pull off a shocking upset.

At a time when many in the media were writing the political obituaries for Donald Trump and religious conservatives as a whole, it showed yet again how indispensable voters of faith were to a winning Republican coalition—and how desperately Democrats needed to find a way to appeal to them. Larger than the African-American, Hispanic, and union vote combined, Evangelicals and pro-life Roman Catholics were the largest and most vibrant single constituency in the electorate. From the day Donald Trump entered the presidential race, he appealed to them with a single-minded focus while Hillary and the Democratic Party ignored and insulted them at their own peril.

Next would come the Trump presidency and a reckoning for the faith community. The media needed a scapegoat. Along with Russia and James Comey, they soon found their villain: Evangelical Christians.

CHAPTER 9

THE FALSE CHARGE OF HYPOCRISY

The media did not find the critical role played by Evangelical voters in the election of Trump amusing, to say the least. In fact, they were horrified. After they had reached for the smelling salts, they turned their attention to trashing Evangelicals and conservative Christians by hurling the false charge of hypocrisy, claiming that churchgoing voters had put partisanship and power ahead of the Bible and their moral beliefs. The first purpose of this smear was (they hoped) to reduce Evangelical voter turnout in 2020, thus making it easier to defeat President Trump. The larger and more important purpose, regardless of what will happen in the 2020 presidential race, was to stigmatize and delegitimize the political engagement of Evangelical and conservative Christians so that their voice could be silenced—or at least ignored—in the larger conversation of democracy.

One of the falsehoods told to advance this strategy was that Evangelicals denounced Bill Clinton for his shortcomings while acting as apologists for allegations of misconduct against Trump. But this is false. When the *Access Hollywood* tape became public during the presidential campaign and revealed lewd comments about women by Trump,

Evangelical leaders expressed a broad continuum of reactions ranging from revulsion to strong disapproval. Jim Dobson denounced Trump's remarks as "deplorable, and I condemn them entirely." Jerry Falwell Jr. called them "horrible" in an interview with radio host Rita Cosby, adding, "There was nothing defensible. It was completely out of order, it's not something I'm going to defend... it was reprehensible."[1] Other Evangelical leaders were appalled. Robert Jeffress, the pastor of First Baptist Dallas who endorsed Trump in the primaries and sat on his campaign faith advisory board, said Trump's remarks were "indefensible." "I find it disgusting," said Tony Perkins, president of the Family Research Council.[2] Franklin Graham said Trump's "crude comments" on the tape "cannot be defended." I wrote on Facebook that the comments were "offensive and inappropriate. As the father of two daughters, I did not appreciate them. The Bible teaches that we are to treat older women as mothers and younger women as sisters, in all purity."

All these statements were in the public domain and available to anyone who wanted to access them. But the liberal media deliberately took these words out of context or published them under misleading headlines to claim that Evangelical leaders "defended" Trump. In fact, they condemned the words and deeds behind them while pointing out the clear differences between the candidates on issues that were important to the faith community. What these critics really resented is that Evangelicals continued to support Trump because they faced a binary choice between him and Hillary (who had her own ethical and character issues), the vacancy on the Supreme Court, and the broader policy implications of the election.

The media responded to this choice by Evangelicals with a toxic mixture of sarcasm and ridicule. On Comedy Central's *The Daily Show*, host Trevor Noah lampooned Evangelical Trump supporters for twisting Christianity like a pretzel to fit their political loyalties. Playing video clips of Gary Bauer, Robert Jeffress, and yours truly explaining our support for Trump, Noah carried on a mock conversation with God, in which the "voice of the Lord" complained, "You see, my child, many use My name when it suits them. But come election time, they change positions faster than my Son changes water into wine."

Another common tactic in the hypocrisy canard is spreading fake news about the polling of people of faith. National Public Radio (NPR) reported on a poll conducted by the liberal Brookings Institution that asked whether it was possible for someone to commit an immoral act in their personal life while still doing a good job in a position of public service. In 2011, only 30 percent of Evangelicals said yes to that question in a poll, while in 2016 that percentage rose to 72 percent. The reason for the shift? No one really knows, and no one has actually asked, most likely because they knew they wouldn't like the answer. But that didn't dissuade NPR from jumping to conclusions, claiming that Donald Trump, in "fending off allegations of sexual misconduct", had somehow "inspired some people to loosen their views on whether it's OK to vote for someone with a questionable past." Get it? Trump persuaded tens of millions of Christians to shed their moral beliefs in order to win an election. Or, as NPR put it, "Evangelicals Have Warmed to Politicians Who Commit Immoral Acts."[3]

Occasionally, the media dress up this smear with a false academic veneer. Two Notre Dame professors looked at the 2018 elections and found that only 16 percent of Evangelicals viewed an immoral act in one's past as a hindrance to doing a good job in public service. Seizing on the survey, HuffPost argued that Evangelicals' willingness to "overlook President Donald Trump's infidelity, his dishonesty, his disparaging rhetoric toward immigrants and refugees, and the multiple accusations of sexual misconduct lodged against him suggests that their views on morality have changed dramatically." Or as Professor David Campbell put it: "They have put politics first." Reverend Adam Taylor, executive director of the liberal group Sojourners, said Evangelicals were making a "Faustian bargain" with Trump, accepting policy victories while turning a deaf ear to "immoral statements, behaviors, and policies" that "contradict the gospel and should assault Christian conscience." The result was "an overtly politicized, intolerant, and nationalistic movement" that "misrepresents Christ."[4]

Not to be outdone, Americans United for the Separation of Church and State published a report in April 2019 that declared, "A new study proves something we've suspected to be true for years: right-wing evangelicals are hypocrites." The report cited the same polling data, none of which supported their overblown conclusions. "For something like 40 years, Religious Right groups have been sanctimoniously lecturing the rest of us about how character counts and why we need 'godly' men and women in public office," the screed continued. Americans United faulted Evangelicals because they "rallied around the most amoral man to hold the highest office in the land since Richard Nixon." It credited Trump with exposing "the Religious Right and its leaders for what they are and always have been: a band of hyper-partisan, morally confused scolds who have failed a simple ethical test of differentiating between right and wrong."

This is hogwash. I have been involved in the pro-family movement almost since its inception and have overseen voter education programs reaching tens of millions of faith-based voters over that period. These voter education efforts provided information on where candidates stood on the issues: abortion, marriage, religious freedom, taxes and spending, education, immigration, support for Israel, and health care. Never have these ads or voter education literature argued who is the more moral or godly candidate. When I served as executive director of the Christian Coalition and Gennifer Flowers and others made charges about Bill Clinton's personal life, we did not mention those personal allegations or argue that they were disqualifying in our voter education literature during my tenure. We did criticize Clinton for vetoing the partial birth abortion ban and repeatedly vetoing welfare reform before finally signing it.

When Faith & Freedom Coalition knocked on over one million doors and distributed voter guides in over one hundred thousand churches to educate Evangelical and pro-life Catholic voters in 2016, we did not mention the *Access Hollywood* tape in our voter education literature or advertising, but we also did not mention Hillary Clinton's private email server, FBI investigation, or the pay-to-play scandal that swirled around the Clinton Foundation. In both cases, these were arguably the largest voter education programs directed at voters of faith during each period.

Waving the bloody shirt and claiming the faith community has spent decades urging people to vote for candidates based on their personal moral character is nonsense—certainly in the case of the major organizations that did the work of registering, educating, and turning out Christian voters. We educated voters on where the candidates stood on key issues and urged them to vote with their moral and biblical convictions. At no time did we claim there was a "Christian" position on the issues, nor did we claim the Bible spoke authoritatively on every issue, although I do believe the Bible speaks in a generalized way to every area of life. Our purpose was singular: to make sure Christians were educated, informed on all the candidates and issues, registered to vote, and went to the polls. The Bible says, "My people perish for lack of knowledge" (Hosea 4:6). Knowledge is power; ignorance is impotence. By equipping Christians with reliable knowledge, we ensure that they are effective citizens. That is our mission, and I don't believe the calling of Christians in the civic arena is to act as modern-day Pharisees seeking out who has committed sins in the past and organizing a mob to embarrass, shame, and rhetorically stone them.

Of course, voters make judgments about the character, honesty, and moral fiber of candidates, as well. But even here, people of faith must ask a simple question: Does the Gospel teach that someone who has had a personal moral failing is disqualified from ever serving in a position of public trust? In fact, the Bible teaches the opposite, offering redemption and hope through faith in Christ to all sinners. Peter denied Christ three times on the night of his betrayal, but he was still elevated to leadership in the early Church. Paul persecuted the Church, rounded up Christians for trial, and participated in the stoning of Christian martyrs, but he went on to write two-thirds of the New Testament. But the media aren't interested in this aspect of the Gospel. Instead, they seek to condemn anyone for their past shortcomings and sins if it serves their real purpose—namely defeating Trump and marginalizing Bible-believing Christians.

For decades, the media and the Left accused Evangelicals of acting like modern-day Anthony Comstocks trying to impose their religion on everyone else. In 1997, an American Civil Liberties Union (ACLU) official claimed that the Christian Coalition aimed to "enshrine one religion, one morality in law and impose it on all."[5] That was certainly news to me, and I ran the day-to-day operations of the organization. Columnist Frank Rich of the *New York Times* found it "galling" that the Christian Coalition "is now legislating a morality for others, especially the poor, that it patently doesn't adhere to itself."[6] Now they are seemingly angry for the opposite reason: because Evangelicals are not condemning enough, not judgmental, and are willing to extend grace to those who have not lived a perfect life. Rather than discard other people who have made poor decisions in the past, Evangelicals are open to seeing their redeeming qualities and giving them a chance to serve. The truth is that they were always willing to do so. Now the same liberal critics who once attacked Evangelicals for being puritanical accuse them of hypocrisy for not being puritanical enough.

In truth, Evangelicals have always possessed a greater measure of grace and mercy in their public witness than is generally understood. In the Sermon on the Mount, Jesus taught that any man who divorces his wife, other than for adultery, and then marries another woman commits adultery and causes the other woman to commit adultery (Matthew 5:32). This is a difficult teaching, and one that has been much debated in the Church over the centuries. But by that literal reading of the Bible and the faux sanctimony of their critics, Christians should not support divorced presidential candidates. But they have done so repeatedly. In fact, Evangelicals backed divorced and remarried candidates for president in 1980, 1984, 1996, and 2008 by huge margins. Kate O'Beirne of *National Review* joked in 2008 when Mitt Romney, Rudy Giuliani, and Newt Gingrich all ran for president that the only candidate who had only one wife was a Mormon.

They never held it against Ronald Reagan that he had gone through a painful divorce. After Governor Mark Sanford was caught in an embarrassing affair and went through a very public divorce, he apologized to the voters of South Carolina and served out the remainder of his term. Mark and I were friends, and he wrote me a moving note personally apologizing for his conduct. I wrote him back and told him he owed me no apology, and I encouraged him to put the past behind him and live for the present, making his life count for good. Several years later in 2013, Sanford made a stunning political comeback and ran for his old congressional seat. He began his campaign by admitting he had made terrible mistakes in the past. Voters of faith forgave him, and many voted for him. (Sanford would later lose reelection in the 2018 primary in part because of his very public criticism of President Trump, but that was based on politics, not his past.) Evangelicals have never asserted that someone who fails to live up to Christ's teachings in their personal life can never make a positive contribution to their community and nation. That is a false and misleading caricature of the Christian faith drawn by those who mean it no good. Christians believe in second chances, in no small measure due to the fact that their own personal stories are about finding a second chance through the salvation and forgiveness they found through faith in Jesus Christ.

My friend Nick Ayers, who served as chief of staff to Vice President Pence, shared a revealing story about his time in the White House that speaks to this point. One day he encountered President Trump in his private office, just off the Oval Office, where the president often works when he is not in formal meetings. At the time, there were charges circulating in the media against the president.

President Trump asked why the Evangelicals continued to support him so strongly.

Nick replied that it was because they had experienced God's forgiveness in their own lives and felt a responsibility to extend the same grace and forgiveness to others. That was the correct answer to a very good question. To the extent that Evangelicals have extended grace to Donald Trump, it has been an expression and a witness of their Christian faith, not a contradiction of it. If there is a criticism that can be leveled at people of faith, it is not in their offering this grace to Trump, but in their failure in the past to always offer it as willingly to others—especially politicians with whom they have disagreed on public policy.

Yet the hypocrisy charge has become a standard talking point among liberal Democrats. "It's something that really frustrates me, because the hypocrisy is unbelievable," Indiana's South Bend mayor, Pete Buttigieg, told Chuck Todd on *Meet the Press*, referring to Evangelical support for President Trump. "Even on the version of Christianity that you hear from the Religious Right, which is about sexual ethics, I can't believe that somebody who was caught writing hush-money checks to adult-film actresses is somebody they should be lifting up as the kind of person you want to be leading this nation."[7] This was a rather ironic charge, given the fact that one presumes that Buttigieg does not want Christians to condemn a candidate because he is gay, yet urges them to judge President Trump because of the biblical injunction against adultery—which in Trump's case involves allegations that are unproven and which he disputes. In the twisted morality of the new secular Puritans on the Left, the Bible's teachings about sexual morality no longer apply, except for the prohibition against adultery, even when the facts are in dispute—but only against Donald Trump. This isn't biblical morality; it is tyranny. It may exist in Iran, but it has never existed in America. Once the cross of Christ is twisted into a crooked finger of accusation, no one is safe. When a society makes the past personal lives of candidates— rather than their public policy positions and qualifications—the primary standard for their eligibility to serve in public office, it has opened the door to a modern-day inquisition. Imagine the horror of the Brett Kavanaugh nomination battle occurring in every election with both major party candidates subjected to investigations of their sexual pasts, kangaroo courts examining high-school yearbooks, lawyers deposing old boyfriends and girlfriends, and the media dumpster-diving into the lives of anyone seeking public office. This is not the world that Evangelicals seek. It is the political system contemplated by the media and urged on by some Never Trumpers, and secular Puritans are trying to usher it in right now for the express purpose of destroying and defeating conservatives—starting with Trump.

Sometimes fellow Evangelicals make this argument with the hearty approval of the liberal media. In December 2019, the day after the Democrat-controlled House of Representatives impeached President Trump in a partisan vote (not a single Republican voted in favor), *Christianity Today*, the Evangelical magazine founded by Billy Graham, wrote an editorial calling for Trump's removal from office. *Christianity Today* claimed Trump should be impeached because he "attempted to use his political power to coerce a foreign leader to harass and discredit one of the president's political opponents," namely Joe Biden. "That is not only a violation of the Constitution; more importantly, it is profoundly immoral." The editorial also attacked Trump's character, claiming he "admitted to immoral actions in business and his relationship with women, about which he remains proud." It also denounced his Twitter feed, "with its habitual string of mischaracterizations, lies, and slanders," as a "near perfect example of a human being who is morally lost and confused."[8] The editorial gave no credit to Trump's strong record on the economy, criminal justice reform, lifting millions out of poverty, protecting the unborn, or defending Israel. It also questioned the spiritual integrity of Evangelicals who supported President Trump, claiming that they had undermined their witness for Christ. The Graham family, offended by the editorial's invocation of Billy Graham's name, reacted swiftly. Franklin Graham wrote on Facebook, "My father knew Donald Trump, believed in Donald Trump, and he voted for Donald Trump" because he believed Trump "was the man for this hour in the history of our nation."

Meanwhile, Ben Howe, an Evangelical and the son of a former Liberty University professor, published the book *Immoral Majority* in 2019, alleging that his fellow Evangelicals were spiritually bankrupt partisans "more concerned with the lives and happiness of their children than whether or not the president is a lying, philandering, unethical charlatan." He accused conservative Christians of selling their souls to gain political power. "For the possibility of worldly influence, they surren-dered their moral voice in the public sphere," he charged. By supporting Trump, Howe argued, Evangelicals have "embrace[d] brutality over compassion, self-interest over persuasion, and deception over repen-tance."[9] Could they therefore regain their moral authority by turning their backs on Trump in 2020 and helping a Democrat win the White House? Howe wasn't convinced. "I don't know that there is a recovery in the sense that people will look to evangelicals for any kind of moral leadership again," he said in an interview on MSNBC's *Morning Joe*. One of the show's hosts, Willie Geist, concurred. "So in some ways the politics trump the word of the Bible," he said of Evangelicals.[10]

In an interview with *The Atlantic*, Howe dismissed the idea that voters of faith chose Trump because his issues aligned more closely with their values. In the end, "Trump's appeal isn't judges, it's not policies. It's that he's a s—t-talker and a fighter and tells it like it is," Howe said. Evangelicals "love the meanest parts of him." When asked about abor-tion, Howe strangely claimed that Trump actually hurts the pro-life cause. "As a Trump-supporting pro-lifer, can I convince anyone that abortion is wrong? He makes it more difficult."[11]

Most Evangelicals would disagree. Two-thirds of them supported some-one other than Donald Trump in the early Republican primaries. In the general election, they held deep reservations about both candidates. But in the final analysis, they viewed the protection of life from conception to natu-ral death as both a biblical and moral issue, considered abortion-on-demand to be the most profound evil of their time, and saw *Roe v. Wade* as a black stain on the history of our country. Based on this calculus, they went heavily for Trump after he said he would appoint pro-life justices to the Supreme Court, said in the third debate with Hillary that it would probably lead to the overturning of *Roe*, and with unusual moral clarity argued that his opponent's position amounted to allowing an unborn child to be "ripped from its mother's womb" moments before birth.

In this context, the people of faith who voted for Trump in 2016 and will do so again in 2020—probably in even larger numbers—are not engaged in an act of spiritual delusion or cognitive dissonance. They are moral actors engaged in civic action that is rich in ethical content and long-term consequences. People of faith, confronted with a less-than-perfect choice between two flawed candidates, chose to do all they could to protect innocent life. Like someone charging into a burning building to save a child, these voters weighed all the options, examined their consciences, prayed fervently, and then voted for the candidate who promised to defend life. Critics of conservative Evangelicals know this, which is why they now dismiss abortion as mere window dressing. Ben Howe has called abortion a "cudgel" that Evangelicals use to bludgeon liberals, wielding it to disguise their partisanship. He cited polls showing that the economy is the number one issue in determining voting behavior for Evangelicals (as it is, by the way, for all voters). Howe concluded without a shred of evidence that this proves Evangelical leaders "have taught their flocks to value the things of the world, rather than the things of Christ."[12]

But Howe misunderstood the data. In my work on eleven presidential campaigns, I have studied public opinion survey data for decades. There is nothing new or remarkable about polling data in the Trump era. With the possible exception of George W. Bush's reelection in 2004, when the war on terror was a major campaign issue, the economy consistently ranked highest for most voters—including voters of faith. This doesn't mean that abortion, religious freedom, or support for Israel are not important issues to these voters; it means that once they have sorted through the candidates based on values criteria (usually led by abortion), they then cast their ballots primarily on the economy, jobs, education, and health care. They exclude pro-abortion candidates who will deny them their First Amendment right to practice their faith, weeding them out of the field, allowing them to vote on a wider range of issues.

It also means they are not single-issue voters. Citizens of faith are thoroughly integrated into the economic and cultural life of the larger society. They don't live in trailer parks, watch only Christian television on satellite dishes, grow their own food, and read only the Bible. Most are college-educated and live in the suburbs or exurbs. Many are small business owners or employees active in their local Chamber of Commerce or industry groups. In states like Texas, Oklahoma, Pennsylvania, and North Dakota, many are involved in the energy industry. A large number are teachers and educators, or they educate their children at home; they care a lot about education. Many are doctors, nurses, and health practitioners. They have a professional understanding of these industries and issues, and it naturally influences their voting behavior—not in contradistinction or opposition to their views on abortion or marriage, but as a substantive part of a larger whole. Their worldview can best be summed up as traditionalist, conservative, and Bible-based. It is a seamless garment, to borrow a phrase from Catholic social teaching, in which the principles of Scripture that teach the essential dignity and God-given rights and responsibilities of every human being inform their views on a broad range of issues. Their pro-life position on abortion is a reflection of this worldview; it does not define it.

The same phenomenon prevails among union members, minority voters, and younger women. Union workers support collective bargaining, but labor issues rarely rank at the top of the issues driving their voting behavior. (Just ask Trump, who won 42 percent of union households in 2016.) Minority voters rarely rank civil rights as their number one issue in exit polls. Hispanic voters list jobs, the economy, and a quality education far above immigration, which usually ranks fifth or sixth in their hierarchy of issues in their voting decisions. And while most young women are pro-choice, the percentage who say abortion determines their vote is in the single digits. The same is true, by the way, for hunters, sportsmen, and members of the National Rifle Association, whose main issues are the economy and jobs—not guns. Try telling them that they are not committed to the Second Amendment right to keep and bear arms. It is absurd on its face. And it is equally absurd to use polling data to argue that life, family, and religious freedom issues are just not that important to voters of faith. If a politician believes that, let him try to run a campaign on a platform of lower taxes, less regulation, and abortion on demand, and then he will see how many Evangelical and pro-life Roman Catholic votes he wins.

The importance of the economy and jobs to people of faith is not a sign of misplaced priorities or spiritual shallowness because the prosperity of families and society is a biblical issue too. Jesus said that man does not live by bread alone, but man cannot live without bread. Jesus fed people wherever he ministered. He showed concern for people's physical needs for food, water, shelter, and health. So too should we. This also fails to grasp the comprehensive biblical worldview of people of faith or the holistic manner in which they approach their civic witness.

The philosophical chasm that separated Trump and Hillary—and will separate Trump from the Democratic nominee for president in 2020—is the widest of our lifetimes. This will weigh heavily in 2020. Hillary (and likely the Democratic nominee in 2020) support abortion on demand; Trump opposes it. The 2020 Democratic nominee will favor funding abortions with tax dollars; Trump opposes it. The 2020 Democratic nominee will support late-term abortion; Trump opposes it. The 2020 Democratic nominee will favor forcing church-affiliated nonprofits, ministries, and colleges to pay for medical services that include abortion; Trump opposes government mandates (like those imposed on the Little Sisters of the Poor by the Obama administration) that violate the religious teachings and the consciences of people of faith. For the first time since Roe, the official position of the Democratic Party today is that abortion for any reason at all at any stage of pregnancy is not only a constitutional right, but must also be directly subsidized with federal tax dollars. The Hyde Amendment, which first became law in 1976, has prohibited taxpayers' dollars under the Medicaid program from being used to perform abortions. Hillary was the first Democratic presidential nominee to call for its repeal. Joe Biden, who supported and voted for the Hyde Amendment for over forty years, flip-flopped in 2019 and caved to the pro-abortion lobby. For people of faith, on the most pressing moral issue of our time, Trump represents life, and the 2020 Democratic Party nominee will advocate making every taxpayer in America complicit in taking the lives of hundreds of thousands of innocent unborn babies.

This fact is backed up by anecdotal evidence and solid reporting. During the 2016 campaign, when my wife, Jo Anne, encountered committed Christian women in church or among her circle of friends who found it difficult to vote for Donald Trump because of his checkered past or coarse language, rather than argue with them, she would simply recite a list of numbers. "Eighty-three, seventy-nine, seventy-seven, seventy-five, etc.," she would say. "Do you know what those numbers represent?" Invariably, the friends did not know. "Those are the ages of the current members of the U.S. Supreme Court," my wife would reply. "In addition to the Scalia seat, whoever is elected president will appoint at least two and probably three or four justices. Do you want that to be Hillary?" Using this simple argument, she never failed to win the vote of the person for Trump. Exit polling backs this up. According to exit polling conducted by Edison Research, about 25 percent of voters said the Supreme Court was the most important factor in their vote, and 56 percent of those voters backed Trump versus the 41 percent who backed Democrat Hillary Clinton. Trump also won a plurality among the 70 percent of the electorate who said that Supreme Court appointments were a factor in their vote, while Hillary won voters who said they were not a factor by a huge margin of 52 to 39 percent. Without the Scalia vacancy and other pending Supreme Court appointments as a campaign issue, Trump might well have not been elected.

In April 2019, *Washington Post* reporter Elizabeth Bruenig traveled to Texas to interview Evangelicals about how they had wrestled spiritually and politically with Trump's candidacy in 2016 and whether they planned to back Trump in 2020. She visited a number of churches, talking to pastors and activists of many different ethnic backgrounds, political persuasions, and denominations. She found no one who had supported Trump in 2016 who expressed regrets about their decision. Bart Barber, an Evangelical pastor who had voted for independent candidate Evan McMullin, expressed a willingness to vote for Trump despite lingering doubts about his temperament. The main reasons were abortion and the Supreme Court. "Trump might say some things that run against the basic ethos of evangelical Christianity," Barber told the *Washington Post*, but he conceded that "he has also put in place two Supreme Court justices who are known to take anti-abortion positions." Southern Baptist and independent voter David Coleman also came to Trump because of abortion. He ruled out Hillary Clinton because she "would not say she was against partial-birth abortion." He could "understand their thinking in the early trimesters. But the killing of a child...." His voice trailed off. Barber and Coleman represent millions of voters of faith who cannot stomach a political agenda that includes the killing of a child who can survive outside the womb, late-term abortion, and infanticide. It will be even worse for the 2020 Democratic presidential nominee among voters of faith. As Bruenig pointed out, the abortion issue will likely loom larger in the 2020 presidential campaign after the passage of legislation allowing late-term abortion in New York and an attempt to pass a similar bill in Virginia sparked national controversy and shone a bright spotlight on the extremism of the Democratic Party.[13]

It is no accident that the seismic shift in voting behavior among self-identified Evangelicals that began in the late 1970s and culminated in Trump's 2016 victory coincided with the Republican Party becoming steadfastly pro-life and the Democratic Party becoming aggressively pro-abortion. Democrats once promised to make abortion "safe, legal, and rare." Today they promise to make it the most common surgical procedure in the nation, paid for with taxpayers' dollars, mandated in every private health insurance policy in the nation, or in a government-run health care plan modeled after Medicare for All. Democratic presidential candidates also refuse to appoint anyone to the Supreme Court who does not share the same view. To pretend that this development has not shaped the voting behavior of Evangelicals and pro-life Catholics is unhistorical and disingenuous. Indeed, in some ways Trump is the not-so-accidental beneficiary of this larger historical trend. Even with his flaws and the mistakes of his past, which he freely acknowledges, he embraced the pro-life agenda with full-throated enthusiasm, telling voters of faith he would appoint federal judges who were "pro-life." No

Republican presidential nominee had ever stated it that explicitly. Rather than focus on the personal foibles of Donald Trump or the alleged hypocrisy and spiritual blindness of Christians who voted for him (and will vote for him again), the media and other critics should consider how abortion has so thoroughly reshuffled the deck of American politics and whether or not it is really in the interest of the Democratic Party to remain a wholly-owned subsidiary of Planned Parenthood and the modern pro-abortion movement.

Fifty years ago, most Evangelicals and faithful Roman Catholics were Democrats. At that time, the South (where roughly 45 percent of Evangelical voters reside) was a one-party region—only for the Democrats. In 1976, when he ran as a "born-again evangelical," Jimmy Carter won two-thirds of the self-identified Evangelical vote and carried every southern state except Virginia. For most of their lives, Evangelicals and ethnic Roman Catholic voters supported Democratic candidates who invoked their Christian faith in expressing reservations about abortion and opposed using taxpayers' dollars to perform them. Many Democratic candidates were moderate to conservative on cultural issues.

This remained the case until recently. Barack Obama said when he ran for president in 2008 that he opposed same-sex marriage because it violated his Christian beliefs. At the Saddleback Civil Forum in April 2008 that was moderated by bestselling author and Evangelical pastor Rick Warren, Obama said of same-sex marriage: "I believe that marriage is the union between a man and a woman. Now, for me as a Christian— for me—for me as a Christian, it is also a sacred union. God's in the mix." But if a Republican candidate says today that "God is in the mix" when it comes to marriage and "as a Christian" he believes it is a "sacred union," he will be denounced as a bigot and homophobe.

It was not always so. Even as late as 2010, several dozen Democratic members of Congress—many from heavily blue-collar, Catholic districts in in the upper Midwest that Trump would carry in 2016—refused to vote for Obamacare unless it included a strict prohibition on taxpayer subsidies for abortion. Led by Bart Stupak of Michigan, almost all of them lost their seats in the 2010 GOP landslide because they accepted a phony compromise on abortion funding crafted by the Obama White House that was made of Swiss cheese. The political graveyards are full of Democratic politicians who lost their careers because of the abortion issue.

It is now unimaginable that the Democratic presidential nominee would ever stand on a debate stage in the fall of 2020 and express reservations based on their Christian faith on abortion, marriage, religious freedom, support for Israel, or probably any other issue. And as we have seen, Democrats have exacerbated their hostility towards faith by denouncing Christians who supported Trump as deplorables, irredeemable, hypocrites, and spiritual frauds. This is not only bad theology; it is bad politics. One doesn't win friends (or votes) by telling citizens who regularly attend church and believe the Bible is the Word of God that they are motivated by selfishness, greed, hunger for political power, spiritual hypocrisy, and racism. Yet this is clearly the strategy of the media and the Democratic Party in 2020 as they are assisted by an Amen chorus of Never Trumpers.

CHAPTER 10

THE MORAL SENSE

Many have claimed that the decision of Evangelicals and faithful Roman Catholics to back Donald Trump in 2016 and since in unprecedented numbers was just shallow partisanship. Certainly, citizens of faith remain the most loyal and resilient members of Trump's political base. For example, a June 2019 survey by Public Opinion Strategies found that Trump's job approval rating among self-identified Evangelicals stood at an astonishing 83 percent.[1]

But as we have seen, Evangelicals did not rush headlong into Donald Trump's arms. They wrestled with their decision, with two-thirds of Evangelical voters initially supporting other candidates in the 2016 Republican primaries. Only when confronted with a binary choice between Trump and Hillary in the general election—and after Trump had powerfully signaled his conservative governing philosophy by selecting Mike Pence as his running mate—did Evangelicals' support for Trump reach the historic level of previous GOP presidential nominees.

The support for Trump among citizens of faith has intensified as he has built a remarkably conservative record as president, such as his federal court picks (including for the Supreme Court), pro-life policies, tax cuts, defunding of Planned Parenthood, defense of religious freedom, and support for Israel. For most Evangelicals, these are moral and biblical issues that give meaning to their lives and shape their souls as citizens. They are also choices between right and wrong with real-life consequences, such as whether or not taxpayers' funds will be used to take the lives of the unborn, or whether a nuclear-armed Iranian regime run by radical mullahs will be able to threaten the survival of Israel.

Given the polarization of our politics in recent years, partisanship has gotten a bad name, and understandably so. But partisan loyalties serve a useful purpose in a democracy. They enable busy and distracted voters to sift through the choices and cut through the clutter and noise emanating from a distrusted media, arriving at a voting decision based on shared values. As the Republican Party has become identified as the party of the right to life, pro-family policies, and conservative judicial nominees, voters of faith have felt comfortable gravitating to its candidates. Similarly, the Democratic Party has now become identified as the party of abortion on demand, socialism, same-sex marriage, gay rights, and hostility to religious freedom for believers who do not share that agenda. The two parties today more closely resemble European ideological parties than the broadly conceived American parties of the past, and they crystallize sharply opposing political philosophies on social and moral issues. As political scientists Jonathan Mummolo of Princeton University, Erik Peterson of Texas A&M, and Sean Westwood of Dartmouth University argued, "conditional partisanship" melds voters to a political party as long as it remains true to their core values on key issues. "Voters show strong allegiance to their party when selecting which candidates to support, but will defect from the party line if candidates diverge from the voter on enough high-salience issues," they concluded.[2]

Given the stark choice offered by the two political parties in both 2016 and 2020, it is more accurate to state that Evangelicals and other devout Christians faced a decision between two candidates holding diametrically opposed political agendas—one of which embraced the intrinsic good while the other advanced grave evil, in their view. In this regard, they were motivated by what the social scientist James Q. Wilson called "the moral sense." In an age of relativism and non-judgmentalism, Wilson posited that human beings remained innately motivated by a desire to choose right from wrong. "We do have a core self, not wholly the product of culture, that includes both a desire to advance our own interests and a capacity to judge disinterestedly how those interests ought to be advanced," Wilson argued. Significantly, he contended that making such judgments required "taking the perspective of a citizen," because these moral judgments are inherently social in nature, involving our conduct and behavior toward others.[3]

It is the success of Evangelicals and the pro-family movement in advancing this policy agenda—not their alleged hypocrisy over Trump's past—which really drives the media crazy. *Boston Globe* columnist Renée Graham lamented that the real goal of Evangelicals isn't everlasting life, but "reshaping the Supreme Court," with the "terrifying potential" that *Roe* could be overturned, abortion laws could be returned to the states, religious freedom laws might be upheld, and gay and transgender rights might not be codified into law. "White evangelicals may not despise God," Graham conceded, "yet their hypocrisy and unflagging devotion leave no doubt that Trump is their true master and savior." Others urged Evangelicals to drop any pretense of concern for character, begging for consistency by accepting rogues of both parties. "So please, evangelical Trump supporters, be honest," pleaded Bonnie Kristian in *The Week*. "If you don't care about politicians' character anymore because you've realized such apathy is politically useful, admit that and apply your disinterest in character consistently across the political spectrum."

The only crime people of faith are guilty of is taking their citizenship seriously. That and asking not to be discriminated against because of their faith. In so doing, they have exercised their citizenship in a manner that is entirely consistent with Scripture. In both the Old and New Testaments, the Bible teaches that God's people can and should appeal to government leaders for protection and justice when possible, especially when their lives or ability to practice their religious beliefs are under attack. We are all familiar with the Bible story of Daniel in the lions' den. What is not as well-known is that the episode occurred because Daniel's political enemies, jealous because he had gained significant power within the kingdom as a senior advisor to the king, manipulated the Medo-Persian ruler Darius into signing an edict that restricted the religious freedom of Jewish exiles to worship their God. As a practicing Jew, Daniel refused to obey the edict, allowing his enemies to charge him with treason. After God delivered Daniel from the lions' den, Darius ordered that the men who had maliciously accused Daniel, as well as their families, be put to death. He also issued a second edict declaring that everyone in his kingdom should respect the Jews and fear their God. The chapter in the Bible that relates this remarkable turn of events closes with this statement: "So this Daniel enjoyed success in the reign of Darius and in the reign of Cyrus the Persian" (Daniel 6:28).

God loves and cares for His people. He honored Daniel for his faithfulness in refusing to obey an edict that denied him the right to practice his Jewish faith. Cyrus, Darius's successor, would eventually return the Jewish exiles to their homeland, giving them protection from their enemies and enabling them to rebuild and repopulate Jerusalem. There are some Evangelicals who have claimed that Trump is a modern-day Cyrus, either to the Jews or the Christians, or to both. I have no particular view on that subject, but I have never made a similar claim—nor would I. God alone knows His heavenly purpose in elevating a leader, and it takes the passage of time and a greater historical perspective from future generations to fully appreciate the role of leaders. During Ronald Reagan's campaign for president in 1980, the media and his liberal critics denounced him as a geriatric, right-wing crackpot itching to push the nuclear button. Only with the fall of the Berlin Wall and the liberation of Eastern Europe (which occurred after he left office) did we fully understand that Reagan's lifelong commitment to defeating and transcending Communism had made him one of America's most pivotal historical figures.

The larger and more salient point is that Daniel rose to a high position in government, remained true to his faith, and relied on both God and a sympathetic government leader to deliver and protect the people of God. Esther did the same in another time, assuming the position of queen after joining the harem of a Persian king, which certainly many would consider to be morally compromising. When the evil royal advisor Haman attempted to have the Jews in Persia exterminated, Esther intervened on behalf of her people, pleading with the king to spare their lives. Unable to retract his edict, the king issued a second decree authorizing the Jews to kill their enemies. In both of these cases and numerous others in the Bible, God's people used their influence in government to plead for their lives and resist evil. When Esther was reluctant to go before the king to plead the case of the Jewish people because appearing at court without being called by the king risked punishment, her uncle Mordecai warned her, "If you remain silent at this time, relief and deliverance will arise for the Jews from another place and you and your father's house will perish. And who knows whether you have not attained royalty for such a time as this?" (Esther 4:14).

This beautiful verse teaches two things that are enormously humbling and counter to everything in our culture. First, it teaches us that deliverance is ultimately from God, not from kings or presidents, and God simply uses whomever He selects. If one person He has chosen declines to show the courage of their convictions, God will raise up someone else. Second, it teaches us that God grants us whatever influence we may have primarily to serve and glorify Him, not to seek favor or power for ourselves.

As with Esther, how do we know that the same is not true for us in our own time? Drawing analogies from the Bible can be overly simplistic and syllogistic, and I am not arguing that either Trump or his supporters are modern-day Daniels, Esthers, or Cyruses. But like all of them, we have been placed in positions as citizens, as those with some measure of influence, or as those serving in elective or appointive office (either today or in the future), and we should use those positions to resist evil, advance righteousness, defend the innocent, and protect God's people. I can think of no higher or nobler purpose for our citizenship or public service.

In carrying out their own dual responsibilities as Christians and earthly citizens, the leaders of the early Church never failed to use their rights as citizens to advance righteousness. When Paul was unfairly arrested in Jerusalem for allegedly inciting a riot while preaching the Gospel, he did not acquiesce to the injustice. Roman centurions tried to flog him, but he resisted, reminding them that he was a citizen of Rome and could not be scourged without a trial. "Those who were about to interrogate him withdrew immediately," the Bible recounts. "The commander himself was alarmed when he realized that he had put Paul, a Roman citizen, in chains" (Acts 22:30). So Paul used his citizenship to strike fear in those who sought to persecute him. When his opponents tried to have him executed in a kangaroo court in Jerusalem, Paul exercised the most precious right of a Roman citizen: appealing his case all the way to Caesar (Acts 25:11).

The Emperor Nero was a corrupt, wicked, and debauched ruler who murdered his own mother and stepbrother, beat his wife to death (thus killing his own unborn child), and routinely executed political opponents. He was also a sexual deviant and pedophile who married a young boy after castrating him. Christians suffered horrific persecution under Nero, and while historians debate whether Christians were actually fed to dogs and lions by the reprobate ruler, both Paul and Peter were executed under Nero. This is who Paul appealed for justice, not because he was unwilling to suffer persecution, but because he took the rights and obligations of his Roman citizenship seriously. Like U.S. citizenship in our own time, Roman citizenship was a precious possession for anyone in the ancient world, but especially for a Jew. Because of Paul's strong belief in defending his rights as a Roman citizen, the message of salvation through faith in Christ reached the very courts of Caesar, and the Bible records that many in the emperor's household became Christians (Acts 25:11).

Our American citizenship is a gift from God, and it should be exercised in a robust and muscular manner—not used to gain political power or win favor from rulers, but primarily to glorify God. Just as Paul was a citizen of Rome, American Christians are U.S. citizens. They have shed their blood on a thousand battlefields on every continent, from Valley Forge to Gettysburg, from Normandy to Korea and Vietnam, and more recently in Afghanistan and Iraq to protect their rights as Americans and defend this nation. It is obviously true that God, not a parliament or president, is our ultimate defender against all forms of evil. It is in God that we must put our ultimate trust and faith—not politicians or government officials.

David says it far better than I can in Psalm 146, verses 3–5:

Do not trust in princes
In mortal man, in whom there is no salvation.
His spirit departs, he returns to the earth;
In that very day his thoughts perish.
How blessed is he whose help is the God of Jacob,
Whose hope is in the Lord his God.

Even the most dominant and powerful political figures only occupy the stage of history for a brief moment in time. Even if he wins reelection (as I hope he does), Trump will be gone in 2025. People of faith should not put their trust in him or any politician to deliver or defend the Church. But it is also true that throughout history God has used government leaders as instruments of His will, often for the protection and deliverance of His people and other innocents. In God's sovereignty, He has placed us in this time as citizens of the greatest nation on earth—a nation where we are free to speak our mind and follow our conscience as informed by our faith and where we are able to share the Gospel without fear of persecution under the rights afforded us under the First Amendment of the Constitution. Those rights come from God. No human agency can grant them, and no government or Congress can take them away. We are called by God and instructed by Scripture to defend those rights with all our might, including the vigorous exercise of our full rights as citizens—to vote, to organize like-minded citizens, to form citizen organizations that advance our values, to donate to candidates who share our views, to serve on juries of our peers, and to lobby elected officials.

We do so not because we fear persecution but because we honor God when we do so. To do otherwise is to fail to fulfill our obligations and responsibilities as citizens with all the attendant rights God has granted us. If after doing all these things we still suffer persecution (as the early Church did) and we are still dragged into court and denied our rights as Americans, then we should pray and seek God's deliverance by other means. But He expects us to be effective citizens. If Paul could appeal to Nero, a reprobate and bloodthirsty emperor, then Christian Americans are fully justified in appealing to President Trump, the Supreme Court, and any other elected or appointed official on behalf of their constitutional rights.

But the critics of modern American Evangelicals urge them to yield to evil by inaction, adopting a strategy of abdication that masquerades as a form of protest. They recommend that Evangelicals avoid any association with the unsavory aspects of politics by essentially withdrawing, allowing evil to triumph. Because both sides are flawed and all candidates disappoint us to some degree, Evangelicals must avoid making a choice at all. Then, when their advice has been rejected, Never Trump Evangelicals charge their spiritual brethren with hypocrisy, racism, bigotry, fear, and hatred of "the other." All this because they support the pro-life, pro-family, pro–religious freedom, pro-Israel Trump administration over extremists who promise to take the lives of millions of unborn children, appoint judges who will give free reign to abortion-on-demand, enact policies that will deny Christians their constitutional rights to freedom of speech and religion, and pledge to turn their back on Israel.

In both 2020 and beyond, we dare not and cannot sit on the sidelines. Retreating to the cold comfort of the stained-glass ghetto and refusing to dirty our shoes with the mire and muck of politics are simply not options for followers of Christ. We are called to put away our "my way or the highway" pride, forsake cynicism and negativity, participate fully, remain always cheerful and always ready to defend our faith, and address the hard moral choices that Providence presents us in our never-ending mission to advance good and resist evil.

Some have claimed that the choice in 2016—and now in 2020—is between flawed individuals who represent simply the lesser of two evils, and that as men and women of conscience we have no stake in the outcome. The exact opposite is true. As Ronald Reagan urged when he addressed the National Association of Evangelicals in 1983, "beware the temptation of pride—the temptation of blithely declaring yourselves above it all and label both sides equally at fault," to simply claim there is a pox on both houses, "and thereby remove yourself from the struggle between right and wrong and good and evil." Reagan spoke of the arms race between the Soviet Union and the West, but he might well have been addressing the evils we confront in our own time.

The courage and moral clarity of men and women of faith in making this choice to support Trump, undertaken with much prayer and soul-searching, has been dismissed and condemned by the chattering class and joined in by more than a few Evangelicals. *National Review* writer David French calls some Evangelicals "religious charlatans" driven by "partisanship and ambition," conceding that still others are "grasping at fading influence by clinging to a man whose daily life mocks the very values Christians seek to advance," causing "the church's witness to degrade further." (French briefly considered running for president as a third-party candidate in 2016. More recently, he proposed that Evangelicals mount a quixotic primary challenge to Trump, which would only strengthen a Democratic presidential nominee in the general election.)

As it turns out, something larger and more interesting than fear and resentment explains Trump's historic support among Evangelicals. Although a large majority of them initially supported someone else in the Republican presidential primaries, once the general election devolved into a binary choice between Trump and Hillary Clinton, whose social and other policy views were anathema to Evangelicals, they voted for Trump in record numbers. As we have seen, they did so despite concerns and reservations about Trump's character, in part because their views of Hillary's character, dishonesty, and ethical lapses—not to mention criminal misconduct in her use of a private email server—were even greater.

This situation will no doubt repeat itself in the 2020 presidential election when whoever the Democrats nominate will run on the most extreme platform on abortion and other social issues in its history. Even Joe Biden, a lifelong practicing Roman Catholic who opposed taxpayer-funded abortion for over forty years as a senator and vice president, cravenly caved to the demands of the abortion lobby within days of announcing his candidacy and now supports codifying *Roe v. Wade* into federal law and making abortion an entitlement under government-run health care.

Evangelicals are not primarily driven by identity politics. They have always supported candidates who shared their policy convictions over those who shared their faith. Led by the likes of Jerry Falwell Sr. (founder of the Moral Majority) and Pat Robertson (founder of the Christian Coalition), the pro-family movement first burst on the national political scene in the late 1970s, mobilizing churches and pastors and registering millions of Evangelical voters against Jimmy Carter, a Southern Baptist Sunday School teacher. This was no small feat. Carter had openly campaigned as a "born again" Christian, routinely invoked his faith, and by all accounts was a faithful husband and father. Instead, Evangelicals cast their ballots by a wide margin in 1980 for Ronald Reagan, a divorced former Hollywood actor who had previously signed the most liberal abortion law in the nation as governor of California. Reagan, though a deeply spiritual man, rarely attended church services and did not subscribe to the label of "born again." But Evangelicals did not hold Reagan's personal past or even his previous public record against him. Reagan had come to share their policy views on life, school prayer, and educational choice. Evangelicals admired Reagan because he was strongly pro-life and cast the Cold War in starkly moral terms. Those stands trumped Jimmy Carter's personal piety.

Some view this political eclecticism as spiritual dissonance. The media lacerated Trump in 2016 for mangling a quote from "Two Corinthians" and referring to Holy Communion as "the little cracker." But Evangelicals are far less judgmental than the common stereotype suggests. They take seriously the Constitution's prohibition on a religious test to serve in government, in part because it could someday be used to exclude them. They will gladly support a candidate of a different religious faith or tradition. This is a sign of civic health, not hypocrisy. The alternative is to support only those candidates who are members of one's sect or swear fealty to one's theology. Such a posture would be intolerant and undemocratic—the very things their critics accuse them of when they aren't calling them hypocrites.

Do we honestly want a balkanized electorate where Evangelicals will only vote for another Evangelical, based not on their policy views but on their religious beliefs? I hope not. America is not Bosnia or the Middle East, with its sectarianism and religious tribalism. And thank goodness. All politics is to some extent tribal, but Evangelicals have shown a willingness to vote for candidates who do not necessarily share their faith. That trait should be celebrated, not criticized.

History has vindicated Evangelicals for the choice they made in 1980. The day after formally becoming the Republican presidential nominee, Reagan presided over the formal marriage ceremony between the faith community and the GOP when he attended a Religious Roundtable meeting and declared, "I know that you can't endorse me...but I want you to know that I endorse you and what you're doing." Some might denounce this statement by Reagan and Trump's more recent embrace of the Evangelical community as "status" politics—a desire by Evangelicals for social status and proximity to power. But it may also be the logical and defensive reaction by the faith community to an attempt by the political and legal culture to silence, harass, and persecute them, denying them their constitutional rights. It is entirely appropriate for Christians to create public policy organizations that reflect their values, form coalitions with others, and back candidates who will advance their public policy views. To do otherwise is to be less than a citizen in a free society.

The argument that supporting flawed leaders who share the policy convictions of believers somehow endangers their Christian witness or degrades the Christian faith does not ultimately hold water. Any fair-minded individual knows that in a rough-and-tumble democracy, Christians must act as citizens, form coalitions, and make less than ideal choices—especially when confronted with one candidate who seeks to advance the common good and another candidate who supports grave moral evil. To support the former does not imply complicity with every excess or wrongdoing. When I served as the executive director of the Christian Coalition in the 1990s, our leadership in Louisiana confronted the Hobbesian choice in a governor's race of choosing between David Duke, a former member of the Ku Klux Klan, and Edwin Edwards, a notoriously corrupt Democrat. They opted for Edwards.

This does not mean that Christians should be advocating for the "lesser of two evils," as the critics of Evangelicals accuse them of doing. When President Trump appointed Neil Gorsuch and Brett Kavanaugh to the U.S. Supreme Court, he was not engaged in the lesser of two evils; he was appointing jurists who were strict constructionists who were supremely qualified and holding to a conservative judicial philosophy. Defending innocent human life by strengthening the Mexico City Policy that prohibits the use of U.S. tax dollars to perform or promote abortion in overseas family planning programs is not the lesser evil; it is the greater good. Recognizing Jerusalem as the capital of Israel and moving the U.S. Embassy from Tel Aviv was not a lesser evil, but a greater good, because it solidified the special relationship between the United States and the Jewish state and codified into law the historic reality of Jerusalem as its capital city. These and other Trump policies do not represent the acceptance of a lesser evil but represent the promotion of what is good and admirable—and none of them would have happened if people of faith had followed the advice of their critics and either stayed home or voted for a third-party candidate in 2016. Incidentally, the same critics were wrong about the outcome of the election, variously claiming that Trump would lose by a landslide, that he was not really interested in being president, and that he was only auditioning to start his own cable channel. They were wrong about all that, too.

At the birth of their movement, the founders of the Religious Right eschewed making it a sectarian movement about shared religious beliefs. Instead, they built a movement about shared values, backing any candidate of any faith—or no faith at all—who was pro-life, pro–religious freedom, and pro-Israel. The ecumenism that characterized the religious conservative movement from its inception and the critics of Evangelicals who selectively quote leaders critical of Bill Clinton's character missed the bigger picture. In a little-noted but significant historical development, Evangelical leaders Jerry Falwell Sr. and Pat Robertson collaborated with the U.S. Roman Catholic bishops and the Mormon Church—institutions that Evangelicals had denounced for centuries—on passing pro-life laws and defending traditional marriage.

Particularly for Falwell, a fundamentalist who spent most of his career avoiding political engagement, this pragmatism revealed a sophisticated understanding of the need to form coalitions and a recognition that the perfect need not be the enemy of the good in politics, as well as the need to make common cause with those who shared their values in spite of deep theological differences. Robertson was the son of a powerful U.S. senator who spent decades in the Byrd Machine of Virginia, and he possessed a seasoned politician's understanding of logrolling, horse-trading, and hardball politics. Both Falwell and Robertson knew that Evangelicals, entering the political arena anew after two generations of self-imposed exile, needed to compromise on issues and legislation without surrendering their principles. This required working with people in both parties, including establishment Republicans and Democrats with whom they disagreed on many other issues. In some cases, it meant working with Chamber of Commerce Republicans and supply-siders to get tax credits for children, families, and stay-at-home moms. In other cases, it meant working with union-backed Democrats to pass the Hyde Amendment and win votes on school prayer and religious freedom. This pragmatism would serve Evangelicals well when, to their collective surprise, Trump emerged as the Republican presidential nominee in 2016.

Nor was Trump the only beneficiary of this pragmatism. At the Value Voters Summit in October 2011, Robert Jeffress urged Evangelicals to reject Mitt Romney, saying that he was not a true Christian. "Every true, born again follower of Christ ought to embrace a Christian over a non-Christian," Jeffress told reporters. Jeffress reflected the theological views of most Evangelicals about Mormonism. Yet Romney went on to win 78 percent of the Evangelical vote in the general election, the highest total ever won by a Republican presidential nominee until Trump came along. While many Evangelical voters may have preferred someone who shared their faith, it was not the only or even the most determinative factor in their voting decision. It turns out, happily, that people of faith vote for many of the same reasons that all citizens do—based on a candidate's qualifications, ability, and public policy views.

This is not to say that the character of a leader doesn't matter; it clearly does. But voters assess the moral fiber of leaders in complex and multifaceted ways, factoring in their public service, accomplishments in the private sector, public policy positions, those who surround them as friends and advisors, endorsements by others they respect, their personal and family life, and their faith testimony. Character often is not the most important issue, as we saw in 1992 when George H. W. Bush lost to Bill Clinton. Voters were under no illusions about Clinton's flaws and past indiscretions, yet they elected him by a landslide. In truth, voters' assessments of character are complicated and not always easy to discern. Nor do voters treat character evaluations as separate and distinct from stands on the issues; for many voters, issue positions reflect and define character.

The 2016 election presented a special case, with polls showing voters harboring deep reservations about both candidates. Fully 61 percent of voters said Hillary was not honest or trustworthy, and 63 percent of voters said the same of Donald Trump. On the fundamental issue of trustworthiness, it was a tie. Hillary's personal unfavorable rating was 55 percent while Trump's was 60 percent—the highest totals for both nominees since exit polling began. This made the election a jump ball on the candidates' personalities, which shifted the final decision to the key issues for most voters, where Trump held an advantage. Tellingly, among voters who held an unfavorable view of both candidates (18 percent, or nearly one out of every five voters), Trump won 47 percent to Hillary's 30 percent. Whatever the media and the chattering class may believe, voters rendered their verdict in 2016, and they considered Hillary's character issues more disqualifying than Trump's. That was true for voters of faith, as well.

The accusation of hypocrisy against Evangelicals comes from the very people who acted as apologists for Bill Clinton and his tawdry conduct in the Oval Office. As we shall see, they are the real hypocrites, claiming that character matters when it comes to Trump—even though they discounted it when it mattered most.

CHAPTER 11

LIBERAL HYPOCRISY

From the moment Donald Trump became the Republican presidential nominee, the media and Democrats attacked his character and temperament, hurling charges of alleged misogyny and sexual misconduct with a laser-like focus. This strategy of character assassination ultimately failed, but there was a method to the liberal media mob's madness. The raw political calculus was to so sully Trump that it would drive suburban Republican women away from him while simultaneously suppressing the Evangelical vote. Achieving either outcome would have put Trump in danger of losing; achieving both would have been fatal. The Democrats and the media will spend billions of dollars in 2020 on a campaign of fear that smears Trump and alleges that his so-called lack of character makes him unsuited for the office of the presidency. It is also the most persistent theme in their attempt to bludgeon voters of faith into silence and shame.

When the Lincoln Project, a dark-money group run by Never Trumpers and disgruntled former Republicans, launched an anti-Trump ad campaign in January 2020, it did so with a video titled "MAGA Church" that mocked Evangelicals for backing Trump. The video intercut clips of faith leaders praising and praying with and for President Trump with sound bites from rallies in which Trump used crude language or profanity. The message was clear: Evangelicals were frauds, hypocrites, and supplicants for prostrating themselves before a man so thoroughly lacking in character as Donald Trump. Not by accident, the video did not mention a single policy of Trump's that animated voters of faith and drew them to support him.

Attacks on Trump's character have been a constant refrain. After the release of the *Access Hollywood* tape in 2016, Vice President Joe Biden wrote on Twitter, "The words are demeaning. Such behavior is an abuse of power. It's not lewd. It's sexual assault." Biden's smear against Trump became somewhat ironic in 2019, when he was accused of multiple unwelcome advances and invasions of the personal space of numerous women—some of whom felt he had hugged or touched them in ways that were highly inappropriate and made them feel uncomfortable.

Four days after the release of the *Access Hollywood* tape, the *New York Times* published an account by two women who alleged that Trump had made unwanted advances against them in the 1980s and 1990s. Both were Hillary Clinton supporters and had contributed to her campaign. Neither of the women went to the authorities or took any action against Trump at the time of the alleged episodes. In one case, the alleged incident occurred on an airplane in full view of other witnesses (none of whom came forward to corroborate the accuser's account), in which Trump was supposed to have reached and partially climbed over an armrest separating their seats.

Trump vehemently denied the allegations, denouncing them as "phony" and "made-up." That didn't prevent the media from reporting the stories ad nauseum and repeatedly providing a platform to his accusers. Having failed to derail Trump during the campaign, the accusers resurfaced at a Manhattan news conference in 2017 to repeat their stories. This "news," nothing more than a rehash of an old story, gave Senator Kirsten Gillibrand of New York the opportunity to denounce Trump's conduct as "criminal" and to call on him to resign. "President Trump has committed assault, according to these women," Gillibrand said in an interview on CNN. "And those are very credible allegations of misconduct and criminal activity, and he should be fully investigated, and he should resign." Gillibrand made no allowance for the presumption of innocence or due process, and she showed no interest in finding the truth with a sober review of the evidence. It was a political hit job, pure and simple. Other feminist leaders and female Democratic members of Congress echoed Gillibrand, calling for a congressional investigation.

With each unsubstantiated accusation against Trump, the media and liberals repeated mantra-like the phrase that "women should be believed." I have members of my family who are victims of sexual assault, and I certainly take such charges very seriously and believe victims should be given every opportunity to tell their stories. But accepting every accusation on its face as true means when carried to its logical extreme that merely making a charge (often years or decades later, with no corroborating evidence) equals guilt. In the case of Trump, that is exactly what the Left and the media want, and there is little attention given to inconsistencies in testimony, lack of contemporaneous witnesses, or evidence of political bias.

Reminding everyone why she lost in 2016, Hillary Clinton waded into the character debate during her book tour in 2017. "We have a man who's accused of sexual assault sitting in the Oval Office, don't we?" Apparently, the irony of her discussing an alleged sexual predator occupying the White House was lost on her. "The very credible accusations against him have not been taken seriously," Clinton said in an interview with 77 WABC Radio's Rita Cosby. "We can't excuse the president from this debate." Clinton said Trump "has disgraced the office."[1]

During Hillary's husband's many scandals and his impeachment in the 1990s, feminists and liberals sang a very different tune. Today, every accusation against the president is the gospel truth; back then, accusers were "sluts and nuts" motivated by greed and a political agenda, cogs in the wheel of a "vast right-wing conspiracy," in Hillary's own words. Or as James Carville, one of Clinton's top political advisors, put it, "If you drag a hundred-dollar-bill through a trailer park, you never know what you'll find." In this case, Carville was referring to Paula Jones. It was a cut-and-dry case of sexual harassment in which then-governor Bill Clinton allegedly used his power (and recruited state law enforcement in the process) to pressure a state employee to perform a sex act. Carville's attack set the tone for the entire Clinton attack machine and made it clear that any woman harassed by Clinton who dared to tell her story would be ridiculed and shamed.

When it became clear that Bill Clinton had an affair with White House intern Monica Lewinsky and committed a felony by lying about it under oath in a civil lawsuit, liberals rallied to his defense. Gloria Steinem absolved him of wrongdoing in an op-ed column in the *New York Times*, also dismissing a serious and credible allegation made by Kathleen Willey during an interview with CBS News' *60 Minutes* detailing attempted sexual assault. She said it was nothing more than a "gross, dumb and reckless pass at a supporter during a low point in her life." She argued that Willey was old enough to be Monica Lewinksy's mother, was more than capable of taking care of herself, and she criticized Willey for shopping a book, implying that her real goal was to make a buck. Paula Jones's claim that then-governor Clinton lured her to a hotel room under false pretense, then dropped his pants and asked her to perform a sex act, wasn't sexual harassment, according to Steinem, but was just another "clumsy sexual pass." Because Clinton's policies were critical to "preserving reproductive freedom," Steinem claimed that "feminists will still have been right to resist pressure by the right wing and the media to call for his resignation or impeachment. The pressure came from another case of the double standard."[2]

Steinem's op-ed was typical of feminists at the time. In the words of one critic, she "slut-shamed, victim-blamed, and age-shamed," urging "compassion for and gratitude to the man the women accused." Nor was she alone. Betty Friedan, one of the founders of modern feminism, showed no interest whatsoever in the Lewinsky scandal, regardless of the facts. "Whether it's a fantasy, a setup, or true, I simply don't care," said the author of *The Feminine Mystique* and one of the pioneers of modern feminism. Feminists dared not criticize Clinton for his shabby and in some cases allegedly violent treatment of women because he had championed their liberal agenda. A steadfast supporter of abortion, Clinton vetoed the partial-birth abortion ban passed by a Republican Congress, defended affirmative action by proposing to "mend it, not end it," and appointed Ruth Bader Ginsburg to the U.S. Supreme Court. Liberal feminists who had spent decades insisting that the "personal is political" now claimed the opposite: public policy and politics trumped personal matters.

Bob Hebert, a columnist for the *New York Times*, reported in January 1998 that "women's advocates have decided, in some cases to their great discomfort, that the more important fight at the moment is about policy and not principle, about practical political matters and not the abuse of political power." Advocates of abortion-on-demand made a cold political calculation during Clinton's scandals and impeachment that preserving *Roe v. Wade*, securing more liberal appointments to the U.S. Supreme Court, and other policies were more important than standing up to the exploitation and abuse of women. Rather than criticize this hypocrisy, the *Times* gave it further credence, noting that "a similar view seems to be reflected in opinion polls. The percentage of women with a favorable overall view of Mr. Clinton remains high." The *Times* also handed its editorial pages to Steinem and other Clinton defenders, who assured liberals that Clinton was not guilty of sexual harassment, and that his defense of "reproductive rights" was more important than treating women with respect and dignity.[3]

Today, the media routinely trash conservatives and Christians for overlooking Trump's occasionally crude language or mean tweets because of his policies and judicial appointments. But twenty years ago, when the nation was plunged into a crisis because of the clearly criminal conduct of a liberal president, they justified his excesses, dismissed his abuse of power, and attacked his critics.

There were few excuses liberals would not make on Clinton's behalf, despite credible evidence that he was guilty of either sexual harassment, sexual assault, or both. "If anything, it sounds like she put the moves on him," feminist author Susan Faludi said of Lewinsky. "It will be a great pity if the Democratic Party is damaged by this," lamented feminist writer Anne Roiphe, who admitted in an interview with *Vanity Fair* magazine, "That's been my response from the very beginning—I just wanted to close my eyes, and wished it would go away." When wishing didn't make it disappear, Clinton's feminist supporters defended the indefensible, if only to advance their political and policy agenda. They surrendered their commitment to protect women against sexual harassment and assault on the altar of preserving the constitutional right to abortion on demand. "We're trying to think of the bigger picture, think about what's best for women," said Eleanor Smeal, the president of the Feminist Majority Foundation.[4] Occasionally, this required descending into the gutter. "I would be happy to give [Bill Clinton] a blowjob just to thank him for keeping abortion legal," feminist writer Nina Burleigh declared in 1998. "I think American women should be lining up with their presidential kneepads on to show their gratitude for keeping the theocracy off our backs."[5] In other words, having the right politics gave Clinton a hall pass to seek sexual favors from women, who should willingly acquiesce as long as he kept abortion legal.

Today, in part because of evolving views of the treatment of women in the workplace and in part because of the #MeToo movement sparked by the Harvey Weinstein scandal, these same liberals and feminists have changed their views on sexual harassment. They now insist that every accuser must be believed, however inconsistent or unverified their testimony. For example, the media kept a running tally of every Trump accuser during the 2016 presidential campaign, breathlessly recounting every detail of each accusation, even when there were no corroborating witnesses. The double standard was obvious, with the unintentional effect of forcing a new examination of the evidence related to Bill Clinton's sexual misconduct—and Hillary's apparent role as his protector and enabler. During Clinton's 1992 presidential campaign, his longtime aide Betsey Wright was put in charge of managing "bimbo eruptions," which meant assembling opposition research to discredit and smear his accusers and disseminating the dirt to friendly and pliant reporters. Hillary participated in this strategy and helped direct a systematic campaign to smear her husband's accusers as sluts, liars, and trailer trash. Rich Lowry, editor of *National Review*, concluded, "[T]here is no doubt Hillary compromised herself, by the standards of feminism 20 years ago, and even more by the standards of today."[6]

Admittedly, Hillary's role was complicated. She was Bill's wife as well as his political partner, and it isn't easy to delve into someone's marriage. But Hillary became a symbol of liberal hypocrisy once she and the Left tried to apply a double standard to Donald Trump. Just as the partisan impeachment of Trump over the Ukraine hoax shone an unwelcome light on the corrupt activities of Joe Biden and his son Hunter in Ukraine, so too did allegations about Trump's treatment of women put the Clintons under the microscope for Bill's past behavior. In both cases, the attacks on Trump had a boomerang effect, hitting Democrats for engaging in the very conduct they accused Trump of committing.

This boomerang effect was vividly demonstrated in the downfall of Senator Al Franken of Minnesota, one of the leading liberals in the U.S. Senate. In 2017, Los Angeles radio host and former model Leeann Tweeden accused Franken of sexually harassing her on a USO tour years earlier. This created a full-blown crisis on the Left. At the very same time, Democrats and the media were attacking Alabama GOP Senate candidate Roy Moore over last-minute allegations of sexual assault and rape as they tried to win a special election in the Deep South. Other embarrassing stories involving groping and unwelcome kisses involving Franken soon surfaced, along with a photo of the comedian jokingly pretending to fondle the breasts of his main accuser while she slept on a transport plane. Like the photo of Gary Hart with an attractive blonde on his lap in 1987, the Franken photo spoke a thousand words, and it rifled across the Internet and the larger media ecosystem at warp speed. How could liberals and feminists countenance this kind of behavior within their own ranks when they were hurling the same charges at

Trump and Roy Moore? Something had to give. If only to help defeat Moore and gain a Senate seat, Franken had to be thrown overboard. Led by women Democratic senators—most prominently Gillibrand—a majority of the Senate Democratic Caucus called on Franken to resign. Franken requested a hearing before the Senate Ethics Committee so that he could refute the allegations and present a defense. But his plea fell on deaf ears. When Senate Democratic leader Chuck Schumer privately warned Franken that he would soon join the call for his resignation, Franken walked the plank, resigning from the Senate in an emotional floor speech, his political career going up in a conflagration of largely unsubstantiated and disputed accusations just weeks after he had been laying the groundwork for a possible presidential run.

I had known Franken going back to my time at the Christian Coalition, when he wrote a chapter about the organization in his book *Rush Limbaugh Is a Big, Fat Idiot and Other Observations*. While doing research on the book, he attended our annual conference in Washington. Our staff ensured that Al received media credentials and was able to interview conference attendees. I think he was surprised that we treated him fairly. Some years later, Al was producing a situation comedy program on ABC that was a send-up of *Nightline*, and he asked me to play myself in one of the episodes and sent me a script. He was flattering and indefatigable, love bombing me with phone calls, telling me he would be fair to me. I politely declined, as neither the character nor the plotline in the script accurately reflected either me or the faith community. I liked Al and was a fan of his comedy, if not his politics. He was a very funny guy.

Several times during this back and forth, Al and I talked about politics and faith, and he told me that although he didn't share my conservative views, he agreed with me about the importance of faith and family. He told me how devoted he was to his wife and family. As we spoke, the Clinton impeachment unfolded in Washington, and I raised the topic just to get his honest opinion.

"Al, you seem like a decent person to me," I said. "So why do you and other liberals put up with Bill Clinton? He lied to the American people, and he lied under oath in a deposition. If you believe in morality, how can you countenance this behavior?"

Al explained that Clinton had lied about his relationship with Monica Lewinsky because had he told the truth at that moment, the ensuing firestorm might have forced him to resign. By lying, Clinton had saved his presidency. Al said he did not agree with what Clinton had done, but he pointed out that liberals were willing to overlook it.

Years later, watching Franken's televised speech as he resigned from the Senate, I recalled that conversation. I was stunned that he had decided to resign over allegations that he insisted were untrue. I wondered: What happened to due process? What about the facts? Did they no longer matter? The truth seemed to be beside the point; the mob had to be pacified. In order to get Trump (and Roy Moore), the liberal mob had turned on one of its own. Like the Salem witch trials, it unfolded as a rush to judgment. Ironically, and perhaps unfairly, Franken paid the price for liberal hypocrisy that Bill Clinton didn't have to pay—a hypocrisy in which he had sadly participated.

Many liberals now express regret over the way Franken was run out of the Senate. Jane Mayer of *The New Yorker*, who coauthored one of the articles leveling an eleventh-hour charge against Judge Brett Kavanaugh, examined the allegations against Franken and found them mostly unproven or suspect. Even here, the self-serving political motive was clear. Franken must now be rehabilitated for the same reason that Clinton had to be saved: because he is on their team. Trump and Kavanaugh must be destroyed, because they are on the other team.

Projection and relativism are classic liberal maladies. The media and the Left routinely accuse others of the very things of which they are guilty. Hypocrisy about the allegations against Trump, compared to those against Bill Clinton, are at the top of the list. They assert that in the 1980s and 1990s, Evangelical leaders said that character mattered and called for Clinton's removal from the presidency because of his sexual misconduct.

But this charge is neither entirely accurate nor entirely fair to the faith community. First, while both Trump and Clinton were accused of misdeeds, the facts and circumstances are dramatically different. Clinton's case involved committing perjury, suborning perjury, obstructing justice, conspiracy, and abuse of power. The deeds for which he was impeached were not related to his personal conduct; they involved the abuse of his office and the use of White House staff and members of the cabinet to obstruct justice. Not everyone agreed with Clinton's argument that his relationship with Monica Lewinsky was a "private" matter "between me, the two people I love the most—my wife and our daughter—and our God." But as Nixon famously told White House chief of staff Bob Haldeman in a conversation captured on the Watergate tapes, it's never the crime; it's always the coverup. The fact that Clinton committed perjury, suborned perjury, and engaged in a conspiracy to obstruct justice is beyond dispute.

Furthermore, the personal allegations against Trump failed to meet a reasonable standard of evidence. Some by their very nature fell into the category of "he said, she said" ambiguity, where who is telling the truth is a matter of conjecture, and the truth is impossible to determine due to the passage of time and unreliable memories or the lack of witnesses. The American system of justice is based on a presumption of innocence, and the impeachment and removal of a president should require an overwhelming preponderance of evidence. Some of the allegations (such as the payments to Stephanie Clifford—more commonly known as Stormy Daniels—and Karen McDougal) were fully investigated by the U.S. Attorney for the Southern District of New York and were closed without any charges. So there is no real equivalence between Trump and Clinton.

It is true that at the time of the Lewinsky affair, many Evangelical leaders called on Clinton to resign or for Congress to impeach him. Richard Land, head of the Ethics & Religious Liberty Commission of the Southern Baptist Convention, urged Clinton to resign after the president admitted to the nation in August 1998 that he had lied about the affair for eight months. Land argued that Clinton "has lost the moral authority and the trust necessary to govern. He has fallen below the threshold of what is necessary to be able to effectively serve in office." Paige Patterson, president of the Southern Baptist denomination, said Clinton should resign "for the good of the country" and seek personal repentance and forgiveness "before he is instrumental in corrupting all our young people." Robert Schuller, founder of the Crystal Cathedral and host of the highly rated *Hour of Power* television program, called on Clinton to resign after the House impeached him. Hardly a partisan figure, Schuller, who had counseled Clinton earlier in his administration and provided him with a Scripture verse about being a "repairer of the breach" that Clinton cited in a State of the Union Address, penned an open letter in the *Wall Street Journal* in which he implored Clinton to spare the nation the trauma of a Senate trial. "I ask that you look within your conscience and summon the will and strength to end this agony," Schuler opined. "By stepping aside, you can spare our nation weeks, perhaps months, of divisive debate and repulsive testimony. Your action can help restore public confidence in the moral fabric that sustains our form of government and the moral standards we have a right to demand in our leaders."

Other Evangelical leaders viewed impeachment as unnecessarily harsh, accepting Clinton's expressions of remorse and announcing they were entirely ready to forgive him. Bill Hybels, then pastor of the influential Willow Creek Community Church in the suburbs of Chicago and a leader in the seeker-friendly megachurch movement, said of Clinton's public apology, "It is crystal clear that he has asked for forgiveness for his mistakes and is on a journey of spiritual restoration and growth." Billy Graham said in an interview on NBC's *Today* show two months after the scandal became public, "I forgive him. I know how hard it is, and especially a strong, vigorous young man like he is; he has such a tremendous personality. I think the ladies just go wild over him." Graham would later privately counsel Hillary to find it in her heart to forgive her husband, and she would later speak movingly of the impact his words had on her.[7] Some interpreted Graham's remarks as giving Clinton a pass for his adulterous conduct, sparking controversy and rare criticism for

Graham in the Evangelical community. I believe Graham was acting and speaking as a pastor, not preaching on biblical morality.

His son Franklin took a different approach, arguing that Clinton's misconduct was not a personal matter because it took place while he was president. He decried the fact that much of the American public "seems to have succumbed to the notion that what a person does in private has little bearing on his public actions or job performance, even if he is the president of the United States." He urged Clinton to show genuine repentance, which he suggested had not happened yet, but he did not directly address whether Clinton should be impeached. "Mr. Clinton's sin can be forgiven, but he must start by admitting to it and refraining from legalistic doublespeak," he wrote in an op-ed in the *Wall Street Journal*. "Acknowledgment must be coupled with genuine remorse. A repentant spirit that says, 'I'm sorry. I was wrong. I won't do it again. I ask for your forgiveness,' would go a long way toward personal and national healing."[8]

In this sense, it was Clinton's evasion of responsibility, his parsing of words, and his legalistic hair-splitting that disturbed Evangelicals. Christians believe that everyone sins and falls short of the mark. They objected more to Clinton's failure to own up to his wrongs, confess them, and repent. "It depends on what the meaning of the word 'is,' is," entered the national lexicon not only as a punchline, but as a symbol of Clinton's prevarication and fundamental dishonesty.

This, however, was a minority view among the American people. The country as a whole seemed prepared, even anxious, to forgive their president and move on. When Clinton held a breakfast with religious leaders in the White House in September 1998, he delivered a confessional so raw and emotionally wrenching that it at least appeared to turn the tide in the impeachment saga. "There is no fancy way to say I have sinned," Clinton began, reading from notes before a crowd of about one hundred pastors and faith leaders in the East Room. "I have asked all for their forgiveness," he continued. "But I believe that to be forgiven, more than sorrow is required. At least two more things: First, genuine repentance, a determination to change and to repair breaches of my own making. I have repented." He acknowledged the need for "what my Bible calls a broken spirit." He expressed a yearning for "God's help to be the person that I want to be" and a "willingness to give the very forgiveness I seek."[9] In the ensuing impeachment and Senate trial, there would be little expression of forgiveness or reconciliation on either side. But Clinton, who said he had come to Christ as a child and who often spoke movingly of attending a Billy Graham crusade as a youth, knew the Evangelical lexicon as well as any politician in recent memory, and he had hit all the right notes.

The faith leaders in attendance gave him a standing ovation that lasted a full minute. Many immediately proceeded to a press gaggle to offer their spiritual support and public absolution to the embattled president. "It was a very powerful and moving appeal that should go far," Reverend Jesse Jackson told reporters after the breakfast event. Clinton had shown that he understood the "need for him to show genuine repentance on one hand and take care of the nation's business on the other." Jackson added, "I was very impressed with his strength and his will to serve." Reverend Fred Davie of the national Presbyterian Church in Brooklyn, New York, agreed, saying, "He couldn't be more contrite. Anybody who couldn't see that has another agenda altogether."[10] Philip Wogaman, Clinton's longtime pastor, applauded the fact that Clinton had "voiced his deep feelings of remorse over his misbehavior, including his regret over the pain he had caused his own family, the Lewinskys, others directly involved, and the nation. He offered no excuses. He blamed no one but himself." He credited Clinton with "working on changing his life, relying especially on pastoral help. He spoke of his need for forgiveness from God and from those whom he had hurt."

The forgiveness of Evangelical leaders and even the American people did not immunize Clinton from the consequences of his actions. The report by independent counsel Ken Starr contained devastating and embarrassing details of Clinton's affair and the extraordinary (and illegal) lengths to which he went to conceal it. The impeachment proceedings convulsed the nation for the next nine months, paralyzing the country more thoroughly than at any time since Watergate, disgracing Clinton while diminishing the office of the presidency and distracting the country's leadership from more urgent and pressing issues.

The scars left by the Lewinsky scandal on the body politic of our country remain deep and abiding, and traumatic effects of impeachment are still with us. In one respect, the willingness of the public to make allowances for and forgive Trump for his past behavior finds its roots in Clinton's successful strategy of expressing public remorse while attacking his attackers. Trump effectively followed the same strategy after the release of the *Access Hollywood* tape. Clinton's Evangelical supplicants (who critics denounced as enablers who had compromised their moral principles) foreshadowed the resilience of Trump's religious supporters. There was much in the Gospel message to recommend their willingness to forgive Clinton and judge not, lest they be judged. But where is the willingness to extend the same grace to Donald Trump? Outside of his churchgoing Evangelical supporters, it is virtually nonexistent. This, too, is about politics. If the critics of Evangelicals who support Trump were so genuinely concerned about fidelity to the Gospel message, they would be willing to forgive Trump for his past transgressions. Jesus didn't join the crowd who eagerly wished to stone the adulterer. He did not condemn her. Instead, he forgave her and told her, "Go, and sin no more."

This is why I had a slightly different view of the character issue during the Clinton presidency than some of my Evangelical brethren. My view was also shaped by realpolitik. As far back as 1992, I had concluded that making Clinton's past sexual sins a major issue in the campaign was a loser. Generally speaking, the American people are not comfortable rummaging through the candidates' closets in search of past personal indiscretions. I knew this to be the case from my study of U.S. history. Some believe that the high tolerance of the American public for the moral failings of political leaders began with Bill Clinton, but it did not.

Federalist pamphleteers skewered Thomas Jefferson in the 1800 presidential election as an infidel, an enemy of Christianity, a supporter of the French Revolution, and a sexual libertine who had fathered children by Sally Hemings, one of his slaves. The latter charge appears to have been true, though no one will ever know for certain; it was certainly widely trafficked in by Federalist Party propagandists. When the voters went to the polls, none of it mattered. Jefferson won the 1800 election by a landslide, and the Federalist Party soon faded into insignificance, disappearing from the national political scene. Andrew Jackson once killed a man in a duel, and his opponents denounced him as a murderer, a drunk, and, according to one historian, "a vindictive monster, a despot who crushed the innocent beneath his boot heel."[11] Jackson still won the popular vote in the 1824 election, but he lost the presidency when no candidate received a majority in the Electoral College and the election was thrown into the House of Representatives; he then won two landslide victories. Jackson effectively won a third presidential election when his vice president, Martin Van Buren, was elected in 1836. So the attacks on Jackson's character failed to derail his political movement for four successive presidential elections, something we would not see again until Franklin D. Roosevelt.

When Grover Cleveland, the governor of New York, ran for president in 1884, a scandal broke claiming that he had previously had an affair with a widow, impregnated her, and then refused to marry her after she gave birth. His opponents claimed this was not an isolated case of debauchery for Cleveland, who was widely known as a confirmed bachelor and a ladies' man in Albany, the state capital. They circulated rumors about other female victims of Cleveland's, denounced him as a drunk and a sexual deviant who preyed on women, and even claimed he had contracted a venereal disease. Republicans taunted Democrats at torchlit parades and rallies by chanting, "Ma! Ma! Where's my Pa? Gone to the White House. Ha! Ha! Ha!" In the fall campaign, the GOP mobilized Protestant ministers who took to their pulpits to deliver sermons warning that putting an adulterer in the White House would usher in a contagion of moral decay. Reverend George Ball of Buffalo delivered a typical jeremiad that read like it was torn from the headlines of the

Clinton scandals. "The issue is evidently not between the two great parties," Ball thundered, "but between the brothel and the family, between indecency and decency, between lust and law, between the essence of barbarism and the first principles of civilization, between the degradation of woman and due honor, protection, and love to our mothers, sisters and daughters." Yet even at the height of the Victorian era, appeals to moral character could not overcome voters' concerns about corruption in Washington and a late ill-advised attack on Catholic voters by Republican presidential nominee James G. Blaine. Cleveland narrowly won what some historians call the dirtiest election in U.S. history, becoming the first Democrat elected president since the Civil War.[12]

As a trained historian, I knew that attacks on Bill Clinton's character would likely have little effect on the outcome of the election. It seemed to me that the biggest obstacles to President George H. W. Bush's 1992 reelection campaign were Ross Perot's independent candidacy and voters' perceptions of a weakening economy. Clinton's zipper problem couldn't fix either of them. During the campaign, I received a handful of unsolicited phone calls offering compromising photos of Clinton with women, or in one case, Clinton burning an American flag at an anti-Vietnam war rally. I ignored them all. Similarly, I tuned out the sensational claims by Gennifer Flowers at a press conference sponsored by a tabloid newspaper that she had been Clinton's lover. I recall a senior staff member at the Bush-Quayle '92 campaign telling me confidently, "Clinton's got more shoes to drop than a centipede." But in the end, few voters cast their ballots over such personal charges. That did not mean I approved of Clinton's extramarital affairs, but I did question whether the issue would move many voters. What Republicans needed in 1992 was a strong economy and Perot out of the race—not more dirt on their opponent.

Clinton, of course, won by a landslide. During his presidency, more allegations surfaced, including those reported by David Brock in the *American Spectator* that as governor he had used Arkansas state troopers to procure women for sexual dalliances. This was explosive stuff, but the American people were largely aware of his past and had elected him anyway. In 1994, the Christian Defense Coalition formed a legal defense fund for Paula Jones, who claimed that Clinton had sexually harassed her as governor. When Jones held a news conference at the Conservative Political Action Conference (CPAC) to publicize her lawsuit against President Clinton, I was invited to attend but declined. At the Christian Coalition, we remained focused on public policy matters, including launching a multimillion dollar campaign to defeat Hillarycare, opposing attempts to repeal the Hyde Amendment, and opposing Clinton's plan for gays in the military. This was not because I thought the characters of our leaders didn't matter; they most certainly do. But I believed those judgments were best left to the voters, not public policy organizations.

In 1996, as Clinton campaigned for reelection, I addressed the question of his character head on in my book *Active Faith*. "I have always deliberately confined my criticism of Clinton to public policy issues, not his character or moral shortcomings," I wrote then. "I oppose President Clinton's policies. But I do not despise him." If only the same could be said today of Donald Trump's critics, who seem to be motivated by a personal animus that borders on an irrational hatred. "If Bill Clinton is a sinner, then he is no worse than you or me," I argued. "[T]he Bible teaches that all have fallen short of the glory of God—and that means every one of us. Has our version of the gospel become so politicized that we no longer believe that His grace extends to Bill Clinton?" This did not mean that I believed criticism of Clinton's character or misconduct in office should be prohibited or circumscribed, only that it should be leavened with God's grace and a willingness to forgive. "[F]ollowers of Christ should temper their disagreements with Clinton with civility and the grace of God," I suggested, "avoiding the temptation to personalize issues or demonize opponents."[13]

My position was not always popular among all Evangelicals at the time. But I believed then, as I do now, that it was a mistake to make someone's personal past the sole or primary criterion in whether they are qualified for public office. We are called to forgive, as we have been forgiven for our own sins. After all, if Clinton had been a perfectly moral man in every respect and completely faithful to his wife, I would have opposed him because of his positions on the issues. Jimmy Carter was a devout Southern Baptist and a Sunday School teacher, but Evangelicals broke heavily for Ronald Reagan, a divorced man from Hollywood, because he opposed abortion and cast the Cold War with the Soviet Union in starkly moral terms.

When the Lewinsky scandal broke, I thought Clinton's behavior was unprofessional and immoral. Whether it met the standard for impeachment and removal from office was a different question. If it did, it was not because of the affair, but because Clinton corrupted his office by suborning perjury, obstructing justice, and using the resources of the White House to hide his misconduct. By then, I had left the Christian Coalition and opened Century Strategies, a public relations firm that also did political consulting for candidates. In August of that year, most of the candidates we represented were positioned for victory, and the Republicans appeared poised to pick up ten to twenty House seats. Then came the Starr Report, with its lurid and prurient details about stained blue dresses and cigars, and Republicans began readying plans to impeach Clinton. Overnight, we saw Democratic support surge as liberal and minority voters rallied to Clinton's side. The leads of our candidates all but disappeared. I reached out to Representative John Linder, chairman of the National Republican Congressional Committee, and Joe Gaylord, the very smart political advisor to Speaker of the House Newt Gingrich, to warn them about the storm clouds that impeachment had cast over our congressional candidates.

On Election Day, Republicans came within twenty-five thousand votes spread across a handful of House seats out of a total of sixty-three million votes cast of losing the House. Newt was forced out as speaker amid finger-pointing and recrimination. Still, impeachment rolled on like a slow train heading off a cliff. No one could stop it, in no small measure because Clinton had in fact committed crimes—not in his affair with Lewinsky, but in his subsequent attempts to hide it. This official misconduct, the abuse of power, the corruption of the presidency, and the obstruction of justice were the reasons Clinton faced impeachment—not his infidelity.

Still, the American people had no stomach for the removal of a president, and it was far more damaging politically for Republicans than for Clinton. His job approval numbers actually went up the more Republicans in Congress went after him. After the election, I wrote an op-ed in the *Washington Post* urging Republicans to pivot to kitchen-table issues like the economy, education, taxes, and health care, and I blamed the near-loss of the GOP House on an unhealthy fixation on Clinton's scandals. "Blinded by their disdain for Clinton, Republicans believed that their own revulsion at the president's misconduct translated into a national mandate for their majority," I observed. "But the Clinton scandals were a mirage, not an oasis. Outside the Republican base, voters disapproved of Clinton personally but cast their ballots on other issues—education, taxes, Social Security, health care. An exit poll by the Voter News Service found that 58 percent of voters wanted the impeachment inquiry dropped entirely; only 33 percent favored impeaching Clinton." I urged the GOP Congress to swiftly dispatch the impeachment inquiry. If they lacked the two-thirds vote in the Senate to remove Clinton, they should consider instead a resolution of censure. "Absent bipartisan support for impeachment, they should vote as soon as possible on a resolution of censure that condemns the president, and then move on with the rest of their agenda for the country."[14] This advice, like my warnings prior to the election, largely fell on deaf ears. Ironically, twenty-five years later, Democrats are repeating the same mistake.

As a political matter, impeachment has little appeal outside the party that does not hold the White House. The same pattern prevails today. A July 2019 *Wall Street Journal*/NBC News poll during the Mueller investigation found that only 21 percent of registered voters favored beginning impeachment hearings against Trump, while 50 percent opposed them and wanted further congressional inquiries instead. Only 6 percent of Republicans favored impeaching Trump.[15] A scandal like Watergate that drives a president from office is a rare occurrence. Even during the impeachment inquiry over Trump's Ukraine policy, an October 2019 *New York Times*/Sienna College poll found that only 43 percent of voters in the top six swing states favored removing Trump from office, while 53 percent opposed impeachment and removal.[16] My strong view during the 1990s was that if Clinton's personal flaws and sexual peccadilloes had mattered to voters, they wouldn't have elected him in the first place. The same is true of Trump; voters have already factored his character into their decision. They are much more concerned with Trump's performance as president, the strength of the economy, and whether their lives are better off under his policies than they are with his personal past.

On the issue of presidential character, I have been consistent, sticking to public policy matters and always trying to season legitimate criticism with grace. I expressed a willingness to look beyond Bill Clinton's past personal failings and have a civil debate about the issues. I agreed with him where I could, confining my criticism to the issues—not his personal character. Indeed, if Evangelicals have erred, it has not been in their defense of Trump, whose policies clearly advance their values and the common good, but perhaps in the harshness of their criticisim directed at Clinton. We must always ensure that the Gospel does not become so politicized that we neglect our call as Christians to extend grace and forgiveness. After all, the Bible teaches that we will be forgiven according to the measure by which we have forgiven others.

This does not mean that character doesn't matter or that we should countenance the abuse of power or the corruption of the presidency. In 1998, I told the *New York Times*, "We care about the conduct of our leaders, and we will not rest until we have leaders of good moral character.'" We elected such a leader in President George W. Bush in 2000. But that verdict was rendered by the American people at the ballot box, not by Congress in a partisan impeachment proceeding. Today, as in the 1990s, it requires a high bar to remove a president, and disqualifying someone because they have come up short of the mark in their past is not the best spiritual or political principle.

The radical Left and the media have been the hypocrites when it comes to the character issue. In defending Clinton, they acted as both apologists and enablers. They orchestrated an ugly "sluts or nuts" strategy designed to malign, intimidate, and shame Clinton's female accusers. Today, they demand that every accuser of President Trump's be believed, regardless of evidence or facts. This violates the rule of law, the presumption of innocence, and the basic spirit of American fairness.

CHAPTER 12

TRUMP'S PRO-LIFE, PRO-FAMILY AGENDA

On a sunny, chilly afternoon on January 24, 2020, a crowd of tens of thousands packed the National Mall near the Washington Monument and spilled out across surrounding avenues in the nation's capital. Wind rippled the backdrop of the outdoor stage, across which were emblazoned a huge red rose and the words "March for Life." Well-bundled in coats and hats, the men, women, and young adults in the crowd cheerfully disregarded the cold, brandishing signs and banners. Cheers surged in the clear winter air as President Donald J. Trump emerged from behind the stage and stepped to the podium.

It was an historic day as Trump became the first sitting president to address the March for Life in its forty-seven-year history. In a split-screen moment that seemed a common thread in the Trump era, Democratic House managers at the impeachment trial prepared to complete opening arguments before the U.S. Senate at the other end of Pennsylvania Avenue. In stark and moving contrast to that partisan sideshow, Trump, surrounded by pro-life leaders, came to reaffirm his commitment to the protection of all human life—born and unborn.

"Every child is a precious gift from God," Trump declared. "Together we must protect, cherish, and defend the dignity and sanctity of every human life. When we see the image of a baby in the womb, we glimpse the majesty of God's creation." He ticked off the greatest hits of his pro-life accomplishments: strengthening and expanding the Mexico City Policy to prevent U.S. taxpayers' funds from being used to promote and perform abortions overseas, reforming Title X in a way that defunded Planned Parenthood from the family planning program, ending the persecution and harassment of the Little Sisters of the Poor and other pro-life Americans through religious freedom and conscience protections, vowing to veto any legislation that weakened protections for the unborn in federal law, defending the freedom of speech of pro-life students on college campuses, supporting the Pain-Capable Abortion Ban, promoting faith-based adoption, and the appointment of 187 federal judges—including two Supreme Court justices. It was an amazing list. "Unborn children have never had a stronger defender in the White House," Trump added in summation to the loud cheers of the crowd.

Trump's appearance at the March for Life was a stunning rebuke to all those who had criticized Evangelicals and other pro-life voters for a lack of spiritual integrity and political hypocrisy in backing Trump in 2016 and for strongly supporting his policies as president. But Trump's address to the pro-life marchers dramatically vindicated the wisdom of their embrace of his candidacy and presidency. Contrary to the charges of naysayers who said Trump would betray pro-lifers, by his presence, Trump granted the prestige of his office and the bully pulpit of the presidency to the pro-life cause. The larger political and cultural significance of that moment will be felt for decades.

Every January since 1974, tens of thousands of peaceful protestors had flocked to Washington for the largest pro-life rally in the country. But in those forty-seven years, the mainstream media had deliberately ignored the march, as far as was possible. (Some even ignored President Trump's appearance, with CNN and MSNBC refusing to break away from impeachment coverage to show even a brief part of his speech.) But in January 2017, Trump had asked the vice president to speak at the event—something which had never happened before. President Trump encouraged the pro-life crowd in a tweet: "The #MarchForLife is so important. To all of you marching—you have my full support!"

With the president's support and Pence's speech, the Trump administration made a strong pro-life statement right out of the gate. The symbolism was not lost on the pro-lifers in the crowd. This provided a dramatic contrast to the feminist-inspired Women's March that had filled the mall just days earlier. That march featured profanity-laced speeches, Madonna confessing she had contemplated "blowing up the White House," and many protesters wearing pink "pussy" hats.

Nor was Pence's appearance the first pro-life move of the new Trump administration. On January 23, Trump had reinstated and strengthened the Mexico City Policy, signing an executive order which prevented U.S. tax dollars from being used to promote or perform abortions in overseas family planning programs. Since Ronald Reagan's establishment of the Mexico City Policy in 1984, the order had been rescinded by every Democratic president and reinstated by every Republican president. Most recently, Obama had abolished the policy in 2009.

But Trump did more than simply reinstate it; he strengthened it by expanding the programs covered by the policy to an estimated $8.8 billion in U.S. global health programs, including maternal and child health, infectious diseases, nutrition, and HIV/AIDS—including the highly-successful President's Emergency Plan for AIDS Relief (PEPFAR), which was started by President George W. Bush and has saved an estimated two million lives in Africa. "Originally a ban covering roughly $600 million in family planning money, the Trump policy now applies to all international health care aid doled out by the U.S. government—nearly $9 billion," the *Washington Times* reported. The administration said they would redirect the money to health organizations that did not promote or provide abortion. Tony Perkins, president of the Family Research Council, enthusiastically endorsed the expansion, saying, "We applaud the Trump administration for not just stopping the pro-abortion policies of the Obama era, but putting in place policies that will reverse the destructive and immoral trends of the last eight years."

In March 2019, Secretary of State Mike Pompeo announced a further strengthening of the Mexico City Policy by prohibiting non-governmental organizations from providing funds to any group that performed abortions. This prevented the organizations from circumventing the Mexico City Policy by engaging in "pass throughs," essentially passing U.S. funds to organizations promoting and performing abortions without permission. Pompeo specifically cited the Organization of American States as an entity targeted for a reduction in U.S. funding. Pro-life groups hailed the decision while the pro-abortion lobby denounced it as a "global gag rule." Whatever the term, it represented one of the most significant pro-life policy victories in U.S. foreign aid in the last forty years, and it set a new standard in prohibiting the use of U.S. funds to advance the abortion agenda around the world.[1]

In his speech at the 2017 March for Life, Pence reminded the crowd of the recent reinstatement and strengthening of the Mexico City Policy. He expressed pride and humility at being the first vice president to ever address them in person. He encouraged the marchers by noting that the cause of life was on the offensive—and was winning. "Life is winning through the steady advance of science that illuminates when life begins," Pence proclaimed to the crowd, the cold air frosting his breath. "Life is winning through the generosity of millions of adoptive families to open their hearts and homes to children in need. Life is winning through the compassion of caregivers and volunteers at crisis pregnancy centers and faith-based organizations who minister to women in towns across this country." He also reminded them of another of Trump's campaign promises: "[N]ext week, President Donald Trump will announce a Supreme Court nominee who will uphold the God-given liberties enshrined in our Constitution in the tradition of the late and great Justice Antonin Scalia."

Trump's promise to nominate a pro-life, conservative judge to the Supreme Court had convinced many voters of faith to cast their ballots for him the previous November. A Pew Research survey asked Evangelical voters in 2016 who would do a better job selecting Supreme Court justices, and 74 percent said Trump.[2] Some, however, wondered if he would actually follow through. Many pro-life activists felt they had been burned before, especially by the appointments of Sandra Day O'Connor and Anthony Kennedy by Reagan and David Souter by George H. W. Bush. "No More Souters" had become a mantra on the Right. During the recent presidential campaign, critics of Evangelicals and pro-lifers roasted them for trusting Trump's word on Supreme Court justices. "There simply is no reason to believe that the same Trump who has contradicted himself on amnesty for illegal immigrants, abortion, NATO, and much else, will stick to his assurances on this," argued Ian Tuttle in *National Review*. Trump's list of Supreme Court candidates, "released under duress," was "promising, if hardly foolproof."[3]

Trump, meanwhile, was closing in on selecting a nominee, a process that had been underway since the transition. From his original campaign list of twenty-one possible judges, he had narrowed it down to four: Thomas Hardiman, Bill Pryor, Amul Thapar, and Neil Gorsuch. Trump personally interviewed the four finalists, keeping his final decision a closely guarded secret until the evening of January 31. Then, in a dramatically staged announcement in the East Room of the White House, Trump announced Neil Gorsuch as his Supreme Court pick. I was honored to be present for the announcement (as I detailed in Chapter 2), and the effect was electric. The next morning, I attended the National Prayer Breakfast, where many of the pastors and religious leaders who had backed Trump were present, and I found them to be euphoric and grateful for the Gorsuch selection. Many had hoped that Trump would keep his word in what surely qualified as one of the most explicit promises by a presidential candidate in recent memory, and Trump had delivered.

The Gorsuch selection was a home run in the broader conservative community, as well. Gorsuch, a graduate of Columbia, Harvard, and Oxford, had a classic high court judge's background, an eloquent speaking and writing style, and a reputation for upholding religious liberty and criticizing liberal legislation from the bench. He was, as the *New York Times* put it, "a reliably conservative figure in Justice Scalia's mold, but not someone known to be divisive." Gorsuch was also a former clerk of Justice Anthony Kennedy, and if confirmed, his tenure would mark the first time a former clerk would serve on the Supreme Court with the justice for whom he once worked. In picking Gorsuch, Trump was also sending a subtle signal to Kennedy: It's alright for you to retire. Should you choose to step down, I will choose someone to replace you of whom you will be proud.

The Far Left immediately swung into opposition, and Democratic senators promptly announced their intention to filibuster Gorsuch's nomination. No Supreme Court nominee had been filibustered since Lyndon Johnson nominated Abe Fortas in 1968—a nominee mired in ethical issues who ultimately withdrew from consideration. To threaten a filibuster before Gorsuch had even received a hearing—and for a nominee so clearly qualified without any hint of ethical problems—had no precedent in modern American history. Even in 1991, when Clarence Thomas was accused of sexual harassment by Anita Hill and ultimately won confirmation by a narrow vote of fifty-two to forty-eight, no one even suggested a filibuster. Senate Majority Leader Mitch McConnell responded to the threat by his Democratic colleagues by invoking the "nuclear option," which changed the Senate rules so that Gorsuch could be confirmed by a simple majority rather than a two-thirds vote.

In the ensuing confirmation fight, both sides spent tens of millions of dollars on television ads, direct mail, phone banks, and digital marketing to gin up their respective supporters to oppose or back the Gorsuch nomination. Faith & Freedom Coalition undertook a one-million-dollar grassroots campaign in support of Gorsuch, mailing 1.5 million "action alert" postcards to pastors and pro-family activists in key states, placing millions of ads on Facebook and other social media sites, making over one million phone calls to Christian voters, and deluging Senate offices with tens of thousands of calls from their constituents. The key targets of these appeals were red-state Democratic senators like Heidi Heitkamp of North Dakota, Joe Donnelly of Indiana, Bill Nelson of Florida, Claire McCaskill of Missouri, and Joe Manchin of West Virginia. But Democrats, still bitter about McConnell's declining to hold a vote on the vacant Scalia seat until after the election and reeling from Trump's shocking victory, marched in lockstep against the new president's nominee. Republicans were joined by only three Democratic senators (Heitkamp, Manchin, and Donnelly), and the Senate confirmed Gorsuch by a vote of fifty-four to forty-five on April 6, 2017.

Trump, meanwhile, kept delivering on his promises, disproving false claims after his election that he was really a Democrat in disguise and an ideological interloper that was more willing to cut deals with Nancy Pelosi and Chuck Schumer than work with Republicans on Capitol Hill. This prediction turned out to be yet another liberal delusion. On April 3, the State Department pulled out of the United Nations Population Fund, claiming that the fund "supports, or participates in the management of, a program of coercive abortion or involuntary sterilization" in foreign countries, particularly China. The United Nations denied the charge, but Trump did not restore the funding. Instead, he redirected the money to the U.S. Agency for International Development, an organization for humanitarian aid. He also tasked Vice President Pence with finding a way to direct aid to Christian and other religious minorities like the Yazidis suffering from discrimination in the Middle East.

On April 13, Trump signed Congressional Review Act legislation that allowed states to deny funding to Planned Parenthood under state Medicaid programs. This reversed an executive order signed by Barack Obama, who had once boasted, "I have a pen and a phone" to advance his liberal agenda. Pro-life leader Marjorie Dannenfelser was present at the signing and praised Trump in glowing terms: "Prioritizing funding away from Planned Parenthood to comprehensive healthcare alternatives is a winning issue. We expect to see Congress continue its efforts to redirect additional taxpayer funding away from Planned Parenthood through pro-life health care reform after the spring break recess." Seema Verma, the administrator for the Centers for Medicare and Medicaid Services, also thought the law was a good move: "I think the president's signature today is an important step and it shows that the president is keeping his campaign promises," Verma said. "This shows that we want states to be in charge of their own decision making."

Meanwhile, Trump was also making changes to the Department of Health and Human Services (HHS), turning it from a "pro-abortion antagonist" into a "pro-life advocate," as a January 2018 story in *Christianity Today* declared. Trump made numerous pro-life appointments to HHS in 2017, transforming its leadership into a vanguard for the protection of life. Scott Lloyd, a member of the Catholic charitable organization Knights of Columbus, became the director of the Office of Refugee Resettlement. Heidi Stirrup, who had worked for me as one of the senior legislative executives at Christian Coalition, became Deputy Assistant Secretary of Policy at HHS. Teresa Manning, a former employee for the Family Research Council and National Right to Life, was chosen as Deputy Secretary for Population Affairs, overseeing federal funds for family planning programs. Manning had spoken out strongly against both abortion and contraception. Charmaine Yoest, head of Americans United for Life, was appointed as assistant secretary for HHS public affairs. And Shannon Royce, a former chief of staff at the Family Research Council, was made director for the Center for Faith-Based and Neighborhood Partnerships. Pro-life advocates cheered each of these significant appointments as strongly as abortion supporters bemoaned them. My friend Congressman Tom Price of Georgia, a fine public servant and a man of faith, became HHS secretary.

Trump also used the bully pulpit of his office to advance the right to life. In October 2017, Trump recognized World Down Syndrome Day, the first president to do so in over a decade. In his comments at the White House, Trump emphasized the incalculable value of individuals with Down syndrome and reminded Americans that they needed to be defended, including the developmentally challenged who were still in the womb. "Sadly, there remain too many people—both in the United States and throughout the world—that still see Down syndrome as an excuse to ignore or discard human life," the president said. "This sentiment is and will always be tragically misguided. We must always be vigilant in defending and promoting the unique and special gifts of all citizens in need. We should not tolerate any discrimination against them, as all people have inherent dignity." Trump issued a similar statement about adopted children, declaring November 2017 to be National Adoption Month. "My administration recognizes the profound importance of adoption for the American family," he said. "Adoption is a life-changing and life-affirming act that signals that no child in America—born or unborn—is unwanted or unloved."

These strong statements promoting adoption, defending the disabled, and promoting what Pope John Paul II called "the culture of life" made a positive difference. They demonstrated that a president not only influences public policy, but he can also change the culture. Taken together, the pro-life policies, personnel appointments, federal court nominations, and public statements fulfilled Trump's promise to act as president in a way that advanced the cause of life. Not incidentally, it also vindicated those Evangelicals and pro-lifers who had backed Trump in 2016 despite being told that they would be betrayed.

Trump had made one of the centerpieces of his campaign the repeal of the Johnson Amendment, an obscure provision in the Internal Revenue Code that made it against the law for any church, ministry, or nonprofit to speak out on political matters at the risk of losing its tax exempt status. Trump had learned about the Johnson Amendment during one of his early meetings with Evangelical leaders in 2015—before he even announced his candidacy. When he asked a group of Evangelical pastors why they didn't have more political influence when Evangelicals numbered roughly sixty million Americans, one of them replied, "the Johnson Amendment."

"What's that?" Trump reportedly asked.

The pastors explained that Johnson had inserted the provision in a tax bill in 1954 to silence a radio preacher in Texas who regularly criticized him. It had been on the books ever since, hanging like a Sword of Damocles over churches and ministries that spoke out on political matters. The IRS had used the Johnson Amendment as a blunt instrument for decades to justify harassment and invasive audits of major Evangelical ministries to ensure compliance, forcing the ministries to spend millions of dollars in legal fees to protect themselves, intimidating Evangelical leaders, and chilling the freedom of speech of the faith community.

"Well, if I become president, we're getting rid of that," Trump replied. He became the first president of either party to make repeal of the dreaded provision a priority.

When he spoke at the National Prayer Breakfast days after being sworn in as president, Trump quoted Thomas Jefferson's statement that the God who gave us life also gave us liberty, and he declared, "Among those freedoms is the right to worship according to our own beliefs." Veering off script, he added, "That is why I will get rid of, and totally destroy, the Johnson Amendment and allow our representatives of faith to speak freely and without fear of retribution. I will do that—remember." The massive crowd of religious leaders packed into the ballroom of the Washington Hilton responded with grateful applause. I later learned from someone in the White House that the president's aides had recommended against including a policy statement in remarks that had traditionally been strictly religious. But Trump had waved them off. That decision revealed his heart and the seriousness with which he took his commitment to the faith community. Trump also spoke in remarkably personal terms, again departing from his prepared text, stating that he knew many of the vastly wealthy who were not happy, and that he considered true success as having a strong faith and a close-knit family. Adding an intimate note about his own faith, he added, "I was blessed to be raised in a churched home. My mother and father taught me that to whom much is given much is expected. I was sworn in on the very

Bible from which my mother would teach us as young children. And that faith lives on in my heart every single day."

In May 2017, Trump issued an executive order called Promoting Free Speech and Religious Liberty, which emphasized federal protections for religious freedom. The order essentially directed the Treasury Department not to enforce the Johnson Amendment as long as a nonprofit was otherwise in compliance with the law. The same executive order directed the revision of health care mandates that violated the consciences of religious employers, such as the Little Sisters of the Poor, who had been heavily fined under Obamacare for refusing to pay for contraception and abortion-inducing medication. Some Christian conservatives expressed dissatisfaction with the broad and general terms of the executive order, but those concerns were misplaced. The more specific rules and regulations would be issued by individual government departments and agencies, not by the White House. During the course of the staff drafting of the order, senior White House aides shared various draft wordings under consideration in confidence with me and explained that the administration intended to delegate the regulatory heavy-lifting to cabinet departments, including HHS and the Justice Department.

The president could protect churches from harassment, but repealing the Johnson Amendment entirely required congressional action. Faith & Freedom swung into action, meeting with Republican leaders in the House and Senate, including Majority Leader McConnell, Speaker Paul Ryan, Senate Finance Committee chairman Orrin Hatch, and Ways and Means Committee chairman Kevin Brady to convey our strong support for repealing the Johnson Amendment. It was one of our top legislative priorities—especially given the backdrop of the scandal-plagued IRS under Barack Obama, when Lois Lerner and other liberal bureaucrats slow-walked tax-exempt applications for pro-life, Tea Party, and pro-Israel groups. The tax cut legislation was reported out of the Ways and Means Committee in November 2017 with language repealing the Johnson Amendment. Getting the language right required an aggressive lobbying effort. Another provision in a House

Appropriations Committee bill required the IRS commissioner to approve any investigation of a church or ministry and to swiftly notify Congress of any church targeted by the agency. Having the White House and Chairman Brady in our corner was an enormous help. The ACLU predictably opposed all these measures to protect freedom of speech for people of faith, denouncing them as a violation of "separation of church and state," claiming, "Unconstitutional religious favoritism has absolutely no place in government."[4]

The full House passed the tax cut just before Thanksgiving with the Johnson Amendment provision included. Unfortunately, the Senate parliamentarian then ruled that the provision was not a revenue provision but a policy change, which meant it could not be included in a revenue bill. We argued vehemently to the contrary to Senate leaders, and Vice President Pence lobbied on our behalf on numerous occasions. The chief advocate in the Senate was Senator James Lankford of Oklahoma, and he kept us posted on behind-the-scenes developments with regular updates. When I spoke with President Trump at the White House in early December, he told me he was fighting hard to get the repeal provision included in the final bill. But in the end, the Senate parliamentarian held firm (we strongly believed erroneously), leaving the Johnson Amendment on the books for now, all but unenforced by the Trump administration. It was another example of the faith community treating an 80 percent victory as a win, not a partial defeat.

Faith & Freedom also lobbied hard for increasing the child tax credit and standard deduction for working families, a major tax cut directed at poor and middle-class families with children. In the mid-1990s, the Christian Coalition had made passage of the $500 per child tax credit its top legislative priority and successfully worked to have it included in the "Contract with America." It was passed by the Republican Congress and signed by Bill Clinton after two vetoes. President Bush had doubled it to $1,000 in his 2001 tax cut. Our goal with Trump was to double it again to $2,000, and we found an invaluable and tireless ally in Ivanka Trump, who lobbied her father (not surprisingly, to great effect), as well as congressional leaders. Ivanka is an MVP on any team she joins, and the accolades I heard from members of Congress who met with her were remarkable. She walked the halls of the Capitol, buttonholing senators and congressmen, impressing everyone who encountered her. Grover Norquist hosted a meeting with anti-tax and pro-family groups with Ivanka at Americans for Tax Reform, where I pledged all the resources of Faith & Freedom to get the $2,000 child tax credit across the finish line. I met with Senator Orrin Hatch, a friend of over thirty years, who pledged he would get it included in the Senate bill, and with Kevin Brady, who told me he supported it, adding that the main issue was making the math add up with cuts in the corporate tax rate. Marco Rubio, as the original sponsor of the child tax credit in the Senate, was a great champion. In the end, the Senate Finance bill came in at our goal of $2,000 per child, while the House Ways and Means bill came in at $1,500. Patrick Purtill, our head of legislative affairs, worked hard with the conference committee, and with help from the White House, the $2,000 child tax credit became the law of the land.

The tax cut bill, signed into law by President Trump, also doubled the standard deduction for a family from $12,000 to $24,000, dramatically lowering the tax burden on middle-class families. By transferring money and power from Washington to mothers and fathers, we strengthened the family, relieved the tax burden on 22 million American families in the process, and also lifted millions out of poverty. In fact, according to the U.S. Census Bureau, the child tax credit has raised 11 million people out of poverty (including 5.5 million children) and made 20 million people less poor, including 12.5 million children.[5] In 2018, 39.4 million families received an average of $2,200, or over $80 billion in tax relief under the child credit. The intact, working family is the most successful and effective anti-poverty program ever conceived. No Washington bureaucrat or government program can replace a loving mother and father who provide for their children—not only financially, but in terms of unconditional love and discipline. None of this would have happened if the pro-family movement hadn't broadened its agenda in recent years to include budget and tax matters—and not just the traditional issues of life and religious freedom.

After eight years of arguably the most anti-Israel administration in history, Evangelicals were also anxious to see President Trump rekindle the special relationship between the United States and the Jewish state. In May, I learned that Trump would have to sign a waiver delaying a decision to move the U.S. Embassy from Tel Aviv to Jerusalem, as required by U.S. law, or announce his intention to begin the move. Every president since 1995 had pledged to move the U.S. Embassy, and every president had signed the same waiver every six months for twenty-two years. We hoped Trump would be the president who finally complied with U.S. law and reaffirmed our commitment to Israel by locating our embassy in the eternal capital of Israel. When asked by White House officials, I told them we had no problem with an initial waiver and deferred to the president's judgment and the counsel of his national security team, but that if the embassy were not moved by the end of his first term, it would present a real problem for Trump's Evangelical supporters. We had key allies on the embassy issue in Jared Kushner, senior advisor and son-in-law to the president, and the U.S. ambassador to Israel, David Friedman, who had worked with Trump for decades as one of his attorneys.

When the embassy waiver came up for renewal again in late 2017, I was told by a senior White House official that Trump held a meeting with his national security team and polled everyone around the table, including Secretary of State Rex Tillerson, Secretary of Defense Jim Mattis, and National Security Advisor H. R. McMaster. Everyone came down on the side of signing the waiver again, buying more time to try to restart the stalled peace process with the Palestinians. According to this senior official, Trump then turned to Mattis, asking if he announced the embassy move and the West Bank, Gaza, and other parts of the Middle East exploded in protest, would he then have everything he needed to defend U.S. forces, bases, and other assets in the region? Mattis replied that he did. Trump then informed his security advisors that he intended to move the embassy. It was a gutsy move and another reminder that his status as an outsider and an unconventional political figure enabled him to make decisions that members of the political establishment likely would not.

The theme of Trump's presidency could be summed up as this: "Promises Made, Promises Kept." Not as well-noted, but of far greater significance in the sweep of history, Trump fought for and advanced a pro-family policy agenda that had developed and matured in conservative think tanks, pro-family public policy organizations, and on Capitol Hill for decades. In partnership with his faith-based supporters, he helped make it a reality, and that is an historic achievement.

CHAPTER 13

THE "BORKING" OF
BRETT KAVANAUGH

On June 27, 2018, I was sitting at a table having dinner with my wife, Jo Anne, at a restaurant on Lake Como while on vacation in Italy when I received a news alert on my cell phone that Justice Anthony Kennedy had announced his retirement from the U.S. Supreme Court. As I gazed out over the glassy, pristine waters of one of the most beautiful lakes in the world with a summer moon rising over the hills of northern Italy, I reflected on how the calm scene before me contrasted with the firestorm that would soon engulf Washington. Six thousand miles away, the nation's capital braced for what promised to be one of the bloodiest Supreme Court confirmation fights in American history.

"This is why we worked so hard to elect Trump," I said to Jo Anne. "Let's hope and pray he delivers." For my part, I was confident that Trump would do so.

The Left reacted to the news of Kennedy's retirement with unhinged hysteria that bordered on madness. "We're f-@-#-$-&-d," screamed the sewer headline on the left-wing news website The Root, which claimed that Trump would nominate someone to the right of Kennedy, "as in Ku Klux Klan worse."[1] Sadly, this reaction was fairly typical. BuzzFeed reported that social media platforms had lit up with women seeking IUDs (intrauterine birth control devices) because Trump's pending pick "has people concerned about their reproductive rights, including access to birth control and safe abortions." On a conference call with members of the Democratic National Committee (DNC), news that Kennedy had retired was greeted with audible groans and "Oh, my God!" DNC chairman Tom Perez thundered, "The rule of law has been replaced by the rule of Trump."[2] Hollywood erupted with over-the-top rhetoric. "THIS BLOW COULDN'T BE MORE SEVERE," rock star Cher wrote on Twitter in one all-caps screed. "IF WE DON'T FIGHT LIKE OUR LIVES DEPEND ON IT, SOME AMERICANS COULD FIND THEMSELVES IN INTERNMENT CAMPS."[3]

Liberals had not been so dispirited since the 2016 election. Now the full consequences of that defeat sunk in, and they vowed to fight—and fight dirty. Brian Fallon, the gut-punching Obama political operative who headed a liberal outfit called Demand Justice, wrote on Twitter, "Every name on Trump's shortlist would be another Neil Gorsuch. Democrats should draw a line in the sand now that they will oppose anyone on that list."[4] Liberal groups went to the mattresses, hiring staff, placing digital ads on Facebook urging activists to contact their senators, organizing "war rooms," and assembling astro-turf armies of protesters for rent-a-riots to disrupt the pending Senate hearings on the nomination. For those paying attention in the days after Kennedy's announcement, the picket lines were already forming, and for the professional Left, Trump's nomination represented an existential struggle for the survival of their liberal agenda—an ideological battle to the death.[5]

The media acted as stenographers for the shrillest claims about Trump's still-unnamed nominee. Jeffrey Toobin, a legal reporter for CNN, wrote on Twitter, "Anthony Kennedy is retiring. Abortion will be illegal in twenty states within 18 months."[6] (Needless to say, this turned out to be false.) And in the *New Yorker*, Toobin sketched a dystopian future right out of *The Handmaid's Tale*, claiming that Trump's pick would lead to the subjugation of women, the persecution of gays, and discrimination against minorities. The catalogue of horrors to be committed by a Trump-influenced Supreme Court was a liberal's worst nightmare:

> It will overrule *Roe v. Wade*, allowing states to ban abortions and to criminally prosecute any physicians and nurses who perform them. It will allow shopkeepers, restaurateurs, and hotel owners to refuse service to gay customers on religious grounds. It will guarantee that fewer African-American and Latino students attend élite universities. It will approve laws designed to hinder voting rights. It will sanction execution by grotesque means. It will invoke the Second Amendment to prohibit states from engaging in gun control, including the regulation of machine guns and bump stocks.[7]

These hysterical attacks offered with no evidence and aimed at a nominee that had not even been named may have appeared scattershot and unhinged. But there was actually a deliberate strategy behind it. Ever since Ronald Reagan nominated Robert Bork, liberals have engaged in a systematic campaign of fear and smear intended to take down conservative Supreme Court nominees. This strategy began on the day of Bork's nomination on July 1, 1987, when Senator Ted Kennedy went to the Senate floor to proclaim:

> Robert Bork's America is a land in which women would be forced into back-alley abortions, blacks would sit at segregated lunch counters, rogue police could break down citizens' doors in midnight raids, schoolchildren could not be taught about evolution, writers and artists would be censored at the whim of government, and the doors of the federal courts would be shut on the fingers of millions of citizens for whom the judiciary is often the only protector of the individual rights that are the heart of our democracy.[8]

Through these gutter tactics, one of the most respected jurists in the nation and a distinguished professor at Harvard Law School had his character assassinated and his public reputation sullied. Sadly, it had the desired effect. Bork's nomination was defeated by Democrats in the Senate, and the Left learned a new lesson: the politics of personal destruction worked.

Ted Kennedy's "Robert Bork's America" speech signaled a new low in the history of Supreme Court nominations, ushering in a polarized era of search-and-destroy missions against any judicial conservative who aspired to sit on the high court. It also introduced a new word into the lexicon of American politics: "to bork," defined by Merriam-Webster's dictionary as to attack or defeat a nominee "unfairly through an organized campaign of harsh public criticism or vilification." Bork's defeat led to the nomination of Anthony Kennedy, a relative moderate, who was confirmed by a vote of ninety-seven to zero in the Senate. The Left knew this history well, which is why Toobin urged liberals to defeat Trump's nominee for the explicit purpose of paving the way for a more moderate-to-liberal justice. "Most of all, they need to remember that fighting Supreme Court nominees, even against formidable odds, can succeed—and produce a better Court than anyone might have expected," Toobin advised.[9]

By the time of his retirement, Kennedy had become the swing vote on the Supreme Court, the linchpin in a five-vote liberal majority on social and moral issues that included four other justices appointed by Bill Clinton and Obama. They upheld Roe, struck down pro-life state laws, and legalized same-sex marriage. Kennedy had made gay rights a personal cause, quietly lobbying his colleagues and writing the majority opinions in the *Lawrence v. Texas* (2003), *U.S. v. Windsor* (2013), and *Obergefell v. Hodges* (2015) cases, all five-to-four decisions that respectively struck down state sodomy statutes, voided the federal Defense of Marriage Act, and struck down the laws of thirty-four states that had defined marriage as a union between a man and a woman. Now Kennedy was gone, and with him perhaps the liberal majority on the court on social issues. The Left was apoplectic.

Republicans knew the vacancy would spark a furor, signaling a possible shift in the philosophical direction of the high court. Although Neil Gorsuch, Trump's first Supreme Court nominee, had a relatively smooth confirmation process, only three Democratic senators voted to confirm him. Republicans had since lost a Senate seat in Alabama in late 2017, reducing the GOP Senate majority in the upper chamber to a single vote. The politics of Supreme Court nominations, meanwhile, simmered with partisan animosity. When the June 2018 vacancy occurred, the stakes were high for both sides. If Trump chose a conservative, originalist judge to replace Kennedy, the ideological balance of the court—which had been a bastion for the Left—would swing to the Right. Democratic leaders were bound and determined to shoot down any Trump nominee. The grassroots of the Democratic Party would accept nothing less.[10] Trump had not even chosen a replacement, and the Democrats and the Left were already at war.

This should have been a warning sign. It was certainly not the first time in Supreme Court history that there had been strong resistance to a president's nominee. But few conservatives were expecting the unprecedented levels of delay tactics, slander, and outright falsehoods that would be brought to bear on Judge Brett Kavanaugh. Perhaps conservatives had been lulled to sleep by the relative ease of Gorsuch's confirmation. More likely, they were so pleased with Kavanaugh's impressive academic and judicial credentials that they could not see him as vulnerable to such an unfair, vicious assault. As a graduate of Yale University and Yale Law School, a clerk to Justice Kennedy, an associate counsel to Independent Counsel Ken Starr, a White House staff secretary, and a judge on the D.C. Circuit Court of Appeals since 2007, Kavanaugh boasted one of the strongest resumes of any recent Supreme Court nominee.

Kavanaugh had been added to Trump's list of potential Supreme Court picks in November 2017, which should have alerted both sides to the president's possible intentions.[11] I never asked anyone at the White House, but at the time I assumed that Kavanaugh had been added so he would be available to be selected. The move could have been interpreted as a sign to Justice Kennedy that he could retire in the knowledge that Trump would pick another one of his former clerks (Gorsuch being the first) as his successor. In any event, Kavanaugh had an impeccable reputation and sterling academic and judicial credentials, and he was quickly considered to be one of the frontrunners for the nomination. On July 5, the *Washington Post* reported that Trump's list had narrowed down to the top three contenders: Amy Coney Barrett, Raymond Kethledge, and Brett Kavanaugh.[12]

I had occasionally crossed paths with Kavanaugh during George W. Bush's administration and had heard nothing but good things about him, but I did not know him personally. In the days after Kennedy's announcement, I reached out to some old friends from the Bush White House and asked them if he was really as good as everyone claimed. Among them was Karl Rove, who related a striking anecdote about Brett's decision to go back to a White House staffer who had submitted a memo to President Bush. Kavanaugh offered suggestions on how to make his argument more persuasive, including specific points he believed would resonate with the president. The staff member was floored by Kavanaugh's generosity, especially because he knew Brett did not share his view on the issue. The superlatives I heard from the Bush 43 administration alumni about Brett were among the most extraordinary in my career.

While conservatives felt encouraged by Trump's reported shortlist and liberals fretted about how likely the candidates might be to overturn *Roe v. Wade*, another series of events was unfolding behind the scenes that would soon provide the Democrats with the fodder they needed against Trump's nominee. On July 6, Christine Blasey Ford, a psychology professor from California, called the office of Democratic representative Anna Eshoo. Ford, concerned about Kavanaugh's possible nomination, wanted to meet with Eshoo. On the same day, Ford sent a message to the *Washington Post*, claiming that Kavanaugh had once attacked her in some way.[13]

At the White House, where the president and his senior staff were oblivious to these developments, the selection process proceeded at an efficient clip. Trump met with each of the finalists individually in the week after Kennedy's announcement, conducting free-wheeling and wide-ranging interviews. Barrett had only sat on the Seventh Circuit Court of Appeals for eight months, so her nomination seemed less likely. One potential hitch for Kavanaugh was his reputation as a Bush loyalist, something not likely to play well in Trumpworld. The *Washington Post*, in a transparent attempt to damage his chances, filled a profile of Kavanaugh with photographs of President Bush standing at his side when he was sworn in as an appellate court judge and of Bush senior advisor Karl Rove wrapping his arm around him in a bear hug.[14] The *New York Times* reported that the photo with Rove was making the rounds in the Trump White House, undermining Kavanaugh's prospects.[15] The *Washington Post* kept up the drumbeat with a dispatch from star political reporter Bob Costa reporting that Kavanaugh faced "questions from social conservatives" and "clamor from those who see him as out of step on health care and abortion, or too tied to George W. Bush's White House."[16]

My sources told me the opposite: Trump was committed to choosing the most qualified and capable nominee and had no intention of holding a grudge against anyone for working for George W. Bush. I found the idea that Trump would allow petty politics of this nature to influence a lifetime appointment to the highest court in the land completely laughable. To Trump's credit, he stayed focused on the judicial philosophy, intellect, and qualifications of the potential nominees. When Costa called me to probe what I was hearing about the nomination, I told him what Faith & Freedom had said publicly: everyone on the president's list was acceptable, and we fully expected him to choose from that list. Because of the public list, the selection process was the most transparent in history. I did not know who the president would choose and made no attempt to influence his decision.

On July 9, Trump announced Kavanaugh as his Supreme Court pick in a televised ceremony in the East Room. Twenty minutes after the announcement, Senate Minority Leader Chuck Schumer issued a statement drawing the battle lines: "I will oppose Judge Kavanaugh with everything I have. I hope a bipartisan majority will do the same. The stakes are simply too high for anything less."[17] At an opposition rally in front of the U.S. Supreme Court building, protesters cheered on socialist former 2016 presidential candidate Senator Bernie Sanders and far-left Senator Elizabeth Warren, who vowed to fight the nomination with all they had. "Are you ready to defend *Roe v. Wade*?" Sanders bellowed. "Are you ready to tell the Supreme Court that we think it's absurd that they give constitutional rights to billionaires to buy elections and then tell women they don't have the constitutional right to control their own bodies?" Behind the building, reporters found discarded pre-printed signs bearing the slogans, "Stop Kethledge" and "Stop Hardiman," referring to federal judges Raymond Kethledge and Thomas Hardiman, who were reportedly also under consideration. The Women's March organization sent out a press release trumpeting its opposition to the nominee but forgot to fill in the blank for his name, making it clear that the press advisory had been written before Trump's announcement. All this proved that the Left didn't care who the nominee was or what their qualifications were because the nominee would be a conservative nominated by Trump, and they would oppose that nominee with all their might.[18]

The Democrats were determined to block Kavanaugh's nomination by any means necessary. Their first strategy was delay, hoping to push the timeline for the nomination past the 2018 midterm elections in hopes that they could regain control of the U.S. Senate in November. The first line of attack in this strategy was the threadbare charge that Trump should not be allowed to fill Kennedy's vacancy as long as he was under investigation by special counsel Robert Mueller. This absurd claim was cable catnip in the usual precincts of MSNBC, but it didn't find many supporters in the Senate. The second line of attack was the so-called "transparency" issue: Democratic senators demanded time to examine Kavanaugh's extensive paper trail, which included legal opinions, emails, and memos, along with all the papers that he handled while serving as White House staff secretary to George W. Bush. This was a ridiculous demand because most of the documents Kavanaugh handled as staff secretary involved merely facilitating the paper flow to the Oval Office and in no way reflected his own views. The number of records was immense—amounting to millions of pages—and the overwhelming majority of it was entirely irrelevant to Kavanaugh's career as a federal judge. Nonetheless, Democrats accused Republicans of not releasing enough of these records to the public and of trying to hide something about Kavanaugh's past career. Their goal was to delay the confirmation hearings past the midterm elections, and they launched an online campaign called #WhatAreTheyHiding on Twitter and Facebook to drive the message.

I had no idea whether there was anything controversial contained in the documents the Democrats sought, but at the Faith & Freedom Coalition, we were not taking any chances. We dropped one million "action alert" postcards to Faith & Freedom members and activists in Missouri, North Dakota, Indiana, and West Virginia, all red states held by Democratic senators. We placed digital ads in those states, adding Florida in order to keep the heat on Senator Bill Nelson, with the bulk of our mail and digital ads landing when the Kavanaugh hearings were scheduled in early September. We prepared for the worst, believing (far more correctly than we knew at the time) that the Left would stop at nothing to defeat Kavanaugh.

Meanwhile, the greatest threat to Kavanaugh's nomination unfolded outside of public view. On July 9, the same day that Trump announced his selection of Kavanaugh, Christine Blasey Ford again spoke with Representative Eshoo's staff over the phone.[19] She arranged a private meeting with Eshoo, and on July 20, she told the congresswoman about her allegations against Kavanaugh. Ford claimed that Kavanaugh had tried to sexually assault her at a party in the 1980s, back when both had been high schoolers in the Washington area. Ford could not recall several crucial details about the purported event—including the exact date or the location where it allegedly occurred. But Eshoo nonetheless believed her and advised her to contact Dianne Feinstein, the ranking Democrat on the Senate Judiciary Committee. Ford then wrote a letter to Feinstein in which she detailed her claims, which was delivered on July 30.[20] At some point during the summer, Ford also spoke with Emma Brown, a reporter with the *Washington Post* who responded to her July 6 tip.[21]

Senator Feinstein replied to Ford on July 31, promising not to share her letter without Ford's explicit consent. At this point, no media outlet had published anything about Ford's allegations. Senate Judiciary Committee protocols and procedures required that Feinstein provide the letter to the committee so it could investigate the claims in a confidential manner, including FBI interviews when warranted. This is the normal procedure for dealing with serious allegations against a Supreme Court nominee, and it had been followed in the case of Anita Hill's allegations against Clarence Thomas in 1991. But Feinstein and her staff deliberately kept the existence of the letter a secret, with the desired result being that Ford's claims could not be investigated in a confidential or timely way. This, too, was part of a deliberate Democratic strategy of obstruction, delay, and hide the ball.

Sometime between July 30 and August 7, Feinstein spoke with Ford over the phone. Feinstein's staff then recommended that Ford engage liberal attorney Debra Katz as her lawyer.[22] Katz was a seasoned litigator, radical feminist, and civil rights attorney with a background of handling sexual harassment cases. After engaging Katz, Ford took a polygraph test, the results of which her attorneys provided to the *Washington Post*. During this time, Michael Bromwich also joined Ford's legal team. Bromwich also represented Andrew McCabe, the disgraced and dismissed FBI deputy director who had been involved in the Russiagate and Hillary Clinton email scandals.[23] Throughout the month of August, as Feinstein assisted Ford in finding lawyers to represent her case and as the Judiciary Committee prepared for hearings on the nomination, she still failed to notify the committee of the allegations.

Meanwhile, Kavanaugh was making the rounds on Capitol Hill, holding meetings with Republican and Democratic senators, especially members of the Judiciary Committee. At first, Democrats had refused to meet with him until there was a deal on their unreasonable demands on document production. But they looked terrible declining to even meet with Kavanaugh, and eventually they caved. On August 20, Kavanaugh met with Dianne Feinstein and Chuck Schumer. By this time, Feinstein had known about Ford's sexual assault allegations for three weeks, spoken with the accuser, and referred her to lawyers. But she did not utter a word about Ford's charges in her meeting with Kavanaugh, a glaring (and deliberate) omission.[24] A week later, on August 28, her staff participated in an official background information call with Kavanaugh, asking him "numerous questions about confidential background information."[25] Again, Ford's charges went unmentioned.

Around this time, I attended a briefing at the White House by counsel Don McGahn regarding the Kavanaugh nomination for conservative organizations. Projecting confidence, McGahn reported that the meetings with senators were going well and that Kavanaugh had answered all the questions directed at him forthrightly while showing an enormous knowledge of constitutional law and precedent. I asked McGahn if the *Lemon* test was used—an obscure and byzantine three-part test from the *Lemon v. Kurtzman* (1971) decision that determined whether or not a government action violated the establishment clause of the First Amendment. McGahn said it had not. He added that Kavanaugh was a "fundamentalist" when it came to the separation of powers, something he expected would play well in the Senate.

When the meeting ended, I pulled McGahn aside. "I recommend we avoid using the term 'fundamentalist' when talking about a Supreme Court nominee," I said. "People might think he's too close to the Religious Right." McGahn broke up laughing. The general mood as people filed out of the White House that day was upbeat, almost as if we couldn't believe our good luck. It was still early, but Kavanaugh appeared to be sailing to an easy confirmation.

On September 4, Brett Kavanaugh's hearings began. For thirty-two hours over four days, Senate Judiciary Committee members grilled Kavanaugh on his background, judicial career, his rulings and opinions as an appellate court judge, and his judicial philosophy. These thorough hearings included a closed session on September 6, during which senators were allowed to question Kavanaugh about sensitive or awkward information, such as possible alcohol addiction or credit card debt.[26] This closed session would have been the place for Feinstein to air Ford's explosive sexual assault charges. Yet Feinstein did not even attend the session, and no one in the four days of hearings brought up Ford's allegations.

During the hearings, Faith & Freedom lit up the phone lines in the red states held by Democratic senators, all of whom were up for reelection in November, placing over 250,000 calls to our members and generating tens of thousands of calls to Senate offices. Heidi Heitkamp of North Dakota and Claire McCaskill of Missouri were the most vulnerable. All of them declined to say how they would vote. No Democratic senator laid a glove on Kavanaugh during the hearings. He answered every one of their queries politely, humbly, and with an impressive understanding of the law, the Constitution, and existing Supreme Court jurisprudence. With the hearings over and not a scratch on him, Kavanaugh looked like a deadlock to be confirmed.

But Democrats were not ready to give up yet. As another delay tactic, they submitted 1,278 follow-up questions to Kavanaugh after the hearings to which they demanded answers. The practice of asking follow-up questions of Supreme Court nominees had started in the 1970s, but the questions posed to Kavanaugh far outnumbered the queries for all previous nominees combined. Neil Gorsuch, whose confirmation the Democrats had also opposed strongly, had only received 324 questions.[27] In this avalanche of questions, Ford's allegations were mentioned nowhere. Despite the Democrats' delay tactics, it appeared that the nomination would go forward relatively smoothly. Kavanaugh and his team worked overtime to provide written answers in the time allotted and submitted them on September 12.

The same day, however, word about Ford's allegations began to leak. On September 12, Ryan Grim of The Intercept published a piece describing rumors of a "Brett-Kavanaugh related document" that Feinstein was refusing to release to her fellow Democratic senators. "Different sources provided different accounts of the contents of the letter," Grim wrote, "but the one consistent theme was that it describes an incident involving Kavanaugh and a woman while they were in high school."[28] So far, Feinstein had pointedly declined to let other Democratic senators see the document, claiming that the letter's author had requested strict confidentiality. But the other Democrats wanted to have a say in whether the letter should be made public.

Rumors began to circulate. The next day, September 13, Senator Feinstein announced that she had referred the letter to the FBI for investigation—forty-five days after she had first received it.[29] She still declined to give out Ford's name or the exact nature of the allegations.

The following day, Ronan Farrow and Jane Mayer of the *New Yorker* published a piece that described the contents of Ford's letter in detail while withholding her name.[30] Hearing the specifics of the allegations, Kavanaugh quickly and unequivocally denied them. The gathering storm exploded on September 16, when the *Washington Post* posted a story on its website that included an interview with Ford and described her decision to go public with her allegations.[31]

I read the account within minutes of its being posted. While the allegations were damaging and lurid, I was struck by the complete absence of corroborating witnesses and the fact that Ford could not recall even basic facts, such as where the alleged party took place, how she got there, or the date on which it occurred. One could discount these missing details as the product of an imperfect memory three decades later. But their absence also conveniently made verifying any of the alleged facts almost impossible. Even one of the friends she cited as a witness could not recall whether Kavanaugh was at the alleged party. I also found their publication by the same media outlet that first published the *Access Hollywood* tape suspicious. Why hadn't Ford gone to the Judiciary Committee with a written account of her story, which would have allowed the FBI and committee staff to investigate it? It all smelled fishy and underhanded.

Like Anita Hill's allegations against Clarence Thomas, the bombshell charges were dropped by a liberal news organization after public hearings had concluded, just days prior to a scheduled vote on a Supreme

Court nominee. As a veteran of the Thomas nomination fight and eleven other Supreme Court nominations, I fully expected a shoe to drop at some point. The opposition was simply too virulent and venomous to allow Kavanaugh to be confirmed without a fight, and these lurid and unsubstantiated charges were a Hail Mary pass thrown by the Left to derail—or at least delay—Kavanaugh's nomination.

But don't take my word for it. Just listen to Ford's own attorney. In a speech to a feminist legal conference at the University of Baltimore in April 2019, Debra Katz made it clear that she and Blasey Ford were "motivated" by preserving abortion rights and delegitimizing efforts to overturn *Roe v. Wade*—not by any civic responsibility to make known to the public concerns about Kavanaugh's character. "We were going to have a conservative [justice]...elections have consequences, but he will always have an asterisk next to his name," Katz said. "When he takes a scalpel to *Roe v. Wade*, we will know who he is, we know his character, and we know what motivates him, and that is important; it is important that we know, and that is part of what motivated Christine." As documented by *National Law Journal* reporter Ryan Lovelace in his book *Search and Destroy: Inside the Campaign Against Brett Kavanaugh*, Ford and her legal team's goal was not to persuade the Senate to reject Kavanaugh, but rather to smear his reputation so completely that if he later voted to curb the availability of abortion, the decision would be discredited among the American people.[32] There's no doubt that abortion politics played a role in Ford's eleventh-hour attack, but Katz's rationale was revisionist history. As with the *Access Hollywood* tape and related charges against Trump in 2016, as well as the sexual assault charges against GOP Senate nominee Roy Moore in 2017, the objective was to win by forcing Kavanaugh to withdraw or to defeat him in a Senate vote. The real goal was to force Trump to nominate a moderate or centrist justice.

Kavanaugh issued a statement denying Ford's charges completely, all but demanding the opportunity to clear his name. There was no wiggle room or parsing of words in Kavanaugh's response. He said he had never met Ford to his knowledge, had never sexually assaulted anyone in his life, and had no recollection of the alleged high school house party. He pronounced himself willing to appear before the Senate Judiciary Committee at a time of its choosing to defend his honor. These were not the words or actions of a guilty man.

With the allegations and the accuser now public, the media exploded with sensational coverage, almost all of it favorable toward Ford. News outlets breathlessly recounted the alcohol-drenched culture at the Catholic prep school Kavanaugh attended. They chased down anyone who might have ever been at a party with him, desperately hoping for some confirmation of inappropriate behavior. As things began to spin out of control, Republicans on the Senate Judiciary Committee realized they needed to provide Ford with a hearing to publicly state her charges. On September 17, Senator Chuck Grassley invited both Kavanaugh and Ford to a special hearing to testify in front of the committee. Kavanaugh immediately agreed; Ford proved harder to reach. Her lawyers delayed until September 23, making demands about calling other witnesses to buttress Ford's case before finally announcing that Ford would be willing to testify on September 27. (Ford's case weakened badly when all three potential witnesses she identified said they had no knowledge of any such incident.)[33]

But on September 23, a second allegation surfaced. In another *New Yorker* article by Ronan Farrow and Jane Mayer, a woman named Deborah Ramirez accused Kavanaugh of more sexual misconduct.[34] She claimed that Kavanaugh had sexually harassed her by exposing himself at a college party when they were both students at Yale. Like Ford, Ramirez could not corroborate her story. She even admitted to being incoherently drunk at the party, making her reliability questionable. I read the Farrow-Mayer piece carefully and could not believe that it had gotten past the famously rigorous fact-checkers at the *New Yorker*. Literally no one could back up Ramirez's allegation. It was a miscarriage of journalism and an embarrassment to the magazine, which despite its liberalism had a reputation for factual accuracy. Farrow had previously written some of the earliest and most devastating accounts of the allegations of sexual harassment against Hollywood producer Harvey Weinstein. But the roughshod journalism, lack of independent verification, and unreliability of the main source gave the attack on Kavanaugh almost no credibility. In the end, Ramirez would decline to even appear before the Judiciary Committee, and her case fell apart.

For the moment, however, the stampede to drive Kavanaugh to withdraw his nomination gained more momentum. The process degenerated into a rogue's gallery of liberal activists and publicity-seekers. Michael Avenatti, the attorney for Trump accuser Stormy Daniels, announced in a tweet that he represented a third woman with "credible information" against Kavanaugh.[35] Avenatti, who had become a fixture on cable news outlets and had even begun flirting with a presidential run, turned out to be a gift. By injecting himself into the story, Avenatti showed that the campaign against Kavanaugh had degenerated into a search-and-destroy mission of lies and smears hurled by trial-bar assassins, pettifoggers, and carnival barkers. On September 26, he released the name and information of his client, Julie Swetnick, who claimed that she had seen Kavanaugh drinking heavily and getting women drunk so they could be gang raped by his friends at several house parties in the 1980s. In a sworn statement submitted to the committee, Swetnick alleged that Kavanaugh and his male friends had targeted vulnerable girls at the parties in order to sexually assault them.[36] Kavanaugh again vehemently denied the allegations. He said that he had no idea who Swetnick was and had never done the things she claimed. Swetnick's story was vague and full of holes, and she later contradicted many of the details in an interview with NBC News before backing down from most of the charges, saying Avenatti had twisted her words.[37] The episode sparked a backlash against Avenatti among liberals who wondered why the publicity-hungry lawyer had bothered to wade into the Kavanaugh fight, undermining their chances to defeat him.

Against the backdrop of this media spectacle, the committee convened on September 27 for its hearing on Ford's allegations. Ford's testimony was compelling and dramatic. But when questioned by Rachel Mitchell, the Arizona sex crimes prosecutor who had been recruited by Republicans to question the witness, many of Ford's basic facts failed to pass muster, including claims of having suffered such psychological damage that she was afraid to fly. Mitchell methodically dismantled the credibility of the witness, demonstrating that she was either not truthful or contradicted herself on a number of issues. But it was not riveting television, and Mitchell did not aggressively go after Ford, leaving the political advocacy to the Democrats. After Ford's testimony, many Republicans were distraught, wondering if they had lost by default by outsourcing their questioning to a prosecutor.

I was never worried. Knowing Kavanaugh's background and character, I was confident he would rise to the occasion. When the committee reconvened, Kavanaugh read a statement fired by moral fervor and righteous fury. He pointed out that all four "witnesses" that Ford claimed were at the party had no recollection of being there or of the party ever taking place. He added that Leland Keyser, Ford's good friend, had said she not only recalled no such party, but that she had never met Kavanaugh—with or without Ford. He welcomed any investigation—by the Senate Judiciary Committee, the FBI, or the Montgomery County Police Department in Maryland—to clear his name. Most importantly, he condemned the media circus that had become an exercise in character assassination. "This confirmation process has become a national disgrace," Kavanaugh said, his face trembling with emotion. "The Constitution gives the Senate an important role in the confirmation process. But you have replaced 'advice and consent' with 'search and destroy.'" When he mentioned that one of his daughters had suggested before evening prayers that they pray for his accuser, one could hear a pin drop in the hearing room. It was a virtuoso performance: deeply moving, evocative, and alternately appealing to due process and basic fairness while correctly condemning the politics of personal destruction to which the judicial confirmation process had sunk.

Senator Lindsey Graham followed up Kavanaugh's testimony with his own broadside, blasting Feinstein and the other Democrats on the committee for smearing and attempting to destroy a good and decent man. He pointed out that he had always treated Democrats with fairness and respect, worked on a bipartisan basis on many issues with his Democratic colleagues, and voted for the confirmations of Sonia Sotomayor and Elena Kagan, two of Obama's nominees to the Supreme Court. "I would never do to them what you've done to this guy," he said, wagging his finger at the Democrats. "This is the most unethical sham since I've been in politics. And if you really wanted to know the truth, you sure as hell wouldn't have done what you've done to this guy." He called the Democrats out for holding the charges until the last minute, then dropping them to delay the confirmation process until after the 2018 elections in order to take the Senate majority back and block any Trump nominee. "Boy, you all want power. God, I hope you never get it. I hope the American people can see through this sham. That you knew about it and you held it. You had no intention of protecting Dr. Ford. None."

Conservatives had not always been huge fans of Graham's, but he gave voice to the anger and righteous indignation of tens of millions of Americans, becoming a conservative hero overnight. Unfortunately, Jeff Flake of Arizona, a frequent critic of Trump's and a lame duck who was retiring from the Senate in a few months, requested a delay until the FBI could conduct a full field investigation of Ford's allegations, as well as any others it considered credible. This action rewarded Feinstein and the Democrats for secretly holding the charge back for forty-five days and failing to follow committee procedures, and it meant the media feeding frenzy would continue for another week while the FBI did its job. But without Flake's vote, the Kavanaugh nomination was likely dead—not only in committee, but on the floor of the Senate. Senator Grassley had no choice but to accede to his request.

After the FBI completed its investigation, its report and summaries of interviews with witnesses were placed in a secure room in the Capitol Building where senators could read and study them before voting. After reviewing the documents, Senator Graham met with our legislative staff and key supporters at a briefing at the Hay-Adams hotel on October 4. He told us there was no corroboration for Ford's allegations and that he was urging his Republican colleagues to do the right thing and confirm

Kavanaugh. I was struck by Lindsey's fiery anger, his revulsion at the tactics of the Left, his conviction that gutter politics should not be allowed to prevail lest it be encouraged, and his understanding that the Kavanaugh confirmation vote now transcended the merits of the nominee. The vote was now a defining moment that revealed the character of the U.S. Senate, and to an equal extent, the country.

Meanwhile, Faith & Freedom operated phone banks and sent action alert text messages and emails to tens of thousands of activists in the home states of the final handful of undecided Democratic senators, generating thousands of calls in the final forty-eight hours before the vote. One by one, all the Democrats announced their opposition, except for Joe Manchin of West Virginia. Republican Lisa Murkowski of Alaska also announced her intention to vote "no," which meant we could only lose one more Republican. The nation waited for the decision of one senator: Susan Collins of Maine. Collins was a moderate from the Northeast, and she was pro-choice. But she had also never opposed a Supreme Court nominee from a Republican president. The radical Left had badly bungled their lobbying campaign directed at Collins, launching a GoFundMe page that raised over a million dollars pledged to her Democratic opponent in 2020—but only if she voted for Kavanaugh's confirmation. It was an amateurish stunt that gave all the appearances of an attempted bribe of Collins, who was well-known for her integrity and rectitude. Liberals also reportedly left profanity-laced voicemails on the phones of her Senate offices, berated and threatened her staff, and sent three thousand coat hangers to her office to send the message that Kavanaugh's confirmation would lead to back-alley abortions. Apparently, there was no tactic too low for the Left.[38]

Finally, in a floor speech on October 5 that echoed the traditions of Senate debate and decorum of a bygone era, Collins methodically reviewed the evidence of the charges against Kavanaugh and announced her intention to vote for him. Manchin followed suit shortly thereafter, giving us his vote as soon as it was no longer needed. But more had been at stake than just Brett Kavanaugh's service on the Supreme Court. His confirmation fight, however distasteful, reminded people of what was at stake in the 2018 midterm elections. The despicable conduct of the Democrats and the attempt by the Left and the media to destroy the reputation, family, and good name of a fine public servant and decent human being would have far-reaching political ramifications. In the short term, we saw a clear uptick in intensity and enthusiasm in the key Senate races, especially in Missouri, Indiana, and Florida—three battleground states where each Democratic senator had opposed Kavanaugh. All three went down to defeat, two of them by large margins.

On October 8, I joined a celebratory crowd for Kavanaugh's swearing-in ceremony in the East Room of the White House. Rather than sticking with *pro forma* diplomatic niceties, Trump used his opening remarks to lambaste the opposition for the shameful way they had conducted themselves. "On behalf of our nation, I want to apologize to Brett and the entire Kavanaugh family for the terrible pain and suffering you have been forced to endure," Trump said, making clear his own distaste for the gutter tactics employed by the Far Left during the political firestorm that had engulfed Kavanaugh's nomination. The president correctly stated that Kavanaugh had been the victim of a "campaign of political and personal destruction based on lies and deception." But Trump said with great generosity to the new justice, "You, sir, under historic scrutiny, were proven innocent."[39]

Not a single Democratic senator attended the ceremony. Their strategy to take down Kavanaugh had failed; it had also backfired. Republican Senate candidates like Josh Hawley in Missouri and Rick Scott in Florida were surging, buoyed by a wave of revulsion and momentum at the grassroots level over the smears and lies directed at Kavanaugh. Nothing more dramatically demonstrated how a Democrat-controlled Senate led by Chuck Schumer with Dianne Feinstein as chairman of the Judiciary Committee would function than the spectacle of the Kavanaugh hearings. After the ceremony, the crowd retired to the State Dining Room for a reception to express relief at the victory and congratulate one another on a job well done. I sauntered over to Don McGahn to offer my congratulations. He expressed relief and gratitude to Kavanaugh for staying in the fight and to the president for never wavering in his support for a moment. McGahn would soon announce his departure from the White House. I hated to see him go, but White House jobs at any time are a grind, and in the Trump era, McGahn had been at the eye of the storm. One could not blame him for seeking the relative sanity of the private sector.

When Kavanaugh and his wife, Ashley, emerged from a room off the State Dining Room, I happened to be standing there and bumped right into them. Justice Kavanaugh shook my hand firmly, and our eyes locked. "Thank you, sir, for all you did," he said.

"Brett, it was a privilege and an honor," I replied. After a brief pause, I added, "The last time I prayed that hard was during the Florida recount in 2000."

Kavanaugh broke up with laughter.

It was nice to be able to laugh, if only for an evening. Outside the warm glow of comaraderie and celebration that bathed the White House that night, the battle still raged. The 2018 elections were only weeks away, and if the Democrats gained control of the House, it was a question of if, not when, they would move to impeach and remove Trump from office. It was as if the 2016 elections in which Evangelicals had played such a major role had never ended. For the Democrats, quit, concession, surrender, and defeat were not words found in their vocabulary. For that reason and many more, we could not quit either.

CHAPTER 14

FAKE NEWS AND THE DEATH OF JOURNALISM

N o one was more wrong about the 2016 election than the elite
media. No one mourned Hillary's loss more or possessed a deeper
longing for a modern-day feminist in the White House than they did.
No one was more gobsmacked by Trump's victory than the media. Once
they recovered from the shock of election night, they set out on a new
and audacious project: to destroy Trump and discredit the Evangelical
community for supporting him. In the process, they destroyed what little
credibility the media had left as an institution, signaling the death of
modern journalism and ushering in a new era of a partisan press, which
had previously existed for much of American history.

The signs were clear to anyone watching on election night in 2016.
Martha Raddatz, the ABC foreign affairs reporter who occasionally
hosts the Sunday news program *This Week*, appeared to become emotional, nearly breaking down in tears on the set. Van Jones, a former
Obama operative and White House aide who is now a CNN commentator, exploded, "This was a whitelash. This was a whitelash against a
changing country. It was a whitelash against a black president, in part."[1]
The host and moderator, Anderson Cooper—a "real" journalist—did

not correct him or suggest that Van might have been motivated more by his partisan leanings than the facts. Over at MSNBC, Rachel Maddow opened her show the day after the election by looking into the camera with total sincerity and saying, "You're awake, by the way. You're not having a terrible, terrible dream. Also, you're not dead and you haven't gone to hell. This is your life now."[2]

For the media, arguably more powerful at that time than at any point in the history of the country (at least in their own minds), Trump's victory was a full-blown, two-fold crisis. First, the election completely shot whatever credibility the liberal media had left. Their smartest minds, sharpest analysts, and best pollsters all assured their readers and viewers for months that the election was over, Trump was finished, the Democratic landslide would be so gigantic that they might retake the House and Senate, and the only decisions remaining for Hillary Clinton were for her to pick her inaugural wardrobe and start selecting her cabinet. During an interview on MSNBC on September 26, former Obama political guru and Clinton campaign advisor David Plouffe said that Trump had no chance of winning and that Hillary's victory was 100 percent certain. "I know 100 percent sounds crazy, but I'm going to stick with it because the Electoral College puzzle here is definitely in Hillary Clinton's favor," Plouffe said. At the time, Trump was tied or within the margin of error in polls in virtually every battleground state. Rather than question whether Plouffe's assertion was supported by the evidence, the MSNBC hosts merely praised Plouffe for the Obama campaign's ground game in 2008 and 2012.[3] In an interview with the online news site Vox, former George W. Bush and John McCain campaign advisor Steve Schmidt said, "The Trump campaign is over—Hillary Clinton is going to be elected president. The question that remains here, the open question, is the degree of the collateral damage, right?" Schmidt confidently claimed that the GOP was "going to lose the U.S. Senate," might "lose the House majority," and wondered aloud "how far below 40 percent is Trump in the popular vote?" The Vox story predicted that after Trump's inevitable loss, the Republican Party would "break in two."[4]

Accompanying the prediction of Trump's certain defeat was an obligatory trashing of Evangelical leaders for supporting him. "These people are
literally the modern-day Pharisees, they are the money changers in the
temple, and they will forever be destroyed from a credibility perspective,"
Schmidt argued. He claimed that faith leaders had surrendered their moral
authority forever. "[T]his country doesn't ever need to hear a lecture from
any one of these people again on a values issue, or their denigration of good
and decent gay people in this country."[5] The media's real agenda was to kill
two birds with one stone on Election Day by taking down Trump and silenc-
ing Evangelicals. Indeed, one wonders how much of the media's irrational
hatred of Trump is rooted in his role as the unlikely champion of Evangelicals
and their pro-life, pro-family agenda.

This didn't just happen at liberal news outlets. The groupthink,
selective manipulation of polling data, and confirmation bias of the
media were institutional, not only ideological. On Fox News, host
Megyn Kelly berated Newt Gingrich on October 25 when he dared to
suggest that Trump had a chance to win and questioned many of the
media's polling. "But your candidate loves [polls], and he has touted them
from the beginning," Kelly replied. "And he's been behind in virtually
every one of the last 40 polls that we've seen over the past month. That's
the reality." On that date, Fox News' decision desk team projected that
Hillary Clinton would win 307 electoral votes to Trump's 174, with
states totaling 57 electoral votes as toss-ups. Larry Sabato's Crystal Ball
went further, predicting 322 electoral votes for Clinton. Charlie Cook,
a nonpartisan political analyst, predicted that Republicans would lose
five to seven Senate seats and lose control of the U.S. Senate. (Democrats
gained only two seats, in Arizona and New Hampshire, and the GOP
held the Senate.) The liberal bias was almost total.[6] Gingrich fired back
by noting that the early Republican vote in Florida, Pennsylvania, and
Iowa was running far ahead of Romney's early vote in 2012 and asserting
that Hillary was "clearly the most corrupt, dishonest person ever nominated by a party." Kelly replied that "if Trump is a sexual predator, then
it's a big story." Outraged, Gingrich accused her of bias because she

raised unproven, explosive sexual allegations. Kelly abruptly ended the interview, suggesting to Gingrich that "you can take your anger issues and spend some time working on them, Mr. Speaker."[7]

Perhaps the most damning indictment of the liberal media was their attempt to dress up their bias with so-called "data journalism," a fad that purported to base its analysis on data analytics and scientific polling. At the *New York Times*, for example, Nate Silver and his team at the FiveThirtyEight "election forecast" website generated reams of charts, graphs, historical evidence, statistics, and analysis proving the case that Hillary's victory was all but assured. Always accompanied by obligatory disclaimers that statistical projections could only assess probabilities, not predict the future, this "journalism" was intended to create the impression that Trump faced insurmountable odds that increased each day. By Election Day, Silver's crack analysts and scientists put Hillary's chances of winning at an astonishing 71.8 percent to Trump's 28.2 percent. In the battleground states, these data-driven predictions were off by even more; Silver gave Hillary an 84 percent chance of winning Wisconsin, 80 percent in Michigan, and 77 percent in Pennsylvania. (She lost them all.)[8] One of the unintentionally comic sideshows of election night occurred when FiveThirtyEight frantically recalculated Hillary's chances of winning in real time as Trump won battleground state after battleground state. As soon as it became apparent that Trump was about to be declared the winner in Wisconsin, which would put him over the necessary 270 electoral votes needed to be elected president, Trump's "likelihood" of winning skyrocketed from around 20 percent to over 80 percent in a matter of minutes. So much for data "science" and analytics-based "journalism."

With Hillary's defeat came a second crisis that was both ideological and institutional. Once elected, Trump's pursuit of a rock-ribbed conservative Republican agenda of tax cuts, regulatory rollback, the repeal of Obamacare, and the appointment of conservative judges gave the lie to the media's wishful portrayal of him as someone who was more centrist and far more comfortable with Democrats. Whatever his previous inclination was as a businessman to play both sides of the aisle for much of his career, Trump's early personnel picks and policy decisions displayed a compass, whether based on philosophy or political instincts (or both), that pointed true north. As we discussed in earlier chapters, Trump came out of the chute in early 2017 with a flurry of executive and legislative action that left no doubt that he was a conservative. For the media, this was an ideological crisis of epic proportions that threatened everything they held dear and all that they cherished. Their sources and friends in the Obama administration, who spoon fed them leaks and socialized with them at Georgetown parties, smoothly assured them that Obama's twin victories had ushered in an enduring progressive majority built on changing demographics and the growing diversity of the country. Old white men were dying off and being replaced by younger voters of color, their models predicted. The future belonged to the Left. Trump's victory not only ended the Obama era with its liberal domestic policies and woolly-headed foreign policies that emboldened our enemies and demoralized our allies, but also ushered in a united conservative government that threatened the entire liberal project.

The average American has no idea how completely and inextricably intertwined the media are with the Democratic Party and the Left. The relationships, the revolving door in which liberal reporters serve in Democratic administrations, and the rewarding of sources for leaks and confidences with lucrative "news" jobs or careers after their government service have been a mainstay of the media-liberal-industrial complex for decades. Just a few of the dozens of examples include Lyndon Johnson aide Jack Valenti, who decamped to the Motion Picture Association of America as the chief lobbyist for Hollywood; Johnson aide Bill Moyers, who spent a career at PBS producing liberal news programs; a former top aide to Democratic senator Daniel Patrick Moynihan, Tim Russert, who became the moderator of *Meet the Press*; former Bill Clinton aide George Stephanopoulos, who became the host of *Good Morning America* and *This Week* at ABC; Clinton political advisors James Carville and Paul Begala, who have spent years as commentators at CNN; and *TIME* magazine political reporter Jay Carney, who joined the Obama administration as a press aide to Vice President Biden and eventually became White House press secretary.

Some of this now occurs on the Right under Trump, particularly with Fox News, which is another reason why the liberal media seek to destroy him. He is now beating them at their own game. Many major news organizations lack the same number of sources who will routinely leak to them, thus enabling them to scoop their competitors. This creates a professional challenge for reporters, whose editors and bosses demand that they get the inside scoop. The Trump White House has dispensed with the daily White House press briefing and primetime presidential news conferences—occasions where reporters performed for the cameras, impressed their bosses with hostile questions, and in many cases became big stars, building their careers and raking in lucrative speaking gigs and book deals. CNN's Jim Acosta did so early during Trump's presidency, going almost overnight from an obscure reporter on a little-watched cable outlet to national fame with the clips of him and Trump exchanging sharp words going viral on social media. Trump actually enjoys parrying with the media and answers many questions, but he does so at "stakeouts" on the South Lawn as he is about to board Marine One for a trip or at press "sprays" in the Oval Office, which are limited to reporters in the press pool. Both settings force reporters to shout their questions and compete for the president's attention, again creating a status crisis for the nation's leading journalists. (Some White House reporters have told me privately that Trump is smart to do this, keeping the focus on him and his answers, not on the press corps.)

Separately, Trump's belittling of the media, calling them out for publishing or airing "fake news," and declining to lend the prestige of his office to their interview programs threatens the unique status of elite journalists as the gatekeepers and power brokers in American society. This status crisis has engendered deep-seated anxiety among media elites about a loss of professional prestige and influence. Trump has declined to attend the White House Correspondents' Dinner, which no president had failed to attend in nearly forty years; he also bypassed the Gridiron Club Dinner, another Washington institution where elected and appointed government officials past and present socialize with reporters in formal gowns and white tie and tails. News organizations spend huge sums on these events, using them to fête sources and curry favor with senior congressional and administration officials. Losing their cache and prestige in the Swamp that is Washington has been a body blow for them. At the 2018 dinner, the press booked foul-mouthed comedian Michelle Wolf, who lampooned and insulted White House press secretary Sarah Huckabee Sanders, who sat just feet away from the podium, in the most vicious terms imaginable, calling her an "Uncle Tom but for white women."[9] Fellow Trump press aide Mercedes Schlapp and her husband, Matt, were so disgusted that they rose from their table and left the dinner. The episode highlighted another popular media tactic: punish all those who serve President Trump by attempting to destroy their reputations and limit their future career opportunities.

Indeed, almost from the moment Trump won the 2016 election, the Left and the media have resorted to the lowest of tactics: word-twisting, selectively quoting the president or his aides out of context, misreporting or misinterpreting the facts, and sometimes outright lying. For this reason, many of their accusations simply don't hold up under closer examination. These biased reports are, in the phrase Trump has popularized, "fake news."

The most extensive—and totally embarrassing—fake news scam was the two-year investigation of Trump's nonexistent "collusion" with Russia. To that charade we will turn in the next chapter. Here, we will look at a host of other false charges that the media have made against Trump. From the mundane to the insane, from the inane to the outrageous, the media have been willing to say almost anything in their attempts to damage the president's public image—and his chances for reelection in 2020.

In the fall of 2016, an attorney for exotic dancer Stephanie Clifford, who went by the stage name Stormy Daniels, contacted Michael Cohen,

Trump's personal attorney, and negotiated a non-disclosure agreement between Cohen and his client that included a payment of $130,000. The agreement arose out of fresh media inquiries to Clifford about an alleged sexual tryst with Donald Trump, which both parties denied. But with Trump's presidential candidacy came renewed scrutiny—and an opportunity for Clifford to extract a financial payment. Cohen made the payment personally by drawing on a home equity credit line and was in turn paid back by the Trump Organization over the course of the next year for performing ongoing legal work.[10]

In February 2018, Clifford met with Michael Avenatti, a California plaintiff bar attorney whose life was at that very moment spinning out of control. Avenatti was going through a messy and very expensive divorce from his second wife, a former law partner was suing him for stealing from him, a coffee company he had started was about to go bankrupt, and his law firm was bleeding money. Whether to distract from his troubles or revive his legal career, Avenatti took on Clifford as a client and soon turned her case into a three-ring media circus that starred him. He filed a lawsuit in Los Angeles to dissolve the nondisclosure agreement, clearly intending to use it as a fishing expedition to depose President Trump and Trump Organization officials. Trump's attorneys did not take the bait, however; they announced they would not seek to enforce the agreement with Daniels, leaving her free to speak to the media and the public. Avenatti filed a separate defamation lawsuit against Trump, claiming he had defamed her simply by denying an affair.

Trump had always denied having an improper relationship with Daniels—as did she for years. But with Avenatti by her side, her story changed, and she claimed a one-night stand occurred in 2006. She wrote a book, launched a nationwide strip-tease tour, and granted dozens of prominent media interviews to level her charges. Former Playboy model Karen McDougal also went public, producing a document she implied had been written contemporaneously that documented her relationship with Trump, dutifully reported on by Ronan Farrow in the *New Yorker* magazine.[11] But an analysis of the stationary paper on which McDougal wrote the notes indicated that they had to have been written in 2016 or later, meaning that she either made it up or reconstructed recollections a decade or so later after the alleged incidents.[12] While this is not proof by itself of prevarication, it raises serious issues of credibility. Why produce a document that is at least a decade older than advertised, especially when memories are so unreliable? Even more damning was the fact that Farrow and the *New Yorker* editorial staff, famously rigorous in their fact-checking, deliberately presented the notes without giving their date, allowing the readers (and other journalists) to mistakenly believe they had been composed contemporaneously. The episode badly undermined McDougal's credibility and called into question the veracity of her testimony.

Avenatti, meanwhile, became a full-blown media star and appeared on television networks constantly as liberal reporters and cable news hosts pitching him softball questions and hung on his every word like fangirls. In a typical star turn on MSNBC in March 2018, he playfully teased more evidence to prove his client's relationship with Trump. Bragging that good lawyers "don't play their entire hand on the first go-around," he claimed to have "a lot of evidence, a lot of documents that haven't come to light yet. Numerous pieces of evidence, numerous facts, and we're not going to show our hand."[13] The Internet lit up with groundless speculation that Avenatti possessed compromising photographs or tapes of Trump. But Avenatti produced nothing. Still, the media hung on his every word because they needed an ambulance-chasing, publicity-seeking, politically motivated lawyer who shared their irrational hatred of President Trump.

The way the media gushed over Avenatti was embarrassing. Granting him the matinee idol status of a magazine profile and photo spread, the *New York Times* admired his ripped 185-pound physique and 9 percent body fat. Though fighting Trump left Avenatti less time at the gym, the *Times* noted that his "cheeks and chin remain Cubist in their geometry, and in motion, head lowered and shoulders hunched, he still has the bearing of a light-heavyweight brawler." CNN president Jeff Zucker showed up on the network's set to greet Avenatti like a conquering hero.[14] Swooning for his "blue eyes that swirled like infinity pools," in the words of *Vanity Fair* reporter Emily Jane Fox, and impressed by his pugnacity, the media and the Left even began to encourage Avenatti to run for president as a Democrat, hoping he could defeat Trump at the ballot box, if not in the courtroom. Not known for his humility, Avenatti launched an exploratory bid for president and traveled to New Hampshire and other Democratic precincts to showcase his pugilistic, take-no-prisoners style. He boasted at one point, "When they go low, we hit harder."[15]

But the Stormy Daniels traveling circus soon unraveled when none of the allegations trumpeted by the media were proven to be true. Courts in multiple jurisdictions tossed Avenatti's nuisance lawsuits, and Daniels was ordered by the judge in her defamation case to reimburse Trump for $293,000 in legal costs.[16] Daniels, belatedly realizing she had been used, fired her celebrity attorney and accused him of fleecing her by setting up an unauthorized GoFundMe page and pocketing the money. In another extraordinary turn of events, Avenatti was arrested by FBI agents in New York City on March 25, 2019, for a $25 million extortion attempt against Nike[17] and was indicted by a grand jury in California for stealing from his clients and law partners, as well as for income tax evasion. Instead of putting Trump in legal jeopardy, Avenatti now faced the prospect of prison. The media ran from the porn star and her attorney like a dumpster fire. They continued to wait for Godot, searching for the latest shiny object (or scandal) they hoped would destroy Trump.

The media also used the Daniels allegations to shame and demoralize Evangelicals, as we saw previously. "With their reactions to...the Stormy Daniels scandal, the Trump evangelicals have scaled the heights of hypocrisy to the summit," declared a columnist for the *Washington Post*.[18] Democrats piled on, and presidential candidate Pete Buttigieg attacked Evangelicals for their alliance with "a porn-star presidency." Asked about the allegations, Franklin Graham said it was "nobody's business," which sent the media into orbit. Tony Perkins of the Family Research Council said Evangelicals had given Trump "a mulligan" on his personal past, which also sent the media into a paroxysm of ridicule and vitriol. My position on Daniels's allegations has always been that no one can say for certain what, if anything, occurred. But Trump has always denied an improper relationship, as did she until she was represented by Avenatti, and as with the allegations of sexual harassment leveled during the 2016 campaign, Trump deserves the same presumption of innocence as any other American. The various ethical and criminal allegations against Avenatti raise serious doubts about the credibility of his client's charges and his representation.

Recognizing that the Daniels sideshow had produced no credible proof of personal wrongdoing by Trump, the media then fixated on the idea that Trump violated federal campaign finance laws by making the nondisclosure payment. This claim rested on the threadbare theory that the $130,000 payment to Daniels constituted a campaign expenditure, and that by using Cohen and the Trump Organization to make it rather than his campaign committee, Trump had broken the law.

This theory gained even greater currency when Michael Cohen, as part of his plea deal with prosecutors, pleaded guilty to violating campaign finance laws and Trump was named in the plea agreement as "Individual One." The media frenzy over Cohen's plea deal was epic; major news organizations booked as guests and quoted as sources liberal "campaign finance experts" and lawyers who assured them that Trump had engaged in a conspiracy and likely faced criminal charges. The *New York Times* breathlessly recounted that Cohen's plea deal and subsequent court filings "laid bare the most direct evidence to date linking Mr. Trump to potentially criminal conduct" and put "the weight of the Justice Department behind accusations previously made by his former lawyer."[19] Although Cohen did not mention Trump by name, he strongly implied that the then-presidential candidate had directed him to make the nondisclosure payment. Cohen's plea deal "directly implicated Mr. Trump in a federal crime," the *Wall Street Journal* claimed.[20] On MSNBC, former federal prosecutor and Obama appointee Joyce Vance could barely contain her glee. "The felony crime is a serious one, it carries a lot of collateral consequences," Vance said. "But most significantly is the threat there is jail time involved, and any amount of jail time in the state system in New York would be very unpleasant for the president of the United States."[21] The media went wild over this accusation, labeling Trump an "unindicted co-conspirator" of the alleged crime.

This language was intentionally inflammatory. Richard Nixon had been an unindicted co-conspirator in the Watergate scandal, which eventually led to his resignation. Evidently the Left was convinced that if they could pin this campaign finance violation on Trump, it could spell his downfall as well.

A few voices in the media warned against the hasty use of this terminology. Alan Dershowitz, a rare voice of reason in the midst of a media lynch mob, wrote in the *Washington Examiner*, "let me state categorically that Trump is not an unindicted co-conspirator and that it is wrong to characterize him as such.... Unlike President Richard Nixon, who had been named an unindicted co-conspirator in an indictment handed down by a grand jury, Trump has not been accused by a grand jury indictment of anything thus far. Cohen's guilty plea and allocution cannot turn the president into an unindicted co-conspirator. Only a grand jury can."[22]

Other legal analysts agreed that there were serious problems with the case. Samuel Estreicher and David Moosmann, writing for Justia. com, warned the media and the Far Left against premature celebration: "Some commentators have suggested that these violations of the Federal Election Campaign Act (FECA) could form the predicate for a bill of impeachment against the president. It may be too soon, however, to pop the champagne corks, for at least with respect to the $130,000 'hush' payment of adult film star Stormy Daniels, it is far from clear that the president has violated federal election law."[23] The specific charge in question was that Cohen had contributed more than $2,700 (the legal cap) to Trump's campaign by paying for Daniels's silence. Estreicher and Moosmann pointed out that this payment could not necessarily be described as a campaign expense: "monies paid for a different purpose—say, to avoid personal embarrassment or family hardship—would not fall within the ambit of the campaign finance laws." Besides that, since Trump reimbursed Cohen, "the Daniels payment ultimately involved the president's own money, which makes it doubtful that a campaign contribution or expenditure within the meaning of federal campaign law occurred in this case."

The accusation that Trump had violated campaign finance laws was specious. In a far more egregious case, federal prosecutors charged former Democratic presidential candidate John Edwards in 2011 with six felony counts for arranging nearly one million dollars in payments from big campaign donors (some of it was cash transported in shoe boxes) to hide his mistress from the media and the public, as well as to keep her pregnancy with their child a secret. The Justice Department claimed that the expenditures were excessive and unreported campaign expenses because Edwards "knew that the public revelation of the affair and pregnancy would undermine his image and force his campaign to divert personnel and resources away from campaign activities to respond to criticism and media scrutiny."[24] But a jury acquitted Edwards, finding that he had many other reputational and personal reasons to keep the affair a secret, delivering a stinging rebuke to the government. The allegations about Daniels were about an alleged incident that had occurred ten years earlier, long before Trump was a candidate. Had the nondisclosure payment been made by his campaign, he could have been charged with using campaign funds to pay for personal or business expenses. In fact, the law forbids a candidate from converting campaign funds to "personal use," and defines "personal use" as spending "used to fulfill any commitment, obligation, or expense of a person that would exist irrespective of the candidate's election campaign."[25] Many candidates have been indicted for using campaign funds for personal expenses, including former congressman Jesse Jackson Jr., who served time in prison. It is a serious offense. The same media critics who brayed that Trump violated federal election law by making the nondisclosure payment to Clifford would have claimed that he had used campaign funds for a personal expense and evaded personal income taxes had he done so with campaign money.

Yet the media raged on, convincing themselves that Trump was in imminent legal jeopardy. As allegations of colluding with Russia began to look like a dry hole, the media claimed that Trump's biggest exposure was not the investigation by Special Counsel Robert Mueller, but the investigation in the Southern District of New York, where the U.S. Attorney's Office was scrutinizing payments by the Trump Organization. This drumbeat went on for months. As was always the case with the liberal media's reporting of "bombshells," it amounted to absolutely nothing. On July 17, 2019, the U.S. Attorney's Office announced in a court filing that the investigation had been closed.[26] Jay Sekulow, a personal attorney for President Trump, claimed vindication. "We are pleased that the investigation surrounding these ridiculous campaign finance allegations is now closed," he told *Politico*. "We have maintained from the outset that the President never engaged in any campaign finance violation.... Another case is closed."[27]

Daniels slipped back into obscurity. Avenatti prepared for multiple trials in New York and California on criminal charges and was later arrested by federal agents for violating the terms of his pretrial release. The media never admitted they were wrong, but simply moved on, refusing to acknowledge that they had misled the public in their fevered pursuit of Trump.

Contrary to the distortions of their critics, for Evangelical Christians, the issue involved in the payments to Clifford and McDougal was not approval of the alleged misconduct, if it did occur. The issue was fairness and the presumption of innocence. In the Old Testament, charges of personal impropriety required more than one witness. Trump's main accusers had no corroborating witnesses and no factual evidence. In the Clifford case, those making the charges were either proven liars or individuals whose reliability was suspect: Cohen had admitted previously to lying under oath to Congress and pleaded guilty to evading taxes. Avenatti had faced multiple criminal charges for attempted extortion and embezzling from his clients. And Clifford had claimed for years that she never had a sexual encounter with Trump before she changed her story. But for the liberal media, every allegation directed at Trump was true, and every charge, however specious, was grist for the mill pointing to impeachment, prison, or both.

There is nothing especially new about the liberal bias of the establishment media. But the sheer number, ferocity, and shamelessness of news media stories that were either distortions or outright lies is probably without precedent in recent American history. Consider just a few of the media's greatest "fake news" hits.

When Trump said that his predecessors had allowed China to take advantage of the U.S. for decades and it had fallen to him to stand up to notorious trade abuses, he glanced heavenward and said, "I'm the chosen one." Rather than treat Trump's comment as a light-hearted remark, the media went into hysterics. CNN proclaimed in a headline on its website, "Yes, Donald Trump really believes he is 'the chosen one.'"[28] Reuters reported that Trump was "claiming a title often used to refer to religious figures such as Jesus and Mohammed," while Axios asserted "the remark was Trump's second messianic comparison of the day," including a retweet of a fan who praised him for his defense of Jews and Israel.[29] The episode revealed "why some evangelicals see him as 'God's Chosen One'—a King Cyrus-like figure, anointed by God to save America from cultural collapse," according to the Religion News Service. It was "a pastiche of certain kinds of evangelical and End Time beliefs that are merging together along with conspiracy theories to empower his presidency with the evangelicals that back him."[30] After days of media hysterics, Trump said on Twitter that the comment had been made in jest and sarcasm, and when he was asked about it as he departed for an international summit with the G-7 countries in France, he denounced the media for knowing he never seriously considered himself to be the Second Coming of the Messiah. But the liberal media will never turn down an opportunity to run with a fraudulent story if they believe it discredits him and his Evangelical supporters.

Another media-generated falsehood claimed that children who crossed the U.S. southern border illegally have been separated from their parents because of a Trump administration policy. The media hype about the humanitarian crisis at the Mexican border and the alleged heartless separation of immigrant children from their families is designed to make Trump look hostile to children and families. Democratic representative Bennie Thompson's accusation to the Capitol Hill newspaper *Roll Call* was typical: "President Trump's zero tolerance and family separation policies inflicted massive pain and trauma on children and their families—but the suffering did not end there," Thompson argued. "Systematic inadequate care, as well as the added chaos that the administration constantly makes worse, created an environment where children suffered from post-traumatic stress and other critical mental health issues. These issues can impact these children for life."[31] Democratic members of Congress and presidential candidates made a publicity-driven rush to the border so they could condemn the facilities in which children and their parents were being held.

I certainly don't support separating children from their parents. In June 2018, I called on the Trump administration and Congress to act to end the practice. "The separation of families illegally crossing the border is heartbreaking and tragic, part of the larger tragedy of a broken immigration system that does not reflect our values or our faith," Faith & Freedom Coalition said in a statement.[32] No doubt there are major challenges in providing adequate care to the surge of minor aliens now being detained at the southern border. But blaming Trump is unfair and inaccurate. Alien minors were separated from the general population of detained illegal immigrants for twenty years prior to Trump's becoming president under the *Flores v. Reno Settlement Agreement* in 1997. The agreement emerged from a series of lawsuits filed against the federal government over the detention of unaccompanied alien minors and ruled that the government must release such children to a parent or guardian "without unnecessary delay." In 2015, Obama-appointed federal district court judge Dolly Gee interpreted the *Flores* settlement to include accompanied alien minors as well. As Matthew Sussis of the Center for Immigration Studies has explained, "Judge Gee...went a step further. *Flores* calls on the government to release children 'without unnecessary delay'. Gee interpreted that to mean twenty days. In other words, now all minors in detention, whether or not they were with their parents, couldn't be detained for more than three weeks. This ruling laid the groundwork for the current crisis at the border, in which children are released while their parents can still be detained awaiting hearings—hence, the 'separation' of families."[33]

Contrary to the media's claims, Trump is the president that finally ended the practice of separating illegal immigrant families in detention. In June 2018, Trump issued an executive order to end the practice of separation at the border: "The Attorney General shall promptly file a request...to modify the Settlement Agreement in *Flores v. Sessions*...in a manner that would permit the Secretary, under present resource constraints, to detain alien families together throughout the pendency of...immigration proceedings."[34] But this executive order did not satisfy either the Left or the media. On National Public Radio, Michelle Brané, director of the Migrant Rights and Justice Program at the Women's Refugee Commission, alleged that Trump's order "effectively creates family prisons." Karen Tumlin at the National Immigration Law Center concurred: "The president doesn't get any Brownie points for moving from a policy of locking up kids and families separately to a policy of locking them up together," Tumlin said. "Let's be clear: Trump is making a crisis of his own creation worse."[35] When the Trump administration took steps to separate several hundred children from adults with criminal backgrounds or who were not their parents as a preventative measure against human trafficking, Michelle Goldstein of the *New York Times* responded, "There are kids in this country being systematically brutalized by the American government, and it's hard to keep that in the forefront of your mind all the time without going mad."[36] The only thing going mad is a media establishment suffering from an extreme case of Trump Derangement Syndrome.

Arguably the most irresponsible accusation from the media is that Trump is a "racist" who said there were "very fine people on both sides" at a white supremacist rally in Charlottesville, Virginia, in August 2017, in which one counter-protester was killed. This false media narrative suggesting that Trump praised neo-Nazis and white nationalists has been repeated so many times that many now believe it is true. As is usually the case with fake news, it is also a prominent Democratic talking point. When Joe Biden announced his presidential candidacy in April 2019, he claimed in a campaign video, "With those words, the president of the United States assigned a moral equivalence between those spreading hate and those with the courage to stand against it."

There's one problem with this claim: President Trump said the exact opposite. After being criticized for initially condemning bigotry on "all sides" after the Charlottesville violence, Trump delivered remarks from the Diplomatic Room in the White House on August 14, 2017, two days after the rally, in which he said:

> [W]e condemn in the strongest possible terms this egregious display of bigotry, hatred, and violence. It has no place in America. And as I have said many times before, no matter the color of our skin, we all live under the same laws; we all salute the same great flag; and we are all made by the same almighty God. We must love each other, show affection for each other, and unite together in condemnation of hatred, bigotry, and violence. We must discover the bonds of love and loyalty that bring us together as Americans. Racism is evil, and those who cause violence in its name are criminals and thugs, including the KKK, neo-Nazis, white supremacists, and other hate groups that are repugnant to everything we hold dear as Americans. We are a nation founded on the truth that all of us are created equal. We are equal in the eyes of our creator, we are equal under the law, and we are equal under our Constitution. Those who spread violence in the name of bigotry strike at the very core of America.[37]

From the White House, Trump condemned bigotry and racism in no uncertain terms in all its ugly forms as inherently evil. He went further, naming names and specifically singling out for condemnation the Ku Klux Klan, white nationalists, and neo-Nazis. The next day, Trump held a news conference on his administration's infrastructure plan at Trump Tower in New York City on August 15, 2017. There were very few questions about infrastructure. The media horde only wanted to ask him about whether he supported racists and white nationalists. After a reporter said that "the neo-Nazis started this" because they "showed up in Charlottesville to protest," Trump said the following, which is provided in its full context:

> TRUMP: Well, I do think there's blame, yes, I think there's blame on both sides. You look at both sides. I think there's blame on both sides. And I have no doubt about it. And you don't have any doubt about it either. And, and if you reported it accurately, you would say it.
> [CROSSTALK]
> TRUMP: Excuse me. You had some very bad people in that group. But you also had people that were very fine people on both sides. You had people in that group, excuse me, excuse me, I saw the same pictures as you did. You had people in that group that were there to protest the taking down of, to them, a very, very important statue and the renaming of a park, from Robert E. Lee to another name.
> REPORTER: George Washington and Robert E. Lee are not the same.
> TRUMP: George Washington was a slave owner. Was George Washington a slave owner? So will George Washington now lose his status? Are we going to take down—excuse me, are we going to take down statues to George Washington? How about Thomas Jefferson? What do you think of Thomas Jefferson? You like him?"

REPORTER: I do love Thomas Jefferson.

TRUMP: Okay, good. Are we going to take down the statue? Because he was a major slave owner. Now, are we going to take down his statue? So you know what, it's fine. You're changing history. You're changing culture. And you had people—and I'm not talking about the neo-Nazis and the white nationalists—because they should be condemned totally. But you had many people in that group other than neo-Nazis and white nationalists. Okay? And the press has treated them absolutely unfairly.[38]

As the transcript makes clear, Trump's reference to "very fine people on both sides" referred to peaceful, law-abiding protesters who either favored or opposed removing a statue of Robert E. Lee and renaming a park that bore his name. He made it clear that he was "not talking about the neo-Nazis and the white nationalists because they should be condemned totally." So Trump did not praise white nationalists; he strongly condemned them. As for the racially motivated violence that led to the death of a counter-protester, Trump said, "I thought what took place was a horrible moment for our country—a horrible moment." The argument that he somehow gave his blessing to white nationalism, neo-Nazism, or racism is a complete lie. Confronted with both transcripts, the media were reduced to condemning Trump's alleged use of "dog whistles," which is another term used when Trump's actual words are not what the media claim they are.

When it comes to Trump, the media don't limit themselves to just smearing the president. Any of his political allies, White House staff, cabinet members, and family members are fair game, too. The examples are too numerous to detail here; these are just the most egregious of the attempts to destroy Trump's friends, family, and supporters on charges that range from petty to out-and-out false.

In March 2018, the media ferreted out an embarrassing story about Ben Carson, the secretary of the Department of Housing and Urban

Development (HUD). Carson had run for the 2016 Republican presidential nomination, but he became one of the first to endorse Trump for president after dropping out from the race. In March 2018—while the department was facing major budget cuts from the White House—word got out that Carson (reportedly with the involvement of his wife) had allegedly ordered a furniture set costing thirty-one thousand dollars to refurbish one of his conference rooms.[39] The media decried this lavish expenditure, "which might have violated a federal law requiring congressional approval for any office renovation expense exceeding $5,000."[40] The former chief administrative officer for HUD claimed that she was punished with a demotion when she objected to the procurement. Carson said he hadn't known about the purchase, and he immediately canceled the order. It was too late to save him from media mockery. CNN's Chris Cillizza predicted that Carson's gaffe would lead to his sacking: "Trump has promised more staff shakeups.... It's impossible for the timing of this story to happen at a worse time for Carson's longevity in the job. Trump is looking for more heads to roll. Carson just voluntarily put his head on the chopping block."[41] Despite this and other gleeful predictions, Ben Carson remained in his position and in Trump's confidence. In September 2019, after more than a year of investigation, the inspector general of HUD cleared Carson of any wrongdoing. The inspector found that the decision to replace the conference room furniture was made by career civil servants, not by Carson, and neither he nor his wife "exerted improper influence on any departmental employee in connection with the procurement."[42]

The Left has also leveled attacks at Trump's senior White House counselor, Kellyanne Conway, who in 2016 became the first woman in American history to successfully manage a presidential campaign to victory. Because Conway, a pro-life conservative and faithful Roman Catholic, represented such a rebuke to the feminist conception of women in power, the long knives were out for her from the moment she entered the White House. In February 2017 during an interview with *Fox and Friends*, one of the hosts asked about the president's daughter Ivanka.

Conway praised Ivanka as a "very successful businesswoman" and a "champion for women empowerment." Nordstrom had just announced it was dropping Ivanka's line of clothing and accessories from its department stores. Defending the president's daughter, Conway—in what was clearly a gesture of kindness and support—praised Ivanka's clothing line, said she owned some items from the line, and mentioned that people should "go buy it today, everybody."[43] Liberals, Democrats on Capitol Hill, and the media quickly pounced. Larry Noble, the left-wing former general counsel of the Federal Election Commission, claimed Conway "may have violated the law." Laurence Tribe, the liberal Harvard constitutional law professor, dutifully told the *New York Times* that Conway was "attempting quite crudely to enrich Ivanka and therefore the president's family."[44] Congressman Elijah Cummings of Maryland signed a letter to a government ethics watchdog calling for disciplinary action and panned Conway's comment as "a textbook violation of government ethics laws and regulations enacted to prevent the abuse of an employee's government position."[45]

When Conway criticized Doug Jones—the Democratic candidate for the U.S. Senate in Alabama—in November 2017, she was accused of violating federal law, even though White House officials in previous administrations had publicly discussed federal candidates for decades. Walter Shaub, a former ethics director under the Obama administration, filed an official complaint against Conway, alleging that she had broken the Hatch Act, "which prohibits White House officials from advocating for or against candidates, even in media interviews."[46] When these attacks did not stop Conway from exercising her right to speak about candidates, the Office of Special Counsel recommended in June 2019 that Trump dismiss her.[47] The president refused and continued to fully support Conway.

But the media still weren't done. While Kellyanne was one of Trump's most trusted advisors, her husband, George, became a critic, sharing his views on Twitter and in the media. During an interview on Fox News in March 2019, Chris Wallace insisted that "this is not something I'm comfortable talking about," then proceeded to ask probing personal questions, including, "Has this hurt your marriage?"[48] Wallace's question had nothing to do with Conway's official duties at the White House. To her credit, Conway stood her ground, declining to answer irrelevant questions about her personal life. But this is how the media treat anyone who defends Donald Trump. The media frequently lash out at Trump for allegedly violating decorum and "constitutional norms," but have no use for protocol or norms when it comes to attacking Trump or those who serve him.

Consider the case of Jared Kushner, the president's son-in-law and senior advisor in the White House. In order to perform his duties, Kushner applied for "Top Secret" security clearance in January 2017. This is a fairly routine classification for a senior White House official with Kushner's responsibilities. But after receiving his interim security clearance, in February 2018, Kushner's status was changed to a "secret" clearance, purportedly due to concerns by career officials about his business dealings and alleged foreign influence, as well as the ongoing Mueller investigation.[49] The media went into overdrive, implying that Kushner posed a potential security threat. The *Washington Post* opined in a news story that "the internal debate over Kushner's clearance revives questions about the severity of the issues flagged in his background investigation and Kushner's access to government secrets."[50] This was nonsense. In May 2018, Kushner was granted permanent "Top Secret" clearance, but the media weren't done throwing dirt at Trump's son-in-law. NBC claimed that "two career White House security specialists after an FBI background check raised concerns about potential foreign influence on him—but their supervisor overruled the recommendation and approved the clearance."[51] The cited concerns included allegations that "officials in at least four countries had privately discussed ways they could manipulate Kushner by taking advantage of his complex business arrangements, financial difficulties, and lack of foreign policy experience. Among those nations...were the United Arab Emirates, China, Israel, and Mexico." Kushner refused to address the controversy beyond pointing out that he had been the target of many baseless charges, all of them proven false. As with his wife, Ivanka, Kushner has been targeted for heavy flak from the biased media specifically because he has been effective in advising President Trump and advancing his agenda. It has been my great privilege to work with Jared on many issues, particularly on criminal justice reform. I found him to be bright, extremely collegial, loyal to his father-in-law, and very effective. The attacks on him have been despicable, but unfortunately it comes with the job in which he serves.

Another example of fake news concerned Anthony Scaramucci, a former White House communications director. In June 2017, CNN published a story on its website linking Scaramucci to "a Russian investment fund supposedly being investigated by the Senate."[52] At the time, with the Mueller inquiry underway and Scaramucci's name circulating as a possible senior member of the White House staff, it was an explosive allegation. Scaramucci immediately denounced the story as false. CNN quickly took down the story and fired the three journalists who wrote it. An internal investigation by CNN found the story had been published without proper fact-checking due to a "breakdown in editorial workflow."[53] The network never admitted that the story was false, merely that it did not meet publishing standards. But the piece's retraction and the subsequent resignation of the journalists clearly showed that the media were intent on destroying the reputation of anyone supportive of or close to Trump. Scaramucci, who only lasted for ten days as White House communications director, publicly swore his loyalty to Trump despite being fired, then later publicly attacked him and eventually joined the resistance, linking arms with the same media that had once smeared him. He may be an example of someone who decided to switch sides rather than endure the punishing hostility of the media towards anyone who serves or supports President Trump.

The result of all this fake news has been a complete collapse in the credibility of the news media, which is not good or healthy for a free society. For example, a recent survey by Gallup found the media to be among the least trusted institutions in American society. Between 2003 and 2016, the percentage of Americans who said they trusted the media fell from 54 percent to 32 percent of those surveyed. Among all adults,

69 percent said their trust in the media had declined. Among conservatives, 95 percent said their trust in the media has decreased in the past decade, and over a third expected that loss of trust to be permanent. The main reasons why are not surprising: bias, inaccuracy, and a lack of transparency.[54] The media are so irreparably damaging their credibility with the American people through a constant and unremitting assault on President Trump and anyone associated with him that they may not be able to recover. Perhaps the media do not care because they are so blinded by their hatred for Trump. But all of us benefit from a free and vibrant press, and our republic suffers when the media are viewed (for good reason) with suspicion and distrust. If the media really cared about a free press and about democracy, they would stop acting like a wholly-owned subsidiary of the Democratic Party, treat all sides fairly, bend over backwards to get the story right or refrain from publishing it, and end the all-out assault on Trump. Their job is to report the news and get the facts right—not "get" someone with whom they disagree politically.

The choice will ultimately be the media's to make. As we saw with the Russia hoax, the media only hurt their own credibility when they chase the phantasm of a story without bothering to see if the fact pattern fits their ideologically inspired hopes and desires. It is to that debacle and its aftermath that we now turn.

CHAPTER 15

RUSSIA, UKRAINE, AND IMPEACHMENT

I t had been a bad week for the *New York Times*.

On August 12, 2019, executive editor Dean Baquet hastily convened a town hall meeting with *New York Times* staff to address the public backlash that the paper had been receiving. The previous week, Baquet had made a humiliating oversight: he ran a headline about Trump that didn't portray him as racist enough.[1] Liberal readers and many in the newsroom were up in arms over the editorial oversight. During his apology, Baquet briefly mentioned another long-running *Times* story that had flopped: the Trump-Russia collusion narrative. "The day Bob Mueller walked off that witness stand...I think that the story changed," the executive editor admitted. "We're a little tiny bit flat-footed. I mean, that's what happens when a story looks a certain way for two years."

A "little tiny bit flat-footed" was a vast understatement. The *New York Times*, which prides itself on being the "paper of record" for the entire media establishment, was suffering a severe crisis of credibility. The *Times* and the entire elite media had to confront the devastating truth that they had poured untold sums of money and editorial resources for two years into systematically developing and promoting a story that turned out to be brazenly false. Of all the fake news that has been woven around Trump and those who support him, none is more misleading— nor more baseless or more nefarious—than the unsupported allegation that he colluded with Russia to steal the 2016 election. Yet many on the Left remain convinced that the president is the compromised asset of a foreign power and has committed treason. Even after the Mueller investigation found no evidence that President Trump colluded with Russia, an astonishing 64 percent of Democrats still wanted Trump impeached largely based on the myth that Trump won the White House because of election interference by Russia.[2]

I have seen this derangement syndrome up close, and it is astonishing. I was in a meeting of business and government leaders in 2018 in which James Clapper, the former Director of National Intelligence (DNI) under Barack Obama, said with a straight face that he believed, based on the number of impressions and individuals reached on Facebook by Russian intelligence, that Russia had thrown the 2016 election to Trump. I listened in disbelief. As someone who oversees digital ad buys reaching tens of millions of Christian voters through Faith & Freedom Coalition, I knew such a claim by a former senior U.S. intelligence official could only be based on willful ignorance or deliberate malice. According to testimony before the Senate Intelligence Committee, the Russians only spent about $46,000 on pre-election digital ads on Facebook, most of them reaching individuals who did not live in battleground states that decided the election. By contrast, the Hillary Clinton and Trump campaigns spent $81 million on Facebook ads prior to the election. Clapper mentioned that the Russian troll farm placed ads that reached 126 million people on Facebook and 20 million people on Instagram. Sounds impressive. But it is not. One out of four of the ads were never seen by anyone, 56 percent of the ads ran after the election, and 99 percent of the Russian ad buys were for less than $1,000. On a platform like Facebook with over 1.4 billion people and billions of impressions, this is like spitting into a hurricane. The Russians were so incompetent that they didn't even upload voter registration information into their targeting, so their ads did not reach actual voters. They scattershot the ads to states like California, New York, and Texas, meaning that the vast majority of the impressions were to non-voters in states that did not affect the election. Even among these individuals the Russian-sponsored ads amounted to less than four-tenths of 1 percent (.004 percent) of over 23,000 stories in their news feed. The idea that in a $2.4 billion presidential election a $46,000 Facebook ad buy that mostly went to unregistered voters decided the outcome is laughable on its face.[3]

Still, for over two years the world's greatest democracy consumed itself with the narrative that Donald Trump had colluded with Russia to win the 2016 election. This narrative drove the appointment of a special counsel by the U.S. Justice Department, sparked an impeachment inquiry by six committees in the House, generated two separate investigations by the House and Senate Intelligence Committees, and became the subject of countless "bombshell" breaking news stories by the establishment media, many of which were misleading or completely false. None of the charges leveled against Trump were proven because none are true. Yet lives and careers were destroyed, numerous people went to prison while others remained under the cloud of suspicion, and otherwise outstanding public servants ran up millions of dollars in legal bills. For what? What are the origins of this narrative, and what has made it persist?

The pervasiveness of the Russia hoax lies in part in the fact that it is not a single narrative. It is based on a loose collection of incidents—some related, some not—that have been thoroughly mashed up, mixed, and poured into the mold of collusion by the Left and the media. Because the real story is far more complex than the narrative the elite news media provide, it has been difficult for the ordinary American to sort out what actually happened.

The Russia hoax has multiple "origin stories." This is partly a result of the partisan struggle over the narrative, a fact that *National Review* writer Andrew McCarthy laments: "The 'when it all began' question is driven by the political battle to dictate the narrative. That should never be the case. Questions about when and why an investigation starts involve matters of objective fact."[4] Sifting out the objective fact from the twisted fact has been a difficult task. Nevertheless, a few important truths have come to light.

Various news outlets have tried to present different events as the first spark of the Russia investigation. One of their first targets was Carter Page. Page, a former naval intelligence officer and businessman with investments in the Russia energy sector, briefly joined the Trump campaign as a foreign policy advisor from March to September in 2016. At the time, Trump had difficulty attracting high-level advisors from the foreign policy establishment because of his outsider status and unconventional views. The amount of work that Page did for the campaign is unclear, and he parted with Trump after a September 26 Yahoo News article reported that intelligence officials were looking into his connections with Russia.[5] Months after Page had left the campaign, the media picked up his story again in an attempt to use it against Trump. In April 2017, the *New York Times* declared ominously that the "Trump Advisor's Visit to Moscow Got the F.B.I.'s Attention."[6] Page had indeed given a speech at the New Economic School in Moscow in July 2016, where he expounded on his pro-Russia policy views. But the *New York Times* report also insisted that Page's suspicious Moscow trips were the "catalyst" for the bureau's investigations into Trump's connections with Russia. But this is getting the story backward. Trump's investigation didn't start because of Page. In fact, Page was being investigated precisely with the aim of damaging Trump.

How do we know this? In October 2016, shortly after Page had left the Trump campaign, the FBI obtained a Foreign Intelligence Surveillance Act (FISA) warrant to monitor Page's communications—apparently because there was "probable cause to believe [he] was acting as an agent of a foreign power, in this case Russia."[7] What was the basis of this "probable cause"? It wasn't just the fact that Page had unorthodox, Russia-friendly foreign policy views. That was not a crime. The FISA warrant was granted to investigate more serious allegations, namely that Page, "while on a trip to Moscow in July 2016, had met with two senior

Russian representatives and discussed matters like lifting sanctions imposed on Russia for its intervention in Ukraine."[8]

These false claims—Page was never accused of any substantive crime and never tried to get U.S. sanctions against Russia lifted—were drawn from the now infamous dossier written by the British ex-spy Christopher Steele for the opposition research firm Fusion GPS. But the dossier was not a piece of solid intelligence work; it was campaign opposition research based on unsubstantiated rumors and uncorroborated charges by anonymous sources. In April 2016, Fusion GPS had been hired by the law firm Perkins Coie to conduct an opposition research project against Trump on behalf of the Democratic National Committee and Hillary Clinton's campaign.[9] So the allegations that allowed the FBI to get a surveillance warrant on Carter Page actually came from a document that had been created for the express purpose of smearing Trump and defeating him. It wasn't Page's conduct that had sparked the Russia investigation; it was a Democrat-funded ploy to bring Trump down, and Page got caught in the crossfire.

But before the biased origins of the Steele dossier had come to light, Special Counsel Robert Mueller had already begun to conduct his two-and-a-half-year-long investigation into Russia's alleged interference in the 2016 election. The series of events that led to Mueller's appointment provide another example of how some FBI officials skirted due process in order to hobble and ultimately destroy the president. It also gives a prime example of how the media contort a complex chain of events into a simple, essentially false narrative.

The trouble started before Trump had been inaugurated. In late December of 2016, outgoing president Barack Obama, after doing little to prevent Russia's meddling in the 2016 campaign or inform the American people of the threat posed by it, imposed sanctions on Russia after the election. The Obama administration also released a declassified report by the six major intelligence agencies concluding that Russia had interfered in the election and had done so in an attempt to assist Trump.[10] Then on January 6, FBI director James Comey and then-Director of National Intelligence

James Clapper briefed Trump on these findings at his office in Trump Tower in New York. It was Trump's first meeting with Comey since being elected president. At the conclusion of the meeting, Comey pulled the president-elect aside and informed him that the FBI possessed explosive intelligence about him, and he mentioned a salacious and unproven allegation about Trump's being in the presence of prostitutes at a hotel in Moscow. Trump informed Comey that the allegation was not true. According to Comey, Trump replied, "Do I look like a guy who needs hookers?" Comey left the meeting, got in the back seat of a government vehicle, and immediately wrote a memorandum of recollection about the conversation. His driver then took him to an FBI secure communications site in New Jersey where he participated in a video conference with Deputy Director Andrew McCabe and other FBI officials. In the worst tradition of J. Edgar Hoover, Comey had hot-boxed Trump, letting him know in a not-so-subtle way that he had embarrassing and damaging information in his files about the president-elect and then recorded for posterity the president's reaction. Unbeknownst to Trump, this entire episode was part of a counter-intelligence investigation launched by the FBI the previous summer—an investigation that included surveilling a former campaign advisor. Also unknown to Trump was the fact that the allegation came from a dossier compiled by an opposition research firm working for Hillary Clinton's campaign. When Trump asked Comey if he was under investigation, Comey assured him he was not.

When the Obama administration imposed sanctions and ejected Russian diplomats from the U.S., Russian ambassador Sergey Kislyak contacted Michael Flynn, Trump's incoming national security advisor. Kislyak and Flynn had a phone conversation during which Flynn simply advised Kislyak not to escalate the situation, assuring him that the Trump administration would review the matter as soon as it took office.[11] He did not promise Kislyak that Trump would lift the sanctions. Flynn also urged Kislyak to delay or oppose a resolution introduced by Egypt at the United Nations condemning Israel over Jewish settlements on the West Bank. The Obama administration, still upset about Prime Minister

Benjamin "Bibi" Netanyahu's 2015 reelection victory (after Obama's political team decamped to Israel to try to defeat him) and reeling over Clinton's losing the U.S. election to Bibi's good friend Donald Trump, had decided not to veto the resolution. So in the waning days of the Obama administration, the U.S. government turned its back on the state of Israel, choosing in the most cowardly fashion imaginable to abstain from voting on a United Nations resolution attacking the Jewish state. Flynn and other incoming Trump officials scrambled to stave off the resolution until they took office.[12]

The FBI was recording this conversation. Even though Flynn had said nothing inappropriate during the phone call, the FBI soon found a way to get Flynn, and by association the president. On January 24, Flynn's second full day working at the White House, Comey sent two agents, including Peter Strzok, to the White House to interview Flynn. In so doing, Comey violated protocol—and did so purposely. As former Assistant U.S. Attorney Andrew McCarthy notes, "an interview of a member of the president's staff is supposed to be sought by the Attorney General through the White House Counsel. That way, there's nothing sneaky: the White House Counsel has an opportunity to be present, and the official sought for an interview can be advised."[13] Comey himself later admitted that he deliberately disregarded due process: "I probably wouldn't have...gotten away with [it] in a more organized investigation, a more organized administration," Comey bragged at an event for his book tour in December 2018. "I thought, 'It's early enough, let's just send a couple of guys over.'"[14] It wasn't the first or last time Comey acted in a duplicitous manner.

During the interview, the agents asked Flynn if he had spoken about sanctions or the anti-Israel U.N. resolution during his phone calls with Ambassador Sergey Kislyak the previous month. Inexplicably, Flynn insisted he had not. The interview took place without the presence of a lawyer for Flynn, either a personal attorney or a lawyer from the White House Counsel's Office. The FBI agents knew this, and they also knew the answers to all their questions; the FBI had recorded the conversation.

Making matters worse, Flynn not only misled the FBI, but he also denied having the sanctions discussion to Vice President Pence and others in the White House.

Within a matter of days, someone leaked the contents of the December calls with Kislyak, and a media firestorm ensued. The media rushed to judgment, implying that Flynn had tried to cover up the content of the calls because he intended to encourage Trump to lift the sanctions on Russia. This was still more proof of Trump's allegedly pro-Russia leanings, which many in the media attributed to Vladimir Putin's "having something" on Trump. There was loose talk that even by talking to the Russian ambassador Flynn had violated the Logan Act, a "a centuries-old law aimed at keeping private citizens out of foreign affairs," as the *Washington Post* described it.[15] This was a ridiculous charge. First, Flynn had acted in his capacity as the incoming national security advisor to the president-elect during a presidential transition. Second, the Logan Act may be "centuries old," but it has resulted in only two indictments and zero convictions in its entire 220-year history. This is because, as Andrew McCarthy explains, the Logan Act is "an almost certainly unconstitutional artifact of the late eighteenth century" that has never been enforced because of its "impossibly vague" wording.[16]

Despite the absurd accusations and the FBI's violating protocol in interviewing Flynn, his career in public service was over. On February 13, 2017, he resigned from his position as national security advisor. The next day, Trump met with James Comey in the Oval Office. During that conversation—according to a memo that Comey wrote shortly afterward—Trump said, "I hope you can see your way clear to letting this go, to letting Flynn go. He is a good guy. I hope you can let this go."[17] Comey would later claim that he interpreted these words to mean that Trump wanted him to end the investigation into Flynn, but Trump never said that. He didn't end the investigation, of course. But he did retain a copy of the memo about the conversation. In fact, he continued to write detailed memos of many of his private conversations with Trump, which he kept in a safe in his home, which constituted a violation of federal law and FBI policy.

In the ensuing weeks, the conflict between Comey and the White House escalated. Slowly and perhaps belatedly, the White House came to realize that Trump was a target of the Russia investigation. On May 9, 2017, Trump, knowing he had done nothing wrong and angry at being placed under a cloud of suspicion by a rogue FBI director, decided he had had enough and fired Comey. A seasoned bureaucratic infighter, Comey retaliated by passing his damning memoranda to a professor at Columbia University who he had placed on a retainer as an "advisor" to the FBI, instructing his friend to give it to the *New York Times*. In this devious (and illegal) manner, Comey leaked highly confidential FBI investigatory material, including private conversations with the president that involved classified information, in clear violation of the law. The *New York Times* predictably treated the February 14 memo as a smoking gun that proved that a coverup and attempted obstruction of justice by President Trump had taken place. Comey later testified that he leaked the memo because he "thought that might prompt the appointment of a special counsel."[18]

Indeed, it did. Attorney General Jeff Sessions recused himself from the case on the dubious grounds that he had been involved in the Trump campaign as a leading surrogate. On May 17, Deputy Attorney General Rod Rosenstein appointed Robert Mueller to investigate attempts by the Russian government to meddle in the 2016 election and any links to the Trump campaign. In one of the most extraordinary abuses of power in modern American history, the FBI opened a counterintelligence operation against a U.S. presidential campaign, obtained secret surveillance warrants from a FISA court using opposition research assembled by the candidate's opponent (without disclosing it to the court), and then attempted to intimidate and ultimately bring down the president of the United States by threatening him with the half-baked evidence. When this failed, a former FBI director violated Justice Department and FBI regulations and the law by leaking contents of internal classified material to the liberal news media.

I do not know James Comey. But I have friends who served with him in the George W. Bush administration, and they warned me at the time

278 FOR GOD AND COUNTRY

that one should never turn their back on him. They also told me he was a shameless self-promoter. Let me give just one example of why in an episode that took place long before Donald Trump ran for president.

In early 2004, the Bush White House was working to extend a critical terrorist surveillance program under the Patriot Act. Some in the Justice Department objected to the program. At the time, Attorney General John Ashcroft was hospitalized after surgery to remove his appendix. Comey, then deputy attorney general, learned that White House chief of staff Andy Card and counsel Alberto Gonzales were on their way to Ashcroft's hospital room to obtain his signature on documents reauthorizing the surveillance program. In Comey's later telling, he heroically rushed to the hospital, the red lights on his official government car flashing, to save the republic. As a result, the Justice Department and the White House negotiated some relatively minor changes to the reauthorization, and Ashcroft later signed off on the program. Several years later, Comey recounted his tale to his friend Preet Bharara, then an aide to Senator Chuck Schumer, and Schumer asked him about it in a public hearing. Comey regaled the senators and the media with the tale of how he had single-handedly defended the Constitution against others in the Bush administration who had tried to manipulate a barely conscious Ashcroft into subverting the rule of law. The episode was typical James Comey: presenting himself as a hero saving democracy, portraying everyone else as ethically challenged or corrupt, and feeding the media a narrative he knew they would endlessly rehash.[19]

Because of Comey and others at the FBI, as well as Sessions's ill-advised decision to recuse himself, President Trump and many of those around him were ensnared in an open-ended special counsel investigation that ultimately interviewed 500 witnesses, issued 2,500 subpoenas, and received over 1.2 million documents from the White House and the Trump campaign. Careers were derailed, lives were destroyed, and many were indicted or went to prison—almost all of them for either process crimes such as misleading the FBI or on unrelated charges. For example, Paul Manafort, Trump's former campaign chairman, was convicted on charges of tax evasion and bank fraud, which had nothing to do with alleged Russian interference in the 2016 election. The media whipped the nation into a frenzy, and our entire government was convulsed and distracted by a false narrative declaring that Donald Trump and his campaign actively colluded with a hostile foreign power—achieving an outcome beyond Russia's wildest hopes and dreams when it had intervened in the first place.

The three main villains in this sad tale are in order: the FBI and other bureaucratic bad actors who foisted the investigation of Trump and his campaign on the country; the media, which fueled the story with fake news, distortions, and outright lies; and the Democrats, who used the Russia hoax as a bludgeon to try to cripple the Trump presidency and ruin the good name and reputation of everyone associated with it.

Let us start with the FBI. James Comey should have been fired on the first day of the Trump administration. As Deputy Attorney General Rod Rosenstein detailed in a letter to President Trump prior to the firing in May, Comey repeatedly violated strict FBI and Department of Justice policies on publicly discussing ongoing criminal investigations during the 2016 campaign.[20] First, on July 5, 2016, he held a news conference to announce that the FBI would not recommend charges against Hillary Clinton for using a home-brewed email server to conduct State Department business and exposing some of the nation's most critical national security secrets to hacking by foreign powers, which the FBI concluded likely took place. Comey had no right to violate FBI policy or usurp the Justice Department, which solely determines whether or not to charge an individual. When confronted about this, Comey used the lame excuse that Attorney General Loretta Lynch was conflicted because of a private meeting she held with Bill Clinton on an airport tarmac, and therefore lacked public confidence. But this was not Comey's decision to make. Comey then compounded this abuse of power by informing Congress on October 28, 2016—just ten days prior to the election—that he had reopened the investigation into Clinton's emails after learning that some of them had been discovered on her aide Huma Abedin's personal computer during the course of an investigation into her husband Anthony Weiner's solicitation of underage girls online. Comey knew it would leak, turning the entire campaign upside down just days before the election when early voting was already underway in many states. What impact this had on the final vote will always be a matter of conjecture, but there is no doubt that it was a major distraction for Clinton. Comey then announced that the investigation had been closed—again just days before the election. So on three separate occasions, Comey interjected himself and the FBI directly into a presidential campaign by abusing his power and discussing an ongoing criminal investigation in clear violation of Justice Department policy. There is no precedent for such a brazen intervention in a presidential campaign by the Justice Department in U.S. history.[21]

Nor was this all. FBI deputy director Andrew McCabe authorized a self-serving leak to the *Wall Street Journal* in October 2016 that made him look like the hero in a story about how the FBI had opened a criminal investigation into the Clinton Foundation. This followed news accounts about foreigners donating millions of dollars to the charity, allegedly to influence Hillary's official actions as secretary of state. McCabe lied to the FBI about the leak and later lied under oath to the inspector general of the Justice Department when the leak was investigated.[22] And as we have already seen, McCabe and Comey launched a counterintelligence investigation of a presidential campaign by using fraudulent and unverified opposition research dug up by a rival campaign to obtain surveillance warrants from a FISA court, misled the court about the origins of the so-called "evidence" to justify government surveillance, and then attempted to use it to intimidate and ultimately destroy President Trump. The abuses of power and politicization of the FBI under James Comey constitute one of the darkest chapters in the history of the agency.

Another strand in the narrative of the Russia hoax flogged endlessly by the media-Democratic-industrial complex was a meeting held in Trump Tower in June 2016 between senior Trump campaign officials and Natalia Veselnitskaya, a Russian attorney representing a pro-Putin

Russian oligarch. The meeting had been set up at the request of a music promoter who was friends with Donald Trump Jr. and had assisted in arranging for the Miss Universe pageant to be held in Moscow. The music promoter had emailed Don Jr., hinting that Veselnitskaya had damaging information on Hillary Clinton. Trump Jr. arranged the meeting, which was also attended by Paul Manafort, who was then the campaign chairman, and campaign advisor Jared Kushner. But in a matter of minutes, it became clear that the meeting had been arranged under false pretenses because Veselnitskaya simply launched into a lawyer's brief on the evils of the sanctions imposed on Russian officials by the Magnitsky Act, a law passed by Congress in retaliation for the killing of a Russian attorney representing a U.S. businessman. Putin had responded by ending adoptions of Russian infants by Americans, which proved devastating to many U.S. families seeking to adopt children overseas. Kushner and Manafort quickly left the meeting, Veselnitskaya provided no information of value to the campaign, and no one associated with the campaign made any effort to revise the Magnitsky Act or propose a loosening of U.S. sanctions against Russia.

Veselnitskaya was in New York City for a court hearing held the previous day regarding the frozen U.S. assets of the Russian oligarch she represented. After the court hearing, she had dinner with the oligarch's U.S. legal team, including Glenn Simpson, the former *Wall Street Journal* reporter and co-founder of Fusion GPS, the opposition research firm that also worked for Hillary Clinton and dug up the dirt contained in the fake Steele dossier. This has led to speculation that the Trump Tower meeting may have been a setup designed to entrap the Trump campaign into colluding with Veselnitskaya. In interviews with the Senate Judiciary Committee and House Intelligence Committee, Simpson denied having any knowledge about the Trump Tower meeting at the time, claiming he barely even talked to Veselnitskaya at dinner the prior evening or at a second dinner the next evening in Washington, in part because she spoke little English.[23] But in those same interviews Simpson refused to identify his clients, declined to discuss how much he was paid, and would not discuss communications he had or the work product he delivered to his clients, claiming it was privileged—a claim with no legal basis whatsoever. Simpson even refused to say whether he informed the Clinton campaign that Steele had provided information from the dossier to the FBI.[24] One doesn't have to be a conspiracy theorist to find it suspicious that the same opposition research firm that peddled dirt on Trump at the same time represented a Russian oligarch close to Putin who was the target of U.S. sanctions. Who were the Russian intelligence sources that Christopher Steele allegedly consulted for the unsubstantiated allegations against Trump contained in the infamous dossier?

Nothing ever came of the Trump Tower meeting, which lasted for all of twenty to thirty minutes, and most of the participants later testified that it was a complete waste of time for all involved. This did not prevent the media from acting with unrestrained hysteria, suggesting that Donald Trump Jr. might be in legal jeopardy for his role in setting up the meeting, trumpeting Democratic calls for Jared Kushner's security clearance to be revoked, alleging that White House aides were exposed to scrutiny by Special Counsel Robert Mueller because of the "scramble" to respond to media inquiries about the meeting, and claiming that one attendee at the meeting who accompanied Veselnitskaya had ties to Russian intelligence.[25] With no evidence to speak of, the media and Democrats portrayed the mere fact that the meeting occurred as proof that the Trump campaign had colluded with the Russian government to influence the 2016 election. As was often the case, the Democrats accused Trump of doing what Hillary Clinton did when she used Russian sources to peddle dirt on her opponent.

In an act of transparency, Donald Trump Jr. released all the emails he exchanged to set up the meeting, hoping to put these conspiracy theories to rest. But the media remained unsatisfied. They continued to scamper down a rabbit trail leading nowhere, airing claims from Democratic members of Congress that "mysterious" calls placed by Donald Jr. to blocked numbers before and after the meeting may have been to brief his father, thus disproving President Trump's claim that he knew nothing about the meeting. The media also continually aired a video clip of Trump at a rally in June saying his campaign was about to release damaging information on the misdeeds of the Clintons, asserting with no evidence that it was somehow related to the Trump Tower meeting. It was not until January 2019, two-and-a-half years after the meeting, that the media had to report that the calls made by Don Jr. to blocked numbers were to friends of the Trump family—not to his father—and had nothing to do with the Veselnitskaya meeting.[26] President Trump took to Twitter to lambaste the media for propagating fake news, claiming vindication and calling the entire controversy "really sad."[27] But by then, Don Jr., White House communications director Hope Hicks, and many others had been harassed by the media, interviewed by Mueller's investigators, dragged before congressional committees and a grand jury, forced to retain criminal defense lawyers, and subjected to document requests from Robert Mueller—all over a meeting that went nowhere.

In the end, the Russia hoax and Mueller investigation were about one thing: distracting and ultimately destroying Donald Trump. Neither had anything to do with actual criminal wrongdoing, as demonstrated by the fact that Mueller concluded at the end of his investigation that he found no evidence of collusion with Russia by the Trump campaign. The fact that this needlessly tragic and wasteful episode in recent American history began with professional misconduct and unlawful media leaks by senior FBI and intelligence officials makes it one of the worst scandals since Watergate, but not for the reasons Trump's accusers alleged. The real scandal was the abuse of power by Comey, McCabe, and others who corrupted the most respected and effective law enforcement agency in the world to try to destroy the Trump presidency.

If there was ever any doubt that this was the real motive behind the Russia hoax, the Ukrainian investigation and impeachment inquiry that followed thoroughly laid it to rest. When President Trump spoke with Ukrainian president Volodymyr Zelensky in July 2019, he asked him to look into whether the hacking of the Democratic National Committee server in 2016, which U.S. intelligence services had concluded was carried out by Russian intelligence, was not a false flag operation designed by Ukraine to make it look like a Russian operation. Trump also asked Zelensky to talk to his personal attorney, former New York City mayor Rudy Giuliani, about the firing in 2015 of a state prosecutor at the behest of then-vice president Joe Biden. The prosecutor was at the time investigating Burisma Holdings, a Ukrainian natural gas company whose founder was under investigation for corruption and money laundering, and on whose board Hunter Biden sat. Reasonable people of good will may disagree about whether it was appropriate for President Trump to discuss these issues on a call with a foreign leader. But given the long history of corruption in Ukraine, they are both legitimate lines of inquiry, especially given the abuses of power detailed above in the Russia hoax. The president's raising them on the call hardly constituted a crime, much less an impeachable offense.

Trump, in a display of transparency, ordered the transcript of his call with Zelenksy to be released, along with a whistleblower complaint filed by an anonymous CIA official based on thirdhand accounts of the call and related information. But Democrats and the media remained unmoved by Trump's remarkable waiver of executive privilege. Instead, Speaker of the House Nancy Pelosi violated precedent by launching a formal impeachment inquiry without first seeing the transcript of the call with the Ukrainian president and without allowing the House to ratify the decision with a recorded floor vote. The latter flaunting of precedent prevented the Republican minority from having subpoena power to compel witnesses and the production of documents. The three previous formal impeachment inquiries in U.S. history—of Andrew Johnson in 1867, Richard Nixon in 1974, and Bill Clinton in 1998—all began with the House of Representatives ratifying the decision with a recorded vote. At a minimum, this would have forced every member of Congress to be on record on one of the most momentous decisions of their career. At a maximum, it is designed to prevent a hyper-partisan Speaker from abusing their power by trying to remove a president from office for political reasons. It also would have allowed for a legitimate investigation with minority rights of inquiry protected. But Pelosi wasn't interested in a real investigation; she wanted impeachment by partisan means and for purely partisan reasons.

Some on the liberal side of the aisle tried to warn Democrats that impeachment was potentially hazardous to them and dangerous for the country. *New York Times* columnist Frank Bruni, no fan of Donald Trump's, said "the prospect terrifies me, and it should terrify you, too." Bruni warned that what was just and wise were not necessarily the same. "At a juncture when we so desperately need to rediscover common ground," impeachment would "be widening fault lines."[28] Others pointed out that the election was only thirteen months away, and prudence argued for leaving the verdict to the American people, not politicians in Washington in a fevered pursuit of a political foe. As someone who lived through the 1998 impeachment of Bill Clinton and advised Republican leaders that it could politically whipsaw them, I know well that impeachment is a Pandora's box. Once opened, it cannot be shut, and it can release a tornado of charges and counter-charges, leaving in its wake a path of destruction and collateral damage that leaves no one untouched. Impeachment is uniquely dangerous in its destructive capability, which is why it has only been used sparingly in American history.

The impeachment investigation conducted by House Democrats was a partisan joke. Rather than waiting for claims of executive privilege by the White House to be litigated in the courts and taking the time to get the witnesses they wanted, the Democrats rammed through the inquiry in a slap-dash rush to judgment. The impeachment investigation lasted only 85 days from start to finish. By contrast, in the case of Bill Clinton's impeachment, then-attorney general Janet Reno appointed Robert B. Fiske, an independent counsel to investigate Whitewater in January 1994. After Ken Starr replaced Fiske, the office of independent counsel was authorized by a federal court to expand the investigation to include Monica Lewinsky in January 1998. So depending on how one does the math, the investigation of Bill Clinton from inception to impeachment took 330 days (dated from January 1998) or 1,793 days (dated from the appointment of the independent counsel). Democrats argued that they had no independent counsel in the case of the Ukraine matter, which is true. But they therefore should have taken the time to complete a full and thorough investigation. Instead, they interviewed only 17 witnesses, 12 of whom testified in public hearings and only one of whom had direct conversations with President Trump regarding aid to Ukraine. The other witnesses had never spoken with President Trump, and most had never even met him.

But for House Democrats, what was best for the country came second to destroying Trump. Impeachment wasn't ultimately about whether Trump committed a crime (he didn't), whether the country is served by a drawn-out, polarizing impeachment saga (it wasn't), or whether there was a slim chance of his conviction and removal from office by a Republican-controlled Senate (there wasn't). After all, the impeachment focused on military aid to Ukraine that was released after being put temporarily on hold over matters of possible corruption that were never investigated. No crime was ever committed or alleged. This is about leaving an asterisk after Donald Trump's name in history. As one congressional Democrat told CNN, "this is for the history books." Just like liberal activist lawyer Debra Katz's bragging about Christine Blasey Ford's unproven, uncorroborated, and discredited charges against Justice Brett Kavanaugh, impeachment was an act of brazen, shameless partisanship designed to discredit Trump's presidency in the eyes of posterity.

My friend Pastor Robert Jeffress, an early Evangelical supporter of Trump's, warned as House Democrats began their formal impeachment inquiry, "If the Democrats are successful in removing the president from office, I'm afraid it will cause a civil war-like fracture in this nation from which this country will never heal."[29] As a trained American historian, I do not believe we are likely to see a conflagration that sunders the bonds of national unity like what occurred during the Civil War. But in many ways, an ideological and cultural fracture has already taken place; impeachment is a reflection of it—not its cause. President Trump has defended life, religious freedom, the state of Israel, and fulfilled his promise to appoint pro-life, conservative federal judges beyond the greatest hopes of his supporters and worst fears of his opponents. Both friends and foes of Trump know that if he were to win a second term in 2020, he would continue these policies, and possibly appoint one or two more justices to the U.S. Supreme Court. This is an unacceptable outcome for the Far Left, the media, and the Democratic Party. Hoping to make it easier to defeat him at the ballot box in 2020, Democrats used impeachment as a partisan weapon designed to weaken Trump in the eyes of some voters.

In this sense, impeachment was just one skirmish in a larger political drama over America's future. The partisan goal of impeachment is to place a cloud of suspicion over Trump and assist the 2020 Democratic presidential nominee. Because of Joe Biden's involvement in threatening to withhold one billion dollars in U.S. aid to Ukraine in 2015 unless Ukrainian officials fired the prosecutor investigating the natural gas company on whose board his son Hunter sat, he may become collateral damage. Biden will learn like many before him that for the liberal grassroots and the media, nothing can be allowed to stand in the way of trying to destroy Donald Trump. It is to that 2020 election, the contesting parties, and the high stakes at hand that we now turn.

CHAPTER 16

2020

I mpeachment was a fool's errand for the Democrats and the elite media, and not just because it failed to remove Trump from office. In fact, impeachment has sparked a fierce backlash among many voters (as it ironically did when Republicans impeached Bill Clinton in 1998–99) by strengthening Trump's core support and allowing the president to portray himself (accurately, in my view) as the victim of a partisan political witch hunt. It also potentially endangers the thirty House Democrats who represent districts Trump carried in 2016, increasing the intensity of Republican opposition in those districts and turning off many independent and swing voters. Polls show independent, unaffiliated voters would prefer for Congress to work on the pressing issues for them and their families, and they consider impeachment to be a distraction at best and a political circus at worst.

Public opinion surveys show the full force of this backlash among swing voters. An October 2019 poll conducted by Public Opinion Strategies found that over two-thirds of voters (68 percent) in swing congressional districts said impeachment is "all about politics," and agree that "Congressional Democrats should be more concerned about addressing the issues of the day." That view was held by 67 percent of independent voters and even 44 percent of Democrats. In the districts held by Democrats that were won by President Trump in 2016, a hypothetical anti-impeachment Republican candidate defeats a pro-impeachment Democrat by a landslide, with 54 percent voting for the Republican and only 38 percent voting for the pro-impeachment Democrat.[1]

Instead of focusing on bettering the lives of American families by growing the economy, creating jobs, ratifying new trade agreements that open up markets for U.S. goods, improving health care, or bettering education, the Democrats have spent over three years trying to gin up the impeachment and removal of a duly elected president. Newt Gingrich has pointed out that the virulent opposition against Trump by the radical Left actually began on November 9, 2016, with rent-a-riot protests and rallies objecting to his victory in major U.S. cities. Within a month, the media began speculating about impeaching him. And on Inauguration Day in 2017, the *Washington Post* used this headline for a story about the Resistance: "The Campaign to Impeach Trump Has Begun."[2] The day after the Trump inaugural, I personally witnessed the Women's March in Washington, the surging crowd wearing "pussy" hats and brandishing obscenity-laced signs, featuring a speech by Madonna in which she said, "I have thought an awful lot about blowing up the White House." The war on Trump's presidency began before he ever took the oath of office, and it continues to this day.[3] The stated reasons—invoking the Twenty-Fifth Amendment, the emoluments clause, campaign finance violations, the Russia hoax, the Ukrainian inquiry—may change, but the goal always remains the same.

Having failed to take Trump out with partisan kangaroo courts and impeachment, the radical Left has only one option remaining: defeating Trump at the ballot box in 2020. For that reason, the 2020 presidential campaign promises to be one of the ugliest, nastiest, most expensive, and most hard-fought elections in American history.

Consider how much the Democrats threw at Trump in 2016. Hillary Clinton spent $768 million to the Trump campaign's $398 million, outspending him nearly two-to-one.[4] According to the campaign finance site OpenSecrets.org, the combined cost of the presidential and congressional races in 2016 was nearly $6.5 billion.[5] In that torrent of spending, an analysis by Bloomberg found that Hillary Clinton and her super PACs raised $1.2 billion while Trump and his super PACs raised only $650 million, again outpacing Trump nearly two-to-one.[6] No presidential candidate of either party who was outspent by this large of a margin has won the presidency since the dawn of the television era. And even this staggering spending advantage by Hillary and the Democrats understates Trump's financial disadvantage in 2016. Outside groups who backed Clinton collected almost triple the amount raised by Trump's outside groups.[7]

Clinton was a conventional, paint-by-the-numbers candidate who waged her campaign by traditional means, mostly airing thirty-second television ads, and Clinton aggressively outspent Trump on television. According to an analysis published by Advertising Age, Clinton outspent Trump on paid advertising by huge amounts.[8] In Colorado, Trump spent only half as much as Clinton on TV and radio ads; in Nevada, only a quarter as much; in Florida, only one-fifth as much.[9] One week before the election, Clinton had spent over $211 million in television advertisements and Trump had spent only $74 million, a three-to-one margin.[10] According to a report by the Center for Public Integrity, Clinton's ads accounted for a whopping 75 percent of all the presidential campaign TV ads aired between June and November of 2016.[11] Priorities USA, the main Democratic super PAC, by itself ran nearly as many advertisements as Trump's campaign did for the entire election season. Key battleground states were inundated with pro-Clinton ads. Between October 1 and Election Day, Clinton aired an average of one ad every five minutes in Nevada, one ad every three minutes in Pennsylvania and North Carolina, and one ad every two-and-a-half minutes in Ohio. In Florida, television channels broadcast one pro-Clinton ad every ninety seconds.[12] Clinton and her allies also focused on attracting Latino voters; they produced over 15,000 Spanish-language TV ads while the Trump campaign and his supporters aired a mere 500—a difference of more than thirty to one.[13]

Despite this avalanche of spending by Clinton, Trump possessed one major advantage: he dominated free media. Every time he visited a battleground state and held a campaign rally, he enjoyed saturation coverage on local television, online, and in newspapers. When it comes to presidential campaigns, earned media is still king. Trump's high-wattage celebrity and willingness to say almost anything drew eyeballs and clicks, earning him the equivalent of $5.9 billion in earned media attention, according to one estimate—more than making up for his smaller paid advertising spend.[14] In addition, Trump spent heavily on digital ads, especially on Facebook, and because of the enthusiasm of his supporters and his edgy message, this resulted in much higher engagement on social media platforms. So while Hillary dominated the airwaves, Trump owned digital.

But money alone does not a president make, and Trump won in 2016 despite Clinton's massive spending advantage. It was an historic victory, but a narrow one. Although Trump was the easy victor in the Electoral College, winning 304 electoral votes to Hillary's 227, he lost the popular vote by 2.9 million votes. Hillary's popular vote margin, however, came mostly in deep-blue states like California and New York. She could have used some of those votes in states that actually mattered. In the swing states that decided the outcome of the election, Trump's margin of victory was razor thin. In Pennsylvania, for example, Trump won 48.2 percent of the popular vote over Clinton's 47.5 percent, winning with 44,292 votes to spare. In Wisconsin, Trump won by 22,748 votes, while in Michigan he won by only 10,704 votes out of 2 million cast.[15] These were impressive victories, since winning these three states in the industrial, upper Midwest had not been done by a Republican presidential nominee since Ronald Reagan did it as a popular incumbent against the hapless Walter Mondale in 1984. Still, a shift of fewer than 40,000 votes spread out over those three states would have made Hillary Clinton president.

The Democrats and the radical Left know this and are bound and determined to do whatever is necessary and spend whatever it takes to add the required number of votes in the key battleground states. Expect 2020 to feature the largest avalanche of spending by the Democrats and liberal outside groups in modern political history, with unprecedented resources poured into voter registration, voter mobilization, door-to-door canvassing, television, and digital ads.

The Left understands that 2020 is the highest-stakes election of our lifetime. Consider just some of what is on the line:

- The next president will appoint at least one and perhaps as many as three Supreme Court justices
- The president elected in 2020 will appoint an additional 150 federal district and appellate court judges who will rule on cases involving state restrictions on abortion, religious freedom, freedom of speech, separation of powers, and gay and transgender rights. This is critical because only a small percentage of cases are decided by the Supreme Court; over 97 percent of cases are decided by lower courts. President Trump appointed 30 appellate court judges in his first two years in office, a historic high-water mark. There are another 60 of 167 federal appellate court judges eligible for retirement
- Protections for innocent human life and whether to provide federal funding of Planned Parenthood, the largest abortion provider in the world today
- Control of the White House, U.S. Senate, and House of Representatives
- Public policies that promote economic growth, business investment, human and financial capital formation, and job creation
- An immigration policy that is both compassionate and respects the rule of law
- Continued support for defending religious freedom here and abroad

- Whether the U.S. will remain the most steadfast ally of Israel in the world
- Control of redistricting, which will draw the lines of congressional and state legislative districts, determining to a great extent which party is most likely to win control of the House of Representatives and the various state legislatures

For a roadmap of the spending and voter turnout strategy of the Democrats and the Left in 2020, one need look no further than the 2018 midterm elections. The increased turnout among minority and younger voters in 2018 compared to previous midterm elections was truly historic. Voter turnout among 18-to-29-year-old voters, a heavily Democratic constituency, increased from 20 percent to 36 percent, a 79 percent increase. Hispanic voter turnout rose by 13 percent, a 50 percent increase. Among all voters, 83.3 million went to the polls in the 2014 midterm elections; in 2018, that number increased to 118.6 million voters who cast ballots, a 42 percent increase. This was the highest turnout of eligible voters in a midterm election since before World War I.[16] As a percentage of the voting-eligible adult population, turnout jumped from 36.4 percent in 2014—the lowest in a midterm election since World War II—to 53 percent in 2018.[17] This dramatic increase is the largest between two midterm elections in modern American history.[18] What caused such a jump in turnout?

The main reasons were the stakes were high, and voter intensity was white-hot. Republicans in the Senate had just confirmed Brett Kavanaugh to the Supreme Court over virulent Democratic opposition. Democrats desperately wanted to win back the Senate and grind to a halt the flurry of Trump-appointed judges. Democrats also wanted to gain control of the House, with a not-so-hidden agenda of impeaching Trump. Voter enthusiasm among liberal voters skyrocketed—as it did among Republicans, conservatives, and Evangelicals. Fundraising broke records: one estimate concluded that federal candidates spent $5.2 billion on their campaigns, surpassing the previous record of $4.2 billion. Democratic candidates alone were expected to raise more than $2.5 billion.[19]

Liberal megadonors like Michael Bloomberg and Tom Steyer poured millions into House and Senate races. Bloomberg alone vowed to spend $100 million during the 2018 election. He spent that amount and more. A post-election analysis by the *New York Times* report found that "overall spending by Mr. Bloomberg and his organizations in the 2018 elections topped $112 million, an amount that included donations to...progressive organizations."[20] Bloomberg also timed his donations to be as effective as possible against Republican members of Congress: in the final three weeks before Election Day, he spent an estimated $30 million on television advertising supporting Democratic congressional candidates in key races, dropping between $1 million and $3 million into every key district in the country from California to Florida.[21]

Bloomberg, whose net worth is estimated by Forbes at $50 billion, will spend even more in 2020. Jumping into the Democratic presidential race in late 2018, he spent $217 million in a matter of weeks, most of it on television ads attacking President Trump. Bloomberg's total spending by January 2020 equaled three-quarters of the entire amount spent by all the other candidates (including Trump) since the beginning of the campaign combined. In online spending alone, Bloomberg spent $23 million on digital ads by early January 2020, compared to $6 million in digital ads by the Trump campaign. Bloomberg also hired 1,000 staffers by January 2020 and pledged to keep paying them to register voters, organize at the grassroots level, and go door-to-door through November 2020—even if he lost the Democratic nomination. He also committed an additional $15–20 million to register 500,000 new Democratic voters in key states. At the rate Bloomberg was spending funds as this went to press, it appears likely that he will spend over $1 billion trying to defeat Donald Trump by himself. There is no precedent for such a level of spending by a single individual in U.S. history.[22]

Along with unprecedented fundraising, Democrats and liberal groups are working overtime to register new voters to expand the electorate and grow their turnout universe. In June 2018, the Democratic National Committee announced a plan to reach 25 million potential Democratic voters who were not registered. The initial $2.5 million investment targeted minority groups such as African Americans, Latinos, Asians, and millennials.[23] These strategies, combined with the Trump Derangement Syndrome suffered by the liberal support base, has fueled a spike in voter registration. In Georgia, failed 2018 Democratic gubernatorial candidate Stacey Abrams led an organization called the New Georgia Project, which focused on helping minorities get to the voting booth. By June 2018, the New Georgia Project had submitted over 220,000 new voter applications.[24] (Not all the applications were accepted, however, due to verification difficulties, which are typical for progressive voter registration efforts, which are plagued by duplication, errors, and outright fraud.) Voters under the age of 30 make up only 14 percent of all voters in Georgia but comprised 45 percent of newly registered voters in 2019. The Voter Participation Center, another liberal group, sent voter registration forms to 560,000 unmarried women, young people under the age of 30, and minorities in Georgia in a single month.[25] In Iowa, Democrats added 23,000 new voters to the rolls, compared to only 1,600 for Republicans.[26] In Pennsylvania, people under the age of 30—who tend to vote for Democrats—made up two-thirds of newly registered voters. Many other states saw a similar upswing in left-leaning voter registration.[27]

These massive efforts in fundraising, voter registration, and get-out-the-vote campaigns have proven effective, especially on the Left. Voters of both parties turned out in record numbers in 2018. The Brookings Institution found that 51 million Republican voters went to the polls in the 2018 races, which represented a 27 percent increase over 2014. These numbers, while impressive, paled in comparison to the opposition: Democratic voter turnout skyrocketed from 36 million in 2014 to 61 million in 2018—a jaw-dropping 70 percent increase.[28]

This was just the beginning. We should expect even greater efforts on the Left in 2020. Liberal billionaires are pouring millions of dollars into voter registration and ground game efforts, often deploying tax-exempt, dark money organizations that are the vehicles of choice, because unlike party or candidate committees, they do not report donors, contributions, or how they spend their money. These ground game operations are already underway in every major battleground state in the country. If conservatives and Christians fail to register, educate, and mobilize a historic turnout of pro-life, faith-based voters, they risk being buried beneath an avalanche of liberal voters turned out by the progressive Left.

The 2020 presidential campaign promises to be the most fiercely contested—and expensive—in history. Both Republicans and Democrats are gearing up to spend more money than ever before during the general election campaign. An analysis by Advertising Analytics and Cross Screen Media projects that the total cost of political advertising by both parties will rise to $6 billion, a 57 percent increase from 2018, with $2.7 billion spent on the presidential campaign alone.[29] Other projections reach similar conclusions. A report from eMarketer also estimated $6 billion in advertising costs, $1.2 billion of which will go toward digital ads.[30] Some firms, including the ad agency GroupM, predict even higher numbers for ad spending—up to $10 billion.[31]

These projections predict the total amount that will be spent by both parties on all levels of the election. Now let us take a look at some of the specific strategies and fundraising efforts on the Democratic side. As we will see, the Left is preparing for a ferocious election cycle in 2020—they want to make sure that Donald Trump and his Republican allies will not survive it.

- On February 21, 2019—more than a year and a half before Election Day 2020—the main Democratic super PAC Priorities USA announced that it had begun a $100 million "early engagement program" targeting voters in Wisconsin, Michigan, Pennsylvania, and Florida—four of the crucial swing states.[32] It later increased this budget to $150 million for the presidential campaign alone; the super

PAC has a separate plan for the Senate races. The organization's chairman, Guy Cecil, explained that he has three priorities, regardless of the Democratic nominee: "defeat Donald Trump, elect a Democratic Senate, and increase voter turnout."[33] The plan includes targeting key counties within the four states and developing a targeted digital ad campaign, which Cecil claimed would be "better" than Trump's 2016 digital campaigning

- American Bridge 21st Century, a liberal super PAC that conducts opposition research, announced in March 2019 that it was raising money for a $50 million expansion in an effort to turn voters in swing states against Trump. The organization claimed that it had over "176 gigabytes of Trump research...including 24,000 video and audio files," which it plans to share with the Democratic nominee if it can find "legal structures" to do so.[34] As a result of this and other efforts, expect more opposition research dumps by the radical Left. They will do everything they can to distract voters from the strong economy, record low unemployment, strong stock market performance, and trade concessions made possible by President Trump's policies. Be forewarned: the media and the radical Left may hold these opposition research attacks until late in the campaign, as they did with the 11-year-old *Access Hollywood* tape in 2016 and George W. Bush's 20-year-old driving-under-the-influence charge in 2000

- Labor unions and a political action organization funded by billionaire Tom Steyer plan to spend $80 million in a campaign to target hard-to-reach voters in a broad group of swing states.[35] Separately, Steyer has spent an estimated $100 million pushing impeachment through a separate nonprofit called Need to Impeach, garnering 8 million signatures and airing ads in key states. Though he looked like Don Quixote at the time, Steyer helped move the center of gravity within the Democratic Party toward impeachment, and ultimately forced Nancy Pelosi and other Democratic leaders to get on board. Even this is not enough for a majority of Democratic voters. An October 2019 poll of Democratic voters in the early caucus and primary states found that 53 percent of Democrats want President Trump imprisoned[36]

- The liberal group Progressive Turnout Project has announced that it will spend $45 million in 2020 hiring 1,100 full-time field staffers and paid canvassers who will deploy a smartphone application with real-time updates of voter information to knock on 4.5 million doors in key states and congressional districts. The group claims it boosted liberal voter turnout in targeted congressional districts by 10.4 percent in 2018. A similar boost in 2020 would turn out an additional 6 million liberal voters against Trump[37]

- In June 2019, the news site Daily Beast reported that Priorities USA is doubling down on a $5 million investment to improve its campaigning analytics.[38] Unable to compete with Trump's fundraising efforts, it is instead focusing on revamping its data analytics to target voters in the most effective way possible. The plan includes hiring up to thirteen new staffers, including "four targeting analysts, three experimental analysts, four data scientists, and a director and coordinator." Under Obama, Democrats gained a huge advantage over conservatives in the area of data analytics and voter targeting. Republicans and conservatives have closed this gap and may have it even better than in 2016. Liberals are determined to reclaim their former advantage and are pouring tens of millions of dollars into doing so

- Democratic candidates are awash in cash, in part due to their significant edge in online small donors. ActBlue, the

Democratic online payment platform, received $420 million from 3.3 million donors supporting liberal candidates and causes in the first half of 2019.[39] This represented a 500 percent increase in fundraising from the previous presidential election cycle; between January and June of 2015, ActBlue processed only $76 million. Executive Director Erin Hill crowed, "We're seeing millions of donors, record-breaking totals every quarter, and a rapidly growing small-dollar army that is ready to help Democrats take back everything from school boards to the White House next year."

- In July, Priorities USA began to spend $1 million per month on online ads attacking Trump's record on the economy,[40] despite the fact that Trump's policies have increased economic growth, created over 7 million new jobs, and reduced unemployment to 3.5 percent, the lowest unemployment rate in 50 years. The attack ads were once again focused on the four swing states of Florida, Pennsylvania, Michigan, and Wisconsin

- Stakes are high in the Senate races, as well, as Democrats raise and spend millions of dollars trying to regain the majority and make Chuck Schumer the Senate majority leader. The news site FiveThirtyEight reported that as of July 2019, Democratic Senate candidates were outraising Republicans. In 14 states considered "competitive" (not solidly Democrat or Republican), Democratic campaigns had gathered $34.1 million to the Republicans' $29.3 million[41]

- Democratic Senate candidates are raising huge amounts of money in short periods of time, indicating a fired-up voter base. *Politico* reported several notable examples: Cal Cunningham of North Carolina raised $500,000 in two weeks. Theresa Greenfield of Iowa pulled in $600,000 in less than a month. Sara Gideon, the Democratic challenger in Maine, raised $1 million in a single week. And Amy McGrath of Kentucky received $2.5 million within a day of announcing her challenge to Senate Majority Leader Mitch McConnell[42]

- At the beginning of August, Democratic megadonor George Soros launched his own super PAC called Democracy PAC. Soros gave his new organization a jumpstart with a check of $5.1 million, the biggest single contribution from any megadonor in the election cycle so far[43]

- On August 14, 2019, OpenSecrets.org released a report revealing the biggest donors to Democratic campaigns and causes to date.[44] David Sussman led the pack with $7.5 million in total donations. Tom Steyer gave $6.5 million. George Soros came in third with his $5 million contribution to his new super PAC

These are just some of the initiatives of the progressive radical Left designed to register, inflame, and turn out a record number of voters to the polls in 2020 to defeat President Trump. The Left and the media know what is on the line, and they recognize that a second term for Donald Trump means even more judicial appointments, probably one— and as many as three—additional Supreme Court appointments, more pro-life and pro-family policies, and the potential for an enduring conservative policy legacy that endangers the liberal project. Trump is fond of saying that the media and the Left are after him because he is fighting for the faith community. Certainly on the sanctity of innocent human life, religious freedom, and unyielding and unwavering support for Israel, President Trump has been a champion for the biblical values of people of faith. The only remaining question is this: Will the faith community step up to the plate and defend its principles as enthusiastically as the Left and the Democrats plan to do in 2020?

I hope and pray the answer to that question is a resounding "Yes!" Never has there been more at stake. Never have I seen the opposition so vicious and virulent, hurling the worst kind of smears imaginable at anyone who stands for our shared beliefs. As I have argued, we have a dual and mutually reinforcing responsibility clearly laid out in the Bible as Christians and citizens to advance the good and resist evil and injustice with all of our civic rights. The 2020 election will determine how serious we are about exercising them.

Faith & Freedom Coalition, which I founded in 2009, will undertake a $50 million voter registration, voter education, and get-out-the vote effort that will focus on approximately 28 million Evangelicals and pro-life Roman Catholic voters in the key states and congressional districts in the country. In addition, we have launched outreach initiatives that will register and educate 1 million African-American Evangelicals and 5 million Hispanic Christians on where the candidates stand on the key issues of life, the family, religious freedom, and Israel. This plan is projected to register 1 million voters in the key states, knock on over 3 million doors of Christian voters, place over 45 million digital ads on Facebook and other platforms, mail 23 million pieces of voter education literature, and distribute 30 million voter guides in an estimated 120,000 churches. Our volunteers will work with a smartphone application that allows them to download each household they visit, pull up a voter's past voting history, conduct a brief survey, record the voter's views on the issues, and leave a voter guide in their hands that they can take to the polls and share with friends and family.

Finally, we need to do more than just educate ourselves, register new voters, and turn out to the polls those voters who share our faith and values. We need to pray. Paul urged that "entreaties and prayers, petitions and thanksgivings, be made on behalf of all men, for kings and all who are in authority, so that we may lead a tranquil and quiet life in all godliness and dignity" (1 Timothy 2:2). The Bible makes a direct connection to intercessory prayer for our political leaders and our own peace and spiritual prosperity. Moreover, Paul goes on to say, "This is good and acceptable in the sight of God our Savior, who desires all men to be saved and to come to the knowledge of the truth" (1 Timothy 2:3–4). In this sense, Paul makes clear that intercession for those in political authority is related to God's compassion for society and for all people, since He desires all to be saved and come to know His Son as their Lord and Savior. What an amazing and world-changing concept! When one compares America's relative peace, prosperity, and political stability over more than two centuries to the bloodshed and civil unrest throughout much of the world, one cannot escape the conclusion that it must be due in no small measure to the prayers of believers for our government and those in authority.

This is always important—now more than ever. Paul wrote his letter to Timothy at a time when the Jews were subjugated under the boot of the Roman Empire, when Palestine was a vassal state occupied by Roman soldiers and governed by leaders appointed by Caesar, and when those who resisted evil were arrested and executed. It was a deeply troubled time in the history of the Jewish people. Today we face nothing so challenging. But the American electorate is deeply polarized, and Washington is paralyzed by partisan rancor. So we must pray as never before for our country, our state, our community, and our leaders.

I pray for President Trump, Melania, his entire family, and those who surround and advise him on a daily basis. I did the same for his predecessors, regardless of party. It is also imperative for us to pray for God's mercy on our nation and for Him to give us godly leaders of character who will make wise and just decisions for America and the world.

I do not claim to know what will happen in 2020, and after Trump's upset victory in 2016, I am reluctant to make predictions. But what I do know for certain is that without an historic and record turnout of Evangelicals and pro-life Roman Catholic voters, it will be very difficult for him to be reelected. There are somewhere between forty and fifty million Evangelical voters in the United States. Should these and other voters of faith turn out in the numbers they are capable of doing, they will make history in 2020 like they did in 2016. Whatever the outcome, let it be said that we did our part, that we did not take the precious gift of American citizenship for granted, and that we were good and effective stewards of our rights under the Constitution to express and share our faith, to associate politically with those who share our values, to speak out on the causes and issues that motivate us, and to contribute financially and vote for the candidates who are uniquely qualified to lead and share our stands on the issues. In so doing, we will have become more than be mere cogs in the political wheel, members of a political party or coalition, or part of an election victory. We will glorify God and be witnesses in our time for the transcendent, heavenly values that can transform society today and will someday usher in a new Kingdom that will never end.

"Promises Made, Promises Kept"

President Trump's Record of Achievement for the American People

This list goes through February 2020. For a full and updated list of the Trump administration's accomplishments, please visit http://www.ffcoalition.com/promises-kept/.

Transforming America's Courts

- The U.S. Senate has confirmed 191 of the judges that President Trump has appointed to America's federal courts—all solid, pro-life constitutionalists who will uphold the rule of law
- Latest count: 2 Supreme Court justices, 50 circuit court judges, 133 district court judges, and 2 judges for the United States Court of International Trade as of January 2020
- The U.S. Senate has confirmed President Trump's two appointments to the U.S. Supreme Court—Justices Neil Gorsuch and Brett Kavanaugh—both solid, pro-life constitutionalists who will uphold the rule of law

- If President Trump is reelected in 2020, he is likely to have a total of four hundred appointments to America's federal courts and between three and five appointments to the U.S. Supreme Court. President Trump's transformation of America's courts will likely be his most lasting legacy

Protecting Religious Freedom

- President Trump ordered the Internal Revenue Service to suspend any further enforcement of the Johnson Amendment, which prohibited churches and ministries from discussing public policy and political issues and was used for decades to harass and persecute Christians
- President Trump issued an executive order prohibiting the U.S. government from discriminating against Christians or punishing expressions of faith
- He signed an executive order establishing the White House Faith and Opportunity Initiative
- Trump signed an executive order upholding religious liberty and the right to engage in religious speech
- He established a Religious Liberty Task Force in the U.S. Department of Justice.
- The Trump administration vigorously defended religious liberty in the courts at every opportunity
- President Trump reversed the Obama-era policy that prevented the government from providing disaster relief to religious organizations
- He signed an executive order that allows the government to withhold money from college campuses that are deemed to be anti-Semitic and fail to combat anti-Semitism
- Trump created "safe zones" in the Middle East for persecuted Christians, Jews, and others of faith—protected by our military

- He committed an additional twenty-five million dollars this year to protect religious sites and relics around the world
- Trump is spearheading the International Religious Freedom Alliance, an alliance of nations dedicated to confronting religious persecution around the world. He has repeatedly called on all countries to stop persecuting religious minorities
- Trump has called on China to respect religious freedom and end its persecution of people of faith—including China's imprisoning of millions of Christians, Jews, Uighur Muslims, Buddhists, Hindus, and others for their faith
- In 2019, President Trump imposed restrictions on certain Chinese officials, internal security units, and companies for their complicity in the persecution of Uighur Muslims and other religious groups in China
- He announced the formation of a coalition of U.S. businesses for the protection of religious freedom. This initiative encourages businesses to protect people of all faiths in the workplace
- The president brought the phrase "Merry Christmas!" back to American public life instead of "Happy Holidays"
- He let it be known that his Justice Department would aggressively prosecute hate crimes committed against Christians, Jews, Muslims, and others for their faith
- The administration is preserving a space for faith-based adoption and foster care providers to continue to serve their communities in a manner that is consistent with their beliefs
- The administration reduced burdensome barriers and allowed Native Americans to keep spiritually and culturally significant eagle feathers found on their tribal lands
- The administration has allowed greater flexibility for federal employees to take time off work for religious reasons

- Trump's administration has partnered with local and faith-based organizations to provide assistance to religious minorities persecuted in Iraq
- President Trump hosted the Global Call to Protect Religious Freedom at the 2019 United Nations General Assembly, calling on global and business leaders to bring an end to religious persecution and stop crimes against people of faith
- The State Department has hosted two Religious Freedom Ministerials, with the 2019 ministerial becoming the largest religious freedom event of its kind in the world
- The Trump administration provided an exemption from the contraceptive coverage mandate to entities that object to services covered by the mandate on the basis of sincerely held religious beliefs, as well as nonprofit organizations and small businesses that have non-religious moral convictions opposing services covered by the mandate. The religious and moral exemptions provided by these rules also apply to institutions of education, issuers, and individuals
- In January 2018, the Department of Health and Human Services (HHS) announced the creation of the Conscience and Religious Freedom Division within the Office for Civil Rights. This new office works to protect health care professionals who do not want to participate in abortion
- On January 16, 2020, President Trump updated a Department of Education guidance regarding protected prayer and religious expression in public schools to safeguard students' rights by giving education providers and students the most current information concerning prayer in public schools. To receive federal funds, local educational agencies must confirm that their policies do not prevent or interfere with the constitutionally protected right to pray outlined in the guidance. The new guidance makes it clear that students can read religious texts or pray during recess and other non-instructional

periods, organize prayer groups, and express their religious beliefs in their assignments

- On January 16, 2020, the Trump administration announced nine proposed rules to protect religious organizations from unfair and unequal treatment by the federal government. The proposed rules would eliminate burdensome Obama-era requirements that unfairly imposed unique regulatory burdens only on religious organizations

- On January 16, 2020, President Trump's Office of Management and Budget (OMB) released a memo requiring federal agencies to ensure that the grant-making practices of state recipients of federal funding respect the rights of faith-based organizations and comply with the First Amendment

Protecting the Right to Life

- President Trump has established a record as the most pro-life president in modern times

- President Trump issued an order preventing U.S. taxpayers' money from going to international organizations that fund or perform abortions

- On January 23, 2017, President Trump signed an order reinstating the Mexico City Policy, which defunded International Planned Parenthood and other organizations that promote foreign abortions. Unlike previous versions of the policy, the Trump administration expanded it to include all global health assistance funding

- On May 15, 2017, the Trump administration massively broadened the scope of the Mexico City Policy to restrict funding to any international health organization that performs or gives information about abortions, expanding the amount of money affected from six hundred thousand dollars to nearly nine billion dollars

- Trump ended the Obamacare mandate that all health insurance coverage must include abortion
- He fought to end taxpayers' funding for Planned Parenthood—which conducts more than 360,000 abortion per year, including late-term and partial-birth abortions
- On April 13, 2017, President Trump signed a bill that allows states to defund Planned Parenthood and prevent it from receiving Title X funds. This bill nullified an Obama administration regulation that prohibited states from doing so. And because this bill was passed under the Congressional Review Act, future administrations cannot reinstate the Obama-era rule
- Trump allowed states to deny Planned Parenthood Medicaid funds. The Obama administration attempted to prevent states from denying Planned Parenthood Medicaid dollars and issued guidance claiming that this may be a violation of federal law. In January 2018, the Trump administration rescinded this guidance, allowing states to defund Planned Parenthood from the Medicaid dollars as they saw fit
- On February 22, 2019, HHS issued the final Title X rule (the Protect Life Rule) to defund any clinic that either provides abortions or refers people to abortion clinics, which reduced Planned Parenthood's funding by roughly sixty million dollars. As a result of the president's policies, Planned Parenthood withdrew from the Title X program
- President Trump is protecting health care entities and individuals' conscience rights—ensuring that no medical professional is forced to participate in an abortion in violation of their beliefs
- The Trump administration provided relief to American employers like the Little Sisters of the Poor, protecting

them from being forced to provide abortion coverage that violates their consciences

- President Trump and Vice President Pence have actively worked to pass life-protecting legislation and have written Congress on numerous occasions encouraging lawmakers to vote to protect innocent human life, including:
  - No-Taxpayer Funding for Abortion and Abortion Insurance Full Disclosure Act of 2019
  - Pain-Capable Unborn Child Protection Act
  - Born-Alive Abortion Survivors Protection Act
- On April 4, 2017, the Trump administration ended U.S. funding of the United Nations Population Fund, which has links to forced sterilizations and coercive abortion programs such as China's one-child policy
- President Trump ended an Obama-era guidance that prevented states from taking certain actions against abortion providers
- On April 20, 2018, the Trump administration ended the Obama-era policy of listing abortion as a "human right" in the State Department's annual human rights report
- On January 18, 2019, President Donald Trump issued a letter to Speaker of the House Nancy Pelosi promising to veto any legislation that would weaken federal pro-life policies. The letter states, "I believe it is the most basic duty of government to guard the innocent. With that in mind, I will veto any legislation that weakens current pro-life Federal policies and laws, or that encourages the destruction of innocent human life at any stage."
- On May 2, 2019, the U.S. Department of Health and Human Services (HHS) Office for Civil Rights (OCR) announced the issuance of the final conscience rule that protects individuals and health care entities from discrimination on the basis of their exercise of conscience

in HHS-funded programs. Just as OCR enforces other civil rights, the rule implements full and robust enforcement of approximately twenty-five provisions passed by Congress protecting longstanding conscience rights in healthcare

- On May 24, 2019, HHS issued a proposed rule amending Obama-era regulations related to Section 1557 of the Affordable Care Act (ACA). Among other things, the rule clarifies that Section 1557 shall not force a recipient of federal funding to provide or pay for an abortion. It shall also be consistent with the First Amendment and with pro-life provisions, conscience provisions, and religious liberty protections in current law. Also, the rule is a timely clarification that the federal definition of sex discrimination in the ACA does not include abortion
- On June 5, 2019, the Trump administration announced it would end research at the National Institutes of Health that uses fetal tissue (which uses aborted human body parts), and it also ended government funding to universities for such research. HHS also announced that it would conduct ethics reviews before funding future private research projects
- In July of 2019, the Centers for Medicare & Medicaid Services (CMS) released guidance requiring hospitals to treat survivors of abortion along with babies born prematurely
- President Trump's administration has worked to fight pro-abortion policies of the Affordable Care Act (Obamacare), such as:
  - In April 2018, CMS issued guidance to allow individuals to claim a hardship exemption from the individual mandate if all affordable plans offered through the federal exchanges in an individual's area included abortion coverage, contrary to the individual's beliefs
  - In January 2019, HHS issued a proposed rule to require that insurance companies that offer ACA plans

covering abortions for pregnancies that do not threaten the life of the mother or result from rape or incest must also offer at least one identical plan in the same geographic area that does not cover these abortions. (The rule would not apply in states with abortion coverage mandates)

- Starting with the 2019 open enrollment period, HHS ensured for the first time that consumers could identify whether a plan covers "non-Hyde" abortion by clearly displaying such information on HealthCare.gov
- On December 20, 2019 (after more than a year's effort), HHS issued a final rule to address the hidden abortion surcharge in many plans purchased under Obamacare. The rule strictly enforces the statutory requirement that the abortion surcharge be collected separately from other insurance premiums. The Obama administration skirted the law and permitted insurance companies to collect payments for elective abortion coverage together with other service fees
- On January 24, 2020, President Trump became the first sitting president to address the March for Life in person in its forty-seven-year history. By lending the prestige of the nation's highest office to the pro-life cause and by using the bully pulpit of the presidency to highlight the sanctity of human life, President Trump underscored the fact that there has never been a greater champion for life in the White House
- Also on January 24, 2020, the Office of Civil Rights (OCR) at HHS announced that it had issued "a Notice of Violation to the state of California, formally notifying California that it cannot impose universal abortion coverage mandates on health insurance plans and issuers in violation of federal conscience laws." On August 22, 2014, the California Department for Managed Health Care

(DMHC) issued a directive mandating that all plans under DMHC authority immediately include coverage for all legal abortions even if a plan excluding certain abortions had been previously approved by DMHC. OCR determined that in doing so, California has violated the Weldon Amendment, which prevents HHS funding recipients from discriminating against health care providers because they refuse to provide, pay for, or refer for abortion. California has thirty days to comply with the Weldon Amendment. If it fails to do so, HHS has announced that "this action may ultimately result in limitations on continued receipt of certain HHS funds."

- Perhaps most importantly, President Trump has appointed 187 pro-life federal judges—including two justices to the U.S. Supreme Court: Justices Neil Gorsuch and Brett Kavanaugh
- If President Trump is reelected in 2020, it is likely he will have appointed four hundred pro-life federal judges and as many as four or five pro-life Supreme Court Justices—transforming America into a nation that cherishes life again

Trump's Record on Taxes and the Economy

- He cut taxes for 85 percent of Americans
- Trump cut the top tax rate for businesses from 35 percent to 21 percent—making America a good place to build a business again. The result is the lowest unemployment rate since 1969
- More than SEVEN MILLION new jobs have been created under President Trump
- The country experienced the lowest unemployment rate among black, Hispanic, Asian, and minority Americans in U.S. history

- For the first time on record, America has more job openings than people looking for jobs. America has SEVEN MILLION job openings. This is causing wages to go up
- More than six million American workers received wage increases, bonuses, and increased benefits, thanks to the Trump tax cuts
- More than ONE TRILLION DOLLARS have poured back into the country since the Trump tax cuts went into effect
- Trump eliminated almost all of the Obama administration's regulations that hurt small businesses—eliminating eight regulations for each new regulation added without endangering public health and safety or hurting the environment. In fact, America's air and water continue to become cleaner under President Trump
- Median household income is up $5,000 per year ($7,000 per year when you include the Trump tax cuts) after just 3 years in office—compared to median household income increasing just $1,400 in the previous 16 years
- The 25 percent lowest-paid Americans enjoyed a 4.5 percent income boost in 2019. This outpaces a 2.9 percent gain in earnings for the country's highest-paid workers. The lowest 10 percent of earners saw income grow at an astounding 7 percent rate over the last year. And for those without a high school diploma, wages increased 9 percent in 2019. In other words, the Trump economy is helping lower-income Americans the most
- Wages overall are growing at 3.4 percent per year under Trump after sixteen years of stagnation
- The unemployment rate for women has been cut to a sixty-five-year low under Trump
- Youth unemployment has dropped to a fifty-year low

- Ninety-five percent of U.S. manufacturers are now optimistic about the future—the highest level of optimism ever
- Small business optimism has hit a thirty-five-year high under Trump
- President Trump has prioritized workforce development to ensure American workers are prepared to fill high-quality jobs
- The president has worked to expand apprenticeship programs, helping Americans gain hands-on training and experience with no student debt
- Since President Trump took office, over 660,000 apprentices have been hired across the country
- President Trump established the National Council for the American Worker, which was tasked with developing a workforce strategy for the jobs of the future
- More than 370 companies have signed the president's "Pledge to America's Workers," pledging to provide more than 14.4 million employment and training opportunities
- President Trump signed an executive order prioritizing Cyber Workforce Development to ensure that we have the most skilled cyber workforce of the twenty-first century
- Five hundred thousand new manufacturing jobs were created in the U.S. so far under Trump after sixteen years of losing manufacturing jobs. Obama mocked Trump in a speech in 2016, saying, "How are you going to bring these jobs back? These jobs are never coming back." Well, they're coming back now under Trump's economic policies

Lifting Millions out of Poverty and Strengthening Middle-Class Families

- The number of people claiming unemployment insurance as a share of the population is the lowest on record
- Since President Trump took office, more than eleven million Americans have been lifted out of poverty

- Since President Trump's election, nearly seven million Americans have been lifted off of food stamps
- The president's historic tax reforms doubled the child tax credit to $2,000 per child, benefitting nearly 40 million American families with an average of over $2,200 dollars in 2019. Also, the president's tax bill nearly doubled the standard tax deduction for families from $12,700 to $24,000 for married couples filing jointly
- A new tax credit for other dependents was created
- The Child and Dependent Care Tax Credit (CDCTC) signed into law by Trump provides a tax credit equal to 20–35 percent of childcare expenses—three thousand dollars per child and six thousand dollars per family. Flexible Spending Accounts (FSAs) allow families to set aside up to five thousand dollars in pre-tax money to use for childcare
- As a direct result of these new and increased tax credits for working families, 39.4 million families have received an average of $2,200 each. This has lifted 11 MILLION Americans out of poverty, including 5.1 MILLION children, and has strengthened the middle class. This, combined with the economic boom under Trump, has been the most effective anti-poverty program in U.S. history
- In 2018, President Trump signed into law a $2.4 billion funding increase for the Child Care and Development Fund, providing a total of $8.1 billion to states to fund childcare for low-income families
- During his Joint Address to Congress and each State of the Union Address, the president called on lawmakers to pass a nationwide paid family leave plan
- The president signed into law twelve weeks of paid parental leave for federal workers
- President Trump's tax reforms provided a new tax credit to incentivize businesses to offer paid family leave to their employees

Helping Black, Hispanic, and Other Minority Americans

- The unemployment rates among black, Hispanic, Asian, and minority Americans plummeted to their lowest levels in U.S. history
- Poverty rates for African Americans and Hispanic Americans have reached their lowest levels ever
- Under Trump's direction, the Environmental Protection Agency (EPA) provided one hundred million dollars to fix the broken water infrastructure in Flint, Michigan, following a water poisoning crisis that primarily affected black and Latino Americans
- In 2018, President Trump signed the groundbreaking First Step Act, a criminal justice bill that enacted reforms to make our justice system fairer and help former inmates successfully return to society
- The First Step Act's reforms addressed inequities in sentencing laws that disproportionately harmed black Americans and reformed mandatory minimum sentences that had often created injustice
- The First Step Act expanded judicial discretion in sentencing for non-violent crimes
- More than 90 percent of those benefitting from the retroactive sentencing reductions in the First Step Act are black Americans
- The First Step Act provides rehabilitative programs to inmates, helping them successfully rejoin society and not return to crime
- Trump is promoting second chance hiring to give former inmates the opportunity to live crime-free lives and find meaningful employment
- Trump increased funding for Historically Black Colleges and Universities (HBCUs) by more than 14 percent

- Trump signed legislation forgiving Hurricane Katrina debt that threatened HBCUs
- The president made HBCUs a priority by creating the position of executive director of the White House Initiative on HBCUs
- Trump received the Bipartisan Justice Award at a historically black college for his criminal justice reform accomplishments
- Trump launched a new "Ready to Work Initiative" to help connect employers directly with former prisoners
- President Trump's historic tax cut legislation included new Opportunity Zone Incentives to promote investment in low-income communities across the country. As a result, even depressed and abandoned cities like Detroit are coming back
- A total of 8,764 communities across the country have been designated as Opportunity Zones
- Opportunity Zones are expected to spur one hundred billion dollars in long-term private capital investment in economically distressed communities across the country

Leveling the Playing Field on Trade

- Trump ended the disastrous North American Free Trade Agreement (NAFTA) that caused America to lose manufacturing jobs for decades and replaced it with the United States–Mexico–Canada Agreement (USMCA) that protects American manufacturing
- Trump stood up to China on trade and continues to do so—further protecting America's manufacturing jobs and stopping China from stealing America's intellectual property
- He signed the Phase One Trade Deal that requires China to crack down on the theft of American technology and corporate secrets, spend two hundred billion dollars to close its trade imbalance with the U.S., and bind Beijing to avoid

currency manipulation to gain an advantage. It includes an enforcement system to ensure that promises are kept
- The president negotiated new trade deals with Japan, South Korea, and the European Union to add more American jobs
- Trump withdrew the U.S. from the job-killing Trans-Pacific Partnership (TPP) deal
- He withdrew the nation from the so-called "Paris Climate Accord," which would have cost the U.S. economy THREE TRILLION DOLLARS, with little evidence that anything would have been accomplished
- The president secured $250 billion in new trade and investment deals in China and $12 billion in Vietnam
- He approved SIXTEEN BILLION DOLLARS in aid for farmers affected by trade retaliation from China
- Trump has replaced "free trade" with reciprocal trade. His goal is zero tariffs with our trading partners who live up to their trade agreements
- The poverty rate fell to a seventeen-year low of 11.8 percent under the Trump administration as a result of the economic boom that Trump's policies have created

Securing America's Borders
- Despite endless obstruction and resistance from Democrats, President Trump is building the wall he promised. He has built nearly 100 miles of new or reconstructed wall so far and estimates that 350 miles of new or rebuilt wall along our southern border will be constructed by the end of 2020
- Illegal border crossings are down 70 percent since May 2019
- More than 977,000 aliens were apprehended or deemed inadmissible at our southern border in 2019—an 88 percent increase from 2018

- Border Patrol agents apprehended more than 851,000 aliens between ports of entry in 2019, an increase of more than 115 percent from 2018
- The U.S. deported tens of thousands of ultra-violent MS-13 gang and drug cartel members, as well as thousands of other violent criminals
- Trump is protecting Americans with the travel ban on terrorist hotspot countries, which was upheld by Supreme Court
- He negotiated agreements with Mexico, Guatemala, Honduras, and El Salvador to require those from Central America who are seeking asylum in America to wait in one of those countries while the U.S. is considering their applications
- He persuaded the president of Mexico to deploy twenty-seven thousand Mexican troops along Mexico's southern and northern borders to stop the caravans of people from coming through Central America and Mexico to the United States
- President Trump ended the Obama-era policy of separating children from their families at the border by requiring asylum-seekers to wait in Mexico or the first safe country they arrive in while their asylum applications are considered by the United States
- The Trump administration is working closely with Mexico and others in the region to dismantle the human smuggling networks that profit from human misery and fuel the border crisis by exploiting vulnerable populations
- Customs and Border Protection (CBP) seized more than 163,000 pounds of cocaine, heroin, methamphetamine, and fentanyl at the southern border in 2019 alone
- The United States Coast Guard seized more than 458,000 pounds of cocaine at sea in 2019 and referred nearly 400 suspected drug smugglers for prosecution

- U.S. Immigration and Customs Enforcement (ICE) Homeland Security Investigations (HSI) seized over 1.4 million pounds of narcotics and made more than 12,000 narcotic-related arrests in 2019
- Trump turned America into the World's number one energy producer
- The president opened up Alaska's Arctic National Wildlife Refuge (ANWR) and other public lands for oil and energy exploration in a way that protects the wilderness and environment
- President Trump approved the Keystone XL and Dakota Access Pipelines
- He ended Obama's war on coal and U.S. energy production—while maintaining common-sense measures to keep our air and water clean
- Under Trump's leadership, America in 2018 surpassed Russia and Saudi Arabia to become the world's largest oil producer
- Thanks to Trump, America is now a net oil and energy exporter, freeing America from dependence on foreign oil—especially freeing America from relying on the Middle East for our oil

Preparing America for the Future

- The president is ensuring that America is prepared to lead the world in the industries of the future by promoting American leadership in emerging technologies like 5G and Artificial Intelligence (AI)
- The administration named artificial intelligence, quantum information science, and 5G, among other emerging technologies, as national research and development priorities
- President Trump launched the American AI Initiative to invest in AI research, unleash innovation, and build the American workforce of the future

- President Trump signed an executive order that established a new advisory committee of industry and academic leaders to advise the government on its quantum activities

Reducing Crime

- President Trump ended Obama's rhetorical war on America's local police
- Violent crime has fallen every year Trump has been in office after rising in each of Obama's final two years as president
- President Trump has revitalized Project Safe Neighborhoods, bringing together federal, state, local, and tribal law enforcement officials to develop solutions to violent crime
- The president is standing up for our nation's law enforcement officers, ensuring they have the support they need to keep our communities safe
- President Trump has made surplus military equipment worth hundreds of millions of dollars available to local law enforcement
- President Trump championed and signed the First Step Act, a bill to help prepare inmates to successfully rejoin society at the end of their sentences, thus reducing recidivism and increasing public safety

Fighting Human Trafficking

- President Trump signed the "Allow States and Victims to Fight Online Sex Trafficking Act" (FOSTA), which includes the "Stop Enabling Sex Traffickers Act" (SESTA), which both give law enforcement officials and victims new tools to fight sex trafficking
- Immigration and Customs Enforcement's Homeland Security Investigations has arrested 1,588 criminals associated with human trafficking

- Trump's Department of Health and Human Services provided funding to support the National Human Trafficking Hotline to identify perpetrators and give victims the help they need
- The hotline identified 16,862 potential human trafficking cases
- Trump's Department of Justice (DOJ) provided grants to organizations that support human trafficking victims—serving nearly nine thousand victims so far
- The Department of Homeland Security has hired more victim assistance specialists, helping victims get resources and support
- In 2018, the DOJ dismantled an organization that was the Internet's leading source of prostitution-related advertisements resulting in sex trafficking
- Trump's OMB published new anti-trafficking guidance for government procurement officials to more effectively combat human trafficking
- Through Trump's Anti-Trafficking Coordination Team (ACTeam) Initiative, federal law enforcement more than doubled convictions of human traffickers and increased the number of defendants charged by 75 percent in ACTeam districts

Improving Health Care While Also Driving Costs Down

- Trump signed a bill this year allowing some drug imports from Canada to drive prescription drug prices down, while at the same time not punishing U.S. medical research and innovation
- He signed an executive order requiring healthcare providers to disclose the cost of their services in advance so that Americans can compare prices and shop for the best deals

- Hospitals will now be required to post their standard charges for services, which includes the discounted price a hospital is willing to accept
- Trump signed an order allowing small businesses to group together when buying insurance to get a better price
- In the eight years prior to Trump's presidency, prescription drug prices increased by an average of 3.6 percent per year. Under Trump, drug prices have dropped in nine of the last ten months
- Trump reformed the Medicare program to stop hospitals from overcharging low-income seniors on their drugs—saving seniors hundreds of millions of dollars this year alone
- The president ended most of the Obamacare mandates—including the very unpopular Individual Mandate
- He modified regulations under the Obamacare law to permit the creation of association co-ops and lower the cost of health care plans that cover the most serious health care issues, but with the option of going without many of the costly "bells and whistles" that many people don't want or need. People now have more than sixty health coverage plans to choose from under the Obamacare law instead of just three
- President Trump signed "Right-To-Try" legislation allowing terminally ill patients to try more experimental treatments that have shown promise in clinical trials, but haven't yet been finally approved by the Food and Drug Administration (FDA)
- He streamlined the FDA's new drug and medicine approval process to get lifesaving medicines in use faster
- Trump secured six billion dollars in NEW funding to fight the opioid epidemic
- In his 2019 State of the Union Address, President Trump announced his administration's goal to end the HIV

epidemic in the United States within ten years. To achieve this goal and address the ongoing public health crisis of HIV, his administration's proposed Ending the HIV Epidemic: A Plan for America will leverage the powerful data and tools now available to reduce new HIV infections in the United States by 75 percent in five years and by 90 percent by 2030

- President Trump proposed $291 million in the FY2020 HHS budget to begin his administration's multiyear initiative focused on ending the HIV epidemic in America by 2030
- The Trump administration provides HIV prevention drugs for free to two hundred thousand uninsured patients each year
- Trump signed the Preventing Maternal Deaths Act that provides funding for states to develop maternal mortality reviews to better understand maternal complications and identify solutions
- The president signed the Autism Collaboration, Accountability, Research, Education and Support (CARES) Act into law, which allocates $1.8 billion in funding over the next five years to help people on the autism spectrum and their families
- Trump signed into law two funding packages providing nearly $19 million in new funding for lupus specific research and education programs, as well an additional $41.7 billion in funding for the National Institutes of Health (NIH)—the most lupus funding ever
- He signed legislation to improve the National Suicide Hotline
- Trump signed the most comprehensive childhood cancer legislation ever into law, which will advance childhood cancer research and improve treatments

Destroying ISIS, Supporting Israel, and Standing Up to Iran—the World's #1 Terrorist Nation

- Trump unleashed America's military to destroy the ISIS caliphate in the Middle East. When Trump took office, ISIS controlled territory in the Middle East that was roughly the size of Indiana and was killing hundreds of thousands of people. Today, ISIS controls no territory
- Trump had ISIS leader Abu Bakr al-Baghdadi killed, thanks to the skill and bravery of America's Special Operations forces. Al-Baghdadi's successor was then killed, along with other ISIS leaders
- After Iran orchestrated an attack on the U.S. Embassy in Iraq, President Trump ordered a military strike killing Iran's top general and terrorist leader Qasem Soleimani, along with his second in command. Soleimani had killed hundreds of American soldiers over the years and was fomenting terrorist chaos across the Middle East. Ridding the earth of Soleimani was as important as the killing of al-Baghdadi
- President Trump signed into law the Taylor Force Act, which halts American economic aid to the Palestinian National Authority until it stops paying stipends to individuals who commit acts of terrorism against Israeli citizens or to the families of deceased terrorists
- Trump moved the U.S. Embassy in Israel to Jerusalem
- He turned Egypt, Saudi Arabia, Turkey, and much of the Middle East into allies of Israel instead of enemies
- The president officially recognized Israel's sovereignty over the Golan Heights
- He recognized the legitimacy of Israeli settlements in Judea and Samaria by returning to the Reagan policy stipulating that Israeli settlements are not illegal

- Trump withdrew from Obama's disastrous Iran nuclear deal. The Obama deal actually assured that Iran would get nuclear weapons
- Trump applied maximum economic sanctions on Iran in an effort to pressure it to abandon its nuclear weapons program and become a member of the civilized world

Rebuilding America's Military and Making America Safer

- Trump secured more than SEVEN HUNDRED BIL-LION DOLLARS in funding per year to rebuild America's military
- He finalized the creation of the Space Force as our sixth military branch
- President Trump pressured North Atlantic Treaty Organization (NATO) countries to increase their financial commitment to NATO. Since he took office in 2017, Trump has criticized NATO countries for failing to meet their 2014 pledge to increase defense spending to 2 percent of GDP. In 2019, nine allies met this benchmark, up from just three allies a few years ago, thanks to Trump's pressure
- The president upgraded our cyber defenses by elevating the Cyber Command into a major warfighting command and reducing burdensome procedural restrictions on cyber operations
- Trump used a combination of very tough economic sanctions and personal diplomacy in an attempt to persuade the North Korean dictator to enter the civilized world. The result so far: no long-range ICBM missile tests by North Korea in nearly three years
- There have been no further incursions by Russia into Ukraine or other neighboring countries—unlike during the Obama years, when Russia invaded Ukraine and Obama did nothing

- Trump imposed tough sanctions on Russia to pressure Vladimir Putin to enter the civilized world
- The president has taken decisive military action to punish the Assad regime in Syria for the barbaric use of chemical weapons on its own people
- The president imposed tough sanctions against those tied to Syria's chemical weapons program
- President Trump is protecting America's defense-industrial base, directing the first whole-of-government assessment of our manufacturing and defense supply chains since the 1950s

Protecting America's Veterans

- Trump signed the VA Choice Act and VA Accountability Act, expanded VA telehealth services, walk-in-clinics, and same-day urgent primary and mental health care
- He created a White House VA Hotline to help veterans and principally staffed it with veterans and their direct family members
- VA employees are being held accountable for poor performance, with more than four thousand VA employees being removed, demoted, and suspended so far
- The president issued an executive order requiring the secretaries of Defense, Homeland Security, and Veterans Affairs to submit a joint plan to provide veterans with access to mental health treatment as they transition to civilian life

Protecting Our Environment without Hurting Jobs

- Trump signed the biggest wilderness protection and conservation bill in a decade and designated 375,000 acres as protected land
- Trump signed the Save our Seas Act, which gives ten million dollars per year toward cleaning up tons of plastic and garbage from the ocean

- America's air and water continue to get cleaner under Trump. America has the cleanest air and water of any large industrialized country
- President Trump signed a bill that creates five national monuments, expands several national parks, adds 1.3 million acres of wilderness, and permanently reauthorizes the Land and Water Conservation Fund
- Trump's U.S. Department of Agriculture (USDA) committed $124 million to rebuild rural water infrastructure to make sure people in rural areas have clean water

Giving Parents Control over Their Children's Education

- President Trump has called on Congress to pass school choice legislation so that no child is trapped in a failing school because of his or her zip code
- The president signed funding legislation in September 2018 that increased funding for school choice by forty-two million dollars
- The tax cuts signed into law by President Trump promote school choice by allowing families to use 529 college savings plans for elementary and secondary education
- Trump signed the first Perkins CTE reauthorization since 2006, authorizing more than one billion dollars for states each year to fund vocational and career education programs
- Trump signed an executive order expanding vocational training and apprenticeship opportunities for students and workers
- President Trump directed the U.S. secretary of education to end the anti-Christian, anti-family, anti-America, and far-left "Common Core" curriculum that the Obama administration was promoting

Acknowledgments

I had a lot of fun writing this book, and I hope it shows. It's a truly amazing story, but it wouldn't have happened without these friends and colleagues.

To President Donald J. Trump, First Lady Melania Trump, and the entire Trump family: Thank you for your willingness to leave a perfectly good life, enter the political fray, and for the sake of a stronger America endure what Shakespeare called "the slings and arrows of outrageous fortune" in order to serve our nation. Tens of millions of your fellow citizens are deeply grateful.

To Vice President Mike Pence: Thank you for being a true friend and an impact player for President Trump, as well as a friend to so many. Your contribution has been indispensable.

To all those who serve in the Trump administration, in the White House, cabinet departments, and throughout the government: Thank you for your sacrifices for our shared values, President Trump, and the country. Also, thank you to all the unheralded heroes I worked with in the Trump-Pence campaigns of 2016 and 2020. You are consummate professionals and patriots.

To Jo Anne and my family: Thank you for giving me the grace and support I needed while writing yet another book. This is your story, too, and I couldn't do it without you.

To my colleagues in the pro-family movement and faith community: Thank you for inspiring me every day with your hard work for faith, family, and freedom. It has been a joy to work with you in bringing about the historic victories recorded in this book.

To my team at Faith & Freedom Coalition: Thank you for mobilizing and equipping Christians to be effective citizens and for lobbying for public policies based on biblical values. I am grateful for all you do and honored to be on the same team with you. Ditto for my assistant, Julie O'Brien, and my colleagues at Century Strategies who do such great work and make me look better than I am.

To my terrific editors, Kathryn Riggs and Erica Rogers, and everyone at Regnery: thanks for believing in this book and giving me such amazing support and guidance.

To my very able research assistant, Mary Woods: Thanks for your enthusiasm, dedication, and willingness to run down so much material that helped me document the facts about what really happened. You are the best!

NOTES

INTRODUCTION TO THE 2024 EDITION

1. Al Hunt, "The Religious Right is About Politics, Not Faith," *Wall Street Journal*, August 20, 1998.
2. HBO, *Real Time*, December 2023.
3. Joe Lombardo, "I'm the Governor of Nevada. This Is Why Trump Is Doing So Well with Our Voters," *The New York Times*, June 10, 2024, https://www.nytimes.com/2024/06/10/opinion/trump -biden-nevada.html.

CHAPTER 1: DONALD TRUMP CALLING

1. MSNBC, *Morning Joe*, June 12, 2019.
2. Frank Bruni, "Trump-ward, Christian Soldiers?" *New York Times*, August 25, 2015, https://www.nytimes.com/2015/08/26 /opinion/frank-bruni-trump-ward-christian-soldiers.html.
3. Michael Gerson, "Trump Evangelicals Have Sold Their Souls," *Washington Post*, March 12, 2018, https://www.washingtonpost .com/opinions/trump-evangelicals-have-sold-their-souls/2018/03 /12/ba7fe0f8-262c-11e8-874b-d517e912f125_story.html.
4. Samuel G. Freedman, "In Revering Trump, the Religious Right Has Laid Bare Its Hypocrisy," *The Guardian*, February 10, 2019, https://www.theguardian.com/commentisfree/2019/feb/10/in -revering-trump-the-religious-right-has-laid-bare-its-hypocrisy.
5. HBO, *Real Time*, November 5, 2016.
6. Michelle Ruiz, "Hillary Clinton Awesomely Defended Abortion Rights at the Debate," *Vogue*, October 19, 2016, https://www .vogue.com/article/hillary-clinton-roe-v-wade-third-debate.
7. David French, "Evangelicals Are Supporting Trump Out of Fear, Not Faith," *TIME*, June 27, 2019, https://time.com/5615617 /why-evangelicals-support-trump/.
8. Rod Dreher, "Trump Can't Save American Christianity," *New York Times*, August 2, 2017, https://www.nytimes.com/2017/08/02 /opinion/trump-scaramucci-evangelical-christian.html.

CHAPTER 2: DEEDS VERSUS WORDS

1. White House, "President Donald J. Trump Nominates Judge Neil Gorsuch to the United States Supreme Court," January 31, 2017, https://www.whitehouse.gov/presidential-actions/president-donald-j-trump-nominates-judge-neil-gorsuch-united-states-supreme-court/.
2. U.S. Justice Department report on recidivism by state prisoners, cited by Matt Clarke, "Long-Term Recidivism Studies Show High Arrest Rates," Prison Legal News, October 31, 2019, https://www.prisonlegalnews.org/news/2019/may/3/long-term-recidivism-studies-show-high-arrest-rates/.
3. Donald Trump, "Remarks by President Trump at 2019 Prison Reform Summit and FIRST STEP Act Celebration," whitehouse.gov, April 1, 2019, https://www.whitehouse.gov/briefings-statements/remarks-president-trump-2019-prison-reform-summit-first-step-act-celebration/.
4. Jennifer Harper, "A Broadcast Tradition: 90% of Trump Coverage Remains Negative, Study Finds," *Washington Times*, January 15, 2019, https://www.washingtontimes.com/news/2019/jan/15/a-broadcast-tradition-90-of-trump-coverage-remains/.
5. "It's Official: The Biased Media Are Incapable of Treating Trump Fairly," *Investor's Business Daily*, May 19, 2017, https://www.investors.com/politics/editorials/its-official-the-biased-media-are-incapable-of-treating-trump-fairly/.

CHAPTER 3: THE NERD PROM

1. Donald Trump, remarks during the Faith & Freedom Coalition's "Road to Majority" policy conference, June 2011.

CHAPTER 4: A WHALE IN A BATHTUB

1. Pew Research Center, "Religion and the 2012 South Carolina Republican Primary," January 23, 2012, https://www.pewforum.org/2012/01/23/religion-and-the-2012-south-carolina-republican-primary/.

CHAPTER 5: CRUZ CONTROL

1. Mark Murray, "NBC/Marist Polls Show Donald Trump Running Strong in Iowa, NH," NBC News, July 27, 2015, https://www.nbcnews.com/meet-the-press/nbc-marist-polls-show-donald-trump-running-strong-iowa-nh-n398401.

2. Eugene Scott, "Trump Believes in God, but Hasn't Sought Forgiveness," CNN, July 18, 2015, https://www.cnn.com/2015/07/18/politics/trump-has-never-sought-forgiveness/index.html.

3. Jonathan Tilove, "'If We Allow Non-Believers to Elect Our Leaders...' Ted Cruz with James Dobson," Statesman, October 12, 2016, https://www.statesman.com/news/20161012/if-we-allow-nonbelievers-to-elect-our-leaders—ted-cruz-with-james-dobson.

4. Quinnipiac University poll, "December 2, 2015–Bump For Trump as Carson Fades in Republican Race, Quinnipiac University National Poll Finds; Clinton, Sanders Surge in Matchups with GOP Leaders," December 2, 2015, https://poll.qu.edu/national/release-detail?ReleaseID=2307.

5. Callum Borchers, "The Inside Story of *National Review's* Big Anti-Donald Trump Issue," *Washington Post*, January 22, 2016, https://www.washingtonpost.com/news/the-fix/wp/2016/01/22/the-story-behind-the-national-reviews-big-anti-donald-trump-issue/.

6. Russell Moore, "Conservatives against Trump," *National Review*, February 15, 2016, https://www.nationalreview.com/magazine/2016/02/15/conservatives-against-trump/.

7. Mark Helprin, "Conservatives against Trump," *National Review*, February 15, 2016, https://www.nationalreview.com/magazine/2016/02/15/conservatives-against-trump/.

8. Andrew McCarthy and Michael Mukasey, "Conservatives against Trump," *National Review*, February 15, 2016, https://www.nationalreview.com/magazine/2016/02/15/conservatives-against-trump/.

9. Michael Medved, "Conservatives against Trump," *National Review*, February 15, 2016, https://www.nationalreview.com/magazine/2016/02/15/conservatives-against-trump/.

10. Thomas Sowell, "Conservatives against Trump," *National Review*, February 15, 2016, https://www.nationalreview.com/magazine/2016/02/15/conservatives-against-trump/.

11. Jack Fowler, *National Review*, "Houston, We Have a Problem," *National Review*, January 22, 2016, https://www.nationalreview.com/corner/houston-we-have-problem/.

12. Steven Ertelt, "Open Letter to Iowa Voters," LifeNews.com, January 26, 2016, https://www.lifenews.com/2016/01/26/leading-pro-life-women-tell-pro-life-voters-dont-vote-for-donald-trump-cant-trust-him-on-abortion/.

13. Donald J. Trump, "My Vision for a Culture of Life," *Washington Examiner*, January 16, 2016, https://www.washingtonexaminer .com/donald-trump-op-ed-my-vision-for-a-culture-of-life.
14. Albert Mohler, "The Briefing 1-26-16," Albertmohler.com, January 26, 2016, https://albertmohler.com/2016/01/26/the -briefing-01-26-16/.
15. David French, "Why I Changed My Mind and Joined the #NeverTrump Movement," *National Review*, March 2, 2016, https://www.nationalreview.com/2016/03/donald-trump-why-i-cant-vote-trump-nevertrump/?target=author&tid=1048.
16. Phillip Rucker, *Washington Post*, "Jerry Falwell Jr.'s Trump Endorsement Draws Objections from His Late Father's Confidant," *Washington Post*, March 1, 2016, https://www. washingtonpost.com/news/post-politics/wp/2016/03/01/jerry-falwell-jr-s-trump-endorsement-draws-objections-from-his-late-fathers-confidant/?noredirect=on.
17. Erick Erickson, "I Will Not Vote for Donald Trump. Ever.", The Resurgent, February 22, 2016, https://theresurgent.com/2016/ 02/22/i-will-not-vote-for-donald-trump-ever/.
18. Rebecca Hagelin, "Meet Donald Trump: The King of Sleaze," Patriot Post, March 6, 2016, https://patriotpost.us/articles/41110-meet-donald-trump-the-king-of-sleaze.
19. Robert George, "An Appeal to Our Fellow Catholics," *National Review*, March 7, 2016, https://www.nationalreview.com/2016/ 03/donald-trump-catholic-opposition-statement/.

CHAPTER 6: YOU CAN'T ALWAYS GET WHAT YOU WANT

1. Burgess Everett and Glenn Thrush, "McConnell Throws Down the Gauntlet: No Scalia Replacement under Obama," *Politico*, February 13, 2016, https://www.politico.com/story/2016/02/ mitch-mcconnell-antonin-scalia-supreme-court-nomination-219248.
2. Barry J. McMillion, "The Scalia Vacancy in Historical Context: Frequently Asked Questions," Congressional Research Service, March 1, 2017, https://fas.org/sgp/crs/misc/R44773.pdf.
3. Henry J. Abraham, *Justices, Presidents, and Senators: A History of the U.S. Supreme Court Picks from Washington to Bush II*, Fifth Edition (Lanham, Maryland: Rowman and Littlefield, 2008), 92.

4. Greg Bluestein, "SEC Primary Could Be the Deciding Point for GOP, Democrats," *Atlanta Journal-Constitution*, February 29, 2016, https://www.ajc.com/blog/politics/the-growing-corporate-backlash-georgia-religious-liberty-bill/cW6dqYMIwJZotTTW7d3aaJ/.

5. Erick Erickson, "Trump Releases Names of Supreme Court Picks; Subject to Change, Offer May Vary," The Resurgent, May 18, 2016, https://theresurgent.com/2016/05/18/trump-releases-names-of-supreme-court-picks-subject-to-change-offer-may-vary/.

6. Denny Burk, "Why Social Conservatives Should Support #NeverTrump," DennyBurk.com, March 17, 2016, https://www.dennyburk.com/why-social-conservatives-should-support-never trump/.

7. David G. Savage, "Trump Announces List of Potential Supreme Court Picks, Including One Who Has Repeatedly Mocked Him," *Los Angeles Times*, May 18, 2016, https://www.latimes.com/politics/la-na-pol-sykes-talk-radio-2017-story.html.

8. Donald J. Trump, Remarks during Faith & Freedom Coalition's "Road to Majority" policy conference, June 10, 2016.

9. Jon Ward, "Transcript: Donald Trump's Closed-Door Meeting with Evangelical Leaders," Yahoo! News, June 22, 2016, https://www.yahoo.com/news/transcript-donald-trumps-closed-door-meeting-with-evangelical-leaders-195810824.html.

10. Katie Glueck, "Evangelicals Still Lack Faith in Trump," *Politico*, June 21, 2016, https://www.politico.com/story/2016/06/donald-trump-evangelicals-christians-224635.

Chapter 7: A Match Made in Heaven

1. The source for the evangelical share of the primary vote comes from network exit polls.

2. Todd Beamon, "Bill Kristol: Dispense with Pence," Newsmax, July 14, 2016, https://www.newsmax.com/Politics/bill-kristol-mike-pence-trump/2016/07/14/id/738743/.

3. David Drucker, "GOP Insiders Cheer Pence, Though Some Trump Skeptics Dismissive, *Washington Examiner*, July 16, 2016, https://www.washingtonexaminer.com/gop-insiders-cheer-pence-though -some-trump-skeptics-dismissive.

4. Katie Glueck, "Evangelicals Still Peeved Over Pence's Religious Freedom Act Flip," *Politico*, July 15, 2016, https://www.politico.com/story/2016/07/trump-vp-pick-mike-pence-evangelicals-225623.
5. Caffeinated Thoughts, "Congressman Mike Pence's Remarks to Iowa Faith & Freedom Coalition Dinner," October 3, 2010, https://caffeinatedthoughts.com/2010/10/congressman-mike-pences-remarks-at-iowa-faith-and-freedom-coalition-dinner/.

CHAPTER 8: CROOKED HILLARY

1. Interview with Marjorie Dannenfelser, November 8, 2019.
2. Katie Glueck, "Why America's Christian Leaders Tolerate Trump," *Politico*, July 24, 2016, https://www.politico.com/story/2016/07/donald-trump-christian-leaders-226075.
3. Interview with Penny Nance, November 8, 2019.
4. Rebecca Hagelin, "Trump, Evangelical Supporters Unfairly Attacked for Efforts to stop Abortion," *Washington Times*, July 14, 2019, https://www.washingtontimes.com/news/2019/jul/14/trump-evangelical-supporters-unfairly-attacked-for/.
5. Amy Chozick, "Hillary Clinton Calls Many Trump Backers 'Deplorables,' and G.O.P. Pounces," *New York Times*, September 10, 2016, https://www.nytimes.com/2016/09/11/us/politics/hillary-clinton-basket-of-deplorables.html.
6. Al Mohler Jr., "Donald Trump Has Created an Excruciating Moment for Evangelicals," *Washington Post*, October 9, 2016, https://www.washingtonpost.com/news/acts-of-faith/wp/2016/10/09/donald-trump-has-created-an-excruciating-moment-for-evangelicals/.
7. Yoni Appelbaum, "Donald Trump's Promise to Jail Clinton," *The Atlantic*, October 10, 2016, https://www.theatlantic.com/politics/archive/2016/10/trumps-promise-to-jail-clinton-is-a-threat-to-american-democracy/503516/.

CHAPTER 9: THE FALSE CHARGE OF HYPOCRISY

1. Sarah Pulliam Bailey, "'We're All Sinners': Jerry Falwell Jr. Defends Donald Trump after Video of Lewd Remarks," *Washington Post*, October 10, 2016, https://www.washingtonpost.com/news/acts-of-faith/wp/2016/10/10/jerry-falwell-jr-the-gop-establishment-could-be-behind-donald-trump-video-leak/.

2. Michael C. Bender and Janet Hook, "Donald Trump's Lewd Comments about Women Spark Uproar," *Wall Street Journal*, October 8, 2016, https://www.wsj.com/articles/donald-trumps-lewd-comments-about-women-spark-uproar-1475886118.

3. Danielle Kurtzleben, "Evangelicals Have Warmed to Politicians Who Commit 'Immoral' Acts," National Public Radio, October 23, 2016, https://www.npr.org/2016/10/23/498890836/poll-white-evangelicals-have-warmed-to-politicians-who-commit-immoral-acts.

4. Carol Kuruvilla, "Trump Has Changed White Evangelicals' Views on Morality in One Major Way," HuffPost, April 26, 2019, https://www.huffpost.com/entry/white-evangelicals-trump-morality_n_5cc20d6de4b031dc07efb940.

5. Barbara Bernstein, "Christian Coalition Has Political Agenda," *New York Times*, January 12, 1997, https://www.nytimes.com/1997/01/12/nyregion/l-christian-coalition-has-political-agenda-109878.html.

6. Frank Rich, "Beverly Russell's Prayers," *New York Times*, August 2, 1995, https://www.nytimes.com/1995/08/02/opinion/journal-beverly-russell-s-prayers.html.

7. Transcript, *Meet the Press*, NBC News, April 7, 2019, https://www.nbcnews.com/meet-the-press/meet-press-transcripts-n51976.

8. Mark Galli, "Trump Should Be Removed from Office," *Christianity Today*, December 19, 2019, https://www.christianitytoday.com/ct/2019/december-web-only/trump-should-be-removed-from-office.html.

9. Ben Howe, *The Immoral Minority: Why Evangelicals Chose Political Power Over Christian Values* (New York: HarperCollins, 2019), 242–43.

10. Transcript, *Morning Joe*, NBC News, August 13, 2019.

11. Emma Green, "Why Some Christians 'Love the Meanest Parts' of Trump," *The Atlantic*, August 18, 2019, https://www.theatlantic.com/politics/archive/2019/08/ben-howe-evangelical-christians-support-trump/596308/.

12. Howe, *Immoral Majority*, 161.

13. Elizabeth Bruenig, "In God's Country: Evangelicals View Trump as Their Protector," *Washington Post*, August 14, 2019, https://opiniontoday.com/2019/08/14/in-gods-country-evangelicals-view-trump-as-their-protector-will-they-stand-by-him-in-2020/.

CHAPTER 10: THE MORAL SENSE

1. Public Opinion Strategies, National Omnibus Survey, June 1–6, 2019.
2. Jonathan Mummolo, Erik Peterson, and Sean Westwood, "Conditional Party Loyalty," Princeton University, September 10, 2018, https://scholar.princeton.edu/sites/default/files/jmummolo/files/mummolo_peterson_westwood_toshare.pdf.
3. For an excellent review of Wilson's book, see Roger Kimball, "James Q. Wilson on the Moral Sense," *New Criterion*, September 1993, https://newcriterion.com/issues/1993/9/james-q-wilson-on-the-moral-sense.

CHAPTER 11: LIBERAL HYPOCRISY

1. Jamie Ducharme, "Hillary Clinton: 'Very Credible' Sexual Assault Allegations against Donald Trump Should Be Investigated," *TIME*, November 18, 2017, https://time.com/5030586/hillary-clinton-donald-trump-sexual-assault/.
2. Gloria Steinem, "Feminists and the Clinton Question," *New York Times*, March 22, 1998, https://www.nytimes.com/1998/03/22/opinion/feminists-and-the-clinton-question.html.
3. Bob Herbert, "The Feminist Dilemma," *New York Times*, January 29, 1998, https://www.nytimes.com/1998/01/29/opinion/in-america-the-feminist-dilemma.html.
4. Marjorie Williams, "Clinton and Women," *Vanity Fair*, May 1998, https://www.vanityfair.com/magazine/1998/05/williams199805.
5. Matt Lewis, "So Feminists Are Finally Admitting It: Bill Clinton Was a Cad (or Worse)," Daily Beast, November 15, 2017, https://www.thedailybeast.com/so-feminists-are-finally-admitting-it-bill-clinton-was-a-cad-or-worse.
6. Rich Lowry, "Yes, Hillary Was an Enabler," *Politico*, May 26, 2016, https://www.politico.com/magazine/story/2016/05/yes-hillary-was-an-enabler-213919.
7. Nancy Gibbs and Michael Duffy, *The Preacher and the Presidents: Billy Graham in the White House* (New York: Center Street, 2007) 321, 324.

8. Franklin Graham, "Clinton's Sins Aren't Private," *Wall Street Journal*, August 27, 1998, https://www.wsj.com/articles/ SB904162265981632000.

9. Brian Knowlton, "'I Sinned,' He Says in Apology That Includes Lewinsky: Clinton Vows He Will Stay and Fight," *New York Times*, September 12, 1998, https://www.nytimes.com/1998/ 09/12/news/i-sinned-he-says-in-apology-that-includes-lewinsky-clinton-vows-he-will.html.

10. Ibid.

11. H. W. Brands, *Andrew Jackson: His Life and Times* (New York: Anchor Books, 2006), 398.

12. Dorothy Rosenberg, "The Dirtiest Election," *American Heritage* 13, no. 5 (August 1962).

13. Ralph Reed, *Active Faith: How Christians Are Changing the Soul of American Politics* (New York: Free Press, 1995), 261.

14. Ralph Reed, "Waiting in Vain for a New Gipper," *Washington Post*, November 15, 1998, C01.

15. NBC News/*Wall Street Journal* Poll, July 14, 2019.

16. Nate Cohn, "What Our Poll Shows about Impeachment Views in 6 Swing States," *New York Times*, October 21, 2019, https:// www.nytimes.com/2019/10/21/upshot/polls-impeachment-battlegrounds-Trump.html.

CHAPTER 12: TRUMP'S PRO-LIFE, PRO-FAMILY AGENDA

1. White House, "Presidential Memorandum Regarding the Mexico City Policy," whitehouse.gov, January 23, 2017, https://www. whitehouse.gov/presidential-actions/presidential-memorandum-regarding-mexico-city-policy/; Nahal Toosi and Dan Diamond, "Trump Beefs Up Funding Ban Aimed at Abortion Providers Overseas," *Politico*, March 26, 2019, https://www.politico.com/ story/2019/03/26/trump-pompeo-abortion-policy-1236397.

2. Sarah Eekhoff Zylstra, "Pew: Most Evangelicals Will Vote Trump, but Not for Trump," *Christianity Today*, July 13, 2016, https://www.christianitytoday.com/news/2016/july/pew-most-evangelicals-will-vote-trump-against-clinton.html.

3. Ian Tuttle, "The Supreme Court Is Not a Sufficient Reason to Vote for Trump," *National Review*, August 4, 2016, https://www.nationalreview.com/2016/08/donald-trump-supreme-court-trump-card-argument-flawed-hillary-clinton-may-not-be/.

4. Ian S. Thompson, "Congress Wants to Let Churches Play Partisan Politics and Keep Tax Exempt Status," ACLU Washington Legislative Office, July 21, 2017, https://www.aclu.org/blog/religious-liberty/government-promotion-religion/congress-wants-let-churches-play-partisan.

5. Jennifer Beltran, "Working-Family Tax Credits Lifted 8.9 Million People out of Poverty in 2017," Center for Budget Priorities, January 15, 2019, https://www.cbpp.org/blog/working-family-tax-credits-lifted-89-million-people-out-of-poverty-in-2017.

CHAPTER 13: THE "BORKING" OF BRETT KAVANAUGH

1. Terrell Jermaine Starr, "We're Fucked," The Root, June 27, 2018, https://www.theroot.com/were-fucked-1827182095.

2. Lauren Strapagiel, "People Are Talking About Getting IUDs Now That Trump Will Get Another Supreme Court Pick," BuzzFeed, June 27, 2018, https://www.buzzfeednews.com/article/laurenstrapagiel/supreme-court-retirement-iud; David Siders, "'Oh, my God': DNC Members React in Horror to Kennedy Retirement," *Politico*, June 27, 2018, https://www.politico.com/story/2018/06/27/oh-my-god-dnc-reaction-anthony-kennedy-retirement-680043.

3. Cher (@cher), "SUPREME COURT NOW COMPLETELY RIGHT WING "trumps SUPREME COURT"WILL TAKE AWAY OUR RIGHTS!! ROE V.WADE,GAY RIGHTS, TOO MANY TO LIST!! THIS BLOW COULDN'T BE MORE SEVERE!! IF WE DONT FIGHT LIKE OUR LIVES DEPEND ON IT, "SOME AMERICANS "COULD FIND "THEMSELVES"IN INTERNMENT CAMPS," Twitter, June 27, 2018, 2:37 p.m., https://twitter.com/cher/status/1012042219224686592?lang=en.

4. Brian Fallon (@brianefallon), "Every name on Trump's shortlist would be another Neil Gorsuch. Democrats should draw a line in the sand now that they will oppose anyone on that list," Twitter, June 27, 2018, 2:25 p.m, https://twitter.com/brianefallon/status/1012039207345442825.

5. Anna Massoglia and Geoff West, "Kennedy's Resignation Sparks Millions in Conservative, Liberal Ad Campaigns," OpenSecrets.org, June 28, 2018, https://www.opensecrets.org/news/2018/06/kennedys-resignation-sparks-seven-figure-ad-campaigns-from-conservative-liberal-groups/.

6. Jeffrey Toobin (@JeffreyToobin), "Anthony Kennedy is retiring. Abortion will be illegal in twenty states in 18 months. #SCOTUS," Twitter, June 27, 2018, 2:06 p.m., https://twitter.com/jeffreytoobin/status/1012034512312832001?lang=en.

7. Jeffrey Toobin, "How Trump's Supreme Court Pick Could Undo Kennedy's Legacy," New Yorker, July 1, 2018, https://www.newyorker.com/magazine/2018/07/09/how-trumps-supreme-court-pick-could-undo-kennedys-legacy.

8. Congressional Record, United States Senate, Vol. 133, No. 110, July 1, 1987, 18518–19.

9. Jeffrey Toobin, "Should Democrats Bother Fighting Brett Kavanaugh's Confirmation? History Suggests Yes," New Yorker, July 31, 2018, https://www.newyorker.com/news/daily-comment/should-democrats-bother-fighting-brett-kavanaughs-confirmation-history-suggests-yes.

10. Carrie Severino and Mollie Hemingway, Justice on Trial (Washington, D.C.: Regnery Publishing, 2019), 11.

11. Ibid., 7.

12. Robert Costa and Seung Min Kim, "Trump Narrows List for Supreme Court Pick, with Focus on Kavanaugh and Kethledge," Washington Post, July 5, 2018, https://www.washingtonpost.com/politics/schumer-urges-trump-to-tap-merrick-garland-for-supreme-court/2018/07/05/ca12f0be-805e-11e8-b0ef-fffcabeff946_story.html.

13. Rachel Mitchell, "Memorandum to All Republican Senators," September 30, 2018, https://assets.documentcloud.org/documents/4952137/Rachel-Mitchell-s-analysis.pdf.

14. Michael Kranish and Ann E. Marimow, "Supreme Court Nominee Has Argued Presidents Should Not Be Distracted by Investigations and Lawsuits," Washington Post, July 1, 2018, https://www.washingtonpost.com/politics/top-supreme-court-prospect-has-argued-presidents-should-not-be-distracted-by-investigations-and-lawsuits/2018/06/29/2dd9c1cc-7baa-11e8-80be-6d32e182a3bc_story.html.

15. Mark Landler and Maggie Haberman, "In Making His Second Supreme Court Pick, Trump Has a Model: His First," *New York Times*, July 6, 2018, https://www.nytimes.com/2018/07/06/us/politics/supreme-court-trump.html.

16. Robert Costa and Josh Dawsey, "Leading Contender to be Trump's Supreme Court Pick Faces Questions from Social Conservatives," *Washington Post*, July 6, 2018, https://religionandpolitics.org/rap-sheet/leading-contender-to-be-trumps-supreme-court-pick-faces-questions-from-social-conservatives/.

17. Senator Chuck Schumer, "SCHUMER STATEMENT ON NOMINATION OF JUDGE BRETT KAVANAUGH TO THE SUPREME COURT," Senate Democrats, July 9, 2018, https://www.democrats.senate.gov/schumer-statement-on-nomination-of-judge-brett-kavanaugh-to-the-supreme-court.

18. Davis Richardson, "Liberal Activist Groups Prepared to Protest All of Trump's SCOTUS Picks," *New York Observer*, July 10, 2018, www.observer.com/2018/07/liberal-activist-groups-protest-trump-scotus-pick/.

19. Mitchell, "Analysis of Dr. Christine Blasey Ford's Allegations."

20. Axios, "Read Christine Blasey Ford's Initial Letter to Dianne Feinstein," July 30, 2018, https://www.axios.com/brett-kavanaugh-christine-blasey-ford-feinstein-letter-9337f417-1078-4334-8a81-c2b4fc051f99.html.

21. Mitchell, "Analysis of Dr. Christine Blasey Ford's Allegations."

22. Ibid.

23. Deroy Murdock, "Feinstein v. Kavanaugh: Anatomy of a Character Assassination," Fox News, October 5, 2018, https://www.foxnews.com/opinion/feinstein-v-kavanaugh-anatomy-of-a-character-assassination.

24. Ibid.

25. Mitchell, "Analysis of Dr. Christine Blasey Ford's Allegations."

26. Murdock, "Anatomy of a Character Assassination."

27. Severino and Hemingway, *Justice on Trial*, 117.

28. Ryan Grim, "Dianne Feinstein Withholding Brett Kavanaugh Document from Fellow Judiciary Committee Democrats," The Intercept, September 12, 2018, https://theintercept.com/2018/09/12/brett-kavanaugh-confirmation-dianne-feinstein/.

29. Murdock, "Anatomy of a Character Assassination."

30. Ronan Farrow and Jane Mayer, "A Sexual-Misconduct Allegation against the Supreme Court Nominee Brett Kavanaugh Stirs Tension among Democrats in Congress," *New Yorker*, September 14, 2018, https://www.newyorker.com/news/news-desk/a-sexual-misconduct-allegation-against-the-supreme-court-nominee-brett-kavanaugh-stirs-tension-among-democrats-in-congress.

31. Emma Brown, "California Professor, Writer of Confidential Brett Kavanaugh Letter, Speaks Out about Her Allegation of Sexual Assault," *Washington Post*, September 16, 2018, https://www.washingtonpost.com/investigations/california-professor-writer-of-confidential-brett-kavanaugh-letter-speaks-out-about-her-allegation-of-sexual-assault/2018/09/16/46982194-b846-11e8-94eb-3bd52dfe917b_story.html.

32. Ryan Lovelace, *Search and Destroy: Inside the Campaign Against Brett Kavanaugh* (Washington, D.C.: Regnery, 2019), 30; Paul Bedard, "Book: Kavanaugh Accuser's Attack 'Motivated' by Defending Roe v. Wade," *Washington Examiner*, September 3, 2019, www.washingtonexaminer.com/washington-secrets/book-kavanaugh-accusers-attack-motivated-by-defending-roe-v-wade.

33. Ballotpedia, "Timeline of Events Related to the Supreme Court Vacancy, 2018," https://ballotpedia.org/Timeline_of_events_related_to_the_Supreme_Court_vacancy,_2018.

34. Ronan Farrow and Jane Mayer, "Senate Democrats Investigate a New Allegation of Sexual Misconduct, from Brett Kavanaugh's College Years," *New Yorker*, September 23, 2018, https://www.newyorker.com/news/news-desk/senate-democrats-investigate-a-new-allegation-of-sexual-misconduct-from-the-supreme-court-nominee-brett-kavanaughs-college-years-deborah-ramirez.

35. Severino and Hemingway, *Justice on Trial*, 161–62.

36. Ibid., 181–82.

37. Ibid., 254.

38. Tal Axelrod, "Collins's Office Received 3,000 Coat Hangers Protesting Kavanaugh," *The Hill*, September 8, 2018, https://thehill.com/homenews/senate/405704-collins-office-received-3000-coat-hangers-protesting-kavanaugh.

39. Mark Sherman and Jill Colvin, "Trump Apologizes to Kavanaugh During Swearing-in Ceremony," Associated Press, October 8, 2018, https://apnews.com/c40afcf2258f4a3b96bad2b1fbb8c682/Trump-apologizes-to-Kavanaugh-during-swearing-in-ceremony.

CHAPTER 14: FAKE NEWS AND THE DEATH OF JOURNALISM

1. Josiah Ryan, "'This Was a Whitelash': Van Jones' Take on the Election Results," CNN, November 9, 2016, https://www.cnn.com/2016/11/09/politics/van-jones-results-disappointment-cnntv/index.html.

2. Jack Shepherd, "Donald Trump Wins: Video of MSNBC Host Rachel Maddow Reminding Viewers 'You're Not Dead' Resurfaces," The Intercept, November 9, 2016, https://www.independent.co.uk/arts-entertainment/tv/news/donald-trump-wins-msnbc-rachel-maddow-youre-not-dead-dreaming-a7406906.html.

3. MSNBC, *Morning Joe*, September 26, 2016.

4. Andrew Prokop, "A GOP Strategist Explains Why the Republican Party Is About to Break in Two," Vox, October 14, 2016, https://www.vox.com/policy-and-politics/2016/10/14/13272322/republicans-after-trump-alt-right.

5. Ibid.

6. Ruairí Arrieta-Kenna, "The Worst Political Predictions of 2016," *Politico*, December 28, 2016, https://www.politico.com/magazine/story/2016/12/the-worst-political-predictions-of-2016-214555.

7. Fox News Channel, *The Kelly File*, October 25, 2016.

8. FiveThirtyEight, "Who Will Win the Presidency," November 8, 2016, https://projects.fivethirtyeight.com/2016-election-forecast/#plus.

9. Emily Stewart, "Wonder What Michelle Wolf Said to Make Everyone So Mad? Read It Here," Vox, April 28, 2018, https://www.vox.com/policy-and-politics/2018/4/30/17301436/michelle-wolf-speech-transcript-white-house-correspondents-dinner-sarah-huckabee-sanders.

10. Rebecca Ballhaus and Michael Rothfeld, "Trump Organization Subpoenaed for Documents Related to Stormy Daniels Hush Payment," *Wall Street Journal*, August 1, 2019, https://www.wsj.com/articles/trump-organization-subpoenaed-for-documents-related-to-stormy-daniels-hush-payment-11564702374.

11. Ronan Farrow, "Donald Trump, a Playboy Model, and a System for Concealing Infidelity," *New Yorker*, February 16, 2018, https://www.newyorker.com/news/news-desk/donald-trump-a-playboy-model-and-a-system-for-concealing-infidelity-national-enquirer-karen-mcdougal.

12. Howard Kurtz, "Ex-Playboy Model's Notes on Alleged Trump Affair Written a Decade Later," Fox News, February 22, 2018, https://www.foxnews.com/politics/ex-playboy-models-notes-on-alleged-trump-affair-written-a-decade-later.

13. MSNBC, *The Last Word with Lawrence O'Donnell*, Transcript, Michael Avenatti, March 19, 2018, http://www.msnbc.com/transcripts/the-last-word/2018-03-19.

14. Matthew Shaer, "The Fast and Furious Michael Avenatti," *New York Times Magazine*, July 10, 2018, https://www.nytimes.com/2018/07/10/magazine/michael-avenatti-stormy-daniels-donald-trump-media.html.

15. Josh Rogers, "'When They Go Low, We Hit Harder,' Michael Avenatti Tells N.H. Democrats," New Hampshire Public Radio, August 20, 2018, https://www.nhpr.org/post/when-they-go-low-we-hit-harder-michael-avenatti-tells-nh-democrats#stream/0.

16. Felicia Sonmez, "Stormy Daniels Ordered to Pay Trump $293,000 for Legal Fees in Failed Defamation Suit," *Washington Post*, December 11, 2018, https://www.washingtonpost.com/politics/stormy-daniels-ordered-to-pay-trump-293000-for-legal-fees-in-failed-defamation-suit/2018/12/11/999d4544-fd8e-11e8-ad40-cdfd0e0dd65a_story.html.

17. Dan Mangan and Kevin Breuninger, "Stormy Daniels' Ex-Lawyer Michael Avenatti Arrested for Alleged $20 Million Extortion Scheme against Nike, Embezzling Client's Money, Defrauding Bank," NBC News, March 25, 2019, https://www.cnbc.com/2019/03/25/michael-avenatti-to-be-charged-with-wire-and-bank-fraud.html.

18. Michael Gerson, "Trump Evangelicals Have Sold Their Souls," *Washington Post*, March 12, 2018, https://www.washingtonpost.com/opinions/trump-evangelicals-have-sold-their-souls/2018/03/12/ba7fe0f8-262c-11e8-874b-d517e912f125_story.html?utm_term=.3589c3bdc2df.

19. Sharon LaFreniere, Benjamin Weiser, and Maggie Haberman, "Prosecutors Say Trump Directed Illegal Payments during Campaign," *New York Times*, December 7, 2018, www.nytimes.com/2018/12/07/nyregion/michael-cohen-sentence.html.

20. Nicole Hong, Rebecca Ballhaus, Rebecca Davis O'Brien, and Joe Palazzolo, "Michael Cohen Pleads Guilty, Says Trump Told Him to Pay Off Women," *Wall Street Journal*, August 21, 2018, https://www.wsj.com/articles/michael-cohen-to-plead-guilty-to-criminal-charges-1534875978.

21. Christina Zhao, "Trump Could Face 'Unpleasant' Jail Time in New York, Former U.S. Attorney Says After Cohen Interviewed for Probe," *Newsweek*, September 11, 2019, www.newsweek.com/trump-could-face-unpleasant-jail-time-new-york-former-us-attorney-says-after-cohen-1458859.

22. Alan Dershowitz, "Alan Dershowitz: Trump Is Not an Unindicted Co-Conspirator," *Washington Examiner*, September 13, 2018, https://www.washingtonexaminer.com/opinion/alan-dershowitz-trump-is-not-an-unindicted-co-conspirator.

23. Samuel Estreicher and David Moosmann, "Trump 'Hush' Payment to Stormy Daniels Likely Does Not Violate Election Law," Justia.com, January 4, 2019, https://verdict.justia.com/2019/01/04/trump-hush-payment-to-stormy-daniels-likely-does-not-violate-election-law.

24. U.S. Department of Justice, "Former Senator and Presidential Candidate John Edwards Charged for Alleged Role in Scheme to Violate Federal Campaign Finance Laws," Office of Public Affairs, Press Release, June 3, 2011.

25. Bradley A. Smith, "Michael Cohen Pled Guilty to Something That Is Not a Crime," *National Review*, December 12, 2018, https://www.nationalreview.com/2018/12/michael-cohen-sentencing-campaign-finance-law/.

26. William K. Rashbaum and Ben Protess, "New Charges in Stormy Daniels Hush Money Inquiry Are Unlikely, Prosecutors Signal," *New York Times*, July 18, 2019, https://www.nytimes.com/2019/07/18/nyregion/stormy-daniels-michael-cohen-documents.html.

27. Darren Samuelsohn, "Feds' Probe into Trump Hush Money Payments Is Over, Judge Says," *Politico*, July 17, 2019, https://www.politico.com/story/2019/07/17/trump-hush-money-payments-probe-over-1418074.

28. Chris Cillizza, "Yes, Donald Trump Really Believes He Is 'the Chosen One,'" CNN, August 24, 2019, www.cnn.com/2019/08/21/politics/donald-trump-chosen-one/index.html.

29. Jeff Mason, "Trump: 'I Am the Chosen One' to Take on China Over Trade," Reuters, August 21, 2019, www.reuters.com/article/us-usa-trade-china/trump-i-am-the-chosen-one-to-take-on-china-over-trade-idUSKCN1VB27K; Ursula Perano, "Trump Says He Is "the Chosen One" to Take on China in Trade War," Axios, August 21, 2019, https://www.axios.com/trump-chosen-one-china-trade-war-b86055c7-14be-4de1-8a1e-a2a665bfe737.html.

30. Anthea Butler, "Why Trump—and Some of His Followers—Believe He Is the Chosen One," Religious News Service, August 23, 2019; religionnews.com/2019/08/23/why-trump-and-some-of-his-followers-believe-he-is-the-chosen-one/.

31. Tanvi Misra, "Trump's Family Separation Policy Amplified Children's Trauma," Roll Call, September 5, 2019, https://www.rollcall.com/news/congress/trumps-family-separation-policy-amplified-childrens-trauma.

32. Brett Samuels, "Faith & Freedom Coalition Calls on Congress to End Family Separation at the Border," *The Hill*, June 19, 2018, thehill.com/latino/393003-religious-conservative-group-calls-on-congress-to-address-family-separation.

33. Matthew Sussis, "The History of the Flores Settlement," Center for Immigration Studies, February 11, 2019, https://cis.org/Report/History-Flores-Settlement.

34. "Affording Congress an Opportunity to Address Family Separation," Whitehouse.gov, June 20, 2018, https://www.whitehouse.gov/presidential-actions/affording-congress-opportunity-address-family-separation/.

35. Richard Gonzales, "Trump's Executive Order on Family Separation: What It Does and Doesn't Do," NPR, June 20, 2018, https://www.npr.org/2018/06/20/622095441/trump-executive-order-on-family-separation-what-it-does-and-doesnt-do.

36. Michelle Goldberg, "The Terrible Things Trump Is Doing in Our Name," *New York Times*, June 21, 2019. https://www.nytimes.com/2019/06/21/opinion/family-separation-trump-migrants.html.

37. White House, "Statement by President Trump," August 14, 2017, https://www.whitehouse.gov/briefings-statements/statement-president-trump/.

38. Angie Drobnic Holan, "In Context: Donald Trump's 'Very Fine People on Both Sides' Remarks (Transcript)," PolitiFact, April 26, 2019, www.politifact.com/truth-o-meter/article/2019/apr/26/context-trumps-very-fine-people-both-sides-remarks/.

39. Glenn Thrush, "Ben Carson Tries to Cancel $31,000 Dining Furniture Purchase for HUD Office," *New York Times*, March 1, 2018, https://www.nytimes.com/2018/03/01/us/ben-carson-dining-table-hud.html.

40. Ibid.

41. Chris Cillizza, "So, HUD Lied about Buying Ben Carson's $31,000 Dining Room Set?" CNN, March 15, 2018, https://www.cnn.com/2018/03/14/politics/ben-carson-dining-room-table/index.html.

42. Brooke Singman, "Carson Cleared as HUD Inspector General Finds No Evidence of Misconduct in Furniture Controversy," Fox News, September 12, 2019, www.foxnews.com/politics/carson-hud-furniture-controversy.

43. Inae Oh, "Did Kellyanne Conway Just Break Federal Ethics Rules by Promoting Ivanka Trump's Clothing Line?", Mother Jones, February 9, 2017, https://www.motherjones.com/politics/2017/02/kellyanne-conway-ivanka-trump-ethics-experts/.

44. Richard Pérez-Peña and Rachel Abrams, "Kellyanne Conway Promotes Ivanka Trump Brand, Raising Ethics Concerns," *New York Times*, February 9, 2017, https://www.nytimes.com/2017/02/09/us/politics/kellyanne-conway-ivanka-trump-ethics.html.

45. Jill Disis and Jackie Wattles, "Kellyanne Conway Unrepentant for Ivanka Trump Plug," CNN, February 9, 2017, www.money.cnn.com/2017/02/09/news/kellyanne-conway-ivanka-brand/.

46. Miranda Green, "Former Ethics Director: Kellyanne Conway Violated Hatch Act with Roy Moore Comments," CNN, November 24, 2017, https://www.cnn.com/2017/11/22/politics/kellyanne-conway-hatch-act/index.html.

47. Renae Reints, "What Is the Hatch Act? Why Kellyanne Conway Is Accused of Violations," *Fortune Magazine*, June 13, 2019, https://fortune.com/2019/06/13/what-is-hatch-act-violations/.

48. Peter Wade, "Kellyanne Conway Takes Offense to Question about Husband on Fox News," *Rolling Stone*, March 31, 2019, https://www.rollingstone.com/politics/politics-news/kellyanne-conway-marriage-question-fox-news-815837/.

49. Shimon Prokupecz, Jeremy Diamond, and Dana Bash, "Source: Mueller Probe Stymies Kushner Security Clearance," CNN, February 27, 2018, https://www.cnn.com/2018/02/22/politics/ jared-kushner-security-clearance-delay-mueller-investigation/ index.html.

50. Tom Hamburger, Rachel Bade, and Ashley Parker, "Jared Kushner Identified as Senior White House Official Whose Security Clearance Was Denied by Career Officials," *Washington Post*, April 3, 2019, https://www.washingtonpost.com/politics/jared-kushner-identified- as-senior-white-house-official-whose-security-clearance-was- denied-by-career-officials/2019/04/03/fefa8dbe-5623-11e9-814 f-e2f46684196e_story.html.

51. Laura Strickler, Ken Delanian, and Peter Alexander, "Officials Rejected Jared Kushner Security Clearance, but Were Overruled," NBC News, January 24, 2019, https://www.nbcnews.com/politics/ donald-trump/officials-rejected-jared-kushner-top-secret-security- clearance-were-overruled-n962221.

52. Michael M. Grymnbaum, "3 CNN Journalists Resign after Retracted Story on Trump Ally," *New York Times*, June 26, 2017, https://www.nytimes.com/2017/06/26/business/3-cnn-journalists- resign-after-retracted-story-on-trump-ally.html.

53. Matthew Boyle, "Three Employees Resign from CNN Amid Very Fake News Scandal," Breitbart, June 26, 2017, https://www. breitbart.com/the-media/2017/06/26/ three-employees-resign-from-cnn-amid-very-fake-news-scandal/.

54. Knight Foundation, "Indicators of New Media Trust," September 12, 2018, www.knightfoundation.org/reports/ indicators-of-news-media-trust.

CHAPTER 15: RUSSIA, UKRAINE, AND IMPEACHMENT

1. Ashley Feinberg, "The *New York Times* Unites vs. Twitter," Slate, August 15, 2019, https://slate.com/news-and-politics/2019/08/ new-york-times-meeting-transcript.html.

2. Politico/Morning Consult Poll, July 25, 2019; Steven Shepard, "Poll: No Impeachment Bump after Mueller's Testimony," *Politico*, July 26, 2019, https://www.politico.com/story/2019/07/26/poll- impeachment-mueller-1437596.

3. Testimony of Colin Stretch, General Counsel, Facebook, "Hearing Before the U.S. Senate Select Committee on Intelligence," November 1, 2017.

4. Andrew McCarthy, *Ball of Collusion: The Plot to Rig an Election and Destroy a Presidency*, Kindle Edition (New York: Encounter Books, 2019), 29.

5. Michael Isikoff, "U.S. Intel Officials Probe Ties between Trump Adviser and Kremlin," Yahoo, September 23, 2016, https://www.yahoo.com/news/u-s-intel-officials-probe-ties-between-trump-adviser-and-kremlin-175046002.html.

6. Scott Shane, Mark Mazzetti, and Adam Goldman, "Trump Advisor's Trip to Moscow Got the F.B.I.'s Attention," *New York Times*, April 19, 2017, https://www.nytimes.com/2017/04/19/us/politics/carter-page-russia-trump.html.

7. Ellen Nakashima, Devlin Barrett, and Adam Entous, "FBI Obtained FISA Warrant to Monitor Former Trump Adviser Carter Page," *Washington Post*, April 11, 2017, https://www.washingtonpost.com/world/national-security/fbi-obtained-fisa-warrant-to-monitor-former-trump-adviser-carter-page/2017/04/11/620192ea-1e0e-11e7-ad74-3a742a6e93a7_story.html.

8. Charlie Savage, "Carter Page FISA Documents Are Released by Justice Department," *New York Times*, July 21, 2018, https://www.nytimes.com/2018/07/21/us/politics/carter-page-fisa.html?hp&action=click&pgtype=Homepage&clickSource=story-heading&module=first-column-region&region=top-news&WT.nav=top-news.

9. Adam Entous, Devlin Barrett, and Rosalind S. Helderman, "Clinton Campaign, DNC Paid for Research That Led to Russia Dossier," *Washington Post*, October 24, 2017, https://www.washingtonpost.com/world/national-security/clinton-campaign-dnc-paid-for-research-that-led-to-russia-dossier/2017/10/24/226fabf0-b8e4-11e7-a908-a3470754bbb9_story.html.

10. Carol E. Lee and Paul Sonne, "U.S. Sanctions Russia over Election Hacking; Moscow Threatens to Retaliate," *Wall Street Journal*, December 29, 2016, https://www.wsj.com/articles/u-s-punishes-russia-over-election-hacking-with-sanctions-1483039178.

11. *United States v. Michael Flynn*, No. 17 Cr. 232 (RC) (District of Columbia, 2017), Statement of the Offense, https://www.justice.gov/file/1015126/download, 3.

12. Seth J. Frantzman, "UN Resolution against Israeli Settlements at Center of Flynn Guilty Plea," *Jerusalem Post*, December 1, 2017, https://www.jpost.com/American-Politics/UN-resolution-against-Israeli-settlements-at-center-of-Flynn-guilty-plea-515776.

13. McCarthy, *Ball of Collusion*, 320.

14. Jonathan Turley, "No Glory in James Comey Getting Away with His Abuse of FBI Power," *The Hill*, December 15, 2018, https://thehill.com/opinion/judiciary/421530-no-glory-in-james-comey-getting-away-with-his-abuse-of-fbi-power.

15. Amber Phillips, "Did Michael Flynn Just Admit to Violating the Logan Act? And What Is the Logan Act?" *Washington Post*, December 1, 2017, https://www.washingtonpost.com/news/the-fix/wp/2016/07/28/democrats-think-donald-trump-just-violated-the-logan-act-what-is-that/.

16. McCarthy, *Ball of Collusion*, 36, 317.

17. Michael S. Schmidt, "Comey Memo Says Trump Asked Him to End Flynn Investigation," *New York Times*, May 16, 2017, https://www.nytimes.com/2017/05/16/us/politics/james-comey-trump-flynn-russia-investigation.html.

18. *Politico*, "Full Text: James Comey Testimony Transcript on Trump and Russia," June 8, 2017, https://www.politico.com/story/2017/06/08/full-text-james-comey-trump-russia-testimony-239295.

19. Benjamin Witte, "James Comey's Damning Testimony," Brookings Institution, May 17, 2007, https://www.brookings.edu/opinions/james-comeys-damning-testimony/.

20. Rod J. Rosenstein, "Memorandum for the Attorney General," Office of the Deputy Attorney General, U.S. Department of Justice, May 9, 2017.

21. Office of the Inspector General, U.S. Department of Justice, "A Review of Various Actions by the Federal Bureau of Investigation and Department of Justice in Advance of the 2016 Election," June 2018.

22. Stewart Baker, "The Low Tragedy of Andrew McCabe," Lawfare.com, April 14, 2018, https://www.lawfareblog.com/low-tragedy-andrew-mccabe.

23. U.S. Senate Judiciary Committee, Interview with Glenn Simpson, August 22, 2017, 132–35.

24. Ibid., 63, 74.

25. CNN Staff, "Trump Tower Russia Meeting: At Least Eight People in the Room," CNN, July 15, 2017, https://www.cnn.com/2017/07/14/politics/donald-trump-jr-meeting/index.html.

26. John Santucci and Matthew Mosk, "Blocked Calls with Donald Trump Jr., Long a Mystery, Went to Longtime Family Friends: Sources," ABC News, January 31, 2019, https://abcnews.go.com/Politics/blocked-calls-long-mystery-longtime-trump-family-friends/story?id=60766720.

27. Donald J. Trump (@realDonaldTrump), "Just out: The big deal, very mysterious Don jr telephone calls, after the innocent Trump Tower meeting, that the media & Dems said were made to his father (me), were just conclusively found NOT to be made to me. They were made to friends & business associates of Don. Really sad!" Twitter, January 31, 2019, 10:02 p.m., https://twitter.com/realdonaldtrump/status/1091170257216159745?lang=en.

28. Frank Bruni, "Impeachment Should Terrify You," *New York Times* Opinion Newsletter, September 25, 2019, https://www.nytimes.com/2019/09/25/opinion/trump-impeachment-.html.

29. Fox News Channel, *Fox and Friends*, September 29, 2019.

CHAPTER 16: 2020

1. Public Opinion Strategies, "Survey of Registered Voters in 95 Swing Congressional Districts," conducted for the National Republican Congressional Committee, October 1–3, margin of error of +/- 3.46%.

2. Matea Gold, "The Campaign to Impeach President Trump Has Begun," *Washington Post*, January 20, 2017, https://www.washingtonpost.com/news/post-politics/wp/2017/01/20/the-campaign-to-impeach-president-trump-has-begun/.

3. Newt Gingrich, Newsletter, October 9, 2019.

4. Christopher Ingraham, "Somebody Just Put a Price Tag on the 2016 Election. It's a Doozy," *Washington Post*, April 14, 2017, https://www.washingtonpost.com/news/wonk/wp/2017/04/14/somebody-just-put-a-price-tag-on-the-2016-election-its-a-doozy/.

5. Niv M. Sultan, "Election 2016: Trump's Free Media Helped Keep Cost Down, but Fewer Donors Provided More of the Cash," OpenSecrets.org, April 13, 2017, https://www.opensecrets.org/news/2017/04/election-2016-trump-fewer-donors-provided-more-of-the-cash/.

6. Bill Allison, Mira Rojanasakul, Brittany Harris, and Cedric
    Sam, "Tracking the 2016 Presidential Money Race," Bloomberg,
    December 9, 2016, https://www.bloomberg.com/politics/graphics
    /2016-presidential-campaign-fundraising/.

7. Sultan, "Election 2016: Trump's Free Media."

8. Simon Dumenco, "State-by-State Map: How the Clinton and
    Trump Camps Spent $595 Million on TV, Radio Ads," Ad Age,
    October 28, 2016, https://adage.com/article/campaign-trail/
    how-clinton-trump-camps-spent-595-million-TV-radio/306496.

9. Ibid.

10. Ken Goldstein, John McCormick, and Andrew Tartar, "Candidates
    Make Last Ditch Ad Spending Push Across 14-State Electoral
    Map," Bloomberg, November 2, 2016, https://www.bloomberg.
    com/politics/graphics/2016-presidential-campaign-tv-ads/.

11. Michael Beckel, "Team Clinton Sponsored 75 Percent of TV Ads
    in 2016 Presidential Race," Center for Public Integrity, November
    8, 2016, https://publicintegrity.org/federal-politics/team-clinton-
    sponsored-75-percent-of-tv-ads-in-2016-presidential-race/.

12. Ibid.

13. Ibid.

14. Sultan, "Election 2016: Trump's Free Media."

15. *Politico*, "2016 Presidential Election Results," December 13, 2016,
    https://www.politico.com/2016-election/results/map/president/.

16. Ella Nelsenella, "The 2018 Midterms Had the Highest Turnout
    Since before World War I: How Trump Made Political Engagement
    Great Again," Vox, December 10, 2018, https://www.vox.com/
    policy-and-politics/2018/12/10/18130492/2018-voter-turnout-
    political-engagement-trump.

17. Jordan Misra, "Voter Turnout Rates Among All Voting Age and
    Major Racial and Ethnic Groups Were Higher Than in 2014,"
    Census.gov, April 23, 2019, https://www.census.gov/library/stories/
    2019/04/behind-2018-united-states-midterm-election-turnout.html.

18. Charlotte Alter, "Voter Turnout in Midterm Elections Hits
    72-Year Low," *TIME*, November 10, 2014, https://time.
    com/3576090/midterm-elections-turnout-world-war-two/.

19. OpenSecrets.org, "Blue Wave of Money Propels 2018 Election to
    Record-Breaking $5.2 Billion in Spending," October 29, 2018,
    https://www.opensecrets.org/news/2018/10/2018-midterm-record-
    breaking-5-2-billion/.

20. Stephanie Saul and Rachel Shorey, "How Michael Bloomberg Used His Money to Aid Democratic Victories in the House," *New York Times*, November 30, 2018, https://www.nytimes.com/2018/11/30/us/politics/michael-bloomberg-democrats-donate.html.
21. Ibid.
22. Tarini Parti and Lukas I. Alpert, "Bloomberg's Huge Spending Transforms 2020 Campaign," *Wall Street Journal*, January 17, 2020, A1.
23. Astead W. Herndon, "Democrats Plan New Effort to Target Minority Voters," *Wall Street Journal*, June 21, 2018, https://www.nytimes.com/2018/06/21/us/politics/democrats-minority-voters-midterms.html.
24. New Georgia Project, "NGP Submits 221,897 Voter Applications!", June 15, 2018, https://newgeorgiaproject.org/blog/ngp_submits_221897_voter_applications/.
25. Mark Niesse, "Voter Registration Surges in Georgia Ahead of 2020 Elections," *Atlanta Journal-Constitution*, October 1, 2019; https://www.wsbtv.com/news/voter-registration-surges-in-georgia-ahead-of-2020-elections/992256476.
26. Evan Siegfried, "Voter Registration Data Suggests Democrats' Longed-for 'Blue Wave' Will Crash over Republicans in November," NBC News, October 1, 2018, https://www.nbcnews.com/think/opinion/voter-registration-data-suggests-democrats-longed-blue-wave-will-crash-ncna915416.
27. Ibid.
28. William A. Galston and Clara Hendrickson, "The Democrats' Choice: The Midterm Elections and the Road to 2020," Brookings Institution, January 30, 2019, https://www.brookings.edu/research/the-democrats-choice-the-midterm-elections-and-the-road-to-2020/.
29. Advertising Analytics and Cross Screen Media, "2020 Political Spending Projections," accessed on October 2, 2019, https://www.politico.com/f/?id=0000016b-b029-d027-a97f-f6a95aca0000.
30. Kristin Myers, "Political Ad Spending to Top $6 Billion for 2020," Yahoo Finance, July 25, 2019, https://finance.yahoo.com/news/political-ad-spending-to-top-6-billion-for-2020-election-162633308.html.

31. Brad Adgate, "The 2020 Elections Will Set (Another) Ad Spending Record," Forbes, September 3, 2019, https://www.forbes.com/sites/bradadgate/2019/09/03/the-2020-elections-will-set-another-ad-spending-record/#7a5cc0d61836.

32. Raymond Arke, "Liberal Super PAC Priorities USA Announces $100 Million Plan for 2020 Presidential Election," OpenSecrets.org, February 21, 2019, https://www.opensecrets.org/news/2019/02/liberal-super-pac-priorities-usa-announces-plan-for-2020/.

33. Ibid.

34. Michael Scherer, "Liberal Groups Plan Early Anti-Trump Campaign Efforts in Key 2020 States," Washington Post, March 22, 2019, https://www.washingtonpost.com/politics/liberal-groups-plan-early-anti-trump-campaign-efforts-in-key-2020-states/2019/03/21/45 22d0d2-4bdc-11e9-b79a-961983b7e0cd_story.html.

35. Ibid.

36. Jacob Knutsen, "Poll: Majority of Dems in Early Voting States Want Trump Imprisoned," Axios, October 14, 2019, https://www.axios.com/impeachment-poll-democrats-early-voting-states-1b9f4a55-4583-4c0f-9102-0e6f49970baf.html.

37. Gabriel T. Rubin, "Washington Wire: Dispatches from the Nation's Capital," Wall Street Journal, October 12–13, 2019, A4.

38. Sam Stein, "Dem Super PAC Has a Plan to Beat Trump with Less Cash," Daily Beast, June 11, 2019, https://www.thedailybeast.com/priorities-usa-democratic-super-pac-has-a-plan-to-beat-trump-with-less-cash.

39. Julie Bykowicz, "Democratic Payment Portal ActBlue Reports Fivefold Jump in Fundraising from 2016 Cycle," Wall Street Journal, July 17, 2019, https://www.wsj.com/livecoverage/campaign-wire-election-2020/card/1563357611.

40. Maggie Severns, "Top Democratic Super PAC Launches Online Barrage against Trump on Economy," Politico, July 23, 2019, https://www.politico.com/story/2019/07/23/priorities-usa-super-pac-trump-economy-1427409.

41. Nathaniel Rakich, "Democrats Are Winning the Fundraising Race in the Senate," FiveThirtyEight, July 17, 2019, https://fivethirtyeight.com/features/democrats-are-winning-the-fundraising-race-in-the-senate/.

42. James Arkin, "Cash Floods Crucial 2020 Senate Races," *Politico*, July 17, 2019, https://www.politico.com/story/2019/07/17/fundraising-senate-2020-1596460.
43. Maggie Severns, "Soros Launches Super PAC for 2020," *Politico*, July 31, 2019, https://www.politico.com/story/2019/07/31/soros-launches-super-pac-2020-1442748.
44. Karl Evers-Hillstrom, "Which Donors Are Giving the Most Ahead of 2020?", OpenSecrets.org, August 14, 2019, https://www.opensecrets.org/news/2019/08/81419-donors-giving-the-most-2020/.

INDEX